D0906714

PASSENGER AND IMMIGRATION LISTS BIBLIOGRAPHY 1538-1900

PASSENGER AND IMMIGRATION LISTS BIBLIOGRAPHY 1538-1900

Being a Guide to Published Lists of Arrivals
in the United States and Canada

Edited by P. William Filby

FIRST EDITION

GALE RESEARCH COMPANY * BOOK TOWER * DETROIT, MICHIGAN 48226

Editor: P. William Filby
Copy Editor and Indexer: Geraldine McIntosh

Production Supervisor-Internal: Laura Bryant
Production Supervisor-External: Carol Blanchard
Production Assistant: Louise Kava

Cover Design: Arthur Chartow

Copyright © 1981 by P. William Filby

831643

LIBRARY
ALMA COLLEGE
ALMA, MICHIGAN

To

Dorothy M. Lower

Head, Genealogy Department

Allen County Public Library, Fort Wayne, Indiana.

A Friend to Genealogists

Table of Contents

Preface

Harold Lancour, a member of the staff of the New York Public Library, first issued his bibliography of published passenger lists in the *New York Public Library Bulletin,* vol. 41, May 1937, and by the time the list was revised in 1963 by Richard J. Wolfe, no fewer than 262 sources of published lists had been found. Although the work was intended to cover the period 1538-1825, Wolfe sensibly included publications he or his helpers found dated after 1825. The year 1825 was chosen because in 1819 a federal act had been introduced whereby all immigrants were required to register at the port of entry, instead of simply coming ashore and making their way to other parts of America, often unregistered, seldom, in any event, recorded systematically. Not everyone complied with the 1819 Act, hence the covering date of 1825, by which time it is probable that most arrivals were being officially recorded.

The third edition of the bibliography, revised by Wolfe in 1963, was reprinted with minor changes, but basically it has 243 sources concerning arrivals prior to 1825 and a further 19 found during the revision. Seventeen years later, the body of published sources of information on immigrants has grown considerably. The present compiler, encouraged by Mr. Frederick G. Ruffner, President of Gale Research Company, Detroit, decided to update Lancour in the fall of 1979, when he had about 900 sources, and, such has been the enthusiasm of helpers, that number has rapidly approached 1,200, thanks to Gunther E. Pohl, Head of the Genealogy and Local History Division at the New York Public Library; Mary K. Meyer, Genealogical Librarian, Maryland Historical Society; Dorothy M. Lower, Head, Historical Genealogy, Allen County Public Library, Fort Wayne, Indiana; and many other librarians and genealogists. Not a week passes without additions being made.

In the beginning, some criteria for inclusion had to be decided upon, and I referred to Richard Wolfe's original definition, contained in the Reviser's Preface to the 1963 third edition:

> It has been my intention in undertaking the revision and enlargement of *Passenger Lists* to preserve as much as possible the identity and practical intent of the original. Only such changes and modifications have been adopted as would improve upon the aim and usefulness of the work or which seemed necessary in order to incorporate into it the many items which have appeared in print since 1938. The standard for including a list in the revised edition is *proof of overseas origin* [of the immigrants named]. I have reserved the right of judgment in this matter, as did Dr. Lancour before me, *usefulness* being the deciding factor in borderline cases. And again no claim is made for unerring judgment or for completeness, though I have made every effort to make the present edition as complete and comprehensive as possible.

This revision of the Wolfe-Lancour work, including almost five times as many entries as there were in the 1963 edition, is offered as an important reference work to be used in conjunction with Gale's *Passenger and Immigration Lists Index* and other consolidations now appearing. Revision and updating of the Lancour-Wolfe bibliography originated when it was decided to consolidate all passenger lists into one alphabet. Researchers have long since found it virtually impossible to check all lists for the names needed—no library has all the sources in Lancour-Wolfe—and, even though consolidations of lists have been made by some publishers, they do not include all sources, so it is still sometimes necessary to check many volumes of consolidations to learn if the names sought are or are not present.

Passenger and Immigration Lists Index, which is an attempt to merge into one all the known, published, passenger lists, contains about 300 sources with over 500,000 names. A further 900 sources (mostly magazine articles) remain to be culled for passenger names, and Gale Research Company is now listing those names—perhaps 400,000 in all—in supplements to be published in the near future. For this reason, the present work is particularly useful: it lists, with complete bibliographical data, every source of published lists known to the compiler at the time of writing.

In preparation of both the bibliography and the passenger index, I have attempted to follow Wolfe's dictum of *usefulness*. Overland migrations such as those which occurred during the Gold Rush are not included. But lists from the many ships which arrived in San Francisco and at other California ports in the late 1840s have been admitted, since I cannot determine whether the passengers leaving New York for West Coast ports were new immigrants or already arrived immigrants. At this juncture, I am sure that researchers are not going to care, as long as they find the name required. To some extent, naturalization lists are included, following the lead of Lancour and Wolfe. It is realized that those being naturalized were not always recent arrivals but, in most instances, very few years elapsed between the date of arrival and the date of naturalization.

This revision has changed many of the features of Wolfe's revision. Genealogy has made great strides since 1963 and, with current aids, the researcher does not need some of the data given by Wolfe. Wolfe arranged his bibliography in geographical, then chronological order, so the researcher is helped if the only information he has is the likely state or port of arrival and the approximate date. Nowadays there are several extensive consolidations of individual passengers' names, and in Gale's *Passenger and Immigration Lists Index,* for example, the researcher can go straight to the personal name instead of referring first to the list of publications in which immigrants' names have appeared. For general information, a subject index to my revision of the bibliography has been made to enable researchers to trace passengers through the names of the particular areas or places from which they came to these shores, at which they arrived, or in which they settled.

Also unlike Wolfe, I have avoided the auxiliary A and B references after entries in the revision of the bibliography, and instead have given each reference a separate number. I have omitted, too, the special index of ship names. Wolfe listed ship names in a separate section, but without the dates of a specific voyage it was a tiresome and irritating task to find information on a particular crossing, especially when over fifty references to one ship might be listed. I have listed ships in the subject index wherever they fall alphabetically, with the dates of particular sailings whenever they were mentioned in a title or an annotation.

Although the Lancour-Wolfe earlier editions had as subtitle, "Being a Guide to Published Lists of Early Immigrants to North America," no Canadian lists were included. Thanks to Eric Jonasson, author of *The Canadian Genealogical Handbook* (Winnipeg, Wheatfield Press, 1978), I have been able to include about seventy-five Canadian lists in this work.

It is true of compilations that unless the compiler receives help from librarians, accuracy and completeness are impossible. Of the libraries consulted, public and historical libraries proved more helpful than university libraries, with the Allen County Public Library, Fort Wayne, Indiana; the New York Public Library; the Maryland Historical Society Library; the Church of Jesus Christ of Latter-day Saints Genealogical Department Library, Salt Lake City, outstanding in assistance throughout this and other projects. This work is dedicated to Miss Dorothy M. Lower, Head, Historical Genealogy, Allen County Public Library, in recognition of her many years of unstinting help to me and to countless other researchers.

It would be impossible to mention every person who has helped me because there were so many. I pay tribute to the following for their outstanding assistance: Gunther E. Pohl (New York Public Library), Mary K. Meyer (Maryland Historical Society), Dorothy M. Lower (Allen County Public Library), Michael D. Kirley and Darell Brown (Los Angeles Public Library), Ann Reinert (Nebraska State Historical Society), David F. Putnam, Jr., and Kip Sperry (Genealogy Department, Church of Jesus Christ of Latter-day Saints), Charles Mann (Pennsylvania State University Library), Wiley Roger Pope (Minnesota Historical Society), Nelda Hinz and Anne Mae Thompson (Public Libraries of Saginaw), and Carolynne L. Miller (Indiana State Library). Librarians surely have the blessing of their chiefs when they go out of their way to supply information or copies, and the cooperation of Rick J. Ashton, Director of Allen County Public Library, Fort Wayne; Dr. Larry E. Sullivan, Head Librarian of Maryland Historical Society, Baltimore (now Head Librarian, New-York Historical Society); and A. Hester Rich (Librarian, Maryland Historical Society), was readily given.

Others, not librarians, were of particular assistance: Clifford Neal Smith, the compiler of many German passenger lists; Willard Heiss, editor of *Genealogy;* Eric Jonasson (whose assistance has already been recorded) and Terrence M. Punch of Nova Scotia; Mrs. Raynold Schmick, Saginaw, for her interest in the immigrant Germans from Russia; Anthony J. Camp, Director, Society of Genealogists, London; and Francis Leeson, editor of *Genealogists' Magazine,* who did much for me with information on British sources.

Gary W. Parks, Susan Sullivan (French and Spanish), and Gary E. Myer (German) did much to assist me with annotations on the works included in this bibliography. A special accolade must be awarded to Gary Myer, a professional genealogist, who annotated most of the German titles and procured many lists from sources in Germany. The comprehensiveness of the German content of this book is his doing.

At all times I have received unstinting help from Gale Research Company. Frederick G. Ruffner, President, suggested the book and encouraged me throughout; Robert C. Thomas, Dennis LaBeau, Miranda C. Herbert, and Barbara McNeil followed the compilation closely and gave advice when necessary. Last but not least, I thank Geraldine McIntosh, who served as copy editor of the bibliography and polished every entry, checked cross references, picked up errors, and prepared the index. Without her skill the work would have been the poorer.

Such is the enthusiasm of librarians and genealogists, I am receiving new lists weekly, so it is intended to update this work at intervals. I therefore request any finders to furnish me with references that may be added: 8944 Madison St., Savage, Md., 20763.

P. William Filby
formerly Director, Maryland Historical Society,
Baltimore, Md.

How to Use This Bibliography

The arrangement of this bibliography is alphabetical by author name or, if there is none or it is unknown, by title of the article, journal, pamphlet, or book. Full publication information is given, including reprint information, followed by an annotation describing the contents of the work and frequently naming the original location of the passenger or ship list, immigration register, church record, naturalization data, or possibly census, military mustering-out roll, or archival source in the "old country." Foreign titles are usually translated in the first line of the annotation.

Item Number

Every entry is preceded by an item number; the numbers are not consecutive, but they do follow one another in ascending order. Gaps were left in the numbering so that late arriving, recently researched, newly prepared items could be inserted in the correct alphabetical sequence right up to press time and for any future revisions. The item number is useful with reference to the three-volume *Passenger and Immigration Lists Index,* where, next to the personal name of an immigrant, along with age, place and year of arrival at a North American port or date of naturalization, is cited the number of the individual item in this bibliography which supplies the source information needed for further research. To sum up: the source number given in *PILI* is the same as the item number in this bibliography. It is the reason these are companion works.

Lancour Number

About twenty percent of the passenger lists described in this work have been described previously in Harold Lancour's *A Bibliography of Ship Passenger Lists* as revised by Richard J. Wolfe in 1963. Entries for these lists appearing in this volume carry within the entry the reference number the item has in Wolfe-Lancour, to alert users to the fact that they may already be familiar with the source.

Subject Index

Following the bibliographical entries is a general index, planned to provide access through the names of the places of emigration or immigration, ports of departure or arrival, and places of settlement, wherever any or some of these are mentioned in a title or annotation. It includes ship names with the dates of particular voyages, if those are cited. Since the information given is not always the same from one item to another, it may be fruitful for a searcher to look not only under the place-names, but also under the collective name of the people(s). The usual specific term relating to the nationality, province, or faith group has been used wherever possible; therefore, in a given quest, look, for example, under Danes or Germans, Moravians, Mennonites, or Quakers (as well as under the place names).

Genealogists and other experienced researchers know how helpful it is to be flexible and expansive in the use of an index, especially one covering this period before as well as after the rise of national states in Europe and before as well as after the colonial era on this side of the Atlantic. Acadia included Maine as well as Nova Scotia; what is now Alabama was "West Florida" at the time of arrival of some immigrants; and one writer, concerned with the New England destination of 1,700 German emigrants, defined the New England states as "the original American colonies from Massachusetts to Georgia." Therefore, specific place-names cited in titles or annotations are entered, unlocated, wherever they fall in the alphabet, and only some of them were able to be consolidated under a larger, obvious political jurisdiction or language group.

Readers are reminded that the index refers to the item number, not the page number.

Passenger and Immigration Lists Bibliography
1538-1900

0008

ABERLE, MSGR. GEORGE P. *From the Steppes to the Prairies: the Story of the Germans Settling in Russia on the Volga and Ukraine, also the Germans Settling in the Banat, and the Bohemians in Crimea: Their Resettlement in the Americas - North and South America and Canada.* (Bismarck, N. Dak.): the author, 1964.

Frequent mention of immigration to the U.S. and Canada. Pages 89 and 90 list families who left Russia for Kansas in October 1874; page 117, others from Russia, 1884; page 127, from Russia to North Dakota, 1887.

*   *   *

0016

ABSTRACTS FROM ALIENS' DECLARATIONS OF INTENTION TO BECOME CITIZENS, and Other Naturalization Proceedings." In *Tree Talks,* vol. 3:3 (Sept. 1963), p. 78 (Immigration- Naturalization, p. 2); vol. 3:4 (Dec. 1963), pp. 109-110 (Immigration-Naturalization, pp. 3-4); vol. 4:1 (Mar. 1964), pp. 16-17 (Immigration-Naturalization, pp. 5-6).

From records in various counties of New York State concerning immigrants from Great Britain and Ireland only, about 1800-1855.

*   *   *

0024

"ABSTRACTS OF NATURALIZATION PAPERS." In *DeWitt County Genealogical Quarterly,* vol. 5:1 (Spring 1979), pp. 1-15.

Mostly declarations of intention, petitions for naturalization, final oaths, discovered in DeWitt County Circuit Clerk's Office, Clinton, Illinois. Covers 1850s-1870s; gives dates of arrival in America. Lists British and other European immigrants.

*   *   *

0032

"AN ACCOUNT OF THE LANDS IN PENNSYLVANIA GRANTED BY WILLIAM PENN, ESQR, Chief Proprietary and Governour of That Province, to Several Purchasers Within The Kingdom of England, Ireland and Scotland, &c., c. 1682 . . . ." In *Pennsylvania Archives,* vol. 1, 1st series, 1852, pp. 40-46.

Provides names of those who were granted lands in Pennsylvania by Penn, 1681-1682. Also in no. 2979, Hazard; no. 7570, Roach; and no. 8370, Sheppard.

*   *   *

0040

ACRELIUS, ISRAEL. *A History of New Sweden, or The Settlements on the River Delaware.* Translated from the Swedish by William M. Reynolds. (Memoirs of the Historical Society of Delaware, 11.) Philadelphia; Historical Society of Pennsylvania, 1874, pp. 189-193. Reprinted by Arno Press, New York, 1972.

Copy of a letter from Pennsylvania along the Delaware River, written by Carl Christopherson Springer to Postmaster John Thelin, "Gotheberg," Sweden, May 31, 1693, which lists persons living in New Sweden in 1693. Also found in no. 0041, Acrelius. And see nos. 7282, Reinders; 1999, Ferris; 3263, Holm; and 9623, Watson.

*   *   *

0041
ACRELIUS, ISRAEL. "Swedish Colonists in Pennsylvania 1693." In *Pennsylvania Traveler,* vol. 5:1 (Nov. 1968), pp. 68-70.

> Taken from Acrelius, *History of New Sweden* (no. 0400), p. 190. "An exact list and roll of all men, women and children which are found and still alive in New Sweden, now called Pennsylvania, on the Delaware River."

*   *   *

0048
ADAMS, ARTHUR. "Adams Emigration Lists, 1572-1640, England." In *National Genealogical Society Quarterly,* vol. 9:3 (Oct. 1920), pp. 38-39.

> A list of emigrants from England whose surnames were Adams, Adam, Haddam, etc., from manuscript emigration lists. Some persons bound for New England and Virginia, 1634-1635. Also in no. 0702, Boyer, *Ship Passenger Lists, National and New England,* pp. 29-30; and no. 9143, Tepper, *New World Immigrants,* vol. 1, pp. 32-33.   (Lancour 8)

*   *   *

0050-0052
ADAMS, BARBARA, contributor. "Naturalizations." In *Shelbyana.*
0050
No. 2 (Jan. 1980), pp. 11-13.
0051
No. 3 (Apr. 1980), pp. 11-12.
0052
No. 4 (July 1980), pp. 11-12.

> Shelby County, Ohio, mainly covered. Information taken from Minute Books in the Clerk of Court's Office, Shelby County, Ohio, on naturalizations between 1820 and 1838. The research continues.

*   *   *

0053
ADAMS, NATHANIEL. *Annals of Portsmouth . . . .* Portsmouth (N.H.): the author, 1825, p. 18.

> Stewards and servants to Portsmouth area, 1631, sent by John Mason. Contains some variations from no. 2056, "First Settlers of New Hampshire."   (Lancour 31)

*   *   *

0061
ADLER, CYRUS. "Jews in the American Plantations between 1600-1700." In *Publications of the American Jewish Historical Society,* no. 1 (1893), pp. 105-108.

> Extracted from no. 3283, Hotten's *Original Lists . . . .* Mostly concerns the years 1621, 1634, and 1679. Also in no. 9143, Tepper, *New World Immigrants,* vol. 1, pp. 13-16. (Lancour 1)

*   *   *

0069
AINSWORTH, FERN. *Index to Naturalization Records, Chester County, South Carolina.* Natchitoches (La.): the compiler, 197?. 26 p.

> Covers 1800-1830s. See also no. 8354, Sellingsloh.

*   *   *

0077
AKINS, THOMAS BEAMISH, editor. "A List of the Families of English, Swiss, &c, Which have been Settled in Nova Scotia Since the Year 1749, and who now (1752) are Settlers in the Places Hereafter Mentioned (Halifax, et al.)." In *Selections from the Public Documents of the Province of Nova Scotia.* 1869, pp. 650-670.

> Names heads of families, with data on number of members in each family, all Halifax or vicinity. Copied from a book in the Crown Land Office dated December 1862. Also in Akins, *History of Halifax City,* 1895, reprinted by Mika Publishing, Belleville, Ontario, 1973 (Canadiana Reprint Series, 52), pp. 246-261.

*   *   *

0080
AKINS, THOMAS BEAMISH, editor. "List of the Settlers who came out with Governor Cornwallis to Chebucto in June 1749." In *Selections from the Public Documents of the Province of Nova Scotia,* 1869, pp. 506-557. Reprinted by Polyanthos, Cottonport, La., 1972, under the title, *Acadia and Nova Scotia: Documents Relating to the Acadian French and the First British Colonization of the Province, 1714-1758,* pp. 506-557.

> Contains passenger lists naming the settlers who came with Governor Cornwallis to Chebucto, Nova Scotia, in 1749. Gives names, quality, ship, etc.

*   *   *

0087
ALANDER, URSEL. "Die Auswanderung von der Insel Foehr in den Jahren 1850 bis 1875." In *Friesisches Jahrbuch 1961: Jahrbuch der Gesellschaft fuer bildende Kunst und vaterlaendische Altertuemer zu Emden,* vol. 41 (1961), pp. 244-262.

> Emigration from the Island of Foehr in the years 1850-1875. From 61 volumes of ship lists for the port of Hamburg, preserved in the state archives at Hamburg, Germany. Concerns 685 emigrants from Foehr. Apart from 55 who gave their destination as Australia, most of them came to America. Name, age, profession, town of origin, place of destination. Listed in chronological order. Also in *Jahrbuch des nordfriesischen Vereins fuer Heimatkunde und Heimatliebe,* vol. 34 (1961), pp. 244-265.

*   *   *

0094
ALLAMAN, D.B. "Some American Oaths of Allegiance, Oquawka, Henderson County, Ill." In *Illinois State Genealogical Society Quarterly,* vol. 8:3 (September 1976), pp. 151-152.

> Gives individual name, date of oath sworn, date and place of

birth, with immigration information. Mostly Germans, 1836-1855.

*   *   *

0108

AMES, AZEL. *The May-Flower and Her Log, July 15, 1620- May 6, 1621, Chiefly from Original Sources.* Boston and New York: Houghton Mifflin, 1907, pp. 166-195.

Age, occupation, and social condition given. For other *Mayflower* references, see the index.   (Lancour 33C)

*   *   *

0115

ANDERSON, RASMUS B. *The First Chapter of Norwegian Immigration (1821-1840), Its Causes and Results* . . . . Madison, Wis.: 1895, pp. 91-93.

Details concerning 53 passengers who sailed from Stavanger to New York, July 5, 1825, on the *Restaurationen.* Also in no. 0714, Boyer, *Ship Passenger Lists, New York and New Jersey,* p. 214; no. 0588, Blegen; no. 7700, Rosdail.   (Lancour 107A)

*   *   *

0117

ANDERSON, RASMUS B. *"Restaurationen -* the Norse Mayflower." In *The American Scandinavian Review,* vol. 13 (Jan. 1925), pp. 348-360.

Biographies of 53 passengers who sailed from Stavanger, Norway, for New York, July 5, 1825. Also in no. 0115, Anderson; no. 0714, Boyer, *Ship Passenger Lists, New York and New Jersey,* p. 214; no. 0588, Blegen; no. 7700, Rosdail; and no. 9144, Tepper, *New World Immigrants,* vol. 2, pp. 371-383.   (Lancour 107)

*   *   *

0119

ANDRUSKO, SAMUEL. "Immigrants from Baden." (Notes on Genealogical Literature.) In *Germanic Genealogical Helper,* no. 2 (1974), pp. 16-19.

Excerpted from Albert Kobele's *Ortssippenbuch Grafenhausen,* 1971. Name of immigrant, year of birth, and, when known, the year of emigration. Considerable family information. A few to Canada and Brazil, with spouses.

*   *   *

0121

ANDRUSKO, SAMUEL M. "An Immigration List from Koebele." In *Germanic Genealogical Helper,* no. 4 (1975), pp. 47-49.

Excerpted from Albert Kobele's *Sippenbuch der Stadt Herbolzheim im Breisgau, Landkreis Emmendingen in Baden,* 1967, a genealogical history of the inhabitants of the city of Herbolzheim in Wuerttemberg-Baden. Lists individuals who migrated to the United States in the late 18th or first half of the 19th centuries.

*   *   *

0124

APPLETON, WILLIAM S., contributor. "More Passengers for New England." Transcribed by H.G. Somerby. In *The New England Historical and Genealogical Register,* vol. 25:1 (Jan. 1871), pp. 13-15.

From manuscripts in the Public Record Office, London. Passengers from Weymouth, England, March 20, 1635. Also in no. 0702, Boyer, *Ship Passenger Lists, National and New England,* pp. 149-151; no. 9151, Tepper, *Passengers to America,* pp. 77-79; no. 6545, *"Passengers for New England, 1635."*   (Lancour 48)

*   *   *

0132

ARMSTRONG, EDWARD. *An Address Delivered at Chester, Before the Historical Society of Pennsylvania; on the 8th of November, 1851.* Philadelphia: J. Penington, 1852, pp. 22-25.

In celebration of the 169th anniversary of the landing of William Penn in the *Welcome.* Also in no. 1342, Cowgill; and no. 4752, "List of the Pilgrims . . . ." For other references to the *Welcome,* see index.   (Lancour 119A)

*   *   *

0140

ARNDT, KARL J.R. "The 1777 Saratoga Surrender of German Mercenaries and Its Importance for American-German Genealogical Research." In *Genealogical Journal,* Utah Genealogical Association, vol. 6:4 (Dec. 1977), pp. 192-199.

Mercenaries from Brunswick, many of whom stayed in North America. Includes the Von Riedesel Parole List of December 13, 1777, at Cambridge, Massachusetts; also the names of those who reached Boston and those omitted from the list after the surrender at Saratoga, as transcribed from the *Boston Public Library Bulletin,* January 1893. Original documents in the Boston Public Library.

*   *   *

0154

"ARRIVALS IN BOSTON, MASSACHUSETTS, THE MONTH OF JUNE 1712. Impost Office Boston from Records of the N.E. Historic, Genealogical Soc. Pub. 1877 in July." In *Genealogical Reference Builders Newsletter,* vol. 2:8 (Sept.-Oct. 1968), pp. 338-340.

Taken from *The New England Historical and Genealogical Register,* vol. 31:3 (July 1877), pp. 309-312. Part of no. 6630 in this volume. Passengers, chiefly from London, listed with their occupations. Mostly lists of ships and their masters. Also part of no. 9151, Tepper, *Passengers to America,* pp. 128-145.

*   *   *

0162

ASPINWALL, ALGERNON AIKIN. "The Mayflower Passengers." In *National Genealogical Society Quarterly,* vol. 6:3 (Oct. 1917), pp. 56-57.

Complete list of 104 passengers who landed at Plymouth in

1620. Also in no. 9143, Tepper, *New World Immigrants,* vol. 1, pp. 4-5. For other references to *Mayflower* passengers, see index.   (Lancour 33B)

*   *   *

0172
AUGER, ROLAND-J. *La Grande Recrue de 1653.* Montreal [P.Q.]: Societe Genealogique Canadienne-Francaise, 1955, pp. 10-28, 41-98. Reprinted by Polyanthos, New Orleans, 1976.

Contains names of the French recruited for the 1653 voyage to Ville-Marie (Montreal) and extensive information, when available, including year of birth, place of origin, terms of contract, money advanced, occupation, marriage, members of household, property, date, place and cause of death, and whether or not there are descendants. Similar lists in nos. 5344-5346, 5374, Massicotte; and no. 5751, Mondoux.

*   *   *

0180
"AUSWANDERER AUS DEM KREIS FRANKEN-THAL." In *Monatsschrift des Frankenthaler Altertumsvereins,* Jahrgang 46: 5 (1938), p. 29.

Emigrants from the district of Frankenthal. A German text not seen by editor.

*   *   *

0209
BACHE, SOREN. *A Chronicle of Old Muskego: the Diary of Soren Bache, 1839-1847.* Translated and edited by Clarence A. Clausen and Andreas Elviken. Northfield, Minn.: Norwegian-American Historical Association, 1951, pp. 227-232.

Passenger list of the *Johanna,* embarked at Drammen, Norway, for New York, May 22, 1843, arrived July 22, 1843. Gives name, home, occupation, and age.

*   *   *

0212
BAEUMER, OTTO. "A Siegerland Emigrant List of 1738." Translated and edited by Don Yoder. In *Pennsylvania Folklife,* vol. 19:2 (Winter 1969-1970), p. 46.

German passengers from Freudenberg, Plittershagen, Boeschen, Anstoss in the Siegen (North Rhineland) area. Some said to have gone to Georgia, U.S.A. Originally published in *Heimatland,* Jahrgang 2:10 (1927), pp. 148-149.

*   *   *

0220
BAILEY, ROSALIE FELLOWS. "Emigrants to New Netherland: Account Book, 1654 to 1664." In *The New York Genealogical and Biographical Record,* vol. 94:4 (Oct. 1963), pp. 193-200.

Contains information from James Riker's copy of the source material in the Manuscript Division, New York Public Library. Also in no. 0714, Boyer, *Ship Passenger Lists, New York*

and New Jersey, pp. 135-136, and no. 9135, Tepper, *Immigrants to the Middle Colonies,* pp. 54-61.   (Lancour 83, note)

*   *   *

0225
BAIR, MRS. S.D., compiler. "Excerpts from *American Colonists in English Records,* by George Sherwood." In *Seattle Genealogical Society Quarterly Bulletin,* vol. 23:4 (June 1974), pp. 161-163.

Ships *Elizabeth, Virginia, Carolina,* and *Susanna,* sailing from London, December 1773, arriving in Virginia in 1774. Data taken from no. 8400, Sherwood.

*   *   *

0228
BAIRD, CHARLES W. *History of the Huguenot Emigration to America.* Vol. 1. New York: Dodd Mead, 1885. Reprinted by Genealogical Publishing Co., Baltimore, 1966. 354 p.

Names of settlers and immigrants are mentioned throughout the volume. In particular, there are the following lists: Attempted settlement, Florida, 1562 - a few names of those who left Le Havre in Normandy, p. 60; Second Expedition, 1564, on the *Elisabeth,* the *Faucon* and the *Breton* from Le Havre to "the Carolines," pp. 63, 65-67; Third Expedition, 1565, from Dieppe to La Caroline, pp. 69-72; "Role des Habitants de Saint Christophe," 1,200 names, with Huguenot families listed, who landed in French West Indies, 1671, and later in New York and South Carolina, pp. 211-212; Inhabitants of Guadelupe, 1671, later to United States, p. 212. List of French and Swiss refugees in Carolina wishing to be naturalized, about 1695, p. 285; Fugitives from La Rochelle who came to Massachusetts and New York in 1681, pp. 287-294.

*   *   *

0236
BALDERSTON, MARION. "Pennsylvania's 1683 Ships and Some of Their Passengers." In *The Pennsylvania Genealogical Magazine,* vol. 24:2 (1965), pp. 69-114.

List of 21 ships arriving between 1682 and 1684 at Philadelphia and the Delaware Bay (p. 110). Also in no. 8370, Sheppard.

*   *   *

0242
BALDERSTON, MARION. "The Real *Welcome* Passengers." In *The Huntington Library Quarterly,* vol. 26:1 (Nov. 1962), pp. 31-56.

Suggests that of the 99 passengers listed as having arrived on the *Welcome* (no. 4752), only 43 were certain to have done so and 17 others probably did. Also in no. 8390, Sheppard, with corrections made to the text; and in no. 9143, Tepper, *New World Immigrants,* vol. 1, pp. 250-275. For other references to the *Welcome,* see index.   (Lancour 120)

*   *   *

0248
BALDERSTON, MARION. "William Penn's Twenty-Three Ships, with Notes on Some of Their Passengers." In *The Pennsylvania Genealogical Magazine,* vol. 23:2 (1963), pp. 27-67.

> List of the ships of Penn's "First Adventure" and dates of arrival at Delaware Bay and Pennsylvania, 1681-1682; one in 1681 and 22 in 1682. Also in no. 8370, Sheppard, pp. 27-67, with corrections and additions, pp. 68-69.

*   *   *

0255
BANKS, CHARLES EDWARD. *The English Ancestry and Homes of the Pilgrim Fathers Who Came to Plymouth on the "Mayflower" in 1620, the "Fortune" in 1621, and the "Anne" and the "Little James" in 1623.* New York: Grafton Press, 1929, 187 p. Reprinted with corrections and additions by Genealogical Publishing Co., Baltimore, 1962.

> Lists of passengers, with other information. For other references to these ships, see index.   (Lancour 34)

*   *   *

0263
BANKS, CHARLES EDWARD. *The Planters of the Commonwealth; a Study of the Emigrants and Emigration in Colonial Times: To Which Are Added Lists of Passengers to Boston and to the Bay Colony; the Ships which Brought Them; Their English Homes, and the Places of Their Settlement in Massachusetts, 1620-1640.* Boston: Houghton Mifflin, 1930. 231 p. Reprinted by Genealogical Publishing Co., Baltimore, 1961.

> Part 1, pp. 1-43, is a study of emigration to New England in colonial times; part 2, pp. 45-207, lists passengers and the ships they arrived on (3,600 passengers on 213 ships). From the Custom House records of English ports. Much of the information is contained in nos. 7906 and 7907, Savage; nos. 1672 and 1674, Drake; and no. 3283, Hotten.   (Lancour 35)

*   *   *

0269
[BANKS, CHARLES EDWARD]. "Scotch Prisoners Deported to New England by Cromwell, 1651-1652." In *Massachusetts Historical Society Proceedings,* vol. 61 (October 1928), pp. 4-29.

> Alphabetical list of passengers on the *John and Sarah* of London. Includes list of prisoners from the Battle of Dunbar who settled at Kittery and Lynn (now Berwick), Maine. Also in nos. 8170, 8171, "Scotch Prisoners sent to Massachusetts in 1652;" no. 0702, Boyer, *Ship Passenger Lists, National and New England,* pp. 158-161; and in no. 9143, Tepper, *New World Immigrants,* vol. 1, pp. 135-160.   (Lancour 53A)

*   *   *

0275
BANKS, CHARLES EDWARD. *Topographical Dictionary of 2885 English Emigrants to New England, 1620-*

1650. Edited, indexed and published by Elijah Ellsworth Brownell. Philadelphia: Bertram Press, 1937. 295 p. Reprinted by Genealogical Publishing Co., Baltimore, 1957.

> Comprehensive listing of early immigrants, in various arrangements to assist the researcher. Pages 1-189 contain passenger lists; pages 193-295 are indexes.   (Lancour 5)

*   *   *

0281
BANKS, CHARLES EDWARD. *The Winthrop Fleet of 1630: an Account of the Vessels, the Voyage, the Passengers and Their English Homes, from Original Authorities.* Boston: Houghton Mifflin, 1930. 119 p. Reprinted by Genealogical Publishing Co., Baltimore, 1961.

> Over 700 names given, with list of 40 heads of families on the *Mary and John,* which sailed with the Winthrop Fleet. See also no. 0388, Bartlett; no. 3323, Hunt; no. 4477, Kuhns; and no. 6600, "Passengers of the *Mary and John,* 1634."   (Lancour 39)

*   *   *

0285
BAREKMAN, JUNE B. "Bremen to Baltimore." In *Genealogical Reference Builders Newsletter,* vol. 8:2 (Sept. 1974), pp. 5-6.

> Passengers embarked on the ship *Johannes,* Bremen, Germany, to Baltimore, Maryland, arriving 1834. Name, occupation, age, and often place of origin. List of 71 names.

*   *   *

0289
BAREKMAN, JUNE B. "A Few 1870 Arrivals, New York." In *Genealogical Reference Builders Newsletter,* vol. 6:1 (Feb. 1972), p. 52.

> Ships, passengers, with ages and places of origin. Included are immigrants from Italy (Messina), West Africa (Sierra Leone), South America (Rio), the West Indies (St. Kitts), and others.

*   *   *

0294
BAREKMAN, JUNE B. *"Louisa:* Passenger List, The Bark *Louisa."* In *Genealogical Reference Builders Newsletter,* vol. 8:1 (June 1974), pp. 7-8.

> From Liverpool, England, to Baltimore, Maryland, arriving May 30, 1834. Names and ages; 124 passengers listed. Taken from U.S. National Archives microfilm, City List, M-255, R-1.

*   *   *

0299
BAREKMAN, JUNE B. "Passenger List, Port of New York, Taken from Xerox of Film Devoted to Passenger List *Guiding Star* Steamship." In *Genealogical Reference Builders Newsletter,* vol. 4:2 (May 1970), pp. 81-85; 4:3 (Aug. 1970), pp. 183-190; 4:4 (Nov. 1970), pp. 265-275.

> The steamship *Guiding Star* arrived on June 29, 1869, bearing

passengers from Sweden, in majority, with a few from Denmark and Prussia. Data in vol. 4, no. 2, is duplicated in vol. 4, no. 3. Reproduced in book form: see no. 0314.

*   *   *

0305
BAREKMAN, JUNE B. "The Ship *Empire State,* Sailed from Liverpool to Arrive in New York, 14 January 1850." In *Genealogical Reference Builders Newsletter,* vol. 6:3 (Nov. 1972), pp. 171-177.

About 700 names, with much information on each passenger. All Irish except five who were from England. Extracted from U.S. National Archives Microfilm Publication 37.

*   *   *

0314
BAREKMAN, JUNE B., and **RUTH BAREKMAN,** abstractors. *Passenger List of the Steamship "Guiding Star" from Copenhagen, Denmark, to New York City, June 29, 1869.* Chicago, Ill: the abstractors, 1970. 37 p.

Published for the Barekman Family Association. Passengers mostly from Sweden, some from Norway and Denmark. Provides 806 names, with age, sex, occupation, and origin for each. See also no. 0299.

*   *   *

0321
BARNES, ROBERT W. *Gleanings from Maryland Newspapers 1727-1775.* Lutherville, Md.: Bettie Carothers, 1976. 72 p.

Marriage, birth, and death notices taken from Maryland newspapers. Names 139 persons who must have arrived as ship passengers.

*   *   *

0323
BARNES, ROBERT W. *Gleanings from Maryland Newspapers 1776-1785.* Lutherville, Md.: Bettie Carothers, 1975. 58 p.

Source contains dozens of names from which 32 arrivals (ship passengers) were able to be extracted because dates of entry were given for them.

*   *   *

0325
BARNES, ROBERT W. *Gleanings from Maryland Newspapers 1786-1790.* Lutherville, Md.: Bettie Carothers, 1975. 71 p.
Names of 52 passengers extracted from the papers.

*   *   *

0327
BARNES, ROBERT W. *Gleanings from Maryland Newspapers 1791-1795.* Lutherville, Md.: Bettie Car-

others, 1976. 110 p.
Names of 48 passengers extracted.

*   *   *

0333
BARNES, ROBERT W. "Maryland Settlers and Their Origins in Europe." In *The Maryland & Delaware Genealogist,* vol. 5:2 (Apr. 1964), p. 34; vol. 5:3 (July 1964), p. 54; vol. 5:4 (Oct. 1964), p. 74.

Mostly taken from wills of Britishers, 1650 to early 1700s. Lists origins and places of settlement.

*   *   *

0354
BARNES, WALTER D. compiler. "A List of Servants Names Brought into Maryland by the *Nightengale,* Ketch of Hull (Eng.), John Hobson, Master, A.D. 1669." In *Barnes-Bailey Genealogy,* Baltimore: the author, 1939, p. A-1.
A family history.

*   *   *

0356
BARNES, WALTER D., compiler. "Transported 1677, Thomas Applewaite, of London (Eng.), Commander of the *Crown Milligo. . . ."* In *Barnes-Bailey Genealogy,* Baltimore: the author, 1939, p. A-2.

Lists 28 people who were transported to America, for which crossing Thomas Applewaite received 1,450 acres of land.

*   *   *

0361
BARRETT, CLARK. "The Glengarry 'Indian Lands.' " In *Ontario Genealogical Society Bulletin,* vol. 8:1 (Winter 1969), pp. 5-6.

A petition listing settlers of the Indian Lands of Glengarry County, Ontario, about 1817. The area called Indian Lands is a strip along the western border of Glengarry County from the St. Lawrence River to St. Elmo near Maxville. From a document in the Public Archives in Ottawa, filed under "Upper Canada Sundries, RF5 A-1, vol. 51." All settlers from Scotland.

*   *   *

0368
BARTHOLOMAEUS, E. "Pfaelzer Amerika-Auswanderer des 18. Jahrh." In *Familie und Volk: Zeitschrift fuer Genealogie und Bevoelkerungskunde,* Jahrgang 5:6 (Nov.-Dec. 1956), p. 239.

Emigrants to America from the German Palatinate in the 18th century. From the Lutheran church register in Wiesbaden-Biebrich as well as from articles by Krebs concerning emigrants from the Palatinate. Only a few emigrants are named.

*   *   *

0378
BARTLETT, ELIZABETH FRENCH. "Two Early Passenger Lists: Additions and Corrections." In *The New England Historical and Genealogical Register,* vol. 79:1 (Jan. 1925), pp. 107-109.

> Passengers from Sandwich, County Kent, bound for New England in the *Hercules,* spring of 1634/35 and late spring of 1637. Corrects no. 7111, Putnam; nos. 0732 and 0744, Boys. Also in no. 9151, Tepper, *Passengers to America,* pp. 120-122; and no. 0702, Boyer, *Ship Passenger Lists, National and New England,* pp. 145-148.   (Lancour 46 and 46C)

*   *   *

0388
BARTLETT, J. GARDNER, communicator. "Leaders in the Winthrop Fleet, 1630." In *The New England Historical and Genealogical Register.* vol. 75 (Apr. 1921), pp. 236-237.

> Taken from Colonial Office (London) Papers, vol. 5, no. 78. Also in no. 9151, Tepper, *Passengers to America,* pp. 8-9. For the best list, see no. 0281, Banks.   (Lancour 39)

*   *   *

0398
BATES, WALTER. *Kingston and the Loyalists of the "Spring Fleet" of A.D. 1783 . . . .* Saint John, N.B.: Barnes & Co., 1889. 30 p.

> Return of the families and individuals embarked on board the *Union* transport, Consett Wilson, Master, at Huntington Bay, Long Island, April 11, arrived Kingston, Ontario, April 16, 1783. List on p. 12 names the passengers, indicates accompanying women and children, records former places of abode and occupations. These were British settlers leaving from Huntington Bay.

*   *   *

0408-0410
BATTAGLIA, MRS. R. B., contributor. "Ship Lists (Ships Arriving in Texas in the 1840's)." In *Our Heritage.*
0408
---Vol. 13:1 (Oct. 1971), pp. 20-21; vol. 13:2 (Jan. 1972), pp. 76-81.
0409
---Vol. 20:2 (Jan. 1979), pp. 63-66; vol. 20:3 (Apr. 1979), pp. 106-108; vol. 20:4 (July 1979), pp. 180-182. (Title changed to "Ship Lists - Arrivals in Texas in the 1840's.")
0410
---Vol. 21:1 (Oct. 1979), pp. 11-14.

> Primarily lists German immigrants who settled in and around New Braunfels, Texas.

*   *   *

0418
BATTLE, J.H. [Passengers on the *Friends' Adventure,* 1682, and the *Endeavor,* 1683.] In *History of Bucks County, Pennsylvania.* Philadelphia: A. Warner and Co., 1887, pp. 440-441.

> Names of several British passengers given. Also in no. 8370,

Sheppard, *Passengers and Ships Prior to 1684,* p. 177. (Lancour 122)

*   *   *

0428
BATTLE, J.H. "A Registry of All the People in the County of Bucks Within the Province of Pennsylvania That Have Come to Settle the Said County." In *History of Bucks County, Pennsylvania.* Philadelphia: A. Warner & Co., 1887, pp. 672-680.

> From the "Book of Arrivals" in the registry office, Doyleston, Pennsylvania. Gives considerable information on the passengers, all British. Also in no. 6463, "A Partial List of the Families Who Resided in Bucks County, Pennsylvania, Prior to 1687 . . . ;" in no. 9120, Tepper, *Emigrants to Pennsylvania,* pp. 19-29. Compared, corrected, and retranscribed by Hannah Benner Roach in no. 8370, Sheppard. And see no. 7385, Roach.   (Lancour 117)

*   *   *

0438
BAUER, ARMAND, and **ELAINE BAUER,** copiers. "Passenger Lists." In *Heritage Review,* no. 13/14 (Apr. 1976), pp. 54-55.

> Germans from Russia, passengers to Baltimore from Bremen, 1874. Names, ages, and occupations given.

*   *   *

0439
BAUER, ARMAND, and **ELAINE BAUER.** "Passenger Lists." In *Heritage Review,* no. 25 (Dec. 1979), p. 36

> List of passengers from Russia via Hamburg to New York on the S.S. *Cimbria,* July 1, 1875.

*   *   *

0448-0449
BAYLESS, JOYCE. "Acts of Naturalization #1, June 5, 1871, to Mar. 30, 1880, Superior Court, County Court, and District Court." [Bakersfield, Calif.] In *Kern-Gen.*

0448
---Vol. 4:1 (Mar. 1967), pp. 5-6; vol. 4:4 (Dec. 1967), pp. 50-52.
0449
---Vol. 5:1 (Mar. 1968), pp. 6-9.

> From records in the Kern County Clerk's office, Bakersfield. Involves many nationalities.

*   *   *

0454
BECKEL, CLARENCE E. *Early Marriage Customs of the Moravian Congregation in Bethlehem, Pennsylvania . . . .* Published as a separate entity in *The Pennsylvania German Folklore Society* [Yearbook], vol. 3, 1938. 32 p.

> Includes dates of 18th century arrivals in America. Many came

in 1743 and 1749 to New York City from Germany. And see nos. 3660-3661, Jordan.

*   *   *

0468

BECKER, WILHELM, and **WILHELM WEBER.** "Remmesweiler Auswanderer im 18. und 19. Jahrhundert." In *Heimatbuch des Kreises St. Wendel,* vol. 6. (1955-1956) pp. 77-84.

Emigration from Remmesweiler in the 18th and 19th centuries. From church registers and civil records of Remmesweiler, Germany. Contains a list, pp. 83-84, of 148 emigrants departing between 1834 and 1897. Names of heads of emigrant groups, their birth dates, year of emigration, number in party, and occupations. Excerpted from the *Remmesweiler Heimatbuch.*

*   *   *

0478

BELL, RAYMOND MARTIN. "Emigrants from Wolfersweiler Parish, Germany, to Pennsylvania before 1750." In *National Genealogical Society Quarterly,* vol. 63:2 (June 1975), pp. 105-109.

List of emigrants from Wolfersweiler, based on Strassburg and Hinke, *Pennsylvania German Pioneers* (nos. 9041 and 9042). Also from the 1719 census of Wolfersweiler parish and other parish records, and from German and Pennsylvania records.

*   *   *

0488

BELL, RAYMOND MARTIN. "The Ensminger Family." In *Pennsylvania Dutchman,* vol. 5:13 (Mar. 1, 1954), p. 12.

German passengers in the 1700s.

*   *   *

0498

BELLINGER, LYLE FREDERICK, compiler. "Our Early Citizens: Names of Those Taking the Oath of Allegiance from 1715 to 1773." In Lou D. MacWethy, *The Book of Names.* . . . St. Johnsville, N.Y.: The Enterprise and News, 1933, pp. 1-7. Reprinted by Genealogical Publishing Co., Baltimore, 1969.

Lists of Palatine immigrants naturalized, taken from Colonial Laws of New York, Munsell's *Annals of Albany,* and other sources. (Lancour 99)

*   *   *

0505

BERGEN, TUNIS (TEUNIS) G. "Dutch Settlers in New Jersey." In *New Jersey Genesis,* vol. 13:2 (Jan. 1966), pp. 544-546; 13:3 (Apr. 1966), pp. 557-558; 13:4 (July 1966), pp. 569, 571; 14:1 (Oct. 1966), pp. 580-582; 14:2 (Jan. 1967), pp. 592-594.

From Kings County, New York: names, some genealogical information, and dates of settlement, mostly 1640s-1660s; settlement in New Jersey in early 1700s. First published in *Our Home,* Somerville, New Jersey, 1873. Appeared in a column headed "Ancestral Notes" in *New Jersey Genesis.*

*   *   *

0508-0509

BERGEN, VAN BRUNT. "A List of Early Immigrants to New Netherland. Alphabetically Arranged, with Additions and Corrections, from Manuscripts of the Late Teunis G. Bergen." In *The New York Genealogical and Biographical Record.*

0508

---Vol. 14:4 (Oct. 1883), pp. 181-190.

0509

---Vol. 15:1 (Jan. 1884), pp. 34-40; vol. 15:2 (Apr. 1884), pp. 72-77.

Alphabetical arrangement of the combined lists in nos. 6291, 6306, and 6326, O'Callaghan. Also in no. 9135, Tepper, *Immigrants to the Middle Colonies,* pp. 31-40, 41-47, and 48-53. (Lancour 84)

*   *   *

0528

BEVERLY, TREVIA WOOSTER, compiler. *Index to Naturalization Records - Grayson County, Texas.* Houston [Texas]: the compiler, 1978. 2nd pr., 35 p.

Includes 421 names, mostly German or English, covering the years 1855-1907.

*   *   *

0538

BEVERLY, TREVIA WOOSTER, compiler. *Waller County, Texas Naturalization Records, with Record of Alien-Owned Lands.* Houston [Texas]: the compiler, 1976. 3rd pr., 1977. 51 p.

Almost 400 names, mostly German and British. Spans 1847-1932, covering especially late 19th and early 20th centuries.

*   *   *

0544

BIERMAN, LEE. "Ship Passenger Lists." In *Branching Out from St. Clair County, Illinois,* vol. 7:4 (Aug. 1980), pp. 139-143.

Lists of passengers on board the ship *General Washington,* Bremen, Germany, to New Orleans, arriving November 1845, and the ship *William D. Sewall,* Liverpool, England, to New Orleans, arriving November 1849. The *General Washington* data gives names, ages, occupations, and origin. The *William D. Sewall* list provides the same information plus location in America.

*   *   *

0548

BIRKFELD, F. "Auswandererschicksale: Reitzengeschwendaer Bauern in Amerika." In *Heimatbuch Kreis Ziegenrueck,* n.p.: 19--, pp. 163-168.

Information on the fate of certain emigrants: farmers from Reitzengeschwenda, Germany, in America. Text not seen by editor.

*   *   *

0558
BISCHOFF, JOHANNES. "Amerika-Auswanderer von Hohentruedingen aus der Mitte des 18. Jahrhunderts." In *Blaetter fuer fraenkische Familienkunde,* Jahrgang 14: 2-3 (1939), p. 203.

Emigrants to America from Hohentruedingen in the middle of the 18th century. From vol. 1 of the church registers in the Evangelical-Lutheran parish office of Hohentruedingen in the district of Gunzenhausen in Middle Franconia, Bavaria, Germany. Eleven emigrants to America, 1740-1752. Names, places of origin, some family data, and further history.

*   *   *

0568
BLACK, J. ANDERSON. *Your Irish Ancestors.* New York: Paddington Press, 1974, p. 235.

Some 1849 emigration from Ireland to America through the port of New York. Page 235 is in the format of an original passenger list. Pages 138-227 give details in the history of great Irish families.

*   *   *

0578
BLASIG, ANNE. "An Abstract of the Original Ship Register of the Wendish Colonists of Texas of 1854." In *The Wends of Texas.* San Antonio, Tex.: Baylor Co., 1954, pp. 92-115.

Germans from Rothenburg and Saxony regions. Also in no. 1067, Caldwell; no. 1858, Engerrand; and no. 2504, Geue.

*   *   *

0588
BLEGEN, THEODORE C. *Norwegian Migration to America, 1825-1860.* Northfield, Minn.: 1931, vol. 1, pp. 395-396. Reprinted by Haskell House Publishers, New York, 1969.

Lists the passengers on the *Restaurationen* in 1825 to New York. Also in nos. 0115 and 0117, Anderson; no. 7700, Rosdail; and no. 0714, Boyer, *Ship Passenger Lists, New York and New Jersey,* p. 214. (Lancour 107B)

*   *   *

0598
BLENDINGER, FRIEDRICH. "Die Auswanderung nach Nordamerika aus dem Regierungsbezirk Oberbayern in den Jahren 1846-1852." In *Zeitschrift fuer bayerische Landesgeschichte,* vol. 27 (1964), pp. 431-487.

Emigration to North America from the government district of Oberbayern (Upper Bavaria), 1846-1852. From the state archives of Oberbayern in the *Hauptstaatsarchiv* at Munich. Concerns 1,144 emigrants from Upper Bavaria in the Kingdom of Bavaria to North America. Names of heads of family groups as well as given names of most accompanying family members, places of origin, and many of the intended places of destination in America, particularly St. Marys and St. Vincents in Pennsylvania. The list is on pp. 464-487, alphabetically arranged by county, then by locality, then by surname. Supplementary information is given in no. 3941, Klueber.

*   *   *

0608
BLUMENTHAL, WALTER HART. *Brides from Bridewell: Female Felons Sent to Colonial America.* Rutland, Vt.: Charles E. Tuttle Co., 1962. 139p.

A study of English female felons sent to Virginia, Maryland, and French Louisiana. Names are throughout the text. On p. 20 there is a "True List of Prisoners Taken from Newgate, and shipp'd on board the *Anne,* bound for Carolina or Virginia, which were delivered this 21st day of Feb. 1723-4 by Jonathan Forward of London, vizt." Of 66 passengers, only the 29 women are listed. Page 94 lists 27 women who were alleged to have come on the *Pelican* to Louisiana in 1704, but Blumenthal found the list and the voyage to be fictitious.

*   *   *

0618
BOCKSTRUCK, LLOYD DEWITT. "Some Amelia County, Virginia, Colonists, 1737-1745." In *National Genealogical Society Quarterly,* vol. 65:3 (Sept. 1977), p. 234.

Extracted from the first court order book of Amelia County, Virginia. Contains the names of individuals claiming their headrights and specifies their places of origin and year of arrival.

*   *   *

0622
BOCKSTRUCK, LLOYD DEWITT. "Some Spotsylvania County, Virginia, Immigrants, 1769-1770." In *National Genealogical Society Quarterly,* vol. 68:1 (Mar. 1980), p. 69.

Describes 60 indentured servants from Ireland aboard the brig *Fanny,* as property of Fielding Lewis, 1769 and 1770. Found in Spotsylvania County Minute Book, 1774-1782, p. 125.

*   *   *

0628
BOER, ELISABETH. "Dresdner Auswanderer 1852-1857." In *Mitteilungen des Roland und der Saechsischen Stiftung fuer Familienforschung, Dresden.* Jahrgang 18: no. 4/7 (Apr/July 1933), pp. 3-5.

Emigration from Dresden, Germany, 1852-1857. From requests for permission to emigrate from Saxony, stored in the municipal archives in Dresden (Ratsarchiv file CXVIII 178). Lists 174 emigrants, 86 giving their destination as America. Name, place of origin, year of emigration, intended destination, and much other data.

*   *   *

0638
BOLAY, THEODOR. "Auswanderung aus Asperg im 18. und 19. Jahrhundert." In *Ludwigsburger Geschichtsblaetter,* vol. 16 (1964), pp. 98-126.

Emigration from Asperg in the 18th and 19th centuries. Information taken from the municipal archives of Asperg, Germany. This documents the emigration to various parts of the world, that for America beginning on p. 108. Names, some ages, several intended destinations in America, and much family data. Asperg is a community in southwestern Germany.

*   *   *

0648
BOLTON, CHARLES KNOWLES. "The Petition to Governor Shute in 1718." In *Scotch Irish Pioneers in Ulster and America.* Boston: Bacon & Brown, 1910, pp. 324-330. Reprinted by Genealogical Publishing Co., Baltimore, 1967.

> From a manuscript in the New Hampshire Historical Society, Concord. Concerns over 250 inhabitants of Northern Ireland who, in 1718, petitioned Samuel Shute for permission to emigrate to New England. Many (pp. 262-264) settled in Londonderry, New Hampshire. Also in no. 0702, Boyer, *Ship Passenger Lists, National and New England,* pp. 130-133. (Lancour 32)

*   *   *

0658
BOLTON, ETHEL STANWOOD. *Immigrants to New England, 1700-1775.* Salem, Mass.: Essex Institute, 1931. 235 p. Reprinted by Genealogical Publishing Co., Baltimore, 1966.

> Alphabetical list of British immigrants to New England, 1700-1775. Includes index. Originally in *The Essex Institute Historical Collections,* vols. 63-67 (April 1927-July 1931). (Lancour 63 and 63A)

*   *   *

0666
BOOGHER, WILLIAM FLETCHER, compiler. "Immigrant List, 1707." In *Gleanings of Virginia History . . . .* Washington, D.C.: the compiler, 1903, p. 8. Reprinted by Genealogical Publishing Co., Baltimore, 1965.

> Reports on 18 persons from Bristol, England, boat hands in the *Joseph and Thomas.* Also in no. 0720, Boyer, *Ship Passenger Lists, The South,* p. 90. (Lancour 225)

*   *   *

0675
BOOSTER PRESS, IOWA, compiler and publisher. *Souvenir History of Pella, Iowa...1847...to the Present Time in 1922.* Pella, Iowa: Booster Press, 1922, pp. 34-142.

> Lists settlers who came to America from Holland, including several who went first to Baltimore, 1847, then to Iowa. Also names French families who settled in the Pella area in the years 1853-1860. Similar data in nos. 9385-87, Van Stigt.

*   *   *

0685
BOSS, FRIEDER, compiler. "Emigrants to North America and Russia-Poland from Hochst, Lichtenberg, and Umstadt." Translated by Hildegard Schwabauer. In *Clues,* 1977, pp. 45-48.

> Compiled from public notices of embarkations, taken from the *Dieburg County Weekly* (Wochenblatt fuer den Kreis Dieburg), 1834-1838. Gives dates of embarkation and individual places of origin. Although it is impossible to determine which emigrants went to America and which to Russian Poland, it is probable that most ultimately came to America.

*   *   *

0689
BOTTENBERG, HELEN, contributor. "Passenger List of Ship *Helene,* July 3, 1849, District of New York, Port of New York." In *Central Illinois Genealogical Quarterly,* vol. 14:4 (Fall 1978), pp. 130-132.

> From Bremen. Much information given. Most settled in Edward County, Illinois.

*   *   *

0695
BOWMAN, GEORGE ERNEST. *The Mayflower Reader. A Selection of Articles from The Mayflower Descendant,* selected by Ruth Wilder Sherman. Baltimore: Genealogical Publishing Co., 1978, pp. 1-8.

> Excerpts from volumes 1-7 of *The Mayflower Descendant,* 1899-1905. Includes Governor Bradford's list of the *Mayflower* passengers, pp. 1-8. For the many versions of the *Mayflower* passenger list, see the index.

*   *   *

0702
BOYER, CARL, 3rd., editor. *Ship Passenger Lists, National and New England (1600-1825).* Newhall, Calif.: the editor, 1977. 270 p.

> Contains passenger lists mentioned in Lancour, *A Bibliography of Ship Passenger Lists, 1538-1825* (1963), nos. 7-10, 11(1), 13 (additions), 15-17(1), 19(1), 22-26, 31-33, 37-38, 40, 42, 45, 46, 48-50, 53-53A, 54A-62, 66, 67, 70, 71. Has an index to ship names, place names, and about 7,000 personal names, with variant surname spellings. In the present work, nos. 9120, 9135, 9143, 9144, and 9151, all by Tepper, have similar lists.

*   *   *

0714
BOYER, CARL, 3rd, editor. *Ship Passenger Lists, New York and New Jersey (1600-1825).* Newhall, Calif.: the editor, 1978. 333 p.

> Contains passenger listings mentioned in Lancour, *A Bibliography of Ship Passenger Lists, 1538-1825.* (1963), nos. 72-76, 78B, 79, 81-83, 83 note, 85, 87A, 88, 89, 98(1), 100, 102(1A), 104-106, 107A, 110-111, 111 corr., 112-114. Includes index to ship names, place names, and about 10,000 personal names, with variant surname spellings. Tepper, in nos. 9120, 9135, 9143, 9144, and 9151, has similar lists.

*   *   *

0717
BOYER, CARL, 3rd, editor. *Ship Passenger Lists: Pennsylvania and Delaware (1641-1825).* Newhall, Calif.: the editor, 1980. 289 p.

> Contains details of 32 passenger lists mentioned in Lancour, *A Bibliography of Ship Passenger Lists, 1538-1825* (1963), from which nos. 116, 118, 129, 137-139, 141-143, 148-151, 157-159, 169, 171-174, 176-182, 190, and 195-197 are quoted in full. Has index of ship names, place names, and about 6,500 personal names, with variant surname spellings. See also Tepper, nos. 9120, 9135, 9143, 9144 for similar lists.

*   *   *

0720
BOYER, CARL, 3rd, editor. *Ship Passenger Lists, the South (1538-1825)*. Newhall, Calif.: the editor, 1979. 314 p.

Contains passenger lists mentioned in Lancour, *A Bibliography of Ship Passenger Lists, 1538-1825*. (1963), nos. 198E, 200-207, 208(1), 213, 215, 219, 220, 222, 225, 227, 229-231, 232A-233, 235-237, 240(1)-243. Boyer has indexed ship names, place names, and about 12,000 personal names, with variant surname spellings. Nos. 9120, 9135, 9143, 9144, and 9151. Tepper's works, have similar lists.

*   *   *

0732
BOYS, WILLIAM. *Collections for an History of Sandwich in Kent*. Canterbury [Eng.]: 1786-1792, pp. 751-752.

Contains the names of emigrants who sailed in the *Hercules* of Sandwich. No. 7111 in this book, Putnam's "Two Early Passenger Lists, 1635-1637," is printed in part in Boys. Also in nos. 1672 and 1674, Drake; and in no. 9151, Tepper, *Passengers to America*, pp. 123-124. And see no. 0744, Boys. (Lancour 46A)

*   *   *

0744
BOYS, WILLIAM. "Emigrants in the *Hercules* of Sandwich." In *The New England Historical and Genealogical Register*, vol. 15:1 (Jan. 1861), pp. 28-29.

Also in no. 0732, Boys; nos. 1672, 1674, Drake; and no. 9151, Tepper, *Passengers to America*, pp. 123-124. And see no. 0378, Bartlett. (Lancour 46C)

*   *   *

0756
BRADFORD, WILLIAM. "Lists of pasengers [sic] to America. From Authentic Sources: Passengers of the Mayflower as Enumerated by Governor Bradford in His *History of Plymouth Plantation*." In *The Genealogist's Notebook*, vol. 1:17 (May 22, 1899), pp. 66-67.

Also in no. 9143, Tepper, *New World Immigrants*, vol. 1, pp. 9-10. For the many versions of the *Mayflower* passenger list, see the index. (Lancour 33D)

*   *   *

0768
BRADFORD, WILLIAM. "Passengers of the *Mayflower;* the Names of Those Which Came Over First, in the Year 1620 and Were by the Blessing of God the First Beginers [sic] and (in a Sort) the Foundation of All the Plantations and Colonies in New England, and Their Families." In *History of Plymouth Plantation, 1620-1647*. Boston: Massachusetts Historical Society, 1912, vol. 2, pp. 397-412.

This list is in all editions of Bradford. Also in no. 0702, Boyer, *Ship Passenger Lists, National and New England*, pp. 134-136. Numerous references to the *Mayflower* will be found in the index. (Lancour 33, 33A-G)

*   *   *

0780
BRAUN, FRITZ. "Amerikaauswanderer aus Odernheim am Glan." In *Nordpfaelzer Geschichtsverein*, Jahrgang 40, no. 2 (June 1960), pp. 438-439.

Emigrants to America from Odernheim on the Glan River. From nos. 9041-9042, Strassburger, and an article of the same title by Krebs (no. 4121). This article serves as a correction and addition to Krebs' article: whereas Krebs could not locate the names of a certain three emigrants in Strassburger's work, Braun, through close examination, appears to find the three arriving together on the ship *Edinburgh* in Philadelphia on Sept. 5, 1748. Names and date of leaving Odernheim given.

*   *   *

0789
BRAUN, FRITZ. "Auswanderer auf dem Schiff *Elisabeth*, Bremen-New York 1832." In *Pfaelzische Familien- und Wappenkunde* (1957), pp. 61-68. (Mitteilungen zur Wanderungsgeschichte der Pfaelzer, Folge 9).

The ship *Elisabeth's* passenger list, stored in the U.S. National Archives, Washington, D.C., covers about 150 immigrants, including many Mennonites, from several parts of Germany to America. Some indicate settlement in New York and Ohio. Name, age, occupation, some places of origin, some family data. (Lancour 247)

*   *   *

0797
BRAUN, FRITZ. "Auswanderer auf dem Schiff *Logan*, Le Havre-New York, 1833." In *Pfaelzische Familien- und Wappenkunde*, (1957) pp. 69-76. (Mitteilungen zur Wanderungsgeschichte der Pfaelzer, Folge 10.)

Emigrants on the ship *Logan*. Concerns 132 persons from Europe (mostly Palatines from Germany), the majority planning to settle in the American Midwest (Illinois, Missouri). Names, ages, occupations, countries of origin, intended destinations, and much additional data. (Lancour 250)

*   *   *

0805
BRAUN, FRITZ. *Auswanderer auf dem Schiff "Samuel M. Fox," Ankunft New York, 4 August 1852*. (Schriften zur Wanderungsgeschichte der Pfaelzer, Folge 21). Kaiserslautern, Germany: n.p., (196?).

Emigrants on the ship *Samuel M. Fox*, which arrived in New York on August 4, 1852. Contains travel descriptions written by several of the 630 passengers during the voyage. The list was sent to Braun by American citizen Albert J. Ruth. Found in the archives of the city of Kaiserslautern and in published and unpublished records of various Mennonite communities. Braun's work is a printed transcription of the passenger list, with much additional information. The list is also in no. 0807, Braun (a resetting of 0805).

*   *   *

0807
BRAUN, FRITZ. "Auswanderer auf dem Schiff *Samuel M. Fox,* Ankunft New York 4.8.1852." In *Pfaelzische Familien- und Wappenkunde,* vol. 5:1 (1964), pp. 25-32: vol. 5:2 (1964), pp. 57-64; vol. 5:3 (1964), pp. 89-96; vol. 5:4 (1964), pp. 121-125. (Mitteilungen zur Wanderungsgeschichte der Pfaelzer, 1964. Folgen 1-4)

> Immigrants on the ship *Samuel M. Fox,* arriving in New York Aug. 4, 1852. For other details, see no. 0805.

*   *   *

0813
BRAUN, FRITZ. *Auswanderer aus der Mennonitengemeinde Friedelsheim im 19. Jahrhundert.* (Schriften zur Wanderungsgeschichte der Pfaelzer, Heft 1.) Ludwigshafen am Rhein [Germany]: Richard Louis Verlag, 1956.

> Church registers of the Mennonite congregation in Friedelsheim in the 19th century. From the registers and from letters of immigrants in the U.S. Most settled in Ohio and Iowa. (Lancour 249)

*   *   *

0821
BRAUN, FRITZ. *Auswanderer aus der Umgebung von Ludwigshafen a. Rh. auf dem Schiff "Thistle of Glasgow" 1730.* (Schriften zur Wanderungsgeschichte der Pfaelzer, Folge 8) Neustadt an der Aisch, Germany; Buchdruckerei Ph. C.W. Schmidt, 1959. 21 p.

> Emigrants from the vicinity of Ludwigshafen am Rhein on the ship *Thistle of Glasgow* in 1730. Contains the names of 77 families who were among 260 Palatines arriving in Philadelphia on August 29, 1730. From church registers in the German community named and three lists of passengers on that voyage of the *Thistle* in nos. 9041 and 9042, Strassburger. Names, without the genealogical data, in no. 0829, Braun. Also in no. 0717, Boyer, *Ship Passenger Lists, Pennsylvania and Delaware,* pp. 125-141. And see nos. 0827 and 0869, concerning Palatines on the *Thistle of Glasgow.*   (Lancour 148)

*   *   *

0827
BRAUN, FRITZ. "Auswanderer aus der Umgebung von Ludwigshafen am Rhein auf dem Schiff *Thistle of Glasgow* 1730." In *Pfaelzische Familien- und Wappenkunde* and the supplement: *Landsleute drinnen und draussen* (Fellow Countrymen Here and There), Folge 5 (1953), pp. 31-32.

> Emigrants from the vicinity of Ludwigshafen on the Rhine on the ship *Thistle of Glasgow* in 1730. Taken from nos. 9041-9042, Strassburger. Includes 73 of the 260 names from the Strassburger list, as a preliminary stage to a later article, no. 0821. The ship arrived in Philadelphia in August 1730. This list by and large has names only, though some entries indicate a place of origin.   (Lancour 148B)

*   *   *

0829
BRAUN, FRITZ. "Auswanderer aus der Umgebung von Ludwigshafen a Rh. auf dem Schiff *Thistle of Glasgow* 1730." In *Pfaelzische Familien- und Wappenkunde,* (1953) pp.31-32. (Mitteilungen zur Wanderungsgeschichte der Pfaelzer, Folge 5) supplement. Folge 3/4 (1959), pp. 253-272.

> For annotation, see no. 0821, Braun. See also no. 0869, Braun. (Lancour 148A)

*   *   *

0837
BRAUN, FRITZ. *Auswanderer aus Enkenbach seit Beginn des 18. Jahrhunderts.* (Schriften zur Wanderungsgeschichte der Pfaelzer, Part 11.) Kaiserslautern [Germany]: Rohr-Druck, 1960? 27 p.

> Emigrants from the Rhenish village of Enkenbach between the years 1715 and 1928. Destinations were to other countries in Europe and to North and South America. Gives last known residence, often established through recent contact with emigrants' relatives or through letters in archives.

*   *   *

0845
BRAUN, FRITZ. *Auswanderer aus Kaiserslautern im 18. Jahrhundert.* (Schriften zur Wanderungsgeschichte der Pfaelzer, Folge 17). Kaiserslautern [Germany]: Rohr Druck, 1965. 32 p.

> Emigrants from Kaiserslautern in the 18th century. Special printing from the *Buergerbuch der Stadt Kaiserslautern,* 1597-1800. Found in Lutheran and Reformed Church registers, civil records of Kaiserslautern, and in published articles. Lists emigrants with destinations not only in America but also in Eastern Europe. Some 19th-century emigrants included. Names, ages, family data, and places of origin and destination.

*   *   *

0849
BRAUN, FRITZ. *Auswanderer aus Steinweiler in drei Jahrhunderten.* (Schriften zur Wanderungsgeschichte der Pfaelzer, Folge 27), Kaiserslautern, Germany: Heimatstelle Pfalz, 1968.

> Emigrants from Steinweiler, Germany, during three centuries. Concerns about 800 departures from Steinweiler to other parts of Europe and overseas; the great majority of these emigrants from about 1700 to mid-20th century went to the Americas. Names, most ages, family data, villages of origin, occasionally places of settlement. Some have detailed genealogies and exact departure and arrival dates, ports of departure and arrival, and ships' names.

*   *   *

0853
BRAUN, FRITZ. "Auswanderung aus dem heutigen Stadtgebiet von Ludwigshafen am Rhein im 18. Jahrhundert." In *Pfaelzische Familien- und Wappenkunde,* including supplement: *Landsleute drinnen und draussen (Fellow Countrymen Here and There),* Folge 5 (1953), pp. 26-31.

Emigration from the present city limits of Ludwigshafen on the Rhine in the 18th century. Covers 20 emigrants to French Guiana and to North America. Much family data. Also includes emigration from Ludwigshafen to Hungary.

* * *

0860
BRAUN, FRITZ. "18th Century Palatine Emigrants from the Ludwigshafen Area." In *The Pennsylvania Dutchman,* vol. 5:13 (Mar. 1, 1954), p. 13.

From records of the district of Neustadt. Tells of eight immigrants to Pennsylvania and one to Nova Scotia. Also in no. 9144, Tepper, *New World Immigrants,* vol. 2, pp. 32 and 33, and in no. 0717, Boyer, *Ship Passenger Lists, Pennsylvania and Delaware,* pp. 189-190.   (Lancour 173)

* * *

0867
BRAUN, FRITZ. "Der Ort Host bei Bernville in Pennsylvanien." In *Pfaelzische Familien- und Wappenkunde,* (Mitteilungen zur Wanderungsgeschichte der Pfaelzer, 1976,3), vol. 8:9 (Dec. 1976), pp. 381-383.

The town of Host near Bernville, Pennsylvania. Records taken from *Host Church Records* by Arthur Shuman and published in a work on Palatine emigration. Basically an historical article concerning the origin of the place-name "Host." Tells of five immigrants and their families, one of whom came to Tulpehocken, Pa., in 1723, and four who settled in Berks County, Pa., about 1740.

* * *

0869
BRAUN, FRITZ. "Palatines on the Ship *Thistle of Glasgow* (1730)." In *The Pennsylvania Dutchman,* vol. 5:13 (Mar. 1, 1954), p. 13.

Has names of 13 persons whose home villages were positively identified. Also in no. 9144, Tepper, *New World Immigrants,* vol. 2, p. 31. Fuller lists are in nos. 0821 and 0829, Braun. (Lancour 148C)

* * *

0877
BRAUN, FRITZ. "Passengers on the *Loyal Judith* (1740)." In *The Pennsylvania Dutchman,* vol. 5:13 (Mar. 1, 1954), p. 12.

Palatine passengers arriving at Philadelphia, November 25, 1740. Names 17 emigrants with their places of origin. The original list was published in *Nordpfaelzer Geschichtsverein,* no. 9/10, (Nov.-Dec. 1953). Also in no. 9144, Tepper, *New World Immigrants,* vol. 2, p. 142.

* * *

0885
BRAUN, FRITZ. *Schweizer und andere Einwanderer sowie Auswanderer im ref. Kirchenbuch Steinwenden (1684-1780)."* Neustadt/Aisch, [Germany]: Buchdruckerei Ph. C.W. Schmidt, 1960. 23 p. (Schriften zur Wanderungsgeschichte der Pfaelzer, Folge 10, 1960). Offprint in the series Mitteilungen zur Wanderungsgeschichte der Pfaelzer, supplement in *Pfaelzische Familien und Wappenkunde,* 1960, Folgen 3-4.

Swiss and other emigrants, including some recorded in the Reformed Church register of Steinwenden. Lists immigrants to Steinwenden as well as emigrants from there to America and other parts of the world. Gives names, ages, family data, places of origin. Sometimes links names with entries in the lists in nos. 9041-9042, Strassburger.

* * *

0889
BRAUN, FRITZ. "Tulpehocken vor 250 Jahren von Deutschen besiedelt." In *Pfaelzische Familien- und Wappenkunde,* vol. 7:10 (Apr. 1973), pp. 357-364; vol. 7:11 (Aug. 1973), pp. 385-396; vol. 7:12 (Nov. 1973), pp. 425-428. (Mitteilungen zur Wanderungsgeschichte der Pfaelzer, nos. 1-3, 1973).

Tulpehocken (Pennsylvania) 250 years ago, settled by Germans. Documents the origins of many of the early Palatine settlers in this community in Berks County, Pa. Of the 100 immigrants, some came in 1709 or 1710 to the province of New York, others came in the 1720s and 1730s to Philadelphia, then settled directly in Tulpehocken. Names, some birth dates, places of origin, some family data.

* * *

0891
BRAUN, FRITZ. "Wege in die Welt." In *Otterberg und seine Buerger.* (Archiv zur Geschichte von Stadt und Kloster Otterberg, no. 1) Ludwigshafen am Rhein [Germany]: Richard Louis, [1956] Part 1, pp. 39-44.

Paths into the world. From sources in Otterberg. Details on about 20 emigrants from Otterberg, from circa 1735 to the middle of the twentieth century. Some family information, name of ship, date of arrival in Philadelphia, and place of settlement in America. See also Krebs, no. 4301.

* * *

0893
BRAUN, FRITZ, and FRIEDRICH KREBS. "Amerika-Auswanderer des 18. Jahrhunderts aus suedpfaelzischen Gemeinden." In *Schriften zur Wanderungsgeschichte der Pfaelzer,* Part 2. Ludwigshafen am Rhein [Germany]: Richard Louis Verlag, 1956. 20 p.

A republication of materials which first appeared in a series on Palatine emigration history: Mitteilungen zur Wanderungsgeschichte der Pfaelzer, supplement to the periodical, *Pfaelzische Familien- und Wappenkunde,* Folge 5 (1956), pp. 29-36; Folge 6 (1956), pp. 37-44; Folgen 11-12 (1957), pp. 83-84. English translation in nos. 0915 and 0922. Information from various Lutheran and Reformed Church registers and elsewhere. Name, age, family data, and often the planned destination. An attempt has been made to link specific names in this list with names in the Strassburger work, nos. 9041-42. A supplement to this material is item no. 0895. (Lancour 139B)

*   *   *

0895

BRAUN, FRITZ, and **FRIEDRICH KREBS.** "Amerika-Auswanderer des 18. Jahrhundert aus suedpfaelzischen Gemeinden: Addition to the supplement of the same name in these pages," Folgen 5 and 6, 1956, p. 83.

Supplement to no. 0893.

*   *   *

0915

BRAUN, FRITZ, and **FRIEDRICH KREBS.** German Emigrants from Palatinate Parishes." Translated by Don Yoder. In *The Pennsylvania Genealogical Magazine,* vol. 25:4 (1967-1968), pp. 246-262.

Lists emigrants from ten parishes in the southern part of the Palatinate, generally in the area west of the Rhine River, between Speyer on the north and Karlsruhe to the south. Gives basic emigration data, with supporting information. Data first appeared in "Amerika-Auswanderer des 18. Jahrhunderts aus suedpfaelzischen Gemeinden," in the supplement *Mitteilungen zur Wanderungsgeschichte der Pfaelzer,* edited by Fritz Braun, to the periodical *Pfaelziche Familien- und Wappenkunde,* 1956 (no. 0893). A translation first appeared in no. 0922, the Braun article, "Pennsylvania Dutch Pioneers from South Palatinate Parishes."

*   *   *

0922

BRAUN, FRITZ, and **FRIEDRICH KREBS.** "Pennsylvania Dutch Pioneers from South Palatine Parishes." Translated by Don Yoder. In *The Pennsylvania Dutchman,* vol. 8:3 (Spring 1957), pp. 39-42.

From Lutheran Church registers in various locations. Published originally in no. 0893; and see no. 0915. Also in no. 9144, Tepper, *New World Immigrants,* vol. 2, pp. 61-74; and no. 0717, Boyer, *Ship Passenger Lists, Pennsylvania and Delaware,* pp. 86-99. (Lancour 139)

*   *   *

0932

BRICKENSTEIN, JOHN C. "The First 'Sea Congregation,' 1742." In *Transactions of the Moravian Historical Society,* vol. 1 (1876), pp. 36-37.

Majority of passengers were German, many of whom had been selected to replace the first colony at Oilgerruh in Holstein but refused and proceeded to America on the *Catharine.* They went from Copenhagen to London, leaving Gravesend in 1742, arriving in New York and thence Philadelphia, 1742. Involves 56 passengers.

*   *   *

0933

BRICKENSTEIN, JOHN C. "The Second 'Sea Congregation,' 1743." In *Transactions of the Moravian Historical Society,* vol. 1 (1876), pp. 108-109.

In 1743, a contingent of 24 passengers left Rotterdam in the

Little Strength. They travelled via Cowes, England, arrived in New York, and proceeded to Philadelphia, 1743.

*   *   *

0943

BRISTOL AND AMERICA; A RECORD OF THE FIRST SETTLERS IN THE COLONIES OF NORTH AMERICA, 1654-1685, Including the Names with Places of Origin of More Than 10,000 Servants to Foreign Plantations Who Sailed from the Port of Bristol to Virginia, Maryland, and Other Parts of the Atlantic Coast, and Also to the West Indies from 1654 to 1685. London: R.S. Glover [1929]. 182 p. Reprinted with index of 16 pages bound in by Genealogical Publishing Co., Baltimore, 1967.

From the archives of Bristol, England, with the title, "Servants to Foreign Plantations." Emigrants to New England, Maryland, Virginia, New York, Pennsylvania, Canada, and the Caribbean Islands. The information was transcribed by R. Hargreaves-Mawdsley, and occasionally the work will be found under his name rather than "Bristol...." An index of 16 pages was issued in 1931 as a separate, but it is now incorporated in the G.P.C. reprint. Pages 1-26 of Book 1 of "Servants to Foreign Plantations" were also in no. 2899, Hargreaves-Mawdsley, and in nos. 3438 and 3440, Gordon Ireland. (Lancour 11)

*   *   *

0953

BROCK, ROBERT ALONZO. *Documents, Chiefly Unpublished, Relating to the Huguenot Emigration to Virginia and to the Settlement at Manakin-Town, with an Appendix of Genealogies, Presenting Data of the Fontaine, Maury, Dupuy, Trabue, Marye, Chastain, Cocke, and Other Families.* (Collections of the Virginia Historical Society, n.s., vol. 5) Richmond, Va.: Virginia Historical Society, 1886. 247 p. Reprinted by Genealogical Publishing Co., Baltimore: 1962. 255 p.

Contents include passenger list of 170 refugees on the *Peter and Anthony,* which came to Jamestown in September 1700; Records Relating to the Huguenot Emigration to Virginia in 1700; "List of All Ye Passingers from London to James River...;" "Liste des Personnes du Second Convoy que Serent Toute l'Annee a Manicanton;" "A List of the Refugees Who Are to Receive of Ye Miller of Falling Creek . . . 1700;" "Rolle des Francois, Suisses, Genevois, Alemans, et Flamans...;" "A List of Ye French Refugees that are Settled att ye Mannachin Town . . .;" and "Lists Generalle de Tous les Francois Protestant Refugies . . . ." The reprint carries, in addition, a "Communication from Governor Francis Nicholson Concerning the Huguenot Settlement, with 'List of ye Refugees,' 1700." (Lancour 224)

*   *   *

0963

BRODHEAD, JOHN ROMEYN. "Names of the Dutch Who Swore Allegiance after the Surrender of New-York." In *Documents Relative to the Colonial History of the State of New-York.* Albany [N.Y.]: Weed, Parsons & Co., 1853, vol. 3, pp. 74-77.

"A catalogue alphabeticall of ye names of such inhabitants of

New Yorke, &c. as tooke the oath . . . October the 21st, 22nd, 24th, and 26th dayes 1664." Also printed in no. 0969.

*   *   *

0969
BRODHEAD, JOHN ROMEYN. "New York Dutch Who Swore Allegiance after the Surrender of New York, October 21st, 22nd, 24th, and 26th, 1664." In *Genealogical Reference Builders Newsletter,* vol. 2:5 (May-June 1968), pp. 179-182, 197.

> Originally published in Brodhead (no. 0963) *Documents Relative to the Colonial History of the State of New York,* vol. 3, pp. 74-77, in a chapter entitled, "New York Colonial Manuscripts." Names only.

*   *   *

0973
BROWN, CHARLOTTE C., and **MARGARET JULIA (B.) LINDSAY.** [Passengers on the *Henry and Francis,* 1685.] In *The New Jersey Browns.* Milwaukee, Wis.: n.p., 1931, pp. 5-6.

> Names 74 persons on the *Henry and Francis* for a crossing in 1685 from Newcastle, England. For numerous other references to the *Henry and Francis,* see the index.   (Lancour 113B)

*   *   *

0983
BROWNING, CHARLES H. *Welsh Settlement of Pennsylvania.* Philadelphia: William J. Campbell, 1912. 631 p. Reprinted by Genealogical Publishing Co., Baltimore, 1967.

> Settlement of "Welsh Tract" lands granted by William Penn, 1681. Mentions many celebrated early immigrants and the ships they took.   (Lancour 123)

*   *   *

0993
BRUMBAUGH, GAIUS MARCUS. "Early Maryland Naturalizations, etc., from Kilty's *Laws.*" In *Maryland Records: Colonial, Revolutionary, County and Church from Original Sources.* Lancaster [Pa]: Lancaster Press, 1928, vol. 2, pp. 311-313. Reprinted by Genealogical Publishing Co., Baltimore, 1975.

> Fuller list in no. 7997, Scharf.   (Lancour 200A)

*   *   *

0998
BRYCE, GEORGE. *The Romantic Settlement of Lord Selkirk's Colonists (The Pioneers of Manitoba).* Toronto: Musson Book Co., 1909. Appendix, pp. 320-328.

> Emigrants from Scotland who settled in Canada at Red River, 1811-1816. They travelled via York Factory. Also in no. 6755, Phillips; no. 5274, Martin; and no. 1000, Bryce.

*   *   *

1000
BRYCE, GEORGE, and **C.N. BELL.** *Papers from the Past. Some Letters of Lord Selkirk, Hitherto Unpublished, and Some of the Early Laws of the Settlement, Read Before the Society, January 17, 1889.* (The Historical and Scientific Society of Manitoba, *Transactions,* 33, 1889) Winnipeg: Manitoba Free Press Print, 1889, pp. 6-9.

> Describes Swiss settlers for the Selkirk Colony, Red River, 1821; most of whom, in 1826, left for Minnesota. Lists Scottish immigrants belonging to the Red River Settlement who arrived at Hudson Bay in 1811, or were brought from York Factory, July 1812. Also Scottish passengers from the *Prince of Wales* destined for the Red River Settlement who arrived at Churchill Factory, Hudson Bay, August 1813, and finally reached the Red River Settlement in 1814. See also no. 0998, Bryce; no. 5274, Martin; and nos. 6755 and 6765, Phillips.

*   *   *

1003
BUECHER, ROBERT. *St. Clair County, Illinois, Naturalization Index, 1816-1905.* Thomson, Ill: Heritage House, 1976. 45 p.

> Lists immigrants of various origins.

*   *   *

1018
BUNTING, MORGAN. "The Names of the Early Settlers of Darby Township, Chester County, Pennsylvania." In *The Pennsylvania Magazine of History and Biography,* vol. 24:2 (1900), pp. 179-186.

> Provides the names of some who arrived in America between the years 1682 and 1686, and who settled between 1687 and 1760. Also in no. 8370, Sheppard, *Passengers and Ships Prior to 1684.*

*   *   *

1021
BURCHALL, MICHAEL J. "Further Light on East Sussex Emigration." In *Sussex Family Historian,* vol. 2:8 (Mar. 1977), pp. 263-268.

> Details on a few emigrations from East Sussex in the south of England to Canada, 1830s and 1840s.

*   *   *

1023
BURCHALL, MICHAEL J. "Heathfield Emigrants to America, 1830-31." In *Sussex Family Historian,* vol. 2:7 (Dec. 1976), pp. 242-244.

> Details concerning emigrants leaving the parish of Heathfield, East Sussex on the English Channel, for America. No ship or place of arrival in America given. Further information may be found in no. 1026, Burchall.

*   *   *

1026
BURCHALL, MICHAEL J. "Parish-Organised Emigration to America; 19th Century Examples from East

Sussex." In *Genealogists' Magazine* (London), vol. 18:7 (Sept. 1976), pp. 336-342.

Records of English emigrants to America from Brede, Framfield, Ewhurst, and Hailsham, Sussex, between 1823 and 1832.

*   *   *

1029
BURCHALL, MICHAEL J. "Sussex Emigrants." In *Sussex Family Historian*, vol. 3:6 (Sept. 1978), pp. 162-169.

From Salehurst parish records in the East Sussex record office at Lewes, England. Lists emigrants to Australia and Canada, 1838-1857; emigrants to Quebec and Montreal, 1840-1862. Names and ages given, with ship and port of origin.

*   *   *

1032
BURGERT, ANNETTE K. "Die fruehen Siedler von Host Church, Berks County, Pennsylvanien, und ihre Herkunft aus Hochstadt, Pfalz." In *Pfaelzische-Rheinische Familienkunde: Pfaelzische Familien- und Wappenkunde*, vol. 9:1 (Apr. 1978), pp. 49-52; 9:2 (Aug. 1978), pp. 89-99; 9:3 (Dec. 1978), pp. 161-180. (Mitteilungen, 1978, 1-3)

The early settlers of Host Church, Berks County, Pennsylvania, and their origins in Hochstadt in the Palatinate. Concerns 75 to 100 German emigrants from the villages of Oberhochstadt and Niederhochstadt in the years 1732-1751. Names, ages, family data, arrival dates.

*   *   *

1034
BURGERT, ANNETTE K. "Some Pennsylvania Pioneers from Hassloch and Boehl in the Palatinate." In *Der Reggeboge: Quarterly of the Pennsylvania German Society*, vol. 12:2 (Apr. 1978), pp. 1-21.

This is a list of 65 German immigrants, with much genealogical information: often the ship, date, and origin, with copious Pennsylvania records. The years covered: 1726-1764. Hassloch and Boehl are located in the Rhineland-Palatinate just east of Neustadt.

*   *   *

1036
BUSHEY, ARTHUR C., JR. *A List of Passengers in the "Ark" and the "Dove" Who Are Known to Have Left Descendants....* [Baltimore]: The Society of the Ark and the Dove [1963]. [4 p.]

A paper submitted to the Society to show the names of persons who came in the *Ark* and the *Dove* in March 1634.

*   *   *

1046
BUTLER, JAMES DAVIE. "British Convicts Shipped to American Colonies." In *The American Historical Review,* vol. 2 (Oct. 1896), pp. 12-33.

Many "convicts" were prisoners of the British, taken in battle

during the 17th and 18th centuries. Destination here was usually New England. No list, but names are contained in the narrative of the article. Good study.

*   *   *

1056
CADBURY, HENRY J. "Four Immigrant Shiploads of 1836 and 1837." In *The Norwegian-American Historical Association Studies and Records,* vol. 2 (1927), pp. 20-52.

From U.S. National Archives, data on 342 passengers of the *Norden, den Norske Klippe, Aegir* and *Enigheden,* New York. Name, age, sex and occupation. Also in no. 9144, Tepper, *New World Immigrants,* vol. 2, pp. 384-416.   (Lancour 254)

*   *   *

1064
CALDER, ISABEL MacBEATH. [Passengers on the *Hector,* 1637-1638.] In *The New Haven Colony,* New Haven [Conn.]: Yale University Press, 1934, pp. 29-31.

Names persons who accompanied John Davenport and Theophilus Eaton to Connecticut (via Boston). Also in no. 0702, Boyer, *Ship Passenger Lists, National and New England,* pp. 201 and 202.   (Lancour 71)

*   *   *

1067
CALDWELL, LILLE MOERBE. *Texas Wends, Their First Half-Century, with Historical, Biographical, and Genealogical Information on the Serbin Wends ....* Salado, Texas: Anson Jones Press, 1961. 283 p.

Texas Wends of Serbin migrated to Texas in 1854 from Upper and Lower Lusatia, a region between the Oder and Elbe rivers in East Germany and southern Poland. Pages 253-276 are a reprint of the original ship register of the Wendish colonists who left Lusatia in 1854 to come to Serbin, Texas. Lists family head, family members, birth dates, status, village and region of origin. There is much information on the Moerbe and Schatte families. The Wends are also listed in no. 0578, Blasig; no. 1858, Engerrand; and no. 2504, Geue.

*   *   *

1072
CALNEK, WILLIAM A. *History of the County of Annapolis, Including Old Port Royal and Acadia.* Edited and completed by Arthur W. Savary. Toronto: William Briggs, 1897, pp. 150-151.

Contains the passenger list of the *Charming Molly* which sailed from Massachusetts to Annapolis Royal, Nova Scotia, in 1760. Also listed in no. 9820, Wilson.

*   *   *

1074-1075
CAMANN, EUGENE, compiler. "Passenger List No. 619 (National Archives, Washington, D.C.), on Board the Barque *Rainbow,* 1843." In *Der Brief.*
1074
---Dec. 1978, [pp. 1-2].
1075
---Jan. 1979, p. 1

> *Der Brief* is the newsletter of the Historical Society of North German Settlements in Western N.Y., Niagara Falls. Name, age, sex, occupation. Settlers were Old Lutherans, from Uekermark region of Pomerania, today just inside East Germany on Poland's border near Stettin. All 118 passengers became part of the New Bergholz settlement, N.Y.

*   *   *

1078
"CAMDEN COUNTY, GEORGIA, HEADRIGHTS. BOOK A, 1785-1790." In *The Georgia Researcher,* vol. 1:1 (March 1963), pp. 36-38.

> Probably all of British origin.

*   *   *

1088
CAMERON, VIOLA ROOT, compiler. *Emigrants from Scotland to America, 1774-1775. Copied from a Loose Bundle of Treasury Papers in the Public Record Office, London, England.* London: the compiler, 1930. 117 p. Reprinted by Genealogical Publishing Co., Baltimore, 1959.

> About 2,000 names, with much additional information. Ships mentioned were bound for New York, Philadelphia, Wilmington (N.C.), Salem (N.C.), South Carolina, Savannah (Ga.), Quebec, St. John's Island, Prince Edward Island, Antigua, and Jamaica. Compiled from a typescript copy. (Lancour 21)

*   *   *

1098
CAMP, ANTHONY J. "Transportation from Hertfordshire, England, to America, 1646-1775." In *The New England Historical and Genealogical Register,* vol. 115:2 (Jan. 1961), pp. 55-57.

> From *Hertfordshire Quarter Sessions Records* (1905-1957), 10 vols. A list of convicts, with much other information, destined for Virginia or Maryland, Barbados or Jamaica. Also in no. 9151, Tepper, *Passengers to America,* pp. 472-474; and in no. 0702, Boyer, *Ship Passenger Lists, National and New England,* pp. 33-36. (Lancour 10)

*   *   *

1110
CAMPBELL, COLIN. "Deportations from Scotland in 1685." In *The New England Historical and Genealogical Register,* vol. 114 (Apr. 1960), pp. 150-151.

> From a document in the Scottish Record Office, H.M. Register House, Edinburgh. Fifteen prisoners sent to New England after capture in an unsuccessful uprising led by the Earl of Argyll in 1685. Also in no. 9151, Tepper, *Passengers to*

America, pp. 171-172; and no. 0702, Boyer, *Ship Passenger Lists, National and New England,* p. 186. And see nos. 2590 and 2596, Glasgow, as well as no. 9840, Wodrow. (Lancour 61)

*   *   *

1114
"CANADIAN AND NOVA SCOTIA REFUGEES WHO JOINED THE AMERICAN CAUSE." In *Daughters of the American Revolution Magazine,* vol. 103:10 (Dec. 1969), pp. 828-829.

> Refugees from Canada who came to the American colonies during the Revolutionary War. Partial listings of those who drew lots for grants of land in the "Refugee Tracts" in what are now Clinton County, New York, and Licking County, Ohio, 1798. Names only.

*   *   *

1120
CAPPEL, ALBERT. "American Emigration Materials from Pfeddersheim." Translated and edited by Don Yoder. In *Pennsylvania Folklife,* vol. 22:4 (Summer 1973), pp. 43-48.

> All records prior to 1787. Concerns passengers to Philadelphia, named in a bundle of loose official documents inscribed, "Abt. XI: Auswanderung ab 1746," in the city archives of Pfeddersheim, Germany. Same data mentioned in the Reformed Church register as well as in Pfeddersheim court records. See also nos. 1126 and 1129, Cappel.

*   *   *

1126
CAPPEL, ALBERT. "Auswanderer im Kirchenbuch der lutherischen Gemeinde Pfeddersheim." In *Pfaelzische Familien- und Wappenkunde,* vol. 4:11 (Aug.-Sept. 1963), pp. 359-360.

> Emigrants listed in the church register of the Lutheran parish of Pfeddersheim, actually combined Lutheran parish of Pfeddersheim and Pfiffligheim, for the years 1750-1794. Indicates five families who emigrated to America between 1753 and 1766. Names, place of origin, and some family data. See also nos. 1120 and 1129, Cappel.

*   *   *

1129
CAPPEL, ALBERT. "Auswanderungsakten in Pfeddersheim." In *Pfaelzische Familien- und Wappenkunde,* vol. 6:10 (Oct. 1969), pp. 347-353; 6:11 (Nov. 1969), pp. 379-386. (Mitteilungen zur Wanderungsgeschichte der Pfaelzer, 1969, Folgen 3-4.)

> Files concerning Pfeddersheim emigration. From various records there in the Palatinate. One hundred emigrants to other parts of Europe, to Brazil, and to North America. Much family data, with some dates of arrival in Philadelphia, apparently provided from nos. 9041-9042, Strassburger. See also nos. 1120 and 1126, Cappel.

*   *   *

1132
CARTER, KATE B., compiler. *Heart Throbs of the West* . . . . vol. 4, pp. 145-157. Salt Lake City, Utah: Daughters of Utah Pioneers, 1943.

> From a chapter entitled, "Ships and Boats of Pioneer Interest." Mentions the names of several immigrants in the 1850s. Also provides a complete list of the ships which carried Latter-Day Saint emigrants from Europe to America between 1840 and 1868, giving dates of sailing, ports of departure and arrival, and the total numbers aboard.

*   *   *

1134
CASTELEIRO, M.A. contributor. "Georgia Immigrants: Names of the Salzburgers, 1734-1741." In *The Southern Genealogist's Exchange Quarterly,* vol. 8:42 (Summer 1967), pp. 45-46.

> Names male immigrants from Salzburg, Austria, who settled in Georgia. Taken from *Urlsperger Nachrichten,* vol. 1, 2307-2310. And see no. 7820, Rupp.

*   *   *

1137
"CATALOUGE OF EIGHTY-SEVEN PUBLIC FRIENDS YT HAVE DIED IN PENNSYLVANIA since ye First Settlement of Friends there Read at ye Yearly Meeting, 1709." In *The Pennsylvania Genealogical Magazine,* vol. 31:2 (1979), pp. 114-121.

> "Public Friends" refers to the Friends who spoke in the Quaker Meeting. Years covered here are 1677-1702. These were settlers from Great Britain and Ireland. Details of places of origin, dates of arrival, and other information on life in America are included. Verbatim copy of a manuscript found at Devonshire House, London, in portfolio 8:89. Originally published by *Quaker History: The Bulletin of the Friends Historical Association,* Swarthmore, Pa., vol. 4, 1913.

*   *   *

1140
CHAPIN, MRS. EDWARD J. "Naturalizations in Federal Courts, New York District, 1790-1828." In *The New York Genealogical and Biographical Record,* vol. 97:1 (Jan. 1966), pp. 1-8; vol. 97:2 (Apr. 1966), pp. 106-114; vol. 97:3 (July 1966), pp. 157-162; vol. 97:4 (Oct. 1966), pp. 219-222.

> Two-thirds of these applicants were from the British Isles; many others from Germany and France. Most lived in New York City. Individual trades are mentioned. Information taken from the Minutes, Southern District of New York, U.S. District Court, New York District.

*   *   *

1148
CHATELAIN, ROGER. "Familles de Tramelan Emigrees en Amerique." In *Actes de la Societe Jurassienne d'Emulation,* 2nd series, vol. 60 (1956), pp. 49-62.

> Article about the Monin and Chatelain families, originally from Tramelan, Switzerland. Includes names of other Swiss emigrants accompanying the Monin family in 1754. Places of

origin given; no ship mentioned.

*   *   *

1153
CHEVES, LANGDON, editor. "A List of All Such Masters, Free Passengers and Servants Which Are Now a Board the *Carolina* Now Ridinge in the Downes. August the 10th 1669." In *Collections of the South Carolina Historical Society,* vol. 5 (1897), pp. 134-143.

> Taken from the Shaftesbury Papers in England and other records relating to Carolina and the first settlement on the Ashley River prior to the year 1676. Masters, servants, seamen, other men's names belonging to the *Carolina,* the *Port Royall,* and the *Albemarle.*

*   *   *

1158
CHILDS, ST. JULIEN R. "The Petit-Guerard Colony." In *The South Carolina Historical and Genealogical Magazine,* vol. 43:1 (Jan. 1942), pp. 1-17; vol. 43:2 (Apr. 1942), pp. 88-97.

> This involves 17th-century French Protestants named in records of the Admiralty, now preserved in the British Foreign Office, London. Names are on pp. 1 and 2. Also in no. 1916, Fairbrother; and in no. 9143, Tepper, *New World Immigrants,* vol. 1, pp. 207-233. (Lancour 233A)

*   *   *

1168
CIFRE DE LOUBRIEL, ESTELA. *La Inmigracion a Puerto Rico Durante el Siglo XIX.* San Juan de Puerto Rico: Instituto de Cultura Puertorriquena, 1964. 441 p.

> History of 19th century immigration to Puerto Rico. Social and geographical analysis of the immigrants. Includes an alphabetical list of the names of settlers, year of arrival or stay, and, when available, occupation, place of origin, family, date of or age at death and cause of death. No ship mentioned. Lists 13,217 names.

*   *   *

1180-1181
CLARK, RAYMOND B., JR. "Frederick County, Maryland, Naturalizations, 1785-1799." In *The Maryland & Delaware Genealogist.*
1180
---Vol. 6:1 (Jan. 1965), pp. 16-18; vol. 6:2 (Apr. 1965), pp. 37-39; vol. 6:3 (July 1965), pp. 58-59; vol. 6:4 (Oct. 1965), pp. 80-81.
1181
---Corrections and additions, vol. 10:1 (Jan. 1969), p. 19.

*   *   *

1182
CLARK, RAYMOND B., JR. *Frederick County, Maryland, Naturalizations, 1799-1850.* St. Michaels, Md.: the author, 1974. 58 p.

> List of naturalizations, designating the origin of each naturalized person. Includes index of witnesses named.

*   *   *

1190
CLARKE, LOUISE BROWNELL. "South'on. A List of Suche Passengrs as Shipt Themselves at the Towne of Hampton in the James of London of iije Tonnes William Coopr Mr, ---Vrs New England in and about V of April 1635." In *The Greenes of Rhode Island, with Historical Records of English Ancestry, 1534-1902.* New York; Knickerbocker Press, 1903, p. 769.

Carries 51 names taken from the "Colonial Documents," vol. 8, folio 67, in the Public Record Office, London. Also in no. 0702, Boyer, *Ship Passenger Lists, National and New England,* p. 152.   (Lancour 49)

*   *   *

1198
"CLARKE COUNTY, GEORGIA, HEADRIGHTS, 1803-1804." In *The Georgia Researcher,* vol. 1:2 (June 1963), pp. 38-43.

Probably all British.

*   *   *

1208
CLAUSEN, C.A. "An Immigrant Shipload of 1840." In *Norwegian-American Studies and Records,* vol. 14 (1944). pp. 54-77.

Pages 63-64 contain a manifest of passengers on the *Emelie* from Drammen, Norway, to Gothenburg (Goteborg), Sweden, en route to New York, arriving August 12, 1840. Involves 89 passengers, with much additional information. Most intended to settle in Missouri. From a document in the U.S. National Archives. Also in no. 9144, Tepper, *New World Immigrants,* vol. 2, pp. 419-442.   (Lancour 255)

*   *   *

1222
COLDHAM, PETER WILSON, compiler and editor. *English Convicts in Colonial America.* Volume 1: *Middlesex 1617-1775.* New Orleans [La.]: Polyanthos, 1974. 309 p.

The County of Middlesex encloses the City of London, so these were largely London departures, transportation bonds, etc. The final eight pages list transport ships to American colonies, 1716-1775, bearing Middlesex convicts only. There is an excellent introduction to transportation of convicts in Middlesex Sessions Records, 4 volumes; Goal Delivery Reports, 1620-1672; Books and Sessions Rolls.

*   *   *

1223
COLDHAM, PETER WILSON, compiler and editor. *English Convicts in Colonial America.* Volume 2: *London 1656-1775.* New Orleans: Polyanthos, 1976. 193 p.

Comprehensive list from the Corporation of London Records Office: Royal Pardons 1662-1693; Transportation Bonds 1661-1772; Landing Certificates 1718-1736, and other records. Names with sentences, ship, date of sailing, and destination. Pages i-ix report Newgate pardons granted on condition of transportation, 1656-1716.

*   *   *

1232
COLDHAM, PETER WILSON. "List of Convicts, 1748." (Genealogical Gleanings in England.) In *National Genealogical Society Quarterly,* vol. 60:4 (Dec. 1972), pp. 256-257.

Found among the collections of Treasury Reports (PRO: T1/330/55) in England. List of convicts transported to America in the ship *Laura* of Gravesend, Kent. No port given.

*   *   *

1242
COLDHAM, PETER WILSON. "Scottish Rebels Transported to Maryland, 1747." (Genealogical Gleanings in England.) In *National Genealogical Society Quarterly,* vol. 63:2 (June 1975), pp. 137-138.

From papers in British Treasury Files (PRO T1/328, 80, 81). Rebels were taken prisoner after the 1745 Scottish uprising. From Liverpool in the *Johnson* to Port Oxford, Md., 1747, and in the *Gildart* for North Potomac, Maryland. *Johnson* passengers also listed in no. 8005, Scharf.

*   *   *

1252
COLDHAM, PETER WILSON. "Some Passenger Lists of 1677." (Genealogical Gleanings in England.) In *National Genealogical Society Quarterly,* vol. 64:3 (Sept. 1976), pp. 216-218.

Names passengers who left England in 1677 on the *Concord* for Virginia and on the *John* for Barbados. Original in a parchment volume (PRO: E157/31) among the series of "Licences to Pass Over the Seas." Also in no. 9540, Walker.

*   *   *

1262
COLKET, MEREDITH B., JR. *Founders of Early American Families: Emigrants from Europe, 1607-1657.* Cleveland: General Court of the Order of Founders and Patriots of America, 1975. 366 p.

Lists the American colonists who arrived in the first half-century of settlement along the Atlantic seaboard from Maine to North Carolina. Approximately 3,500 names, not restricted to the Order of Founders and Patriots of America.

*   *   *

1272
COLONIAL RECORDS OF VIRGINIA. "Lists of the Livinge & the Dead in Virginia, February 16, 1623." In *Colonial Records of Virginia,* Richmond, Va.: R.F. Walker, Superintendent of Public Printing, 1874, pp. 37-66.

Provides names only, arranged under places of residence. Includes many more names than the census of 1624-1625, cited in no. 3520. Published by the Joint Committee on Library (Senate Document, Extra); State Paper Office, Virginia. Colonial, vol. 3, no. 2. Originally from the Public Record Office, London. Also in no. 0720, Boyer, *Ship Passenger Lists, the South,* pp. 23-39.   (Lancour 208/1)

*   *   *

1282-1283
"COMMISSION BOOK, 82." In *Maryland Historical Magazine.*
1282
---Vol. 26:2 (June 1931), pp. 138-158; vol. 26:3 (Sept. 1931), pp. 244-263, vol. 26:4 (Dec. 1931), pp. 342-361.
1283
---Vol. 27:1 (Mar. 1932), pp. 29-36.

> Some of the records of the Council of Maryland containing miscellaneous entries from the years 1733 to 1773. Contains commissions, ship registries, naturalizations, denizations, etc. No entries for the years 1751 to 1761.

*   *   *

1288
CONOVER, CAROLYN (Mrs. George). "English Colonists in Georgia." In *Ancestry: Quarterly Bulletin of the Palm Beach County Genealogical Society,* vol. 9:2 (Apr. 1974), pp. 49-50.

> This account of the establishment of an English settlement in South Carolina [not present-day Georgia, despite the title] was copied from the Shaftesbury Papers in England, major source of documentary evidence on the founding of Charles Towne [now Charleston, S.C.]. The source material is entitled, "A list of all such masters, free passengers and servants which are now a board the *Carolina* now ridinge in the Downes. August the 10th, 1669."

*   *   *

1291
CONRAD, OTTO. *Geschichte der Auswanderung aus Fellbach.* Fellbach-Stuttgart: Volksbund fuer das Deutschtum im Ausland, Landesverband Wuerttemberg, April 1934. 44 p.

> History of emigration from Fellbach, near Stuttgart, Germany. Mostly contained in church books I-VI at Fellbach. Contains names of 1,581 emigrants from Fellbach between 1735 and 1930, of whom 1,221 came to the Americas beginning in 1804. Names of individual adult emigrants or heads of families with number of accompanying family members, year of emigration, and intended destination or country of immigration.

*   *   *

1292
COOK, LEWIS D. "Fenwick, Adams, Hedge, and Champneys, of Salem, N.J." In *The Genealogical Magazine of New Jersey,* vol. 35:3 (Sept. 1960), p. 108.

> Passenger list of the *Griffin* (or *Griffith*) which came to the Salem River in 1675 and brought Major Fenwick with the first permanent English-speaking settlers in the Delaware Valley. The complete list is to be found in no. 8450, Sickler. No. 9144, Tepper, *New World Immigrants,* vol. 2, p. 530, includes a listing (excerpt). For other references to the *Griffin,* see the index. (Lancour 110B)

*   *   *

1297
COPPAGE, A. MAXIM, III, contributor. "List of Passengers Who Came with Lewis Burwell, June 12,

1648." In *The Southern Genealogist's Exchange Quarterly,* vol. 8, no. 42 (Summer 1967), p. 14.

> In an article, "Virginia Coppage Families and Their Neighbors, from Research by A.M. Coppage, pp. 13-14."

*   *   *

1302
CORBIT, W.F. "Welsh Emigration to Pennsylvania. An Old Charter Party." In *The Pennsylvania Magazine of History and Biography,* vol. 1:3 (1877), pp. 330-332.

> Articles of agreement between Owen Thomas, owner of the *William Galley,* and David Powell, John Morris, and 17 others, for passage to Pennsylvania in 1697 or 1698. Also in no. 9120, Tepper, *Emigrants to Pennsylvania, 1641-1819,* pp. 30-32. (Lancour 130)

*   *   *

1312
COULTER, ELLIS MERTON, editor. "A List of the First Shipload of Georgia Settlers." In *The Georgia Historical Quarterly,* vol. 31:4 (Dec. 1947), pp. 282-288.

> Names 118 of the British on the *Anne* who were sent to Georgia in November 1732 to establish the colony there. A fine genealogical study of the settlers. See also nos. 3388 and 6494. Also in no. 9144, Tepper, *New World Immigrants,* vol. 2, pp. 75-81. (Lancour 239)

*   *   *

1322
COULTER, ELLIS MERTON, and **ALBERT B. SAYE,** editors. *A List of the Early Settlers of Georgia.* Athens, Ga.: The University of Georgia Press, 1949. 2nd ed., 1967. 111 p.

> From a manuscript volume in the University of Georgia Library. Covers 3,000 immigrants to Georgia, 1732-1742, with much information. The 1967 edition contains item no. 1312 as well. See also no. 3388 (Lancour 240)

*   *   *

1342
COWGILL, E.B. "The Passengers on the *Welcome.*" In *Transactions of the Kansas State Historical Society,* vol. 6 (1897-1900), pp. 56-59.

> Contains names of 99 of the estimated 100 passengers who accompanied William Penn. Also in no. 0132, Armstrong; no. 9143, Tepper, *New World Immigrants,* vol. 1, pp. 246-249; no. 4752, "List of the Pilgrims of the *Welcome.*" For other references to the *Welcome,* see the index. (Lancour 119B, spelled "Cogwill")

*   *   *

1352
COX, JOHN, JR. "Notes on the Eight Names Marked as Quakers in the *Speedwell* Passenger List, 1656." In *The New York Genealogical and Biographical Record,* vol. 65:1 (Jan. 1934), pp. 45-47.

> Lists 41 persons who landed at Boston in 1656. Also found in

no. 4910, "Lyst of the Pasingers abord the *Speedwell* . . .," nos. 1672, 1674, Drake; no. 9135, Tepper, *Immigrants to the Middle Colonies*, pp. 149-151; and in no. 0702, Boyer, *Ship Passenger Lists, National and New England*, pp. 162-163. (Lancour 54A)

*   *   *

1362

COX, RICHARD J. "Servants at Northampton Forge, Baltimore County, Maryland, 1772-1774." In *National Genealogical Society Quarterly*, vol. 63:2 (June 1975), pp. 110-117.

List of 91 "servants," perhaps convicts, since some convicts were hired into domestic service. Ages and additional record of each person. Taken from Ridgely Papers at the Maryland Historical Society, MHS 691.

*   *   *

1372

COX, RICHARD J. "Some Maryland Recruits of 1776." In *National Genealogical Society Quarterly*, vol. 64:4 (Dec. 1976), pp. 261-270.

From documents at the Maryland Historical Society. Composite of five muster rolls. Recruits were from Maryland, predominantly of European origin: 29% were Irish and 16.5% English. All were immigrants to Maryland prior to 1776.

*   *   *

1382

CRAIG, ROBERT D. *German Immigrants from the Pfalz.* [Laie, Hawaii]: n.p., 1962? 17 p.

A listing of families who left the German Palatinate for America. In many entries, the information includes parentage, date of birth, place of birth, marriage, children. Mostly 19th century.

*   *   *

1384

CRAMTON, LOUIS C., contributor. "Passenger List of the *Sarah Sheaffe*, May 1836." In *The Detroit Society for Genealogical Research Magazine*, vol. 5:10 (Aug.-Sept. 1942), p. 208.

A copy of a list attached to a letter owned by Cramton from Robert Taylor of Philadelphia to Messrs Abraham Bell & Co., New York. Names 60 passengers from Belfast arriving at Philadelphia via New York, May 1836. Also found in no. 9144, Tepper, *New World Immigrants*, vol. 2, pp. 417-418. (Lancour 252)

*   *   *

*1386-1398

CRIGLER, ARTHUR D., GRACE R. SCOTT, ET AL., contributors. "Naturalization Entries 1833-1871: Court Minute Books, Mobile County, Alabama." In *Deep South Genealogical Quarterly.*

1386

---Vol. 2:2 (Nov. 1964), pp. 301-305; vol. 2:3 (Feb. 1965), pp. 338-342; vol. 2:4 (May 1965), pp. 405-410; vol. 3:1 (Aug. 1965), pp. 484-488; vol. 3:2 (Nov. 1965), pp. 538-543; vol 3:3 (Feb. 1966), pp. 585-590; vol 3:4 (May 1966), pp. 631-636; vol. 4:1 (Aug. 1966), pp. 700-705; vol. 4:2 (Nov. 1966), pp. 767-771; vol. 4:3 (Feb. 1967), pp. 809-814.

1387

---Vol. 5:1 (Aug. 1967), pp. 43-47; vol 5:2 (Nov. 1967), pp. 98-102; vol. 5:4 (May 1968), pp. 194-198.

1388

---Vol. 6:1 (Aug. 1968), pp. 27-32; vol. 6:2 (Nov. 1968), pp. 85-89; vol. 6:3 (Feb. 1969), pp. 136-139.

1389

---Vol 7:1 (Aug. 1969), pp. 43-47; vol. 7:2 (Nov. 1969), pp. 73-76; vol. 7:3 (Feb. 1970), pp. 146-149; vol. 8.2 (Nov. 1970), pp. 318-322; vol. 8:3 (Feb. 1971), pp. 353-356; vol. 8:4 (May 1971), pp. 413-417; vol. 9:1 (Aug. 1971), pp. 486-490.

1390

---Vol. 9:3 (Aug. 1972), pp. 19-25; vol. 9:4 (Nov. 1972), pp. 89-93.

1391

---Vol. 10:1 (Feb. 1973), pp. 26-30; vol. 10:2 (May 1973), pp. 63-67; vol. 10:3 (Aug. 1973), pp. 138-140; vol. 10:4 (Nov. 1973), pp. 181-185.

1392

---Vol 11:1 (Feb. 1974), pp. 32-34; vol. 11:2 (May 1974), pp. 69-73; vol. 11:3 (Aug. 1974), pp. 150-152.

1393

---Vol. 12:1 (Feb. 1975), pp. 31-33; vol. 12:2 (May 1975), pp. 98-100.

1394

---Vol. 13:1 (Feb. 1976), pp. 35-38; vol 13:2 (May 1976), pp. 90-93; vol. 13;3 (Aug. 1976), pp. 152-155; vol. 13:4 (Nov. 1976), pp. 199-203.

1395

---Vol. 14:1 (Feb. 1977), pp. 36-41; vol. 14:2 (May 1977), pp. 93-95; vol. 14:3 (Aug. 1977), pp. 152-155; vol. 14:4 (Nov. 1977), pp. 212-214.

1396

---Vol. 15:1 (Feb. 1978), pp. 40-42; 15:2 (May 1978), pp. 99-102; 15:3 (Aug. 1978), pp. 157-162.

1397

---Vol. 16:2 (May 1979), pp. 95-98; 16:3 (Aug. 1979), pp. 155-159;

1398

---Vol. 17:1 (Feb. 1980), pp. 29-35; vol. 17:2 (May 1980), pp. 68-69.

Various nationalities, citizenship dates, and approximate dates of arrival, up to 1857. For passengers arriving at the port of Mobile, 1832-1853, see nos. 5203-5204, Mallon. Crigler became the contributor early on in the series and was still in that capacity to the last issue listed, although it was Mrs. Grace Scott who began the series.

*   *   *

1414

CROSGAERT, MARIE, contributor. "Ship Passenger List - *Ceynosure* - from Liverpool to New York, William H. Sweet, Master, April 23, 1855." In *M.C.G.S. Reporter* (Milwaukee County Genealogical Society), vol. 11, 1-2, pp. 26-28.

Name, age, sex, occupation, country of origin. Passengers from England and Ireland, two-thirds being from Ireland.

1416
CROUSE, C. GORDON. "Immigrants in Ops, 1829." In *The Ontario Register,* vol. 2:4 (1969), pp. 223-224.

Record found in the Upper Canada Sundries at the Public Archives of Canada, Ottawa, as "List of emigrants located in the Township of Ops by Mr. A. McDonell up to the 15th of October 1829." Ops is in Victoria County, Ontario. Many Irish names, lot number and concession granted each settler, and family details.

* * *

1422
CURRY, KATE SINGER. "Naturalizations—during the Court Sessions of January, 1798, Washington Co., Maryland." In *National Genealogical Society Quarterly,* vol. 23:4 (Dec. 1935), pp. 111-113.

Names 45 aliens naturalized, and their countries of origin. Also in no. 9144, Tepper, *New World Immigrants,* vol. 2, pp. 240-241; and in no. 0720, Boyer, *Ship Passenger Lists, the South,* pp. 20-21. (Lancour 207)

* * *

1432
CUSHING, DANIEL. "A List of the Names of Such Persons as Came Out of the Town of Hingham and Towns Adjacent in the County of Norfolk in the Kingdom of England, and Settled in Hingham [Mass.] in New England, 1633-1639." In Samuel G. Drake, *Result of Some Researches . . . Relative to the Founders of New England,* 1860.

Source material by Drake is listed as nos. 1672. and 1674.

* * *

1442
DALBY, BARBARA M. "Naturalization Record. Minors in the U.S. District Court for the Southern District of Illinois, from October 20, 1856, to November 5, 1864." In *Illinois State Genealogical Society Quarterly,* vol. 6:1 (Spring 1974), pp. 36-37.

Contains an index to Record Group 21 of Region 5, Chicago Federal Archives and Records Center. Has good summary of the laws concerning naturalization records. Lists only names and page numbers in the official records. Several Irish names.

* * *

1448
"DARKE COUNTY OHIO NATURALIZATIONS 1856-1873." In *Gateway to the West,* vol. 10:3 (July 1977), pp. 112-118.

Copied from "Naturalization record, first papers, no. 1," now in the Archives Division, Wright State University, Dayton, Ohio. Date and place of arrival, age, and place of origin. Involves immigration in the years 1831-1868.

* * *

1450
DARLINGTON, JANE E. "Marion County [Indiana]

Naturalizations 1832-1842." In *The Hoosier Genealogist,* vol. 20:3 (Sept. 1980), pp. 51-60.

Abstracts of the extant portion of the naturalization records, 1832-1903. The remainder were destroyed.

* * *

1452
DAY, A.J., compiler. "Naturalized Citizens (of Iroquois County, Illinois)." In *The Iroquois Stalker,* vol. 1:1 (Spring 1971), p. 15; vol. 1:2 (April 1971), pp. 1-3; vol. 1:3 (July 1971), pp. 8-10.

For the periods 1867-1868, 1888-1889. Name, date of naturalization, country of origin. Various nationalities.

* * *

1455
DAY, PHILLIP E. "Peterborough Names: 1825 and 1975." In *Families,* vol. 15:2 (Spring 1976), pp. 64-66.

Paupers from Ireland to Upper Canada, an immigration project of Peter Robinson in 1825. Surnames only.

* * *

1462
DEBIEN, GABRIEL. "Engages pour le Canada au *XVIIe siecle, vus de la Rochelle.*" In *Revue d'Histoire de l'Amerique Francaise,* vol. 6:2 (Sept. 1952), pp. 177-233; vol. 6:3 (Dec. 1952), pp. 374-407.

Recruits for Canada from La Rochelle during the seventeenth century. A chronological list for the years 1634-1715 of 830 recruits from La Rochelle committed to work in New France in return for their fare to the North American continent. Contains information and remarks on development of the colonization, its origins and means. Carries names on pages 221-233 and 374-407, with place of origin, age, occupation, and terms of contract for each recruit.

* * *

1472
DE BOER, LOUIS P. "Delaware Papers. Passenger List of Colonists to the South River (Delaware) Colony of New Netherland, 1661." In *The New York Genealogical and Biographical Record,* vol. 60:1 (January 1929), pp. 68-70.

Two lists, the first undated, with names of 15 "Colonists and other Freemen who have already applied for going to the Colony of the City in New Netherland." The second is the passenger list of the vessel *"De Purmerender Kerck"* [sic] for the voyage from the Dutch island of Texel, 1661, to New Amstel, Delaware. Illustration taken from original document in Old City Archives, Amsterdam. Data is also in no. 9135, Tepper, *Immigrants to the Middle Colonies,* pp. 75-77. For the second list (1661), see no. 1722, Dunlap, who cites the ship name as *"Purmerlander Kerck."* Also in no. 0717, Boyer, *Ship Passenger Lists, Pennsylvania and Delaware,* pp. 214-217. (Lancour 195)

* * *

1482
DEBOR, HERBERT WILHELM. "German Soldiers of the American War of Independence as Settlers in Canada." Translated by Udo Sautter. In *German-Canadian Yearbook: Deutschkanadisches Jahrbuch,* Toronto, Ont.: n.p., 1976, vol. 3, pp. 71-93.

Concerns Brunswick soldiers discharged in North America in 1783 from the Hesse-Hanau Rangers. Lists soldiers of the Hesse-Hanau Regiment Erbprinz and Cannoneers of the Hesse-Hanau Artillery Company who remained in Canada. Material drawn from the unpublished "German Regiments in Canada, 1776-1783."

*   *   *

1492-1493
"DECLARATIONS OF INTENTION TO BECOME AN AMERICAN CITIZEN, 1838-1849, Found in the Circuit Court of the City of St. Louis, Missouri." In *Saint Louis Genealogical Society Quarterly.*
1492
---A - BEG. In vol. 3:1 (March 1970), pp. 16-19.
BEM - DOL. In vol. 3:2 (June 1970), pp. 32-35.
DOL - FUR. In vol. 3:3 (Sept. 1970), pp. 60-61.
GAR- HEIT. In vol. 3:4 (Dec. 1970), pp. 71-78.
1493
---HEIT - LOE. In vol. 4:1 (Mar. 1971), pp. 17-20.
LOE - REG. In vol. 4:2 (June 1971), pp. 41-44.
REH - ZEIS. In vol. 4:3 (Sept. 1971), pp. 61-67.

Copied and indexed by Janice Fox, D.A. Griffith, R.R. Henrick, and others. Title varies, compilers vary. Gives name, age, country of origin, date of declared intention, and reference in court records.

*   *   *

1502
DEMAIZIERE, EMILE. "Les Colons et Emigrants Bourguignons au Canada." In *Rapport de l'Archiviste de la Province de Quebec,* 1923-1924, pp. 394-399.

Contains the names of Burgundian immigrants to Canada and explains the reasons for their emigration from France. Includes the first immigration in 1653 and the increased movement of the 18th century. Supplies names, occupation, year of arrival, place of origin, and, for some, place of intended settlement. No ships mentioned.

*   *   *

1512
DENNIS, MRS. ALBERTA V., contributor. "District Court of Finney County, Kansas. Declaration of Intention to Become a Citizen of the United States of America." In *Four States Genealogist,* vol. 2:1 (Oct. 1969), pp. 15-17.

Applications all dated 1886. Aliens from various countries.

*   *   *

1513
DENNIS, MRS. ALBERTA, contributor. "Finney County, Kansas, Miscellaneous Records: Declaration of Intention - Citizenship, April-October 1886." In *Treesearcher,* vol. 18:1 (1976), pp. 5-6.

Lists aliens who appeared before E.G. Bates, Clerk of the District Court in and for the County of Finney, in the 16th Judicial District of the State of Kansas.

*   *   *

1542
DE VILLE, WINSTON, translator and compiler. *Louisiana Colonials, Soldiers and Vagabonds.* Mobile, Ala.: n.p., 1963, 81 p. Distributed by Genealogical Publishing Co., Baltimore.

Passengers on seven vessels that came to Louisiana in 1719 or 1720, pp. 1-53. Mostly soldiers of the new recruitment who embarked in the service of the Company of the Indies to serve in Louisiana. Original records deposited in the Archives des Colonies, Paris. Transcripts in the Library of Congress, Washington, D.C. See also no. 3418, "Immigrants to Louisiana, 1719."

*   *   *

1548
DE VILLE, WINSTON. *Louisiana Recruits 1752-1758. Ship Lists of Troops from the Independant ˌsic] Companies of the Navy [Compagnies Francais de la Marine] Destined for Service in the French Colony of Louisiana.* Cottonport [La.]: Polyanthos, 1973. 99 p.

Data includes soldier's name, that of his father, mother, birthplace, and his prior occupation.

*   *   *

1568
DEXTER, MARY L., abstractor. "Naturalization Records from Book of Naturalization Papers-1816-1870, on File in the County Clerk's Office in the Cortland County [New York] Court House." In *Tree Talks,*

12:1 (March 1972) p. 10	(Imm.-Nat. p. 40);
12:2 (June 1972) pp. 67-68	(Imm.-Nat. pp. 41-42);
13:1 (March 1973) pp. 11-12	(Imm.-Nat. pp. 45-46);
13:2 (June 1973) pp. 68-69	(Imm.-Nat. pp. 47-48);
13:3 (Sept. 1973) pp. 132-133	(Imm.-Nat. pp. 49-50);
15:1 (March 1975) pp. 19-20	(Imm.-Nat. pp. 55-56);
15:2 (June 1975) pp. 115-116	(Imm.-Nat. pp. 57-58);
17:1 (March 1977) pp. 27-28	(Cortland County, pp. 84-85);
17:2 (June 1977) pp. 85-86	(Cortland County, pp. 86-87).

Title varies slightly. When the series was last published (June 1977), abstracting had reached the year 1848. Chiefly involves emigrants from Great Britain and Ireland.

*   *   *

1578
DICKORE, MARIE. "Der Deutsche Pionier Verein von Cincinnati Membership." In *Bulletin of the Historical and Philosophical Society of Ohio,* vol. 21:3 (July 1963), pp. 217-219; vol. 21:4 (Oct. 1963), pp. 278-282.

The purpose of the German society called the Verein was to

"renew and strengthen old friendships, and to collect the history and experiences of German pioneers." This membership list, for 1869-1870, gives full names and places of birth in Germany. German immigrant members had to have lived in the vicinity of Cincinnati for 25 years and be over 40 years of age. Thus, the immigration period covered would be 19th century. List is also in the publication *Der Deutsche Pionier* (Cincinnati, 1869-70).

*   *   *

1582
DICKORE, MARIE. "Klauprecht's *Chronik . . . Des Ohio Thales* Abounds in Genealogical Data About German Pioneers." In *Bulletin of the Historical and Philosophical Society of Ohio,* vol. 20:1 (Jan. 1962), pp. 92-95.

Names German settlers found in Klauprecht, *German Chronicle of the Ohio Valley and Its Capital Cincinnati Expecially . . . . (Deutsche Chronik in der Geschichte des Ohio-Thales und seine Haupstadt Cincinnati in's Besondere . . .).* Cincinnati: Jacobi, 1864. Some have date of arrival, landowner details, and date of naturalization, 1807-1830.

*   *   *

1587
DICKSON, L. TAYLOR. "The Sailing of the Ship *Submission* in the Year 1682, with a True Copy of the Vessel's Log." In *Publications of the Genealogical Society of Pennsylvania,* vol. 1:1 (Jan. 1895), pp. 7-13, Miscellany no. 1.

Names and ages of 49 passengers from Liverpool, 1682, to the Choptank River, Maryland. Mostly from Wales, Cheshire, and Lancashire. Also in no. 8370, Sheppard, with corrections; in no. 9143, Tepper, *New World Immigrants,* vol. 1, pp. 235-241; and in no. 0717, Boyer, *Ship Passenger Lists, Pennsylvania and Delaware,* pp. 9-11.   (Lancour 118)

*   *   *

1594
DICKSON, ROBERT J. *Ulster Emigration to Colonial America, 1718-1775.* (Ulster Scot Historical Series, 1) London: Routledge & Kegan Paul, 1966, Appendix F, para. B, pp. 290-291. Reprinted by Ulster Scot Historical Foundation, Belfast, 1976. 320 p. Available from D.R. Hotaling Assoc., 2255 Cedar Lane, Vienna, VA 22180.

Names 51 passengers from Larne, Ireland, who sailed to Charlestown *(sic),* South Carolina, on the ship *Lord Dunluce* in the year 1773. Also in no. 8980, Stephenson.

*   *   *

1612
DIENER, WALTER. "Die Auswanderung aus dem Amte Gemuenden [Hunsrueck] im 19. Jahrhundert. Nach den Buergermeistereiakten." In *Rheinische Vierteljahrsblaetter,* Jahrgang 5 (1935), pp. 190-222.

Emigration from the jurisdiction of Gemuenden in the Hunsrueck region in the nineteenth century. From files concerning German emigration, 1808-1900, in the Gemuenden mayor's office. Records overseas movement only. Pages 215-222 give names of 423 emigrants to Brazil and elsewhere in North and South America in the years 1827-1897. Individuals and heads of emigrant groups, some first names of accompanying family members, some ages, places of origin, places of destination. Pages 190-215 contain additional information on several of the emigrants. See also no. 1616 for data on more than 2,000 emigrants and no. 8652 for an English-language version.

*   *   *

1616
DIENER, WALTER. "Die Auswanderung aus dem Kreise Simmern (Hunsrueck) im 19. Jahrhundert." In *Rheinische Vierteljahrsblaetter,* vol. 8 (1938), pp. 91-148.

Emigration from the district of Simmern (Hunsrueck region of Germany) in the 19th century. Supplement to no. 1612, Diener. Lists, pp. 124-148, over 2,000 emigrants to the Americas from the Simmern area between 1825 and 1900, with varying details, some of which are very complete. Also lists emigrants to other parts of the world. See no. 8652, Smith, for English translation.

*   *   *

1632
DIFFENDERFFER, FRANK RIED. *The German Immigration into Pennsylvania Through the Port of Philadelphia from 1700 to 1775. Part 2: The Redemptioners.* (Narrative of Critical History . . . Pennsylvania, the German Influence in Its Settlement and Development, 7.) In *The Pennsylvania-German Society Proceedings and Addresses,* vol. 10 (1900). 328 p. Reprinted with slightly changed title by Genealogical Publishing Co., Baltimore, 1977.

Pages 40-42 have "A List of Ye Palatine Passengers Imported in Ye Ship *William and Sarah,* Will'm Hill, Mast'r, from Rotterdam, Phlid'a Ye 18 Sept'bre 1727." Pages 213-216 have a partial list of passengers who arrived on the *Britannia,* September 18, 1773. The list from the *William and Sarah* is also printed in no. 1804, Egle; nos. 9041-9042, Strassburger; and no. 0717, Boyer, *Ship Passenger Lists, Pennsylvania and Delaware,* pp. 114-116. For more on the *Britannia,* see no. 4662, "A List of German Emigrants, 1773."   (Lancour 142)

*   *   *

1636
DINGEDAHL, CARL HEINZ. "Einbecker Auswanderer nach Texas, 1845-1848." In *Norddeutsche Familienkunde,* Jahrgang 29, Part 1 (Jan.-Mar. 1980), pp. 19-22.

Emigrants from Einbeck to Texas, 1845-1848. Names taken from Geue, nos. 2484 and 2504, and church registers of Einbeck. Concerns about 30 German emigrants, with most ages and birthdates given, date of emigration and name of ship.

*   *   *

1642
DONOVAN, GEORGE FRANCIS. *The Pre-Revolutionary Irish in Massachusetts, 1620-1775.* Menasha, Wis.: George Banta Publishing Co., 1932. 158 p.

Irish immigrants, 1621-1769, but mostly 1753-1769. Pages 30 to 40 give passenger lists of ships arriving between these dates. Only names of Irish origin are given, extracted almost entirely from no. 9750, Whitmore's *Port Arrivals . . . to Boston, 1715-*

1716 and 1762-1769. Donovan's work originally a doctoral dissertation, St. Louis University, 1931.   (Lancour 36)

*   *   *

1652

DORRHEIM, MERLYN D., copier. "Passenger Lists." In *Heritage Review,* no. 19 (Dec. 1977), p. 49.

Germans from Russia on the S.S. *Eider* to New York City, May 10, 1889.

*   *   *

1656

DOUVILLE, RAYMOND. "Notes Additionnelles sur Quelques Engages de 1658." In *Memoires de la Societe Genealogique Canadienne-Francaise,* vol. 9:3-4 (July-Oct. 1958), pp. 239-242.

Notes on some recruits of 1658. Biographical data on four of the Canadian colonizers: Chavignaux, Rissavouin, Guichart, and Millet. Names, ages, aliases, marital status, and contractual obligations given when available. Supplements information supplied in no. 2642, Godbout.

*   *   *

1658

DOW, GEORGE FRANCIS. "The French Acadians in Essex County and Their Life in Exile." In *Historical Collections of the Essex Institute,* vol. 45:4 (Oct. 1909), pp. 293-307.

Throughout the article are references to families who settled in Massachusetts, having been driven from Nova Scotia in the 1750s. Pages 304-307 have "A list of the French inhabitants in the County of Essex as they were settled, & proportioned to the several towns, after 16 of Andover & 3 of Haverhill were sett off to the County of Hampshire." Names and ages.

*   *   *

1660

DRAKE, SAMUEL G. "The Founders of New England." In *The New England Historical and Genealogical Register,* vol. 14:4 (Oct. 1860), pp. 297-359.

Part of the other Drake items, nos. 1672 and 1674. Lists immigrants in the years 1634-1635. Also in no. 9151, Tepper, *Passengers to America,* pp. 10-72.   (Lancour 44A)

*   *   *

1666

DRAKE, SAMUEL G. "A List of Names Found Among the First Settlers of New England." In *The New England Historical and Genealogical Register,* vol. 1:2 (Apr. 1847), pp. 137-139.

Additions and corrections to no. 1936, Farmer, *Genealogical Register of the First Settlers of New England. . . .* The reprint of Farmer by the Genealogical Publishing Company, Baltimore, 1964, included Drake's corrections and additions. Also in no. 9151, Tepper, *Passengers to America,* pp. 468-470. (Lancour 43A)

*   *   *

1672

DRAKE, SAMUEL G. *Result of Some Researches Among the British Archives for Information Relative to the Founders of New England: Made in the Years 1858, 1859, and 1860: Originally Collected for and Published in* The New England Historical and Genealogical Register, *and Now Corrected and Enlarged.* Boston: The New England Historical and Genealogical Register, 1860. 143 p. Reprinted with corrections by Genealogical Publishing Co., Baltimore, 1964. 131 p.

A collection of British lists of emigrants to New England in the years 1634 and 1635, with some in the period 1631 to 1671. To be found also in part, with some variation, in item no. 1666. A third edition, privately printed in 1865, is no. 1674. See also note for no. 0263, Banks.   (Lancour 44)

*   *   *

1674

DRAKE, SAMUEL G. *Result of Some Researches Among the British Archives for Information Relative to the Founders of New England. . . .* 3rd ed. Boston: John Wilson and Son, 1865. 122 p.

This edition was privately printed in 75 quarto copies for W. Elliot Woodward. Same as the octavo edition of 1860, with an additional section, "The First Settlers of Plymouth," pp. 115-122. Research done 1858-1860, originally for *The New England Historical and Genealogical Register,* now corrected and enlarged. For original edition, 1860, see no. 1672. (Lancour 44B)

*   *   *

1682

DREILING, NORBERT R. *Official Centennial History of the Volga-German Settlements in Ellis and Rush Counties in Kansas 1876-1976.* Hays, Kan.: Volga-German Centennial Association, 1976, pp. 52-79.

Includes names of earliest arrivals from Liebenthal, Catherine, Herzog, Munjor, Pfeifer, and Schoenchen, in the 1870s, with dates of arrival and places of settlement. See also no. 4497, Laing; and no. 4019, Knoll.

*   *   *

1692

"DUBOIS COUNTY [INDIANA] NATURALIZATION RECORD, 1852-1869." In *The Hoosier Genealogist,* vol. 16:4 (Dec. 1976), pp. 77-85.

Compiled from a microfilm of the Declaration of Intention Record in the Genealogy Division of the Indiana State Library. Original is in the Dubois County Courthouse, Jasper, Indiana. Name, age, country of origin, place and date of arrival in America, date of declaration of intent, page reference. Dates of arrival cover 1820-1869; the majority were 1833-1869. Most of these immigrants were from Germany.

*   *   *

1694

DUDEK, PAULINE BRUNGARDT, compiler. "The Germans from Russia in Franklin County, Nebr., 1880 Census of the United States." In *Clues* (publication of the

American Historical Society of Germans from Russia), 1979, part 2, pp. 49-51.

> Enumerates the families who apparently were among a group of Volga Germans from Norka arriving on the S.S. *City of Berlin,* Dec. 6, 1875. This group went first to Sandusky, Ohio, and later to the town of Sutton and Franklin County, Nebraska, in 1880. A number then went to Marion County, Kansas, Buffalo precinct. Names, ages, places of birth given.

       *   *   *

1697
DUDEK, PAULINE BRUNGARDT. "Passenger Lists from Canada." In *Clues* (publication of the American Historical Society of Germans from Russia) 1979, part 2, pp. 66-68.

> Ship lists, 1893, in Quebec for vessels sailing from Hamburg to Antwerp, Belgium, then to Quebec City, Canada. German immigrants from Russia to Gretna and Hastings, Nebraska, and Winnipeg, Manitoba, Canada.

       *   *   *

1702
DUDEK, PAULINE, and **NORMAN DUDEK.** "Researching the First People Who Came to America from Our Ancestral Village [Kolb]." In *Journal of the American Historical Society of Germans from Russia,* vol. 1:2 (Fall 1978), pp. 9-15

> Names throughout article. Page 15 lists 43 persons from Kolb who came to America on the ship *Donau* in 1876.

       *   *   *

1712
DUMONT, WILLIAM H. "French Emigrants to Richmond County, Georgia." In *National Genealogical Society Quarterly,* vol. 52:2 (June 1964), pp. 75-76.

> Extracted from tombstone inscriptions, cemetery records, and the 1850 and 1860 censuses. Lists 77 French immigrants, latter part of 18th and early 19th centuries, many from Santo Domingo.

       *   *   *

1722
DUNLAP, A.R. "Three Lists of Passengers to New Amstel." In *Delaware History,* vol. 8:3 (March 1959), pp. 310-311.

> From the Historical Society of Delaware's microfilm copy of originals in the archives of the City of Amsterdam. Three lists of 37 persons or families bound for the Delaware River area on the *Purmerlander Kerck* [sic] (Church of Purmerland) and the *Gulden Arent* (Golden Eagle). The 1661 *Purmerlander Kerck* list is cited in no. 1472, DeBoer, where the spelling of the ship's name differs. Also found in no. 9143, Tepper, *New World Immigrants,* vol. 1, pp. 194-195; and no. 0717, Boyer, *Ship Passenger Lists, Pennsylvania and Delaware,* pp. 218-219. (Lancour 196)

       *   *   *

1732
DURNBAUGH, DONALD F., compiler and transla-

tor. *European Origins of the Brethren.* Elgin, Ill.: Brethren Press, 1958, pp. 296-302.

> Concerns the Church of the Brethren in the early 18th century. Lists passengers in the ship *Allen* from Rotterdam, September 11, 1729, to Pennsylvania. Includes 59 Palatine families, 126 persons in all, pp. 296-298. Other movement, four men and families, of the Church of the Brethren to Pennsylvania, 1731-1735, pp. 301-302.

       *   *   *

1736
THE DUTCH SETTLERS SOCIETY OF ALBANY. *Yearbook,* vol. 45, 1974-1977. Albany, New York: The Society, [1977?], pp. 42-66.

> The *Yearbook* has details of the Society, and on pp. 42-66 is a section entitled, "Ancestors and Descendants." This lists original settlers in New York and their progeny. Each original settler arrived between 1624 and 1664. The list changes slightly from yearbook to yearbook. This is the last published up to 1979.

       *   *   *

1739
EAKER, LORENA SHELL. "The Germans in North Carolina." In *The Palatine Immigrant,* vol. 6:1 (Summer 1980), pp. 3-34.

> Contains naturalization records and details on settlers west of the Catawba, North Carolina. Most were German Reformed or Lutheran. Date of arrival often given; all 18th century.

       *   *   *

1742
EARLY, CHARLES MONTAGUE. "Passenger Lists from *The Shamrock or Irish Chronicle,* 1815-1816." In *The Journal of the American Irish Historical Society,* vol. 29 (1930-1931), pp. 183-206.

> Names over 3,000 passengers on 60 ships arriving at New York, 11 at Philadelphia, and one at Baltimore. Ships listed on pp. 205 and 206. A reprint by Genealogical Publishing Company, Baltimore, 1965, contained passenger lists compiled by Hackett, no. 2859, and Early (above): *Passenger Lists from Ireland,* pp. 5-22 and 23-46, which were excerpted from *The Journal of the American Irish Historical Society,* vols. 28-29. Also in no. 9144, Tepper, *New World Immigrants,* vol. 2, pp. 347-370; and no. 8099, Schlegel, who covered the years 1811-1817. Supplementary to no. 2859, Hackett. (Lancour 28)

       *   *   *

1748
"EARLY AMERICAN SETTLERS." "In *Bulletin of the Seattle Genealogical Society,* vol. 28:2 (Winter 1978), pp. 115-120; vol. 28:3 (Spring 1979), pp. 221-222; vol. 28:4 (Summer 1979), pp. 313-314.

> A series presenting biographical sketches of 17th-century immigrants having the same surnames as those submitted by the Seattle Genealogical Society members for their Surname Index Project. Most have date of arrival and further genealogical bibliography.

       *   *   *

1752
"EARLY EAST TEXAS CITIZENS: FOREIGNERS SETTLED AT NACOGDOCHES." In *Records of East Texas,* vol. 3:3 (Apr. 1969), pp. 494-496.

From the Nacogdoches Archives, University of Texas Transcript, vol. 20. Covers period 1824-1834. Includes "foreigners" received as citizens, with some information concerning them and the dates of their presentation for citizenship. "Foreigners" to those in East Texas were persons from another state. Names, previous location in America, date of citizenship, and other information. See also no. 4079, Krause.

*   *   *

1762
"EARLY IRISH EMIGRANTS TO AMERICA, 1803-1806." In *The Recorder: Bulletin of the American Irish Historical Society,* vol. 3:5 (June 1926), pp. 19-23.

Much information about emigrants, from records in the British Museum, London. Lists passengers on three ships for New York, two for New Castle and Philadelphia, and one for Philadelphia only. Also in no. 0702, Boyer, *Ship Passenger Lists, National and New England,* pp. 108-112; and in no. 9144 Tepper, *New World Immigrants,* vol. 2, pp. 289-294. More information is contained in no. 2151, Fothergill, and no. 3450, Ireland.   (Lancour 25)

*   *   *

1765
ECKMAN, JOSEPHINE (Welder), compiler. "Passenger List." In *Heritage Review,* vol. 10:2 (Apr. 1980), p. 43.

Passengers on the *Fulda* from Bremen to New York, 1889, all Germans from Russia. Copied from microfilm 237, roll 435, National Archives, Washington, D.C.

*   *   *

1768
EDWARDS, CONLEY L., contributor. Abstracts of Reports of Aliens, Alexandria County, 1801-1832. In *The Virginia Genealogist,* vol. 24:2 (Mar./June 1980), pp. 112-116. (In progress.)

Abstracts taken from a volume in the Archives and Records Division, Virginia State Library, accession 25081, item 93. Name, sex, place of birth, age, country of origin, place of allegiance, etc.

*   *   *

1772
EDWARDS, CONLEY L., contributor. "Citizenship Applications in the Virginia General and Richmond District Court, 1784-1794." In *Virginia Genealogical Society Quarterly,* vol. 18:1 (Jan. 1980), pp. 7-10.

Lists individuals who applied for citizenship in Virginia, according to material in the British Public Record Office (T. 79/94, pp. 164-165). Supplies names and specifies date on which each qualified as citizen of the State of Virginia.

*   *   *

1782
EDWARDS, CONLEY L., contributor. "Citizenship Applications 1783-1794, Henrico County [Virginia]." In *Virginia Genealogical Society Quarterly,* vol.17:1 (Jan. 1979), pp. 18-22.

List of individuals from Henrico County who applied for citizenship, taken from material in the British Public Record Office (T. 79/94, p. 166 ff.) All British names. Not a complete list; more can be found by consulting the county books in Virginia.

*   *   *

1788
EDWARDS, JOHN. "List of Foreigners Imported in the Ship *Queen Elizabeth,* Alexander Hope, Master, September 16, 1738, to Philadelphia and Took the Oath of Allegiance." In *The Pennsylvania Traveler,* vol. 1:1 (Nov. 1964), pp. 34-35.

Taken from no. 1804, *Pennsylvania Archives,* 2nd ser., vol. 17, pp. 160-162. Provides names and ages. Mostly Germans, but various nationalities represented.

*   *   *

1794
EDWARDS, L.W. LAWSON. "Emigration of Bicester (Market End), Oxfordshire, Paupers to New York, 1830." In *Genealogists' Magazine* (London), vol. 16:6 (June 1970), pp. 275-279.

List of 71 adults and 40 children intended for emigration. From original records housed at the Bodleian Library, Oxford.

*   *   *

1798
EDWARDS, MORGAN. "History of the Baptists in Delaware." In *The Pennsylvania Magazine of History and Biography,* vol. 9:1 (1885), pp. 47-61; vol. 9:2 (1885), pp. 197-213.

Lists Welsh immigrants to Pennsylvania, 1701-1713, founders of a colony in Delaware. Also in no. 1894, Evans. Some differences in the spelling of names.

*   *   *

1804
EGLE, WILLIAM HENRY, editor. *Names of Foreigners Who Took the Oath of Allegiance to the Province and State of Pennsylvania, 1727-1775, with the Foreign Arrivals, 1786-1808.* (Pennsylvania Archives, series 2, vol. 17) Harrisburg [Pa.]: E.K. Meyers, 1892. 787p. Reprinted by Genealogical Publishing Co., Baltimore, 1967.

Taken from original manuscripts in the state archives. Names given throughout pages 1-677. Foreigners arriving in Pennsylvania named on pages 521-667. No 3776, Kelker, supplements this.   (Lancour 145)

*   *   *

1811
EHLE, BOYD, compiler. "Palatine Heads of Families from Governor Hunter's Ration Lists, June 1710 to September 1714." In Lou D. MacWethy, *The Book of Names*.... St. Johnsville, New York: The Enterprise and News, 1933, pp. 65-72. Reprinted by Genealogical Publishing Co., Baltimore, 1969.

> Governor Hunter's claim against the British government for the subsistence account of the Palatines, 1710-1713. Involves 847 debtors, according to records in London. Also in no. 4003, Knittle. (Lancour 97A)

*   *   *

1815
EHMANN, KARL. *Die Auswanderung in die Neuengland-Staaten aus Orten des Enzkreises im 18. Jahrhundert. (Suedwestdeutsche Blaetter fuer Familien- und Wappenkunde,* special supplement, 1977), 61p.

> Emigration to the New England states from localities of the Enz district in the 18th century. Concerns about 1,700 emigrants from the area around Enz in central western Germany to New England, defined by Ehmann as the original American colonies from Massachusetts to Georgia. Much family data, with same dates of arrival as are found in Strassburger. From minutes of the *Rentkammer* and *Hofrat* in the *Generallandesarchiv* in Karlsruhe, Germany, and from nos. 9041-42, Strassburger.

*   *   *

1826
ELLIS, EILISH. "State-Aided Emigration Schemes from Crown Estates in Ireland, c. 1850." In *Analecta Hibernica,* vol. 22 (1960), pp. 329-394.

> From documents in the Quit Rent Office, Dublin. Emigrants from Ireland to New York (with a few to Quebec, 1848-1849). Period covered overall is 1847-1855. Much information given. Also in no. 9144, Tepper, *New World Immigrants,* vol. 2, pp. 448-511. (Lancour 258)

*   *   *

1830
"EMIGRANT FILES." In *Germanic Genealogist,* nos. 9-12 (in 1), 1977, pp. 172-209.

> Extracted from Germanic Emigrants Card File maintained at The Augustan Society Library in Torrance, California. Much information; many 19th century.

*   *   *

1834
ENGEL, JOHANN. "Auswanderung aus der Buergermeisterei Illingen." In *Saarheimat: Zeitschrift fuer Kultur, Landschaft und Volkstum,* Part 8/9 (Aug.-Sept. 1960), pp. 27-28.

> Emigration from the mayoral jurisdiction of Illingen [Germany]. Involves 30 emigrants, 1833-1836. Names of heads of emigrant groups, some wives' maiden names, number of family members in each group, places of origin, some ages.

*   *   *

1842
ENGEL, JOHN C., contributor. "Wisconsin Immigrants from Manifest of the Ship *Republik,* Arrived at New York, 10 July 1856." In *Wisconsin State Genealogical Society Newsletter,* vol. 25:4 (Apr. 1979), pp. 174-175.

> From Bremen, Germany, selected names. Each item gives, as well, age, sex, occupation, origin, and destination Wisconsin.

*   *   *

1850
"ENGEL MISCELLANY." In *The Pennsylvania Traveler,* vol. 3:4 (Aug. 1967), pp. 55-57.

> Immigrants named Engel, Engell, Engels, Engle. Extracted from Rupp, no. 7820. Names in full, date of arrival, ship, and master or captain, with Rupp page references. Period covered: 1737-1773.

*   *   *

1858
ENGERRAND, GEORGE C. "[List of Wends Who Came with the 1854 Emigration . . . .]" and "[A List Compiled by Charles W. Ramsdell, Jr., of Some Founders of Wendish Families in Texas, ca. 1870]." In *The So-Called Wends of Germany and Their Colonies in Texas and Australia.* Austin: University of Texas Press, 1934. Reprinted by R. & E. Research Co., San Francisco, 1972, pp. 155-156.

> Provides 25 names. Ramsdell's article was originally published in the *University of Texas Bulletin.* See also no. 0578, Blasig.

*   *   *

1864
ENO, JOEL N. "New York 'Knickerbocker' Families: Origin and Settlement." In *The New York Genealogical and Biographical Record,* vol. 45:4 (Oct. 1914), pp. 387-391.

> Dutch immigrants to New York in the seventeenth century. No ship mentioned. Also in no. 9135, Tepper, *Immigrants to the Middle Colonies,* pp. 1-5; and in no. 0714, Boyer, *Ship Passenger Lists, New York and New Jersey,* pp. 9-14. (Lancour 72)

*   *   *

1867-1868
ERICSON, TIMOTHY L. "Index to Pierce Series 26, Immigration & Naturalization Papers." In *Wisconsin State Genealogical Society Newsletter.*
1867
---Vol. 26:1 (June 1979), pp. 43-44. A-Esanbock; vol. 26:2 (Sept. 1979), pp. 103-104. Esef - Johnson, Charles; vol. 26:3 (Jan. 1980), pp. 157-158. Johnson, Charles J. - Nelson, Gregor; vol. 26:4 (April 1980), pp. 217-218. Nelson, Gustav through Tim.
1868
---Vol. 27:1 (June 1980). (In progress.)

> From the Area Research Center, University of Wisconsin,

River Falls. Entries cover the years 1907-1925. The Pierce Series consists of three types of document: I. Collections of Declarations of Intent to become a citizen; II. Stubs from Certificates of Naturalization issued to those who became citizens; III. Notice of Application for Admission (to ceremonial swearing-in). Immigrants from Germany, Great Britain, Bohemia, and — the largest group — Scandinavia.

*　　　*　　　*

1871
ERTEL, RONALD J. "Germans from Russia who Settled in Sheboygan, Wisconsin, area and Earned Their Citizenship." In *Clues* (publication of the American Historical Society of Germans from Russia), 1979, part 2, pp. 37-48.

Names, birthdates, birthplaces. A list of Volga-area Germans who settled along the west coast of Lake Michigan. Dates covered: 1864-1922.

*　　　*　　　*

1874
ESPENSCHIED, LLOYD. "Erstansiedler aus dem Rheinland in Wayne County, N.Y., USA." Translated and edited by Fritz Braun. In *Pfaelzische Familien- und Wappenkunde: Mitteilungen zur Wanderungsgeschichte der Pfaelzer,* vol. 3:6 (June 1959), pp. 185-192.

First settlers from the Rhineland in Wayne County, New York. This article first appeared in English in December 1958 in the periodical, *The Lyons Republican and Clyde Times.* Concerns about 40 emigrants from the Rhineland and Alsace-Lorraine in the years 1820-1850. Most ages, dates of immigration, some family data, places of origin, and details of their fate after arrival in America.

*　　　*　　　*

1882
ESSIG, ALICE, contributor. "Passenger Lists." In *Heritage Review,* no. 22 (Dec. 1978), pp. 45-46.

Passengers from Bremen to Baltimore, May 19, 1876, and from Hamburg to New York, September 19, 1880. Only those who stated they were from Russia are listed, and most of them were from the Gluecksthaler Gebiet, Odessa.

*　　　*　　　*

1888
ETEROVICH, ADAM S., editor. "San Francisco, California, Voting Records for 1869-1872; (1873-1876). In *Balkan and Eastern European American Genealogical and Historical Society Quarterly,* vol. 4:2 (June 1967), pp. 123-132.

Gives name, age, occupation, and date naturalized between 1856 and 1875.

*　　　*　　　*

1890
ETEROVICH, ADAM S. "Santa Clara County, California, Voting Records." In *Balkan and Eastern European American Genealogical and Historical Society*

Quarterly, vols. 1-2 (1964-1965), p. 4.

Taken from the "Index to the Great Register" at the Sacramento State Library. Central European names. For each entry, there is name, age, occupation, origin, date naturalized, 1848-1872.
The "Great Register" is a compilation of voter registration lists which were formerly the poll lists. The first voter registration records of California were the county poll lists. In 1866, through passage of the Registry Act, the poll lists were replaced by voter registration lists known as the "Great Register." The Political Code of 1872 required all counties to print an alphabetical list of voters every two years, and updated printed supplements were required before each election. These printed lists constituted an index to the Great Registers, which are manuscripts. About 80% of the California counties printed indexes to the Great Registers. In 1909, maintenance of the Great Registers ceased. Since then, most of the ms. Great Registers remain in the county courthouses and are listed in the *Guide to the County Archives of California.*

*　　　*　　　*

1894
EVANS, JAMES DANIEL. *History of Nathaniel Evans of Cat Fish Creek and His Descendants.* [Philadelphia: the author, 1905,] pp. 4-6.

Welsh immigrants to Pennsylvania, 1701-1713. Also in no. 1798, Edwards. Some differences in name spelling.

*　　　*　　　*

1898
EVJEN, JOHN O. *Scandinavian Immigrants in New York, 1630-1674. With Appendices on Scandinavians in Mexico and South America, 1532-1640; Scandinavians in Canada, 1619-1620; Some Scandinavians in New York, in the Eighteenth Century; German Immigrants in New York, 1630-1674.* Minneapolis: K.C. Holter Publishing Co., 1916. 438p. Reprinted by Genealogical Publishing Co., Baltimore, 1972.

Biographical pieces on Norwegian, Danish, and Swedish immigrants who settled in New York.　　(Lancour 77)

*　　　*　　　*

1906
"EXCERPTS FROM LAWS OF THE STATE OF NEW YORK, vol. 1. Albany, 1886 . . . ." In *Tree Talks,* vol. 3:3 (Sept. 1963), p. 77 (Immigration & Naturalization, p.1).

Mostly British and German immigrants naturalized upon taking the U.S. oath of allegiance. Names excerpted from chapter 32, Fifth Session, April 9, 1782; chapter 37, Sixth Session, March 20, 1783; and chapter 55, Seventh Session, May 4, 1784. For naturalizations in New York state in the years 1782 and 1785, see no. 5841, Moyer.

*　　　*　　　*

1911
EYSTER, ANITA L., compiler and translator. "Notices by German and Swiss Settlers Seeking Information of Members of Their Families, Kindred, or Friends Inserted Between the Years 1742 and 1761 in the Pennsylvanische

Berichte and Between the Years 1762 and 1779 in the Pennsylvanische Staatsbote." In *The Pennsylvania German Folklore Society* [*Yearbook*], vol. 3, 1938. 41p.

> Much information on families, with names of ships and dates of arrival.

*   *   *

1916
FAIRBROTHER, E.H., communicator. "Foreign Protestants for Carolina in 1679." In *Proceedings of the Huguenot Society of London,* vol. 10 (1912-1914), pp. 187-189.

> From records of the Admiralty in the Public Record Office, London. Reports on 67 persons in the *Richmond* and another 90 French Protestants willing to be transported to the Ashley River region of South Carolina. Also in no. 1158, Childs; no. 0720, Boyer, *Ship Passenger Lists, the South,* pp. 155-157; and no. 9143, Tepper, *New World Immigrants,* vol. 1, pp. 204-206. (Lancour 233)

*   *   *

1926
FARMER, JOHN. "First Settlers of Rhode Island." In *The New England Historical and Genealogical Register,* vol. 1:4 (Oct. 1847), p. 291.

> Names 93 passengers who arrived in the year 1636. No ship mentioned. Also in no. 9151, Tepper, *Passengers to America,* page 471. (Lancour 68, erroneously cites p. 91 instead of p. 291.)

*   *   *

1936
FARMER, JOHN. *A Genealogical Register of the First Settlers of New-England; Containing an Alphabetical List of the Governours, Deputy-Governours, Assistants or Counsellors, and Ministers of the Gospel in the Several Colonies, from 1620 to 1692; Graduates of Harvard College to 1662; Members of the Ancient and Honourable Artillery Company to 1662; Freemen Admitted to the Massachusetts Colony from 1630 to 1662; With Many Other of the Early Inhabitants of New-England and Long-Island, N.Y., from 1620 to the Year 1675 . . . .* Lancaster, Mass.: Carter, Andrews, & Co., 1829. 352p. Reprinted with additions and corrections by Genealogical Publishing Co., Baltimore, 1964.

> Excellent directory of the first settlers of New England. Drake's additions and corrections (no. 1666) are found in the G.P.C. reprint and in no. 9151, Tepper, *Passengers to America,* pp. 468-470. (Lancour 43)

*   *   *

1946
FAUST, ALBERT B. "List of Emigrants from Zurich to Carolina and Pennsylvania, 1734-1744; List of Those Persons Who Left the Parish Uster for Carolina, 1736 and 1743." In *National Genealogical Society Quarterly,* vol. 7:4 (i.e. 8:1-2) (Jan. 1919), pp. 17-18.

> Found in the official archives of Zurich, Switzerland. From Zurich, p. 17; from Uster, Switzerland, p. 18.

*   *   *

1952
FAUST, ALBERT BERNHARDT. *Lists of Swiss Emigrants in the Eighteenth Century to the American Colonies.* Vol. 1. Washington, D.C.: The National Genealogical Society, 1920. Reprinted by Genealogical Publishing Co., 1976.

> Swiss emigrants from the Canton of Zurich to Carolina and Pennsylvania, 1734-1744, with index of surnames. About 2,000 persons listed. For nos. 1952 and 1960 in one volume, with Leo Schelbert's "Notes on Lists of Swiss Emigrants," see item. no. 8040. (Lancour 131)

*   *   *

1960
FAUST, ALBERT BERNHARDT, and **GAIUS MARCUS BRUMBAUGH.** *Lists of Swiss Emigrants in the Eighteenth Century to the American Colonies.* Vol. 2. Washington, D.C.: National Genealogical Society, 1925. Reprinted by Genealogical Publishing Co., Baltimore, 1976.

> Contains lists of emigrants from the Cantons of Bern and Basel, 1709-1795, taken from the official archives of those cities. Items nos. 1952 and 1960, with Leo Schelbert's "Notes on Lists of Swiss Emigrants" from item no. 8040, pp. 245-255, are all in the reprint in one volume. (Lancour 131)

*   *   *

1976
FELTY, HAROLD G. "Germans Voted in Hamilton County, Illinois, 1842." In *Illinois State Genealogical Society Quarterly,* vol. 8:3 (Sept. 1976), p. 138.

> Lists nine former subjects of Leopold, Duchy of Baden, filing declarations of intention to become citizens in the Court of Hamilton County, Illinois, in 1845. Seven had entered through the port of New York, 1841; two, the port of New Orleans, 1843.

*   *   *

1984
FERNOW, BERTHOLD. "Form of Oath Taken by the Englishmen on and about Manhattan Island with Their Signatures." In *Documents Relating to the History of the Early Colonial Settlements Principally on Long Island, With a map of Its Western Part, Made in 1666.* Albany, N.Y.: Weed, Parsons & Co., 1883. pp. 24-25.

> Old series, vol. 14, new series, vol. 3, of *Documents Relative to the Colonial History of the State of New York.* Names eight Englishmen who took an oath of allegiance to the Dutch Government and to the Colony of New Netherland, August 1639. See also no. 0714, Boyer, *Ship Passenger Lists, New York and New Jersey,* p. 94. (Lancour 81)

*   *   *

1988
FERNOW, BERTHOLD. "Letter from the Burgomasters of Amsterdam to Stuyvesant: Boys and Girls

from the Almshouses sent to New Netherland." In *Documents Relating to the History of the Early Colonial Settlements Principally on Long Island.* Albany, N.Y.: Weed, Parsons & Co., 1883, pp. 325-326.

Old series, vol. 14; new series, vol. 3, of *Documents Relative to the Colonial History of the State of New York.* Has names and ages of 17 children sent from almshouses in Amsterdam, 1655. No ship mentioned. Also in no. 0714, Boyer, *Ship Passenger Lists, New York and New Jersey,* pp. 136-137.　(Lancour 85)

*　　　*　　　*

1992
FERNOW, BERTHOLD. "West Jersey Settlers." In *The New York Genealogical and Biographical Record,* vol. 30:2 (Apr. 1899), pp. 114-118; vol. 30:3 (July 1899), pp. 175-176.

List of people who, remaining in England, bought land there from the West Jersey Society, John Fenwick, or William Penn, or who came over and settled on land bought in England or acquired upon immigrating. Refers to the year 1664. No ship mentioned. Also in no. 9135, Tepper, *Immigrants to the Middle Colonies,* pp. 78-83.　(Lancour 108)

*　　　*　　　*

1999
FERRIS, BENJAMIN. "[List of the Swedish Families Residing in New Sweden 1693, with the Number of Individuals in Each Family.]" In *A History of the Original Settlements on the Delaware . . . .* 1846, pp. 304-308. Reprinted by Kennikat Press, Port Washington, N.Y., 1972.

Ferris states that only a few of the 938 persons listed were born in Sweden. See also no. 3263, Holm; and no. 7282, Reinders.

*　　　*　　　*

2003
FESER, PHYLLIS HERTZ. [Passenger Lists.]　In *Heritage Review,* No. 25 (Dec. 1979), p. 37.

Passenger list of the S.S. *Kaiser Wilhelm,* Bremen to New York, May 24, 1903, with immigrants from Landau, Russia, to Mandan, North Dakota.

*　　　*　　　*

2006
FETZER, JOHN E. *The Men from Wengen and America's Agony: the Wenger-Winger-Wanger History, Including Christian Wenger, 1718.* [Kalamazoo, Mich.] Fetzer Foundation, 1971, pp. 430-431.

Partial list of known Wenger immigrants, with individual names and year of each arrival, 1717-1868.

*　　　*　　　*

2016
FFOLLIOTT, ROSEMARY, extractor. "The Irish Passengers Aboard the *New World,* Liverpool - New York, October-December 1853." In *The Irish Ancestor,*

vol. 7:1 (1975), pp. 6-10.

Of 754 passengers, mainly Irish and German, about 240 names have been extracted of persons who gave their birthplace as Ireland. Names, ages, and occupations specified.

*　　　*　　　*

2026
FIELDS, S. HELEN. "Covenanters and the Work of Rev. John Cuthbertson." In *National Genealogical Society Quarterly,* vol. 21:1 (Mar. 1933), pp. 16-18.

Pages 17 and 18 have "Names of Those Who Sailed on the *Henry and Francis,* 1685," being a List of Scottish Covenanters who landed at Perth Amboy in December 1685. Published also in nos. 2590 and 2596, Glasgow; no. 0973, Brown and Lindsay; no. 9738, Whitehead; no. 0714, Boyer, *Ship Passenger Lists, New York and New Jersey,* pp. 237-239; and no. 9143, Tepper, *New World Immigrants,* vol. 1, pp. 421-423. (Lancour 113)

*　　　*　　　*

2044
FILBY, P. WILLIAM, contributor. "We the Passengers, Redemptioners, and Servants, in All One Hundred and Seventy, from Belfast to America . . . June 30, 1789 . . . ." In *The Maryland and Delaware Genealogist,* vol. 20:1 (January 1979), p. 13.

A note of thanks published in *The Delaware Gazette,* vol. 5, no. 211, (Saturday, July 4, 1789) [page 3, columns 2-3,] to Captain James Jefferis for his care and humanity to every person on board the brig *Brothers* which came from Belfast and arrived in Wilmington June 30, 1789. A total of 70 passengers signed the document.

*　　　*　　　*

2046
FILBY, P. WILLIAM, contributor. "We the Passengers Who Sailed with Captain Jefferis in the brig *Brothers,* from Belfast to Wilmington . . . 1790." In *The Maryland and Delaware Genealogist,* vol. 20:1 (Jan. 1979), pp. 13-14.

A note of thanks published in *The Delaware Gazette, or General Advertiser,* vol. 6 (July 3, 1790), no. 275 [page 3, columns 1-2], addressed to Captain James Jefferis, for his humane treatment of the 220 passengers on the brig *Brothers,* which arrived in Wilmington, Delaware, late in June or early in July 1790. Of 220 passengers, 38 are listed as having signed the document.

*　　　*　　　*

2048
FILBY, P. WILLIAM, with **MARY KEYSOR MEYER,** editor. *Passenger and Immigration Lists Index: A Guide to Published Arrival Records of about 500,000 Passengers Who Came to the United States and Canada in the Seventeenth, Eighteenth, and Nineteenth Centuries.* Detroit: Gale Research Co., 1981. 3 vols.

Identifies over 480,000 passengers who arrived between 1600 and 1900, with data on when and where they landed and who came with them. Entries name the books, magazines, and documents to consult for further details. Draws on about 300 sources, some 100 of which are not to be found in Harold Lancour's *Bibliography of Ship Passenger Lists, 1538-1825* (3rd ed., 1963). The source numbering accords with the item numbers in this, the present work.

* * *

2053
FINKE, GUENTHER. "Norddeutsche in Aller Welt. Auswanderer aus der Probstei (Ostholstein)." In *Norddeutsche Familienkunde,* vol. 8:3 (July-Sept. 1969), pp. 223-226; vol.8:4 (Oct.-Dec. 1969), pp. 252-254.

Emigrants from the Probstei region (Eastern Holstein) in Northern Germany. Death registers in the parish of Schoenberg for the period 1838-1859 contain the names of deceased parishioners' children who emigrated. Places of residence include Iowa (Davenport), New York, California. Mahrenholtz inaugurated this series, "Norddeutsche in Aller Welt," (Germans the world over) but, on his death, Finke took it over. See no. 5085 and other Mahrenholtz articles.

* * *

2056
"FIRST SETTLERS OF NEW HAMPSHIRE." In *The New England Historical and Genealogical Register,* vol. 2:1 (Jan. 1848), pp. 37-39.

Contains "The names of stewards and servants sent by John Mason, Esq., into this province of New Hampshire," p. 39. Date of arrival is believed to have been somewhere around 1630. Published with variations in no. 0053, Adams; also in no. 9151, Tepper, *Passengers to America,* pp. 464-466; and no. 0702, Boyer, *Ship Passenger Lists, National and New England,* pp. 127-129. (Lancour 31)

* * *

2070
FLECK, LOUISE. "Auswanderer nach Amerika aus der Gemeinde Jabel b. Waren. Meckl." In *Zeitschrift fuer Niederdeutsche Familienkunde,* Jahrg. 47:3 (May 1972), pp. 127-131.

Emigrants to America from the community of Jabel near Waren in Mecklenburg. Information taken from the church register of the community of Jabel, Germany. Lists 77 emigrants, 1850-1857. Much other information is included.

* * *

2075
FLEEHARTY, M. KENDALL, contributor. "Lawfully Transported into This Province [Maryland] by Capt. Wm. Jones in a Seafare Ketch. Anno 1678." In *Maryland Magazine of Genealogy,* vol. 3:1 (Spring 1980), p. 33.

Reports 10 names taken from the Maryland Land Office Records (WC #2, fol. 187).

* * *

2080
FLEMING, GRACE. "Lists of Irish Immigrants to America, 1833 to 1835," In *St. Louis Genealogical*

Society Quarterly, vol. 4:2 (June 1971), pp. 27-30.

Six lists of Irish immigrants to Canada and the United States, with extensive information. Transcribed from records in the Public Record Office of Northern Ireland, Belfast. Copies of originals are in the St. Louis Genealogical Society Library, St. Louis Public Library.

* * *

2100
FORSYTH, ALICE D., and **EARLENE L. ZERINGUE,** compilers and translators. *German "Pest Ships," 1720-1721.* New Orleans: Genealogical Research Society of New Orleans, 1969. 30p. Interleaved with reprints of original documents.

Facsimiles of French holograph passenger lists of five ships that carried German and Swiss families to Louisiana.

* * *

2110
FORSYTH, HEWITT L., and **ERVIN PETER SMITH, SR.** "Naturalization Record Index, New Orleans, Louisiana." In *New Orleans Genesis,* vol. 1:1 (Jan. 1962), pp. 4-7; vol. 1:2 (Mar. 1962), pp. 120-124; vol. 1:3 (June 1962), pp. 221-226.

Entire span of coverage is from the year 1839 to the year 1898. Pages 4-7 cover 1844-1882, 1852-1857, 1857-1861; pages 120-124, the years 1846-1856; all by Forsyth. Smith, on pages 221-226, reports on the years 1868-1898, 1839-1844, 1863-1868. (Lancour 245)

* * *

2120
FOTHERGILL, GERALD. "Emigrant Ministers . . . " [Additions]. In *The New England Historical and Genealogical Register,* vol. 59 (Apr. 1905), pp. 218-219.

Additions to item no. 2144, Fothergill's *List of Emigrant Ministers.* Also in no. 9151, Tepper, *Passengers to America,* p. 475; and in no. 0702, Boyer, *Ship Passenger Lists, National and New England,* pp. 37-38. (Lancour 13, note)

* * *

2128
FOTHERGILL, GERALD. *Emigrants from England, 1773-1776.* Boston: New England Historic Genealogical Society, 1913. 206p. Reprinted by Genealogical Publishing Co., Baltimore, 1965.

About 6,000 names from treasury records in the Public Record Office, London. Much information on each passenger. Reprinted from Fothergill's own articles in *The New England Historical and Genealogical Register,* vols. 62-65. Also in no. 9151, Tepper, *Passengers to America,* p. 222-403. (Lancour 20 and 20A)

* * *

2135
FOTHERGILL, GERALD. "List of Emigrant Liverymen of London." In *The New England Historical and*

Genealogical Register, vol. 60 (October 1906), pp. 399-400.

Short list, giving little other than name and livery or guild for the year 1800 (approximately). Also in no. 9151, Tepper, *Passengers to America,* pp. 476-477; and in no. 0702, Boyer, *Ship Passenger Lists, National and New England,* pp. 60-61. (Lancour 23)

*   *   *

2144
FOTHERGILL, GERALD. *A List of Emigrant Ministers to America, 1690-1811.* London: Elliot Stock, 1904. 65p. Reprinted by Genealogical Publishing Co., Baltimore, 1965.

Ministers and schoolmasters of the Church of England who went to western colonies in return for a bounty from the King. From the Rawlinson MSS. Receipt Book of Secret Service Money, April 20, 1689, to June 1691, in the Bodleian Library. Oxford, England, and from other papers in the Public Record Office, London. For additions, see no. 2120, Fothergill. (Lancour 13)

*   *   *

2151
FOTHERGILL, GERALD. "Passenger Lists to America." In *The New England Historical and Genealogical Register,* vol. 60:1 (Jan. 1906), pp. 23-28; vol. 60:2 (Apr. 1906), pp. 160-164; vol. 60:3 (July 1906), pp. 240-243; vol.60:4 (Oct. 1906), pp. 346-349; vol. 61:2 (Apr. 1907), pp. 133-139; vol. 61:3 (July1907), pp. 265-270; vol. 61:4 (Oct. 1907), pp. 347-353; vol. 62:1 (Jan. 1908), pp. 78-81; vol. 62:2 (Apr. 1908), pp. 168-171; vol. 66:1 (Jan. 1912), pp. 30-32; vol. 66:3 (July 1912), pp. 306-308.

Lists passengers from Ireland to America, 1803-1806, but is regarded as inaccurate. From manuscripts in the British Museum, London. Settlers to all parts of America. Also in no. 9151, Tepper, *Passengers to America,* pp. 411-458; and no. 0702, Boyer, *Ship Passenger Lists, National and New England,* pp. 61-107. And see no. 1762, *Early Irish Immigrants;* no. 3450, Ireland; and no. 9198, Trainor. (Lancour 24)

*   *   *

2162
FRANCE, R. SHARPE. "Early Emigrants to America from Liverpool." In *Genealogists' Magazine* (London), vol. 12:7 (Sept. 1956), pp. 234-235.

Concerns 34 indentured servants destined for Virginia or Maryland from Liverpool in the year 1686. From a manuscript in the Lancashire Record Office, County Hall, Preston, England. Reprinted by Genealogical Publishing Co., Baltimore, in *Some Early Emigrants to America* and in *Early Emigrants to America from Liverpool,* 1965, 110p. The France article is on pp. 98-100; the remainder of the reprint volume concerns no. 6179, Nicholson. The France article is also in no. 0720, *Boyer, Ship Passenger Lists, the South,* pp. 84-86; and in no. 9143, Tepper, *New World Immigrants,* vol. 1, pp. 424-425. (Lancour 220)

*   *   *

2172
FRANK, KARL FRIEDRICH VON. "Auswanderer

aus Goisern nach Nordamerika 1850 bis 1882." In *Senftenegger Monatsblatt fuer Genealogie und Heraldik,* vol. 3:7-8 (Jan.-Feb. 1956), columns 233-240.

Emigrants from Goisern [Austria] to North America, 1850-1882. Names taken from civil family registers maintained by the parish of Goisern beginning in 1856. Lists 49 family names, representing 200 to 300 emigrants, with places of origin, dates of emigration, ages, and some intended destinations in America. Goisern consisted of 31 communities in the Salzkammergut region of Austria. (Lancour 260)

*   *   *

2182
"FRANKLIN COUNTY, INDIANA, NATURALIZATION RECORDS, Book 1, 23 September 1826 - 11 March 1839." In *The Hoosier Genealogist,* vol. 18:4 (December 1978), pp. 59-72.

Name, date and place of birth, arrival in the United States, locations thereafter, and family information. Mostly Franklin County. Index to the names is on pp. 71 and 72.

*   *   *

2192
FRECHEN, FRANZ. "Die Ankunft einiger Auswanderer aus Woerrstadt (Rheinhessen) in Philadelphia (Pennsylvanien)." In *Hessische Familienkunde,* vol. 6:8 (Oct. 1963), cols. 411-412.

The arrival of some emigrants from Woerrstadt (Rhenish Hesse) in Philadelphia, Pennsylvania. Derived from no. 7820, Rupp. Lists fifteen emigrants, 1743-1754, who appear to have origins in Woerrstadt and who emigrated to Philadelphia. Names and arrival dates only.

*   *   *

2202
FREEMAN, WALLACE R. "Scotch Emigrants to New York 1774-1775." In *The Niagara Frontier Genealogical Magazine,* vol. 4:5 (Feb. 1944), pp. 89-90; vol. 4:7 (Apr. 1944), pp. 124-125; vol. 4:8 (May 1944), pp. 136-137 and 145.

List of Scots who arrived from Stranraer, Scotland, in the *Gale,* 1774, and in the *Commerce,* 1775. Names, ages, occupations, origins. Extracted from no. 1088, Cameron. List derived from manuscripts in the New York Public Library. Appears in no. 9144, Tepper, *New World Immigrants,* vol. 2, pp. 217-223. (Lancour 103)

*   *   *

2212
FRENCH, ELIZABETH. *List of Emigrants to America from Liverpool, 1697-1707.* Boston: New England Historic Genealogical Society, 1913. 55p. Reprinted by Genealogical Publishing Co., Baltimore, 1962.

From the records of the Corporation of Liverpool, England. Names 1,500 indentured servants destined for Virginia, Maryland, Pennsylvania, New England, and the West Indies. Much additional information. Originally appeared in *The New England Historical and Genealogical Register,* vols. 64-65, 1910-1911. Also in no. 9151, Tepper, *Passengers to America,* pp. 173-220. (Lancour 14 and 14A)

* * *

2222

**"FRENCH ROYALISTS IN UPPER CANADA:
Sketch (Political and Financial) of an Establishment to
be formed in Canada for the Settlement of the French
Emigrants."** In *Report on Canadian Archives* by Doug-
las Brymner, Archivist, 1888. Ottawa, [Canada]: Queen's
Printer, 1889, note F, pp. 73-87.

Contains a list on pages 85-87 of Royalists who left London for
Canada with Count Joseph de Puisaye, Includes a statement of
Sept. 3, 1799, on the actual condition of the French emigrants
under Puisaye at York, Upper Canada.

* * *

2232

FREY, JULIUS. "Auswanderungen nach Nordamerika
aus der Landschaft zwischen Vogelsberg und Spessart im
18. Jahrhundert." In *Heimat-Jahrbuch des Kreises
Gelnhausen,* 1962, pp. 56-57.

Emigration to North America from the region between the
Vogelsberg and the Spessart in the 18th century. From nos.
9041-9042, Strassburger. Contains names of 134 male adults
emigrating in the period 1738-1751 from Germany to Philadelphia.

* * *

2242

FRICKE, KARL. "Auswanderung nach Amerika." In
Heimat-Blaetter fuer die Grafschaft Diepholz, Folge 9
(20 June 1953), p. 64.

Appears as a random series in supplement to *Diepholzer
Kreisblatt.* From church registers of the parish of Drebber
(Mariendrebber and Jacobidrebber) in the former earldom of
Diepholz, now in the state of Lower Saxony in the Federal
Republic of Germany. Concerns three persons who emigrated
from the villages named above to North America on the
Pauline, sailing from Bremerhaven to New York, April 1-
May 6, 1839.

* * *

2262

FRIES, ADELAIDE L. "Arrivals in Georgia." In *The
Moravians in Georgia, 1735-1740.* Raleigh, N.C.: the
author, 1905, pp. 236-238.

Lists 47 settlers who emigrated to Georgia, 1734-1775, and
their countries of origin. Also in no. 0720, Boyer, *Ship
Passenger Lists, the South,* pp. 164-165. (Lancour 240/1)

* * *

2272

FRIES, ADELAIDE L., editor. "[Lists of Moravian
Immigrants to North Carolina, 1753-1759]" In *Records
of the Moravians in North Carolina* (Publications of the
North Carolina Historical Commission), Raleigh [N.C.]:
Edwards & Broughton, 1922, vol. 1, pp. 68-69, 73-74.

Two lists, one giving 26 names drawn from certificates of land

grants in the Herrnhut (Saxony) archives, the other being a list
of colonists sent to North Carolina in 1753. Also in no. 0720,
Boyer, *Ship Passenger Lists, the South,* pp. 127-129.
(Lancour 231)

* * *

2282

FROEHLICH, HUGO. "Auswanderer im lutherischen
Kirchenbuch von Staudernheim." In *Mitteilungen zur
Wanderungsgeschichte der Pfaelzer (Supplement: Pfael-
ische Familien- und Wappenkunde),* Folge 10 (1954), pp.
55-62.

Emigrants recorded in the Lutheran Church register of
Staudernheim on the Nahe [Germany]. Lists 90 departures to
America, 1738-1750. Includes also emigrants to Poland,
Prussia, and Hungary. Name, age, place of origin other than
Staudernheim, some destinations. Froehlich matched his data
with Strassburger entries where possible. For English version
see no. 2292. (Lancour 158A)

* * *

2292

FROEHLICH, HUGO. "Pioneers from Staudernheim."
In *The Pennsylvania Dutchman,* vol. 8 (Fall-Winter
1956-1957), pp. 43-46.

From the Lutheran church register in the village of Staudernheim. Names 90 emigrants to Pennsylvania, mostly 1739-1741,
with much other information. Published originally in German:
no. 2282, Froehlich. Translated by Don Yoder. Also in no.
9144, Tepper, *New World Immigrants,* vol. 2, pp. 123-132; and
in no. 0717, Boyer, *Ship Passenger Lists, Pennsylvania and
Delaware,* pp. 167-176. (Lancour 158)

* * *

2302

FRY, PHILIP H. "Importations." In William Wallace
Scott, *A History of Orange County, Virginia, from its
Formation in 1734 (O.S.) to the End of Reconstruction in
1870* . . . . Richmond [Va.]: Everett Waddey Co., 1907,
pp. 225-229. Reprinted by Chesapeake Book Co., Berry-
ville, Va., 1962, and by Regional Publishing, Baltimore,
1974.

Persons who proved their importation to obtain "head rights"
to land in the Colony. Also in no. 0720, Boyer, *Ship Passenger
Lists, the South,* pp. 91-95. And see nos. 5831, Morton; and
3816, King. (Lancour 227)

* * *

2313

FUTHEY, JOHN SMITH, and **GILBERT COPE.** "A
Partial Registry of Arrivals Was Made Between the
Years 1682 and 1687." In *History of Chester County,
Pennsylvania, with Genealogical and Biographical
Sketches.* Philadelphia: Louis H. Everts, 1881, pp. 22-24.

Original in The Historical Society of Pennsylvania. Corrected
and re-transcribed in no. 7585, Roach, and no. 8370, Sheppard. Also in no. 6451, "A Partial List . . . ." (Lancour 124A)

* * *

2324
GALENSON, DAVID. "Agreements to Serve in America and the West Indies, 1727-31." In *Genealogists' Magazine* (London), vol. 19:2 (June 1977), pp. 40-44.

From records in the Corporation of London Records Office at the Guildhall. Totals 65 entries, additions to no. 3690, Kaminkow. See also no. 2328, Galenson.

*   *   *

2328
GALENSON, DAVID. "Servants Bound for Antigua 1752-56." In *Genealogists' Magazine* (London), vol. 19:8 (December 1978), pp. 277-279.

Abstracts of indentures of servants bound by Charles Tudway to serve at Parham Hill Plantation, Antigua, West Indies. From the Tudway Papers in the Somerset Record Office in England.

*   *   *

2334
GAMMON, WILLIAM J. "Emigrants to Bath County, North Carolina, 1695-1702." In *National Genealogical Society Quarterly*, vol. 25:1 (March 1937), pp. 28-30.

Chronological list of immigrants taken from an old deed book in Craven County, N.C. Bath County was formed from territories south of Albemarle and north of the Pamtecough (now Tar and Pimlico Rivers) in 1696. Also in no. 0720, Boyer, *Ship Passenger Lists, the South*, pp. 125-127; and in no. 9143, Tepper, *New World Immigrants*, vol. 1, pp. 436-438. (Lancour 230)

*   *   *

2344
GAUDET, PLACIDE. "Acadiens a Cherbourg en 1767." In *Report Concerning Canadian Archives*, 1905, vol. 2:3, Appendix G, pp. 142-146.

A list of Acadians and the amounts of pensions provided them by the French government. Prefaced by a letter requesting either refuge for them on the islands of Miquelon and St. Pierre or better pensions. Name, age, members of household given; occupation and state of health often mentioned. Contains a separate list of ill and incapacitated or bedridden pensioners.

*   *   *

2354
GAUDET, PLACIDE. "Familles acadiennes qui sont maintenant aux iles St Pierre et Miquelon suivant le recensement d'icelles, fait le 15 Mai 1767." In *Report Concerning Canadian Archives*, 1905, vol. 2:3, Appendix G, pp. 171-176.

Acadian families that are presently on the islands of St. Pierre and Miquelon according to the islands' census of May 15, 1767, Names, ages, and members of household given.

*   *   *

2374
GAUDET, PLACIDE. "A List of the French Who Desire to go to Old France, with Letter of Aug. 24th, 1763." In *Report Concerning Canadian Archives*, 1905, vol. 2, part 3, Appendix F, pp. 134-137.

The letter referred to is signed by the Hon Andrew Oliver and concerns immigrants (French Canadians) who had to come to Boston and wished to go to a tract of land lying on the Bay or River Merrimeche in the Gulf of St. Lawrence, Canada. Each head of family, with name of wife and other family data. There were 1,019 who wished to go.

*   *   *

2384
GAUDET, PLACIDE. "Listes des familles acadiennes de Beausejour qui se sont refugiees a Miquelon et autres embarquees par ordre de M. le Gouverneur et les notres, sur le brigantin *Les Deux Amis*, pour etre remises a terre au premier port de France . . . ." In *Report Concerning Canadian Archives*, 1905, vol. 2:3, Appendix G, p. 171.

Lists of the Acadian families from Beausejour who found refuge on the island of Miquelon and others deported by the governor's order on the brigantine *Les Deux Amis*, to be put ashore at the first French port. These were passengers who came to Canada in 1765. Ages and members of household given.

*   *   *

2394
GAUDET, PLACIDE. [Petition of Acadians to Governor of Massachusetts for Permission to Emigrate to Hispaniola 1764.] In *Report Concerning Canadian Archives*, Ottawa: King's Printer, 1905, vol. 2, part 3, Appendix E, p. 91.

Most of the petitioners appear to have gone to Quebec eventually, about 1766. Family head and number of family members given. See other items by Gaudet.

*   *   *

2404
GEBLER, ERNEST. *The Plymouth Adventure: a Chronicle Novel of the Voyage of the Mayflower*. Garden City, N.Y.: Doubleday, 1950, pp. 372-377.

Complete list of passengers on the *Mayflower*, all named with details of what happened to them. For other references to the *Mayflower*, see the index.

*   *   *

2414
GEISEL, KARL. "Hessische Auswanderer auf dem 1854 vor Spiekeroog Gestrandeten Schiff *Johanne*. In *Hessische Familienkunde*, vol. 11:3 (Sept. 1972), columns 123-126.

Hessian emigrants on board the ship *Johanne* which went aground near Spiekeroog, one of the Frisian Islands off the northern coast of Germany, 1854. Mentions that 68 of the 139 survivors had already continued their voyage to Baltimore by the end of 1854. Another 30 mentioned as saved probably proceeded to America in 1855 and are therefore included here.

*   *   *

2417

GEISS, MARVIN, contributor. [Passenger Lists.] In *Heritage Review* (Germans from Russia Heritage Society), vol. 10:3 (Aug. 1980), p. 48.

German passengers from Russia who settled in North and South Dakota and Canada, 1901.

*   *   *

2424

GENSBURGER, ROBIN. [Passengers on S.S. *Brandenburg,* Bremen to New York, 1907, and to Philadelphia, 1910; S.S. *Oldenburg,* Bremen to Baltimore, Maryland, 1903; S.S. *Tennyson,* Buenos Aires to New York, 1907; S.S. *Ivernia,* Liverpool to Boston, Mass., 1903.] In *Heritage Review,* no. 21 (Sept. 1978), pp. 43-44.

Only emigrants from Russia listed, all being Germans from Russia. Many went to North Dakota. Originals in the U.S. National Archives.

*   *   *

2434

GERBER, ADOLF. *Beitraege zur Auswanderung nach Amerika im 18. Jahrhundert aus Altwuerttembergischen Kirchenbuechern.* Stuttgart [Germany]: J.N. Steinkopf, [1928] 32p.

Emigrants from the Duchy of Wuerttemberg, the names arranged alphabetically under the towns from which they came. From local church records. For ship names, see the English edition, no. 2444, Gerber. Supplement: see no. 2464. (Lancour 133)

*   *   *

2444

GERBER, ADOLF. "Emigrants from Wuerttemberg; the Adolf Gerber Lists." Edited by Donald Herbert Yoder. In *The Pennsylvania German Folklore Society* [*Yearbook*], vol. 10 (1945), pp. 103-237.

An English edition of the original and supplementary Gerber lists combined. Lists are on pp. 132-237. They include only individuals in the local church records who are identified as emigrants in the Ludwigsburg files and specifically designated in the record book as going to America. See also no. 4445, Krebs. Also in no. 9964, Yoder. (Lancour 135)

*   *   *

2454

GERBER, ADOLF. *Die Nassau-Dillenburger Auswanderung nach Amerika im 18. Jahrhundert; das Verhalten der Regierungen dazu und die Spaeteren Schicksale der Auswanderer.* Flensburg [Germany]: Flensburger Nachrichten, Deutscher Verlag, 1930. 51p.

Eighteenth century emigration to America from Nassau-Dillenburg; the conduct of the regime there and the eventual

lot of the emigrants. Newspaper reports taken mostly from manuscript sources in the *Staatsarchiv* at Wiesbaden, Germany. Includes an index of surnames. See also no. 2690, Goebel, and no. 3233, Hoffman. Also in no. 0717, Boyer, *Ship Passenger Lists, Pennsylvania and Delaware,* pp. 17-47.

*   *   *

2464

GERBER, ADOLF. *Neue Beitraege zur Auswanderung nach Amerika im 18. Jahrhundert aus Altwuettembergischen Kirchenbuchern unter Hinzuziehung anderer Quellen.* Stuttgart [Germany]: J.F. Steinkopf [1929?]. 44p.

Supplementary volume from larger source of material, including state archives. Has index of surnames lacking from no. 2434, Gerber. (Lancour 134)

*   *   *

2474-2476

GEUE, CHESTER W., translator. "Verein Immigrants to Texas in 1845." In *Stirpes.*
2474
---vol. 7:3 (Sept. 1967), pp. 87-89.
2475
---vol. 9:2 (June 1969), p. 64.
2476
---vol. 10:3 (Sept. 1970), p. 110.

Indexed list of Verein immigrants to Texas taken from the German list in the Verein Collection in the University of Texas archives, Austin. Contains names of those who left the port of Bremen in 1845 but does not include those who left from the port of Antwerp. Place of residence in Germany and ship used are given. Geue intended to continue this work but died shortly after the last contribution.

*   *   *

2484

GEUE, CHESTER W., and **ETHEL HANDER GEUE,** compilers. *A New Land Beckoned: German Immigration to Texas 1844-1847.* 1966. New and enlarged ed. Waco [Texas]: Texian Press, 1972. 178p.

Names 7,000 immigrants, giving European home place, ship taken, and usually birth and death dates. See no. 2504, Geue, for the years 1847-1861.

*   *   *

2494

GEUE, CHESTER W., and **MRS. CHESTER W. GEUE.** "Passagierliste des Schiffes Nr. 109 *Sophie* aus Hamburg . . . . 1852 nach Galveston und Indianola in Texas, USA." In *Footprints* (Fort Worth, Texas, Genealogical Society), vol. 12:3 (Aug. 1969), pp. 96-97.

Names and places of origin of passengers on the ship *Sophie* from Hamburg, 1852.

*   *   *

2504

GEUE, ETHEL HANDER, compiler. *New Homes in a New Land: German Immigration to Texas, 1847-1861.* Waco [Texas]: Texian Press, 1970. 166p.

From German newspapers in Texas, records on microfilm of passenger lists of those who arrived at the port of Galveston. Also names from Hamburg Archives. Includes about 6,000 immigrants, of whom 588 were Wends. Listed on pages 4 and 5 are names of early German settlers in Texas, before 1836. See also Wends in no. 0578, Blasig; no. 1067, Caldwell; and no. 1858, Engerrand. Another Geue title, no. 2484, covers the years 1844-1847.

*   *   *

2514

GEUE, ETHEL HANDER (Mrs. Chester W.). "Passagierliste des Schiffes, *Reform* (und *Magnet*), Galveston from Bremen, 1851." In *Footprints* (Fort Worth Genealogical Society), vol. 12:2 (May 1969), pp. 66-67.

Taken from the *Galveston Zeitung,* 1851. Names and places of origin. See also no. 8317, Seele.

*   *   *

2524

GHIRELLI, MICHAEL. *A List of Emigrants from England to America, 1682-1692, Transcribed from the Original Records at the City of London Record Office.* Introductory notes by Marion J. Kaminkow. Baltimore: Magna Carta, 1968. 106p. Available from Tuttle Company, Rutland, Vt.

From the Lord Mayor's Waiting Books. Mostly involves bonded servants.

*   *   *

2529

GIESINGER, ADAM. "A Passenger List from Canada." In *The American Historical Society of Germans from Russia Journal,* vol. 2:1 (Spring 1979), p. 72.

Passengers on the S.S. *Brooklyn* from Liverpool to Halifax on April 29, 1885. The group left the Black Sea area of Dobruja in 1885. After settling briefly at New Tulcea (now Edenwold) northeast of Regina, Saskatchewan, most moved on to Cathay, North Dakota. The ship's name was given in the *Journal* as S.S. *Manitoban* in error, according to a correction published in a later issue.

*   *   *

2534

GILLESPIE COUNTY HISTORICAL SOCIETY. *Pioneers in God's Hills: a History of Fredericksburg and Gillespie County [Texas] People and Events.* Austin, Texas: printed by Von Boeckmann-Jones, 1960, pp. 239-257.

Concerns Fredericksburg, Texas, settlers, most of whom came on ships arriving in Galveston in 1845 and 1846. A skillfully constructed list compiled from the settlement and ship lists.

*   *   *

2544

GILLINGHAM, HARROLD E. "Passengers from the Rhineland to Pennsylvania." In *Publications of The Genealogical Society of Pennsylvania,* vol. 14:1 (Oct. 1942), p. 79.

Fifteen Palatines named in a warning in the *Pennsylvania Gazette,* March 22, 1732 or 1733, that their passage payment must be met to avoid prosecution. Article signed H.E.G. Also in no.9144, Tepper, *New World Immigrants,* vol. 2, p. 531; and in no. 0717, Boyer, *Ship Passenger Lists, Pennsylvania and Delaware,* pp. 141-42. (Lancour 149)

*   *   *

2554

GILLINGHAM, HARROLD E. "Philadelphia Arrivals, 1738." In *Publications of The Genealogical Society of Pennsylvania,* vol. 12:2 (Mar. 1934), p. 150.

From the Reynell Papers at the Historical Society of Pennsylvania. Seven indentured servants on the *Elizabeth* from London, July 1738. Also in no. 9144, Tepper, *New World Immigrants,* vol. 2, p. 533; and in no. 0717, Boyer, *Ship Passenger Lists, Pennsylvania and Delaware,* p. 167. (Lancour 157)

*   *   *

2564

GIUSEPPI, MONTAGUE SPENCER, editor. *Naturalizations of Foreign Protestants in the American and West Indian Colonies (Pursuant to Statute 13 George II, c.7).* (Publications of The Huguenot Society of London, 1921, vol. 24). Manchester [England]: The Huguenot Society of London, 1921. 196p. Reprinted by Genealogical Publishing Co., Baltimore, 1964.

Data derived from return-forms connected with the naturalization of foreign Protestants, papers that were sent from the Colonies to the Lords Commissioners for Trade and Plantations. Transcribed from two Entry Books, once the property of the Board of Trade and Plantations, now with the Colonial Office in the Public Record Office, London. Much other information. Contains returns from the West Indies, North and South Carolina, Virginia, Maryland, New York and Pennsylvania. A more complete record of New York naturalizations can be found in no. 9860, Wolfe, and for Pennsylvania in no. 6680. (Lancour 19)

*   *   *

2574

GLACKING, JAMES R. "Norwegian Ancestors." In *Illinois State Genealogical Society Quarterly,* vol. 5:3 (Fall 1973), p. 162.

Details concerning some of the *Restaurationen* passengers who came to La Salle and Kendall Counties, Illinois, 1835-1837. For other references to the *Restaurationen,* see the index.

*   *   *

2580

GLACKING, JAMES R. "Norwegians in Adams Township, La Salle County, Illinois." In *Illinois State*

Genealogical Society Quarterly, vol. 7:2 (June 1975), pp. 85-89.

Biographical and genealogical notes about Norwegians who were early settlers in La Salle County or who settled in the vicinity of the village of Leland in Adams Township prior to 1870. Gives names, Norwegian origins, and dates of arrival in America, 1836-1850s.

* * *

2590
GLASGOW, WILLIAM MELANCTHON. [Scottish Prisoners Banished to Pennsylvania and New Jersey (Perth Amboy), 1685.] In *History of the Reformed Presbyterian Church in America . . . .* Baltimore: Hill & Harvey, 1888, pp. 230-231.

A better list is found in no. 9840, Wodrow. For other references, see the index. (Lancour 113A)

* * *

2596
GLASGOW, WILLIAM MELANCTHON, "Some Scot Emigrants." In *Santa Clara County Historical and Genealogical Society* [*Quarterly*], vol. 6:2, (Oct. 1969), pp. 18-19.

Lists Scots on board the *Henry and Francis* from Leith, Scotland, to Perth Amboy, New Jersey, December 1685. All were dissenters who scattered throughout New York, Connecticut, and Eastern Pennsylvania. Data extracted from no. 2590, Glasgow's *History of the Reformed Presbyterian Church in America* (Baltimore: Hill & Harvey, 1888, pp. 230-231). Also in no. 1110, Campbell; and no. 9840, Wodrow. For other references to the *Henry and Francis,* see index.

* * *

2602
GLEIS, P. "Einige Westfalen und Lipper der 1848er Revolutionszeit in Nordamerika." In *Der Ravensberger: Heimatkalender fuer das Minden-Ravensberger Land,* Jahrgang 25 (1953), pp. 47-50.

Some natives of Westphalia and Lippe in America (as a result of) the 1848 revolution in Germany. Concerns eleven persons from Westphalia and Lippe who emigrated to America in mid-19th century. Includes names, places of origin and, for most, ages, dates of emigration, places of settlement, and biographical sketches.

* * *

2612
GOBILLOT, RENE. "L'Emigration Percheronne au Canada." In *Nova Francia,* vol. 3:1 (Oct. 1927), pp. 17-31.

Emigration from Perche to Canada. A general history of these 17th-century French settlers and of the first efforts to colonize Canada. Gives names and some biographical data.

* * *

2632
GODBOUT, PERE ARCHANGE. "Emigration Ro-

chelaise en Nouvelle-France." From *Rapport des Archives Nationales de Quebec,* vol. 48 (1970), pp. 113-367. Quebec: Ministere des Affaires Culturelles, 1971.

Emigration from La Rochelle to New France in the 17th and 18th centuries.

* * *

2642
GODBOUT, ARCHANGE. "Engages pour le Canada en 1658." (Etudes Genealogiques.) In *Memoires de la Societe Genealogique Canadienne-Francaise,* vol. 9:2 (Apr. 1958), pp. 78-84.

Recruits for Canada in 1658. A description of *Le Taureau,* the vessel on which the 16 listed emigrants made their journey to Quebec in 1658. Contains the contract for the ship, the passengers' contracts, and names of the 16 passengers. Gives, as well, place of origin, age, salary, and other biographical information. Additional notes: see no. 1656, Douville.

* * *

2652
GODBOUT, PERE ARCHANGE. "Familles Venues de la Rochelle en Canada." From *Rapport des Archives Nationales du Quebec,* vol. 48, 1970. (1971), pp. 129-367.

Posthumous edition presented and annotated by Roland J. Auger. Contains passenger lists, with biographical notes. Names families who left La Rochelle, France, for Canada in the 17th and 18th centuries. Pages 113-128 contain introductory matter and bibliography.

* * *

2662
GODBOUT, PERE ARCHANGE. *Les Passagers du Saint-Andre: la recrue de 1659.* (Publications de la Societe Genealogique Canadienne-Francaise, 5.) Montreal: Societe Genealogique Canadienne-Francaise, 1964, 48p.

Comprehensive genealogies of passengers on the *Saint Andre:* recruits of the year 1659 headed for Montreal. See also no. 5364, Massicotte.

* * *

2672
GODBOUT, ARCHANGE. "The Passenger List of the Ship *Saint-Jehan* and the Acadian Origins." Translated by J.P. Hebert. In *French Canadian and Acadian Genealogical Review,* vol. 1:1 (Spring 1968), pp. 55-73.

Subtitled "Genealogy and Emigration." Translated from the original in Quebec Provincial Archives: see no. 2682. The *Saint-Jehan* sailed for New France, April 1, 1636. Names, family, often occupations. Also in no. 5811, Moras.

* * *

2682
GODBOUT, PERE ARCHANGE. "Le role du *Saint-Jehan* et les origines acadiennes." In *Memoires de la Societe Genealogique Canadienne-Francaise,* vol. 1

(1944), pp. 19-30.

The passenger list of the *Saint-Jehan*, the ship that brought French settlers to Acadia in 1636. Name, members of household, occupation, place of origin. Detailed biographies of seven passengers and information surrounding the voyage. The English translation of this article appears in no. 2672. Also in no. 5811, Moras.

*   *   *

2688
GODMAN, STANLEY. "West Sussex Emigration to Canada in 1832." In *West Sussex Gazette & South of England Advertiser,* Nov. 8, 1962.

Details of the crossing of the ships *Lord Melville* and *Eveline* from Portsmouth on the English Channel to Montreal, Quebec, with 603 emigrants on board, most from West Sussex. Taken in part from no. 8775, Sockett, first edition, with some additional names. See also no. 9979, Young.

*   *   *

2690
GOEBEL, JULIUS. "Briefe deutscher Auswanderer aus dem Jahre 1709." In *Deutsch-Amerikanische Geschichtsblaetter; Jahrbuch der Deutsch-Amerikanischen Historischen Gesellschaft von Illinois,* vol. 12 (1912), pp. 124-189.

Letters of German emigrants in the year 1709, from copies in the archives of the former principality of Nassau-Dillenburg. Concerns approximately 115 settlers in America. Gives names of family heads and a few of the family members accompanying them; places of origin, some places of settlement (New York, New Jersey). An amplification of E. Schierenberg's article in the German publication *Nassovia* (1903). See also no. 2454, Gerber.

*   *   *

2692
GOLDMANN, L. "Obereichsfeldische Auswanderung nach Amerika in der zweiten Haelfte des 19. Jahrhunderts." In *Unser Eichsfeld,* Jahrgang 23:12 (Dec. 1928), pp. 257-262.

Emigration from Obereichsfeld to America in the second half of the 19th century. From a file containing requests for permission to emigrate, stored in the *Landratsamt* in Muehlhausen (in Thuringia, now East Germany). Concerns 1,095 emigrants to America, 1832-1891: name, place of origin, number of persons accompanying the applicant.

*   *   *

2713
GOODWIN, JOHN A. *The Pilgrim Republic: an Historical Review of the Colony of New Plymouth . . . .* Boston: Ticknor & Co., 1888. 2nd ed., Boston and New York: Houghton Mifflin, 1920, pp. 183-186, 190-191, 242-244, 297-300.

Contains lists from the *Mayflower* in 1620; the *Fortune* in 1621; and the *Anne* and the *Little James* in 1623. These taken from the second edition. The whole story is told in no. 0255, Banks. For other references to the *Mayflower,* see index. (Lancour 34B)

2722
GOOKIN, FREDERICK WILLIAM. "Mr. Danniell Gookines Muster." In *Daniel Gookin, 1612-1687 . . . .* Chicago: privately printed, 1912, pp. 47-48.

Names 27 servants transported from the British Isles to Newport News, Va., in the *Flying Hart* in 1621, and the *Providence* in 1623. Also in no. 2851, Gwynn; no. 3520, Jester and Hiden; and no. 9143, Tepper, *New World Immigrants,* vol. 1, pages 2 and 3. (Lancour 214)

*   *   *

2732
GOSSAGE, F.T. "Irish Railroad Builders." In *National Genealogical Society Quarterly,* vol. 57:1 (Mar. 1969), pp. 51-52.

Extracted from the 1850 census record for Franklin County, Tennessee, where there were labor camps for the Nashville and Chattanooga Railroad. Lists the railroad laborers, over half of them foreign born, mostly from Ireland, some from Germany and England. All prior to 1850.

*   *   *

2742
GRADY, JOHN C., compiler. "Passenger List of the British Ship *Euphemia* from Liverpool, Arriving Port of New Orleans, La., October 20, 1849." In *Louisiana Genealogical Register,* vol. 20:3 (Sept. 1973), p. 207.

Passengers from Ireland and England boarding at Liverpool and Cardiff.

*   *   *

2762
GRAUPNER, LUDWIG. *Die Amerikawanderung im Guessinger Bezirk.* (Burgenlaendische Forschungen, Part 3) Vienna [Austria]: Verlag Ferdinand Berger, 1949. 50p., plus appendix.

Migration to America from the Guessing district. Statistical analysis of a 1940 questionnaire requesting information on family members who had emigrated. Details on the emigration of over 5,500 individuals (1884-1939) were lost in World War II, but the names of 14 emigrants are given.

*   *   *

2764
GREAT REGISTER OF MENDOCINO COUNTY, STATE OF CALIFORNIA. 1898. Ukiah, Calif.: Dispatch-Democrat Print, 1898. 96p. Reprinted and published by Pomo Chapter, Daughters of the American Revolution, 1979.

Registrations date from 1891 through 1898 and are numbered 1 through 5,306. A supplemental register in the precinct covers registrations numbered 5,307 through 7, 226. Entries include name, age, height and other physical features, occupation, country of birth, place of residence, precinct, post office address, date of naturalization, and/or date of registration. For explanation of the Great Register, see no. 1890.

*   *   *

2765-2768
GREAT REGISTER, TULARE CO. [CALIFORNIA], 1888, NATURALIZATION DATA. In *Sequoia Genealogical Society Newsletter.*
2765
---Vol. 1:1 (Jan. 1975), p. 4; vol. 1:2 (Feb. 1975), p. 3; vol. 1:3 (Mar. 1975), p. 4; vol. 1:4 (Apr. 1975), p. 4; vol. 1:5 (May 1975), p. 4.
2766
---Vol. 2:1 (Sept. 1975), p. 3; vol. 2:2 (Oct. 1975), p. 4; vol. 2:3 (Nov. 1975), p. 4 vol. 2:4 (Jan. 1976), p. 4; vol. 2:5 (Feb. 1976), p. 4; vol. 2:6 (Mar. 1976), p. 4; vol. 2:7 (Apr. 1976), p. 4; vol. 2:8 (May 1976), p. 4
2767
---Vol. 3:1 (Sept. 1976), p. 4; vol. 3:2 (Oct. 1976), p. 4; vol. 3:3 (Nov. 1976), p. 4; vol. 3:4 (Jan. 1977), pp. 3-4; vol. 3:5 (Feb. 1977), p. 4; vol. 3:6 (Mar. 1977), p. 4: vol. 3:7 (Apr. 1977), p. 4; vol. 3:8 (May 1977), p. 4.
2768
---Vol. 4:1 (Sept. 1977), p. 4; vol. 4:3 (Nov. 1977), pp. 5-6; vol. 4:4 (Jan. 1978), pp. 5-6; vol. 4:5 (Feb. 1978), pp. 5-6; vol. 4:6 (Mar. 1978), pp. 5-6; vol. 4:7 (Apr. 1978), pp. 5-6; vol. 4:8 (May 1978), pp. 5-6.

From vol. 2:2 (Oct. 1975), the title became *1888 Great Register of Tulare Co., California.* Name, age, occupation, origin, date of arrival or naturalization. Immigrants from various countries. Covers entries 13 through 7,054 in the Great Register for the years 1884-1888. The Great Register is described in no. 1890. This research is believed to have ended with the May 1978 issue cited above.

* * *

2772
GREER, GEORGE CABELL. *Early Virginia Immigrants, 1623-1666.* Richmond [Va.]: W.C. Hill Printing Co., 1912, 376p. Reprinted by Genealogical Publishing Co., Baltimore, 1978.

Includes 25,000 names from records of the Virginia State Land Office. Excerpts of the Irish names from the Greer list were published in no. 6258, O'Brien, *Early Immigrants to Virginia . . . .* (Lancour 216)

* * *

2782
GREINER, W. "Auswanderer aus Lauscha (Thueringen)." In *Archiv fuer Sippenforschung und alle verwandten Gebiete,* vol. 32:22 (May 1966), pp. 527-528.

Emigrants from Lauscha in Thuringia, Germany. Found in church registers of Lauscha from their beginning to about 1900. Concerns emigrants to other parts of Europe as well as to America. At least 110 indicated their destination as America, some specifying New York and Baltimore. Very full information given.

* * *

2792
GRIMES, MARILLA R. "Some Newspaper References to Irish Immigrants in Oneida Co., New York." In *The Irish Ancestor,* vol. 6:2 (1974), pp. 97-98.

Covers period 1827-1867.

2802
GRUCHALLA, ROBERT, contributor. "Verzeichniss der Personen, welche mit dem Segel Schiffe *Liebig* . . . nach Quebec zur Auswanderung durch Unterzeichneten engagirt sind." In *Bismarck-Mandan Historical and Genealogical Society [Newsletter],* vol. 5:4 (Dec. 1976), pp. 8-24.

A list of persons emigrating by the sailing vessel *Liebig* from Hamburg to Quebec, 1868. Most of the 536 passengers settled in Minnesota, and their descendants moved to the Jamestown area of North Dakota. Full details on the passengers.

* * *

2822
GRUHNE, FRITZ. *Auswandererlisten des ehemaligen Herzogtums Braunschweig; ohne Stadt Braunschweig und Landkreis Holzminden 1846-1871.* (Quellen und Forschungen zur Braunschweigischen Geschichte, vol. 20, 1971) Brunswick [Germany]: Braunschweigischer Geschichtsverein, 1971. 293p. Index.

Lists of emigrants from the former Duchy of Braunschweig, or Brunswick, not including the city of Braunschweig (Brunswick) and the county of Holzminden, 1846-1871. From notices in *Braunschweigische Anzeigen* and church registers. The notices appeared as the result of an ordinance enacted in the Duchy of Brunswick-Lueneburg, which called for all officially requested permits for emigration to be publicized. These notices were compared against entries in church registers. Carries names of 7,305 persons whose intended destinations included North and South America, and elsewhere. Name, age, occupation, family data, place of origin, intended destination, and the date of the notice.

* * *

2828-2829
GUENTHER, KURT. "Hessian Emigrants to America." in *Germanic Genealogist.*
2828
---No. 14 (1978), pp. 302-306, Part 1: 1832; no. 15 (1978), pp. 374-377, Parts 2,3: 1833-1834.
2829
---No. 19 (1979), pp. 69-76, Part 4: 1835.

All from counties of the Province Nether-Hesse, northeastern part of the former territory of Hesse-Cassel.

* * *

2832
GUILLET, EDWIN C., editor. *The Valley of the Trent.* Toronto: Champlain Society for the Government of Ontario, 1957, pp. 92-109.

Irish passenger lists to Canada, 1825, often referred to as Peter Robinson Emigration because they were under the control of Robinson. Ships were the *Resolution,* the *Albion,* the *John Barry,* the *Amity.* Lists 474 passengers, with mention of families.

* * *

2842
GUNSCH, HAROLD, copier. "Passenger Lists." In

Heritage Review, no. 20 (Apr. 1978), p. 45.

Germans from Russia, crossing from Bremen to New York, with final destination South Dakota, 1902. Antwerp to New York, 1902, with three destinations: Harvey and Fessenden, North Dakota, and Tripp, South Dakota. National Archives microfilm.

*   *   *

2847

GUTTENDORF, VIRGINIA, (and **ROBERT DEVLIN**). "Federal Courts Relating to Early Western Pennsylvania. Naturalization Lists, 1820-1840, U.S. District Court - Western District of Pennsylvania." In *Western Pennsylvania Genealogical Quarterly,* vol. 5:1 (Aug. 1978), pp. 12-14; vol. 5:2 (Nov. 1978), pp. 59-61; vol. 5:3 (Feb. 1979), pp. 113-116.

Gives date, type of list (petitions, declarations, and/or registry), with full name. All British names. Vol 5:1 by Guttendorf; vol. 5:2-3 by Devlin.

*   *   *

2851

GWYNN, AUBREY. "Documents Relating to the Irish in the West Indies." In *Analecta Hibernica,* no. 4 (Oct. 1932), pp. 165-166.

Servants transported to Newport News, Virginia, in the *Flying Hart,* 1621, and the *Providence,* 1623. Names 24 persons. Also in no. 2722, Gookin; and in no. 3520, Jester and Hiden. See also no. 9143, Tepper, *New World Immigrants,* vol. 1, pp. 2-3. (Lancour 214A)

*   *   *

2856

HACKER, WERNER. *Auswanderungen aus dem fruehen Hochstift Speyer nach Suedost-Europa und Uebersee im 18. Jh.* (Schriften zur Wanderungsgeschichte der Pfaelzer, Part 28.) Kaiserslautern [Germany]: Heimatstelle Pfalz [1969], 145p.

Emigrations from the early diocese of Speyer to southeastern Europe and overseas in the 18th century. From files in the Generallandesarchiv at Karlsruhe, Germany. Covers 1,600 families or individuals who emigrated to Hungary, as well as 400 families or individuals who emigrated overseas, 1720-1800, some to America.

*   *   *

2859

HACKETT, J. DOMINICK. "Passenger Lists Published in *The Shamrock or Irish Chronicle,* 1811." In *The Journal of the American Irish Historical Society,* vol. 28 (1929-1930), pp. 65-82.

Over 2,000 names from lists in 1811 issues of a New York weekly published between 1810 and 1817. Some lists were printed in nos. 8795, 8797, *The Recorder.* This names passengers on 29 ships arriving at New York, six at Philadelphia, one at Baltimore, and one at New London. A reprint by Genealogical Publishing Co., Baltimore, 1965, 46p., contained lists compiled by Hackett (above) and Early in *Passenger Lists from Ireland:* pp. 5-22, by Hackett; pp. 23-46

by Early; excerpted from *The Journal of the American Irish Historical Society,* vols. 28-29. Also in no. 9144, Tepper, *New World Immigrants,* vol. 2, pp. 329-346. And see no. 8099 for the years 1811-1817. (Lancour 27 and 27A)

*   *   *

2875

[HAKLUYT, RICHARD]. *Explorations, Descriptions, and Attempted Settlements of Carolina, 1584-1590.* Edited by David Leroy Corbitt. Raleigh, NC.: State Department of Archaeology and History, 1948. Reprinted by Department of Cultural Resources, Raleigh, 1953, pp. 32-33, 108-109.

"The names of those, as well Gentlemen as others, that remained one whole year in Virginia, under the government of Master Ralph Lane," pp. 32-33. For the year 1584, there are 106 persons listed. "The names of all the men, women and children which safely arrived in Virginia, and remained to inhabit there," 1587, pp. 108-109. That year, 118 were named.

*   *   *

2883

HALL, CHARLES M. *"Pal-Index:" A Surname Index of Eighteenth-Century Immigrants.* Salt Lake City: Global Research Systems, 1979. 147p.

Data on immigrants from France (Alsace-Lorraine), Switzerland, Southern Germany, and some adjacent places, arriving between 1727 and 1775. "Palatines" was a term adopted from British merchants and the people of Philadelphia whose first contact with large migrations from continental Europe in the 1700s was with Palatines (Pfaelzer in German), people from the Palatinate (Pfalz). A third of the immigration in this period was from what later became Baden-Wuerttemberg. Information includes name, origin, date, place of settlement, and sometimes the religion. About 6,500 names gathered from about 50 sources.

*   *   *

2887

HALL, MIRTH, contributor. "Settlers from Rhode Island to Falmouth, Nova Scotia." (Canadian Notes and Records.) In *Seattle Genealogical Society Quarterly Bulletin,* vol. 22:2 (Dec. 1972), pp. 70-73.

The first settlers arrived on the sloops *Sally* and *Lydia* in May 1760 from Newport. The article gives details of town lots assigned and names the recipients of grants in the township of Newport, Nova Scotia, 1761. Taken from an article by R. G. Huling, no. 3309.

*   *   *

2891-2893

HAMLIN, CHARLES HUGHES. "Proof of Importations." In *Virginia Ancestors,* Powhatan, Va.: the author, 1967--1973. Reprinted, 3 vols. in 1, by Genealogical Publishing Co., Baltimore, 1975.
2891
---vol. 1, 1967, pp. 23-24.
2892
---vol. 2, 1969, pp. 88-91.

2893
---vol. 3, 1973, pp. 60-63.

Mostly Virginia arrivals, early 1700s.

*   *   *

2899
HARGREAVES—MAWDSLEY, R., transcriber. "The Bristol Records: A Representative List of Names of Persons Who Emigrated to America Between the Years 1654 and 1679." In *Apollo: a Journal of the Arts,* vol. 6:31 (July 1927), pp. 29-31.

This list concerns the names on pp. 1-26 of the Bristol city records, with British places of residence indicated. Description of the discovery of these records by Hargreaves-Mawdsley in June 1927 is in vol. 6, no. 30, June 1927. The emigration data is also in no. 9143, Tepper, *New World Immigrants,* vol. 1, pp. 161-65. See also no. 0943, *Bristol and America,* and no. 3283, Hotten. (Lancour 11, note)

*   *   *

2917
HARTMANN, GABRIEL. "Emigrants from Dossenheim (Baden) in the 18th Century." Translated and edited by Don Yoder. In *Pennsylvania Folklife,* vol. 21:2 (Winter 1971-1972), pp. 46-48.

List of 84 emigrants from Dossenheim to America, mostly to Carolina and Pennsylvania. In records extracted from the family register of the Reformed Congregation of Dossenheim, Germany, belonging to the Electoral Palatinate, in the 18th century. German title of the article is, "Amerikafahrer von Dossenheim im 18. Jahrhundert," published in the series, *Mannheimer Geschichtsblaetter, vol. 27 (1926), columns 55-58.*

*   *   *

2920
HARVEY, KATHERINE A., editor. 'The Lonaconing Journals: the Founding of a Coal and Iron Community, 1837-1840." In *Transactions of the American Philosophical Society,* vol. 67, pt. 2 (Mar. 1977) Appendix, pp. 70-71.

In two parts: (A) Passenger list of the barque *Tiberias,* arrived at the port of Baltimore, Sept. 10, 1838. Carried immigrants from Newport, Wales, destined for George's Creek Company, Allegany County, Maryland. (B) Naturalization Record of George's Creek Coal and Iron Company employees, 1839-1840, Allegany County Circuit Court. Names, ages, occupations (nearly all colliers.)

*   *   *

2924
HASBROUCK, KENNETH E. "The Huguenots of New Paltz, N.Y." In *De Halve Maen,* vol. 36:4 (Jan. 1962), pp. 7-8, 12, 15.

Has names of 12 Huguenot patentees who founded the Ulster County community of New Paltz in 1678, with dates and places of their births and dates of their departure from the Palatinate. Also printed with genealogical notes in no. 4592, LeFevre; and

in no. 9143, Tepper, *New World Immigrants,* vol. 1, pp. 196-203. (Lancour 87)

*   *   *

2932
HAUSCHILD-THIESSEN, RENATE. *Die ersten Hamburger im Goldland Kalfornien.* (Verein fuer Hamburgische Geschichte, Vortraege und Aufsaetze, Part 17.) Hamburg [Germany]: Hans Christians Verlag, 1969. 106p.

The first citizens of Hamburg in the gold country of California: catalogue of citizens of Hamburg who emigrated to California up to and including 1854, pages 78-105. ("Verzeichnis von Hamburgern, die bis 1854 einschliesslich nach Kalifornien auswanderten.") Names 250 citizens who either came to California or announced their destination as California in the period 1845-1854. Some were merchants who operated branches of their firms for a few years in California but later returned to Hamburg, where they are buried. Much family data is given. From various records in Hamburg, Germany.

*   *   *

2940
HAUTH, WILHELM. "Deutsche Pioniere im Staate Illinois der USA." In *Familiengeschichtliche Blaetter,* Jahrgang 33:5 (May 1935), cols. 137-142; 33:6/7 (June-July 1935), cols. 223-231; 33:8 (Aug. 1935), cols. 263-270.

German pioneers in the state of Illinois. Concerns about 200 immigrants in the period 1783-1850s. Some lived on the Eastern seaboard before settling in Illinois. Name and year of arrival; some ages, family data, and short biographies.

*   *   *

2946
HAUTH, WILHELM. "Deutsche Pioniere im Staate Iowa der USA." In *Familiengeschichtliche Blaetter, Jahrgang 31:9 (Sept. 1933), cols. 215-220; 31:10-11 (Oct.-Nov. 1933), cols. 263-270; 31:12 (Dec. 1933), cols. 317-324.*

German pioneers in the State of Iowa. From works published in Iowa prior to 1933, particularly Joseph Eiboeck, *Die Deutschen von Iowa und deren Errungenschaften* (Des Moines: 1900). About 400 immigrants involved, 1840s to 1870s. Data includes name and date of first appearance in Iowa and place of origin in Europe. Arranged alphabetically: Part 9, A-Geh; Parts 10-11, Gei-Matte; Part 12, Matth-Z; and supplement A-F in col. 324. See also nos. 8580-8581, Smith.

*   *   *

2956
HAVENS, HENRY H. "Aliens Authorized to Purchase and Hold Real Estate in This State." In *General Index to the Laws of the State of New York 1777-1901, both Dates Inclusive.* Archie E. Baxter, ed. Albany[N.Y.]: 1902, vol. 1, pp. 130-190.

Period concerning aliens is 1777-1870. An earlier edition dated 1866 is usually quoted, but the later one, with its extended lists, is preferable. Also in no. 0714, Boyer, *Ship Passenger Lists, New York and New Jersey,* pp. 175-208; Boyer, however, uses the 1866 edition, which covers only the years 1777-1857. (Lancour 104)

2960
HAYNES, EMMA SCHWABENLAND. "Arrival Dates in New York of Steamships Given in *Work Papers 9 Through 14.*" In *Journal of the American Historical Society of Germans from Russia,* vol. 3:1 (Spring 1980), pp. 60-61.

Gives date of departure from Hamburg and date of arrival in New York between 1873 and 1878 of the ships mentioned in *Work Papers* 9 through 14, all by Gwen Pritzkau, nos. 6920-6925. Included in this article are a few names omitted from the lists in *Work Papers* 9 through 14.

*   *   *

2966
HAYNES, EMMA S. "Passenger Lists." In *Journal of the American Historical Society of Germans from Russia,* vol. 1:1 (Spring 1978), pp. 76-78.

Names 400 German passengers, most from Bremen to New York, 1875-1876, and one to Baltimore, 1875.

*   *   *

2969
HAYNES, EMMA S. "Passenger Lists." In *Journal of American Historical Society of Germans from Russia,* vol. 1:3 (Winter 1978), pp. 70-75.

Arrivals in New York and Baltimore, 1873-1876. Contains (among others) the 1875 passenger list of the S.S. *Ohio,* to New York, which brought the first group of Volga German Catholics to the United States. Names in full, with ages.

*   *   *

2970
HAYNES, EMMA SCHWABENLAND. "Passenger Lists." In *Journal of the American Historical Society of Germans from Russia,* vol. 2:1 (Spring 1979), pp. 68-71.

Lists of Mennonites, Volga German Protestants of pietist bent. Hamburg and Liverpool to New York, 1875-1876.

*   *   *

2971
HAYNES, EMMA SCHWABENLAND. "Passenger List, October 24, 1876, Arrival in New York, S.S. *Mosel,* Bremen to New York." In the *Journal of the American Historical Society of Germans from Russia,* vol. 2:2 (Fall 1979), pp. 91-93.

Primarily from the Central European colonies of Neu Jagodnaja, Schoental, Schoenfeld, and Schoendorf on the Wiesenseite. Most settled near Otis, Kansas.

*   *   *

2972
HAYNES, EMMA SCHWABENLAND. "Passenger Lists." In *Clues,* 1979, part 2, pp. 61-65.

Lists of immigrants crossing from Hamburg and Bremen to New York, 1874-1876; Bremen to Baltimore, 1876; Liverpool to New York, 1876. Germans from Russia. *Clues* is the

publication of the American Historical Society of Germans from Russia.

*   *   *

2973
HAYNES, EMMA SCHWABENLAND. "Passenger Lists." In *Clues* (1980), Part 1, pp. 77-85.

Passengers originally from Russia, 1875-1876, 1889-1900. Many were Mennonites from the Volga area. Compilers along with Haynes of some of the lists were Louise Glantz England and Delores Iggulden. See note on *Clues* in item 2792 (above.)

*   *   *

2979
HAZARD, SAMUEL. *Annals of Pennsylvania, from the Discovery of the Delaware, 1609-1682.* Philadelphia: Hazard and Mitchell, 1850. pp. 637-643.

Part of this (Appendices 2 and 3) is "An account of the lands in Pennsylvania granted by William Penn, Esq., chief proprietary and governour of that province, to several purchasers within the kingdom of England, Ireland, and Scotland, etc., ca. 1682, intending for settling the present colony embarked this Autumn at London and Bristol for Pennsylvania." See also no. 8370, Sheppard; no. 7570, Roach; and no. 0032, "An Account of the lands . . . ."

*   *   *

2989
HEADLAM, CECIL, editor. *Calendar of State Papers Colonial Series, America and West Indies, January 1716-July 1717.* London: His Majesty's Stationery Office, 1930, vol. 29, pp. 166-171.

Lists some 600 Scottish rebel prisoners transported to the American colonies in 1716. Also in no. 8690, Smith.

*   *   *

3000
HEIDGERD, RUTH, and **WILLIAM HEIDGERD.** *The Goetschy Family and the Limping Messenger.* New Paltz, N.Y.: Huguenot Historical Society, 1968. pp. 20-27.

Retraces the Goetschy Family, using a pamphlet from Swiss archives, *Der Hinkinde Bott* [sic] (or The Limping Messenger), 1735, by Ludwig Weber. Names those who travelled to England and members of the group taken from no. 7820, Rupp, "List of Foreigners Imported in the Ship *Mercury* . . . from Rotterdam, qualified at Philadelphia, May 29, 1735." Transcribed with notes taken from no. 1952, Faust. It is probable that the spelling in this list is vastly superior to that given in Rupp. See also no. 4487, Kupillas; no. 3161, Hinke; no. 9630, Weber; and no. 1804, Egle.

*   *   *

3004
HEILINGBRUNNER, ELISABETH. "Hessische Auswanderer nach Amerika 1846-1849." In *Hessische Familienkunde,* vol. 6 (Apr. 1963), cols. 319-320.

Hessian emigrants to America, 1846-1849, covers about 80

departures from Hesse during the years specified, with much family information. Data taken from five ships' passengers lists stored in the Haupstaatarchiv in Munich (reference: Geh. Arch., file nos. 11649, 11652, Anl. 3-6).

* * *

3010

HEISS, WILLARD, contributor. "Naturalization Records, Tippecanoe County, Indiana." In *Illiana Genealogist,* vol. 4:3 (Summer 1968), pp. 67-69; 4:4 (Fall 1968), pp. 101-103.

Naturalizations 1834-1850. Taken from Circuit Court Order Books. Name, date, and reference to citation in court records.

* * *

3015

HELMS, KATE, and **GENE LUNDERGAN.** "Index to the Naturalization Papers of Brown County, Located at the Area Research Center, The University of Wisconsin, Green Bay." In *Wisconsin State Genealogical Society Newsletter,* vol. 25:3 (Jan. 1979), pp. 131-132 (Brown County, pp. 37-38); vol. 25:4 (Apr. 1979), pp. 185-186 (Brown County, pp. 39-40); vol. 26:2 (Sept. 1979), pp. 75-76 (Brown County, pp. 41-42); vol. 26:3 (Jan. 1980), pp. 133-134 (Brown County, pp. 43-44); vol. 26:4 (Apr. 1980), pp. 189-190 (Brown County, pp. 45-46); vol. 27:2 (Sept. 1980), pp. 47-48. To be continued.

For the years 1841-1978: Full name, date of naturalization, and index reference. In September 1980, the last *Newsletter* received, the names had reached the letter J, the year 1920.

* * *

3020

HEMPERLEY, MARION R., compiler. "Federal Naturalization Oaths, Charleston, South Carolina, 1790-1860." In *The South Carolina Historical Magazine,* vol. 66:2 (Apr. 1965), pp. 112-124; vol. 66:3 (July 1965), pp. 183-192: vol. 66:4 (Oct. 1965), pp. 218-228.

From Federal Court records, District of South Carolina, Books 1-12, 1789-1861. Not a complete list. No. 8965, Stephenson, lists naturalizations between 1792 and 1800.

* * *

3030

HENDERSON, F.J.R. "Scots in Cuba." In *The Scottish Genealogist,* vol. 11:4 (Nov. 1964), p. 20.

Contains the name, age, profession, parentage, marital status, and date and place of the naturalization petition for 15 native Scots, 1818-1858.

* * *

3040

HERALDIC ARTISTS, LTD. *Handbook on Irish Genealogy: How to Trace Your Ancestors and Relatives in Ireland.* 2nd impr., enl. Dublin [Ireland]: Heraldic Artists, 1973, pp. 102-131.

Passenger lists of emigrants to America, 1803-1855. All from

Ireland to various American ports, mostly New York, with additional information.

* * *

3050-3051

HERPIN, JULIEN. "Les Malouins colonisateurs au Canada: les Acadiens deportes dans la region Malouine." (Les Provinces de France et la Nouvelle France.) In *Nova Francia.*

3050

---Vol. 2:4 (Apr. 1927), pp. 181-186; vol. 2:5 (June 1927), pp. 229-234.

3051

---Vol. 3:2 (Dec. 1927), pp. 111-118; vol. 3:5 (June 1928), pp. 311-314.

Colonizers from St. Malo [France] in Canada; deported Acadians in the St. Malo region. An explanation for the exploration of Canada by adventurers from the St. Malo region, including Jacques Cartier, the men accompanying him, and their successors. Some personal names and ships' names given. The fall of Port Royal, Nova Scotia, to the English and the deportation of its inhabitants to St. Malo.

* * *

3075

HETT, KAREN MC CANN, copier. "Report and Manifest of the Cargo Laden on Board the Brig *Ceres* whereof W. Patterson is Master . . . from Belfast . . . 29 May 1817 Bound for Philadelphia." In *Valley Leaves,* vol. 10:4 (June 1976), p. 194.

Names 14 cabin passengers, from U.S. National Archives' original document.

* * *

3080

HEYNE, BODO. "Ueber bremische Quellen zur Auswanderungsforschung." In *Bremisches Jahrbuch,* vol. 41 (1944), pp. 368-369.

Concerning Bremen sources for emigration research. Two ships, the *Ferdinand* to Baltimore, April 1, 1834, and the brig *Wallace* to New York, September 3, 1834. Involves 152 emigrants, with much family information. See also no. 9640, Wehner.

* * *

3090

HIDEN, MARTHA W., editor. "Accompts of the *Tristram and Jane.*" In *The Virginia Magazine of History and Biography,* vol. 62:3 (July 1954), pp. 424-447.

"A booke of accompts for the shippe called the *Tristram and Jeane* of London which came from Virginia, anno domini 1637." From the Public Record Office, London. Refers to two paying passengers and 74 indentured servants. Also in no. 0720, Boyer, *Ship Passenger Lists, the South,* pp. 72-84; and in no. 9143, Tepper, *New World Immigrants,* vol. 1, pp. 83-108. The *Tristram and Jane* probably left England in the fall of 1636, arriving in Virginia in time to take on tobacco, returning to London early in 1637. (Lancour 219)

3100

HIEBERT, CLARENCE, compiler. *Brothers in Deed to Brothers in Need: a Scrapbook about Mennonite Immigrants from Russia, 1870-1885.* Newton, Kan.: Memorial Library and Archives, Faith and Life Press, 1974. 419p.

Many lists of passengers are reproduced in these pages where space exists between offset clippings from the publication, *Herald of Truth.* Passengers mostly from Hamburg. Includes articles selected from issues of the *Herald of Truth* (Elkhart, Indiana) for period 1870-1885.

*　　　*　　　*

3110

"THE HIGHLAND PRISONERS. Journal of Committee of Safety June 5, 1776-July 5, 1776; Monday the 24th of June 1776." In *Tyler's Quarterly Historical and Genealogical Magazine,* vol. 5:1 (July 1923), pp. 59-63.

General list of the Highland prisoners taken by Captain James and Richard Barron in the ship *Oxford,* and the assignment of them into fourteen divisions to be sent to various counties in Virginia.

*　　　*　　　*

3130

HILL, MRS. GEORGIE A, "Passenger Arrivals at Salem and Beverly, Mass., 1798-1800." Introduction by Meredith Colket, Jr., of Washington, D.C. In *The New England Historical and Genealogical Register,* vol. 106:3 (July 1952), pp. 203-209.

Copied from customs records in the National Archives, Washington, D.C. Also in no. 9151, Tepper, *Passengers to America,* pp. 404-410; and in no. 0702, Boyer, *Ship Passenger Lists, National and New England,* pp. 194-197. (Lancour 67)

*　　　*　　　*

3140

HILL, WARREN. "Those Who Sailed the *Mayflower."* In *The Genealogist's Post,* vol. 1:4 (Apr. 1964), pp. 10-16.

Lists the passengers on the *Mayflower* and tells of their fate subsequent to the landing in 1620. For further references to the *Mayflower,* see index.

*　　　*　　　*

3152

HILLS, LEON CLARK. *History and Genealogy of the Mayflower Planters and First Comers to Ye Olde Colonie.* Washington, D.C.: Hills Publishing, 1936, vol. 1, pp. 20-22, 79-80, 84-87. Reprinted by Genealogical Publishing Co., Baltimore, 1975.

Passengers on the *Mayflower,* 1620, pp. 20-22; the *Fortune,* 1621, pp. 79-80; the *Anne,* 1623, pp. 84-86; the *Little James,* 1623, p. 86; and the *Mayflower,* 1629, pp. 86-87. Totals 66 passengers from London and 38 from Leyden. For other references to these ships, see index. The 1629 crossing of the *Mayflower* is also in no. 0702, Boyer, *Ship Passenger Lists, National and New England,* p. 137. (Lancour 37 and 34C)

*　　　*　　　*

3161

HINKE, WILLIAM J. "Early Swiss Settlers." In *Notes and Queries, Historical, Biographical and Genealogical, Relating Chiefly to Interior Pennsylvania.* Edited by W.H. Egle. Annual volume: 1900 (1901), pp. 121-122. Reprinted by Genealogical Publishing Co., Baltimore, 1970.

From a pamphlet, *Der Hinkinde Bott von Carolina* (The Limping Messenger) no. 9630, by Ludwig Weber, Zurich, 1735, found by Hinke among Swiss archives. Names 48 Swiss emigrants who left Zurich in October 1734 and arrived in Philadelphia May 29, 1735, on the *Mercury.* A more complete list of this voyage, with 186 names, can be found in no. 7820, Rupp, and no. 1804, Egle. See also no. 3000, Heiderd, and no. 4487, Kupillas. (Lancour 153)

*　　　*　　　*

3171

HINKE, WILLIAM J., compiler. "Lebanon County Moravians — 1752." In *The Pennsylvania Dutchman,* vol. 2:13 (Dec. 1, 1950), p. 6.

List of Moravian families in Quitopehille, a Moravian settlement, in the year 1752. Gives the European birthplaces of emigrant ancestors. Entitled, "Catalogus der Geschwister in Quitopehille den 25. Oktober 1752," the original is preserved in the Moravian Archives at Bethlehem, Pa. The list is from Hinke's papers in the Historical Society of the Evangelical and Reformed Church at Franklin and Marshall College.

*　　　*　　　*

3179

HINKE, WILLIAM J. "Moravian Brethren in Heidelberg — 1752." In *The Pennsylvania Dutchman,* vol. 2:15 (Jan. 1, 1951), p.6.

Lists Moravian emigrants belonging to the Congregation at Heidelberg, Pennsylvania, 1752. Transcribed from the original document, "Catalogus der Geschwister in Heidelberg, Oct. 1752," now in the Moravian archives in Bethlehem, Pa. Also in no. 9144, Tepper, *New World Immigrants,* vol. 2., pp. 183-185; and no. 0717, Boyer, *Ship Passenger Lists, Pennsylvania and Delaware,* pp. 201-203. (Lancour 180)

*　　　*　　　*

3183

HINKE, WILLIAM J. "Moravian Pioneers in the Swatara Valley — 1752." In *The Pennsylvania Dutchman,* vol. 2:14 (Dec. 15, 1950), p. 6.

Names ten Moravian emigrants belonging to the Congregation at Swatara, Pa., 1752. Transcribed from the original document, "Catalogus der Geschwister in Swatara den 25. Oct. 1752," now in various archives at Bethlehem, Pa. Also in no. 9144, Tepper, *New World Immigrants,* vol. 2, pp. 181-182; and no. 0717, Boyer, *Ship Passenger Lists, Pennsylvania and Delaware,* pp. 199-201. (Lancour 179)

*　　　*　　　*

3193

HINKE, WILLIAM J., and **JOHN BAER STOUDT,** editors. "A List of German Immigrants to the American Colonies from Zweibruecken in the Palatinate, 1728-

1749." In *The Pennsylvania German Folklore Society* [*Yearbook*], vol. 1 (1936), pp. 101-124.

> From a document in the Bavarian State Archives at Speyer, Germany. German text was published in the *Valley Citizen*, weekly newspaper of Valley View, Pennsylvania, in 1933. Covers 404 emigrants destined for Pennsylvania and Carolina. Also in no. 9964, Yoder. For the years 1750-1771, see nos. 4357 and 4364, Krebs.   (Lancour 147)

* * *

3203-3204
HINS, ALLAN GUSTAV, copier. "Passenger Lists." In *Heritage Review*.
3203
---No. 18 (Sept. 1977), pp. 39-40.
> Some passengers from Kulm, Bessarabia, Russia, to New York City, 1878-1879, settled in Hutchinson County, South Dakota. Names ages and occupations.

3204
---No. 19 (Dec. 1977), pp. 47-48.
> Germans from Russia, some of whom settled in Hutchinson County, South Dakota.

* * *

3213-3215
HODGES, MRS. GEORGE W., contributor. "A List of Persons Naturalized by Particular Acts." In *The County Court Note-Book. A Little Bulletin of History and Genealogy.* Edited by Milnor Ljungstedt. Reprinted by Genealogical Publishing Co., Baltimore, 1972.
3213
---Vol. 2:1 (Feb. 1923), pp. 1-2; vol. 2:3 (June 1923), pp. 18-19; vol. 2:5 (Oct. 1923), pp. 33-34.
3214
---Vol. 3:1 (Jan. 1924), p. 6; vol. 3:2 (Mar. 1924), pp. 10-11; vol. 3:4 (July 1924), p. 29; vol. 3:6 (Nov. 1924), pp. 45-46.
3215
---Vol. 4:1 (Feb. 1925), pp. 6-7.

> From Bacon's *Laws of Maryland.* Many British, 1600s-1700s.

* * *

3219
HODGES, MARGARET. "Passenger List of the *Mayflower.*" In *Hopkins of the Mayflower: Portrait of a Dissenter.* New York: Farrar, Straus and Giroux, 1972, pp. 249-250.

> The list is divided into four parts: pilgrims by persuasion, planters recruited by London merchants, men hired to stay for one year, family servants and young cousins. For the many versions of the *Mayflower* passenger list, see index.

* * *

3223
HOEVEL, RUTH. "Auswanderer der Stadt Wesenberg im Mecklenburg." In *Mitteldeutsche Familienkunde,* vol. 3:4 (Oct.-Dec. 1972), pp. 381-382.

> Emigrants from the city of Wesenberg in Mecklenburg. From 19th century Lutheran Church registers of Wesenberg, stored in the Cathedral archive in Ratzeburg, West Germany. Ten emigrants, 1850-1862; one to Australia, the others to America. Names, some birth and marriage dates, and other family data.

* * *

3233
HOFFMAN, WILLIAM J. " 'Palatine' Emigrants to America from the Principality of Nassau-Dillenburg." In *National Genealogical Society Quarterly,* vol. 29:2 (June 1941), pp. 41-44.

> From records in the state archives at Wiesbaden. Contains the names of 54 persons petitioning to go to Pennsylvania or the Carolinas. Names only. Printed in part in no. 2454, Gerber. Based on material in the German magazine *Nassovia,* vol. 4 (1903), p. 194ff. Also in no. 0702, Boyer, *Ship Passenger Lists, National and New England,* pp. 44-46; and in no. 9143, Tepper, *New World Immigrants,* vol. 1, pp. 449-452. (Lancour 16)

* * *

3243-3244
HOFFMAN, WILLIAM J. "Random Notes Concerning Settlers of Dutch Descent." In *The American Genealogist.*
3243
---Vol. 29:2 (Apr. 1953), pp. 65-76; vol. 29:3 (July 1953), pp. 146-152.
3244
---Vol. 30:1 (Jan. 1954), pp. 38-44.

> Notes on servants and employees hired in New Netherland between 1629 and 1663. Volume 30, pp. 38-44, has a table giving copious details on each settler. Also in no. 0714, Boyer, *Ship Passenger Lists, New York and New Jersey,* pp. 94-116; and in no. 9143, Tepper, *New World Immigrants,* vol. 1, pp. 109-134. (Lancour 82)

* * *

3249
HOLCOMB, BRENT H., abstractor. "Pickens District, S.C., Naturalizations, Taken from Records now on file in [South Carolina] State Archives." In *The Georgia Genealogical Magazine,* no. 57 (Summer 1975), pp. 227-230.

> Many from Germany, especially Hanover, 1846-1871.

* * *

3253
HOLLANDER, JACOB HARRY. "The Naturalization of Jews in the American Colonies under the Act of 1740." In *Publications of the American Jewish Historical Society,* no. 5 (1897), pp. 103-117.

> From records of the Commissioners for Trade and Plantations, now in the Colonial Office in the Public Record Office, London. Names Jews naturalized in South Carolina, Pennsylvania, Maryland, and New York. Also in no. 2564, Giuseppi; and in no. 9144, Tepper, *New World Immigrants,* vol. 2, pp. 143-157. See also no. 3303, Huehner, and no. 9860, Wolf. (Lancour 18)

* * *

3258

HOLLENBACK, RAYMOND E., contributor. "Albany Township, Berks County, Early Taxables." In *Central Pennsylvania Genealogy Magazine,* Dec. 1959, pp. 16-18.

From a list published in Berks County in 1909, then in Rupp, *History of Berks and Lebanon Counties,* and Montgomery, *History of Berks County.* Persons named are identified with the ship on which they arrived in Pennsylvania between 1727 and 1757. Many names spelled incorrectly.

*   *   *

3263

HOLM, THOMAS CAMPANIUS. "A List of the Swedish Families Residing in New Sweden in the Year 1693, with the Number of Individuals in Each Family." In *Short Description of the Province of New Sweden, Now Called by the English, Pennsylvania in America . . . .* Philadelphia, Pa.: M'Carty & Davis, 1834, pp. 164-166. Reprinted by Kraus Reprint Co., Millwood, NY., 1975.

Also in no. 7282, Reinders, and in no. 1999, Ferris.

*   *   *

3273

HOLMAN, WINIFRED LOVERING. "Marriages of Emigrants to Virginia." In *The Virginia Magazine of History and Biography,* vol. 40:1 (Jan. 1932), p. 80.

Names five couples married on the Isle of Wight, England, just before leaving for Virginia. Also in no. 0720, Boyer, *Ship Passenger Lists, the South,* p. 68; and in no. 9144, Tepper, *New World Immigrants,* vol. 2, p. 529.   (Lancour 213)

*   *   *

3280

HOTTEN, JOHN CAMDEN. "List of what Ticqtts have been Granted Out of the Secretary's Office of the Island of Barbadoes for Departure off this Island of the Several Psones Hereafter Menconed, Beginning in January, 1678, and Ending in December Following." In *The Original Lists of Persons of Quality . . . .* London: Chatto and Windus, 1874. Reprinted by Genealogical Publishing Co., Baltimore, 1974.

Names 84 persons who sailed for Virginia, the Carolinas, and other American colonies. One vessel, the *True Friendship,* listed six passengers. Also printed in no. 6280, O'Brien's *Irish Settlers in America,* pp. 18-19.

*   *   *

3283

HOTTEN, JOHN CAMDEN, editor. *The Original Lists of Persons of Quality; Emigrants; Religious Exiles; Political Rebels; Serving Men Sold for a Term of Years; Apprentices; Children Stolen; Maidens Pressed; and Others Who Went from Great Britain to the American Plantations, 1600-1700. With Their Ages, the Localities Where They Formerly Lived in the Mother Country, the Names of the Ships in Which They Embarked, and Other Interesting Particulars. From MSS. Preserved in the*

State Paper Department of Her Majesty's Public Record Office, England. London: Chatto and Windus, 1874, 604p. Reprinted by Genealogical Publishing Co., Baltimore, 1974.

Standard work. Includes lists of ships to Bermuda, Barbados, and continental North America. Indexes family names. Names of Jews are excerpted in Adler, no. 0061.

Care should be taken when using Hotten. There are two versions, one with accurate text and index, the other with poor text and the better index which does not entirely match the text. Therefore it is essential that only the following editions be used: all 1874 printings; 1931, New York; 1935, New York; and the G.P.C. printings from 1974 on. G.P.C.'s earlier printings had the poor text and the better index.   (Lancour 1)

*   *   *

3303

HUEHNER, LEON. "Naturalization of Jews in New York under the Act of 1740." In *Publications of the American Jewish Historical Society,* no. 13 (1905), pp. 1-6.

Wolfe's "The Colonial Naturalizations Act of 1740 . . . ," no. 9860, provides the whole list of 300 names. The Huehner list is also in no. 9144, Tepper, *New World Immigrants,* vol. 2, pp. 158-163. See also no. 3253, Hollander.   (Lancour 102, note)

*   *   *

3309

HULING, RAY GREENE. "The Rhode Island Emigration to Nova Scotia." In *The Narragansett Historical Register,* vol. 7:2 (Apr. 1889), pp. 101-136.

Pages 102-103 have "A List of Settlers Brought from Newport, Rhode Island, to Falmouth [Nova Scotia] . . . in the sloop *Sally* and in the sloop *Lydia* . . . in May, 1760." The article has other details on the settlers at Falmouth, Newport, and Sackville, Nova Scotia. This list is also in no. 2887, Hall.

*   *   *

3313

HULL, WILLIAM I. *William Penn and the Dutch Quaker Migration to Pennsylvania.* (Swarthmore College Monographs on Quaker History, 2) Swarthmore, Pa.: Swarthmore College, 1935, pp. 395-421. Reprinted by Genealogical Publishing Co., Baltimore, 1970.

Two lists: "The Dutch Pioneers of Germantown, 1683," pp. 395-398; and "Dutch and German Settlers in Germantown, 1683-1709," pp. 399-421. Complete list of early Dutch and German settlers in Germantown, with places of origin given. Supplements no. 5924, Myers.   (Lancour 127)

*   *   *

3323

HUNT, JOHN G. "Some Passengers of the *Mary and John* in 1630." In *National Genealogical Society Quarterly,* vol. 63:1 (Mar. 1975), pp. 25-27.

Mentions thirteen families bound for Massachusetts. Discusses fears that passengers might not obtain leave to depart from England. See also no. 0281, Banks; no. 4477, Kuhns; and no. 6600, "Passengers of the *Mary and John.*"

3327
HUNTER, JOSEPH, Communicator. "Suffolk Emi-
grants: Genealogical Notices of Various Persons and
Families Who, in the Reign of King Charles the First,
Emigrated to New England from the County of Suffolk
[England]." In *Collections of the Massachusetts Histori-
cal Society,* vol. 10, 3rd ser., Boston, 1849, pp. 147-172.
        Period covered is 1600-1649.

*   *   *

3333
HURST, CHARLES W. *French and German Immigrants into Boston 1751.* Milford, Conn.: the author,
1968. 15p.

> Condensation of manuscript appearing in *The American
> Genealogist,* vol. 43:3 (July 1967), pp. 168-177 (item no. 3335)
> and the corrections in vol. 44:2 (Apr. 1968), p. 110. Manuscript
> is deposited in key genealogical libraries in America. Pages
> 5-11 contain almost complete list of passengers on the *Priscilla:*
> see nos. 3335 and 3341.

*   *   *

3335
HURST, CHARLES W. "French and German Immigrants into Boston 1751." In *The American Genealogist,*
vol. 43:3 (July 1967), pp. 168-177.

> Passengers on the *Priscilla;* a list 70% - 90% complete.
> Corrections in vol. 44:2 (Apr. 1968), p. 110. See also no. 4210,
> Krebs; and no. 3333, Hurst.

*   *   *

3341
HURST, CHARLES W. "German Settlers at Broad
Bay, Maine, 1757." In *The American Genealogist,* vol.
44:2 (Apr. 1968), pp. 127-128.

> From *Massachusetts Archives,* vol. 117, pp. 356-358. Petition
> dated August 1757, signed by 61 Germans, asking the General
> Court for aid at their Broad Bay settlement. The names appear
> as passengers on the *Priscilla,* which landed in Boston in 1751.
> The names were deciphered by Friedrich Krebs. See also nos.
> 3333 and 3335.

*   *   *

3351
HUSCHKE, WOLFGANG. "Amerika-Auswanderer
aus dem Hessischen Odenwald von 1830 bis 1840." In
Genealogie, vol. 11:4 (Apr. 1973), pp. 510-513.

> From documents in the Hessian State Archives in Darmstadt,
> Germany. Concerns the former district of Erbach: 106 emi-
> grants, 1830-1840. Wife and children are mentioned without
> forenames.

*   *   *

3358
HUSCHKE, WOLFGANG. "Amerika-Auswanderer
aus dem Odenwald, 1853-1855; mit Hinweisen auf Quellen zur Geschichte der Auswanderung aus dem Gross-
herzogtum Hessen im 19. Jahrhundert." In *Genealogie,*
vol. 9:7 (July 1969), pp. 639-643; vol. 9:10 (Oct. 1969),

pp. 751-758; vol. 9:12 (Dec. 1969), pp. 823-827.

> Emigrants to America from the Odenwald, 1853-1855, with
> references to sources on the history of emigration from the
> Grand Duchy of Hesse in the 19th century. These are lists of
> emigrants preserved in the county offices of Lindenfels for the
> years 1853 and 1854, and of Erbach for 1854 and 1855. It is a
> sampling of the wealth of data available in county offices of
> Hesse on emigrants from the Odenwald, supplementing data in
> three card-files maintained in Darmstadt. Much information,
> including names of emigrants, ages, places of origin, port
> and date of departure.

*   *   *

3368
HUTCHISON, FLORENCE. "Applicants for Naturalization Papers, Morgan County, Illinois." In *Illinois
State Genealogical Society Quarterly,* vol. 6:2 (Summer
1974), p. 101.

> Names, places of origin, and date of application. Mostly
> British, 1835-1894, but mainly 1835-1856.

*   *   *

3372
IGGULDEN, DELORES SCHAN, contributor.
[Passenger Lists.] In *Heritage Review* (Germans from
Russia Heritage Society), vol. 10:3 (Aug. 1980), p. 47.

> Lists of Germans from Russia, with eventual destinations
> North and South Dakota.

*   *   *

3378
**"[IMMIGRANTS - DISTRICT AND PORT OF NEW
YORK. List or Manifest of All the Passengers Taken on
Board the Ship** *West Point* **Whereof Allen is Master from
Liverpool, September 1849.]"** In *Santa Clara County
Historical & Genealogical Society* [*Quarterly*], vol. 4:3
(Jan. 1968), pp. 22-24.

> All British and Americans, with names, ages, sex, occupations.

*   *   *

3388
**IMMIGRANTS FROM GREAT BRITAIN TO THE
GEORGIA COLONY.** Morrow, Ga.: Genealogical
Enterprises, 1970. 27p.

> Over 1,000 names, with much information, including occu-
> pations and land grants accorded. Arrivals mostly in the 1730s
> and 1740s. Lists all persons found in the colonial records of
> Georgia. See also nos. 1312 and 1322, Coulter; and no. 6494,
> "Passenger List of the *Ann."*

*   *   *

3408
"IMMIGRANTS ON THE PILGRIM SHIPS." (The
Mayflower Series of Papers, 5.) In *The Historical
Bulletin,* Washington, D.C., vol. 5:2 (Aug. 1904),
pp. 34-36.

> Submitted by Mrs. W. W. Bolles. Lists drawn from the book,

The Pilgrim Republic, by Goodwin, no. 2713. Concerns the crossing of *The Fortune* in 1621 and the *Anne* in 1623. The Mayflower Series of Papers had six numbers, but only two - nos. 2 and 5 - (items 6540 and 3408 in this work) have lists. Also in no. 9143, Tepper, *New World Immigrants,* vol. 1, pp. 10-12. (Lancour 34A)

*   *   *

3418
"IMMIGRANTS TO LOUISIANA, 1719." In *French Canadian and Acadian Genealogical Review,* vol. 1:3 (Fall 1968), pp. 197-209.

List of grant recipients, private passengers, infantry, officers, cadets, soldiers, people exiled by order of the King, and all others who were taken on board at La Rochelle, France, to come to Louisiana from the first day of 1719. The ships were *Les Deux Freres, Le Marechal d'Estrees, Le Duc de Noailles* and *La Duchesse de Noailles.* See no. 1542, De Ville.

*   *   *

3428
"THE IMMIGRATION OF THE KLEIN FAMILY TO AMERICA." In *The Pennsylvania Traveler,* vol. 2:4 (Aug. 1966), pp. 32-36.

Taken from no. 7820, Rupp's *A Collection of Upwards of Thirty Thousand Names* . . . . Gives full personal names, ship names, and dates of arrival. Period covered 1732-1774.

*   *   *

3432
"AN INDEX OF THE NATURALIZATIONS AND DECLARATIONS OF INTENTION from the Ledgers of the United States Circuit Court of Baltimore City, Maryland, volume one, for the years 1797-1853." In *Maryland Genealogical Society Bulletin,* vol. 20:4 (Fall 1979), pp. 287-288.

Date and name in full for each individual, specifying date naturalized or date of intention to become a citizen, with accompanying court record.

*   *   *

3438
IRELAND, GORDON. "Servants to Foreign Plantations from Bristol, England, 1654-1686." In *The New York Genealogical and Biographical Record,* vol. 79:2 (Apr. 1948), pp. 65-75.

An extract from no. 0943, *Bristol and America,* listing 155 servants bound for Maryland, three for New York, 17 for Pennsylvania, and two for Virginia. Gives tables of bondmasters, ships, and ship masters, and names of places from which the emigrants came. Also in no. 9135, Tepper, *Immigrants to the Middle Colonies,* pp. 62-72.   (Lancour 199)

*   *   *

3440
IRELAND, GORDON. "Servants to Foreign Plantations from Bristol, England, to New England, 1657-1686." In *The New England Historical and Genealogical*

Register, vol. 93 (Oct. 1939), pp. 381-388.

Extract from no. 0943, *Bristol and America,* listing servants for New England. Name of person to whom bound and date of arrival, with other references. Provides a table of bondmasters and ships. Also in no. 0702, Boyer, *Ship Passenger Lists, National and New England,* pp. 163-170; and in no. 9151, Tepper, *Passengers to America,* pp. 150-157.   (Lancour 55)

*   *   *

3450
IRELAND, NORTHERN. "American Passenger Lists, 1804-1806 (British Museum Transcripts)." In Northern Ireland Public Record Office, *Report of the Deputy Keeper of the Records for the Year 1929,* Belfast: His Majesty's Stationery Office, 1930, pp. 15, 21-49.

Emigrants from Antrim, Armagh, Down, Fermanagh, Londonderry, and Tyrone, Ireland, sailing for New York, Philadelphia and Newcastle (*sic*), Boston, Baltimore, Charleston, and New Bedford between June 1804 and March 1806. Adds to no. 2151, Fothergill; and no. 1762, *Early Immigrants.* Also in no. 0702, Boyer, *Ship Passenger Lists, National and New England,* pp. 113-125; and in no. 9144, Tepper, *New World Immigrants,* vol. 2, pp. 295-324.   (Lancour 26)

*   *   *

3458
ISCRUPE, WILLIAM L., compiler. *Naturalization Records 1802-1854, Somerset County, Pennsylvania.* Laughlintown, Pa.: Southwest Pennsylvania Genealogical Services, 1979. 16p.

Name, homeland, declaration, date admitted to U.S. Almost all are German.

*   *   *

3460
ISCRUPE, WILLIAM L., compiler. *Naturalization Records 1802-1852, Westmoreland County, Pennsylvania.* Laughlintown, Pa.: Southwest Pennsylvania Genealogical Services, 1978. 382p.

Name, country of origin and, usually, date and port of arrival. Separate index of sponsors. Records in the keeping of the Prothonotary of Westmoreland County.

*   *   *

3470
IVES, J. MOSS. *The Ark and The Dove: The Beginning of Civil and Religious Liberties in America.* London: Longmans Green, 1936, p. 110.

For other references to these two ships, see the index. (Lancour 198B)

*   *   *

3474
IWAN, WILHELM. *Die altlutherische Auswanderung um die Mitte des 19. Jahrhunderts.* Ludwigsburg [Germany]: Eichhorn Verlag Lothar Kallenburg, for the

Johann Hess Institute, Breslau, 1943. 2 vols.

Emigration of "Old Lutherans" around the middle of the nineteenth century. Covers the years 1835-1854. About 5,000 were from the provinces of Pomerania, Lower Silesia, Brandenburg, Saxony, and a few from the city-state of Hamburg; these were bound for North America. More than 2,000 from the same provinces and from that of Poznan (Posen) set out for Australia. Old Lutherans in the United States and Canada formed the Buffalo Synod (see further comments in annotation of no. 8655). Names individual emigrants, heads of emigrant groups, and some accompanying family members. Includes maiden names of some of the wives aboard, some ages and intended destinations. This work forms the basis for no. 8655, Smith, *Nineteenth Century Emigration of "Old Lutherans"*.... The names are listed on pages 241-304 in volume 2 of the Iwan title above.

* * *

3480
[JAMES, MRS. F.O.] "Passenger Lists Taken from Manifests of the Customs Service, Port of New Orleans, 1813-1837." In *New Orleans Genesis,* vol. 1:1 (Jan. 1962), pp. 23-28.

Chronological list of passengers who landed at New Orleans, with manifests for arrivals between 1813 and 1821. The article notes that the remainder (1821-1837 arrivals) were to appear later but apparently they were not published. This list is in no. 0720, Boyer, *Ship Passenger Lists, the South,* pp. 223-228. (Lancour 243)

* * *

3490
JAMESON, J. FRANKLIN, editor. "Answer to the Representation of New Netherland, by Cornelis van Tienhoven, 1650." In *Narratives of New Netherland, 1609-1664.* New York: Charles Scribner's Sons, 1909, pp. 359-377.

The defense by Cornelis van Tienhoven of the existing system of government in New Netherland, 1650. Contains the names of eleven colonists who signed the "Remonstrance," and their arrival dates. Also in no. 6331, O'Callaghan; no. 9400, Van Tienhoven; and in no. 0714, Boyer, *Ship Passenger Lists, New York and New Jersey,* pp. 82-92. (Lancour 78B)

* * *

3500
JEHN, JANET. *Acadian Exiles in the Colonies.* Covington, Ky.: Acadian Genealogy Exchange, 1977, 366p.

Records what happened to the Acadian exiles listed in no. 7430, Rieder & Rieder, *Acadian Exiles.* Many returned to Canada, most to Quebec. The data are taken from archives at Ottawa and Boston.

* * *

3503
JEHN, JANET. [Two lists of Acadians sent to New York, 1756.] In *Acadian Genealogy Exchange,* vol. 5:4 (Oct. 1976), pp. 100-102.

Tells of Acadians who left Nova Scotia and some who were

sent from Georgia, where they were not allowed to stay because they were Catholic. Many names are spelled phonetically and are therefore incorrect. Taken from no. 6414, O'Neill.

* * *

3507
JENKINS, FRANK D. "Naturalization Records, Menard County, Texas." In *Stirpes,* vol. 20:3 (Sept. 1980), p. 190.

Details on eleven persons who made declarations of intent between 1881 and 1886. Dates and places of arrival, with countries of origin, covering 1868-1884.

* * *

3510
JERVEY, THEODORE D. "The White Indented [*sic*] Servants of South Carolina." In *The South Carolina Historical and Genealogical Magazine,* vol. 12:4 (Oct. 1911), pp. 163-171.

Pages 170-171 contain a "List of Convicts Imported from Bristol to the Province of So Carolina on board the Ship called the Expedition . . . (1728)." Also in no. 0720, Boyer, *Ship Passenger Lists, the South,* pp. 157-158; and in no. 9144, Tepper, *New World Immigrants,* vol. 2, p. 532. (Lancour 235)

* * *

3520
JESTER, ANNIE LASH, and **MARTHA WOOD-ROOF HIDEN.** "Musters of the Inhabitants in Virginia 1624/1625." In *Adventurers of Purse and Person; Virginia, 1607-1625.* N.P.: Order of First Families of Virginia, 1607-1620 [Princeton University Press], 1956, pp. 5-69.

From state papers in the Public Record Office, London, a census of the inhabitants of Virginia taken between January 20 and February 7, 1624 or 1625. Lists 1,232 names, with ages and ships taken. Item no. 1272, Colonial Records of Virginia, has many more names than the 1624-25 census (above). Also in no. 0720, Boyer, *Ship Passenger Lists, the South,* pp. 43-64. And see no. 5907, "Muster of the Inhabitants . . . . " (Lancour 210)

* * *

3530
JEWETT, VIVIAN HOLLAND. "Abstracts of Naturalization Records, Circuit Court, District of Colombia." In *National Genealogical Society Quarterly.*
3530
---Vol. 41:2 (June 1953), pp. 41-44; vol. 41:3 (Sept. 1953), pp. 90-92; vol 41:4 (Dec. 1953), pp. 130-131.
3531
---Vol. 42:1 (Mar. 1954), pp. 22-24; vol. 42:2 (June 1954), pp. 68-73; vol. 42:4 (Dec. 1954), pp. 149-150.
3532
---Vol. 43:1 (Mar. 1955), pp. 20-21; vol. 43:4 (Dec. 1955, pp. 146-147.
3533
---Vol. 44:1 (Mar. 1956), pp. 16-19; vol. 44:3 (Sept. 1956), pp. 109-111; vol. 44:4 (Dec. 1956), pp. 147-149.

3534

---Vol. 45:1 (Mar. 1957), pp. 21-26.

Petitions received between 1817 and 1850. Coverage apparently unfinished. From records in the U.S. National Archives. Name, age, year of petition, places of origin and arrival, witnesses, naturalization date. Involves ports on the Atlantic Coast. The first issue, vol. 41:2, names the author as Vivian Holland, in error. Information also in no. 0720, Boyer, *Ship Passenger Lists, the South,* pp. 95-124, and in no. 9144, Tepper, *New World Immigrants,* vol. 2, pp. 249-288. (Lancour 229)

*   *   *

3540

JEWSON, CHARLES BOARDMAN. *Transcript of Three Registers of Passengers from Great Yarmouth to Holland and New England, 1637-1639.* (Norfolk Record Society Publications, 25) Norwich: Norfolk Record Society, 1954. 98p. Reprinted by Genealogical Publishing Co., Baltimore, 1964.

From documents in the Bodleian Library, Oxford, and the Public Record Office, London. Passengers to New England on the *John and Dorothy* and the *Rose,* pp. 21-23; passengers to New England on the *Marey Anne,* pp. 29-30; passengers to Holland not indexed. Full information on each passenger. Emigrants for New England previously included in Hotten, no. 3283. (Lancour 51)

*   *   *

3550

JOERNS, EMIL, and **A. DIECK.** "Johann Dietrich Holzhausen wandert von Denkershausen (Kr. Northeim) nach Amerika." In *Norddeutsche Familienkunde,* Jahrg. 5:6 (Nov.-Dec. 1956), p. 146.

Johann Dietrich Holzhausen emigrants from Denkershausen (County of Northeim) to America. From a church register in the German parish of Langenholtensen-Denkershausen. Relates the genealogy back to the early part of the eighteenth century of one family which emigrated from that community to Baltimore, Maryland, in 1831. Gives names, ages, places of origin, place of destination, and family data.

*   *   *

3560

JOHNSON, AMANDUS. "Lists of Officers, Soldiers, Servants, and Settlers in New Sweden, 1638-1656." In *The Swedish Settlements on the Delaware 1638-1664,* vol. 2. Philadelphia: 1911. Reprinted by Genealogical Publishing Co., Baltimore, 1969. Appendix B, pp. 699-726.

Gives details of ships used, dates of arrival, passengers who returned to Sweden, male inhabitants of New Sweden, 1643-1644, and roll of the people who were alive in New Sweden on March 1, 1648, with facts on families and occupations in the colony, 1654-1655.

*   *   *

3565-3570

JOHNSON, MRS. ARTA F., editor. "Immigrant Ancestors." In *The Palatine Immigrant.*

3565

---Vol. 3:1 (Summer 1977), pp. 21-25.

3566

---Vol. 3:2 (Fall 1977), pp. 19-22.

3567

---Vol. 3:3 (Winter 1978), pp. 27-29.

3568

---Vol. 3:4 (Spring 1978), pp. 23-27.

3569

---Vol. 4:1 (Summer 1978), pp. 25-26; vol. 4:2 (Fall 1978), pp. 65-67; vol. 4:3 (Winter 1979), pp. 102-105; vol. 4:4 (Spring 1979), pp. 152-155.

3570

---Vol. 5:1 (Summer 1979), pp. 44-46; vol. 5:2 (Autumn 1979), pp. 87-91; vol. 5:3 (Winter 1980), pp. 138-143 (In progress.)

Lists German immigrants, mostly Mennonites, with family information. The majority were from Baden-Durlach (in the German Palatinate); they settled in Pennsylvania between 1710 and 1815. This provides the dates of arrival and the present addresses of descendants.

*   *   *

3580

JOHNSON, ROBERT G. "Memoir of John Fenwicke, Chief Proprietor of Salem Tenth, New Jersey." In *Proceedings of the New Jersey Historical Society,* vol. 4:2 (1850), pp. 53-89.

Passenger list, on page 60, of the *Griffin* (or *Griffith*) which arrived in the Salem River on November 23, 1675, bringing Major John Fewicke and the first permanent English-speaking settlers in the Delaware Valley. Gives several ships names and dates of arrival at Salem, New Jersey, between 1674 and 1681. A more complete and correct passenger list appears in no. 8760, Smith, but Johnson's "Memoir" (above) also contains a list of corrections. Original list also in no. 0714, Boyer, *Ship Passenger Lists, New York and New Jersey,* pp. 221-222, and in no. 9144, Tepper, *New World Immigrants,* vol. 2, p. 530. For other references to the *Griffin (Griffith),* see index. (Lancour 110A and 111A, note)

*   *   *

3590

JOHNSTON, DOUGLAS V. "Passenger Lists." In *Heritage Review,* no. 22 (Dec. 1978), p. 46.

List of passengers on the S.S. *Roon* from Bremen, probably to New York, with most of the passengers from Russia, 1912.

*   *   *

3596

JOHS, LEO A. [Passenger Lists.] In *Heritage Review,* no. 24, (Sept. 1979), p. 41.

Passengers on the S. S. *Kasserin Maria Theresa* from Kleinliebental via Bremen, Germany, to New York, October 11, 1900.

*   *   *

3600

JONASSON, ELIZABETH, editor. "The First of the Selkirk Settlers at Red River, 1812-1814." In *Genera-*

tions: Journal of the Manitoba Genealogical Society, vol. 1:1 (Sept. 1976), pp. 15-19.

> Facsimile reprint of the lists contained in no. 5274, Martin. See also no. 6755, Phillips, and no. 0998, Bryce.

*   *   *

3610
JONES, HANK. "Emigrants from Germany to Colonial America, 1720-1760, Traced in Their Ancestral Villages (a Partial Listing)." In *The Palatine Immigrant,* vol. 4:1 (Summer 1978), pp. 20-22.

> Mostly to New York and New Jersey, with a few to Pennsylvania and Georgia.

*   *   *

3620
JONES, HANK. "The Palatine Families of New York . . . ." In *The Palatine Immigrant,* vol. 3:2 (Fall 1977), pp. 3-8.

> A partial list of 1709-1710 emigrants, documented and traced in their ancestral German home churches, found during a study of Palatines.

*   *   *

3630
JONES, WILLIAM MAC FARLANE, transcriber and editor. "A List of Ye French Refugees That are Settled att Ye Mannachin Town . . . ." In *The Douglas Register: Being a Detailed Record of Births, Marriages and Deaths Together with Other Interesting Notes, as Kept by the Rev. William Douglas, from 1750 to 1797.* Richmond [Va.]: J.W. Fergusson & Sons, 1928, pp. 369-371. Reprinted by Genealogical Publishing Co., Baltimore, 1966.

> Names 79 French Huguenot refugees who lived at Manakin Town, Va. Also in no. 0953, Brock. See index under Huguenots for further references. (Lancour 221)

*   *   *

3633
JONES, WILLIAM MAC FARLANE, editor. "A List of Ye Refugees." In *The Douglas Register . . . .* Richmond [Va.]: J. W. Fergusson & Sons, 1928, pp. 378-379.

> Concerns Huguenot settlement in Virginia, 1700. Original appeared in no. 7850, *The Virginia Historical Society Collections,* new series, vol. 6, 1887, pp. 65-67. See also no. 4622, Lilly. For other references, see index.

*   *   *

3640
JONES, WILLIAM MAC FARLANE, transcriber and editor. "Liste Generalle de Tous les Francois Protestants Refugies Etablys dans la Paroisse du Roy Guillaume d'Henrico en Virginia, y compres les Femmes, Enfans, Veuves, et Orphelins." In *The Douglas Register . . . Kept by the Rev. William Douglas, from 1750 to 1797.* Richmond, Va.: J.W. Fergusson & Sons, 1928, pp. 372-374. Reprinted by Genealogical Publishing Co., Baltimore, 1966.

> General list of the French Protestant refugees settled in the Parish of Roy Guillaume d'Henrico in Virginia, including women and children, widows and orphans. Taken from no. 6710, W. S. Perry's *Papers Relating to the History of the Church in Virginia, A.D. 1650-1776.* Also printed in no. 0953, *Documents . . . .* (Lancour 226)

*   *   *

3650
JORDAN, JOHN W. "Moravian Immigration to Pennsylvania, 1734-1765." In *The Pennsylvania Magazine of History and Biography,* vol. 33:2 (1909), pp. 228-248.

> Several ship lists with commentary. See also nos. 3652, 3654, 3660-3661. Also in no. 9120, Tepper, *Emigrants to Pennsylvania,* pp. 33-53. (Lancour 155)

*   *   *

3652
JORDAN, JOHN W. "Moravian Immigration to Pennsylvania, 1734-1767, with Some Account of the Transport Vessels." In *Transactions of the Moravian Historical Society,* vol. 5 (1899), pp. 51-90.

> Dates given in no. 3650 appear to be at variance with these, but upon investigation, both prove correct. Various voyages, with ship lists. See also nos. 3660 and 3661.

*   *   *

3654
JORDAN, JOHN W. "Moravian Immigration to Pennsylvania, 1734-1767." In *The Pennsylvania Traveler,* vol. 2:1 (Nov. 1965), pp. 40-48.

> Refers to Moravian arrivals at Philadelphia and New York. Taken from *Transactions of the Moravian Historical Society,* Bethlehem, Pennsylvania, 1896. Also published in nos. 3650, 3652, 3660, and 3661.

*   *   *

3660-3661
JORDAN, JOHN W. "A Register of Members of the Moravian Church Who Emigrated to Pennsylvania, 1742-1767." In *Notes and Queries . . . .* Edited by William H. Egle. Reprinted by Genealogical Publishing Co., Baltimore, Md., 1970.
3660
---4th ser. vol. 1 (1893), no. 58, pp. 162-163; no. 59, pp. 167-170; no. 62, pp. 174-175; no. 73, pp. 208-211; no. 97, pp. 303-304.
3661
---4th ser. vol. 2:1 (Jan. 1894), no. 102, pp. 1-3.

> Lists of Moravian arrivals at Philadelphia and New York, most later settling in Bethlehem, Pa., some in North Carolina. Supplements no. 3650, Jordan. See also no. 0454, Beckel; and others by Jordan, nos. 3652 and 3654. (Lancour 164)

3670

"JOURNAL OF COLONEL ALEXANDER HARVEY OF SCOTLAND AND BARNET, VERMONT." In *Proceedings of the Vermont Historical Society,* (1921-1923), pp. 199-262.

Page 204 has names of the seamen and farmers who sailed with Colonel Harvey from Scotland to New York on the *Matty* in 1774. These immigrants later settled at Barnet, Vermont. Also in no. 9670, Wells; no. 0714; Boyer, *Ship Passenger Lists, New York and New Jersey,* p. 174; and in no. 9144, Tepper, *New World Immigrants,* vol. 2, p. 534.   (Lancour 102/1)

*   *   *

3686

JUNG, HANS. "Hellertown in Pennsylvanien: nach Auswanderern Heller aus Pfeddersheim benannt." In *Pfaelzisch-Rheinische Familienkunde: Pfaelzische Familien- und Wappenkunde,* (Mitteilungen zur Wanderungsgeschichte der Pfaelzer, no. 3, 1974) vol. 8:3 (Dec. 1974), pp. 113-114.

Hellertown in Pennsylvania, named after the Heller family, immigrants from Pfeddersheim [Germany]. Concerns seven of them in number, who came to Bucks, later Northampton County, Pennsylvania, in 1738. Names, family data, and further history of the family.

*   *   *

3690

KAMINKOW, JACK, and **MARION KAMINKOW,** transcribers. *A List of Emigrants from England to America, 1718-1759.* Baltimore: Magna Carta Book Co., 1964, 288p. (Available from Tuttle, Rutland, Vt.)

Indentured servants, with exceptionally full information, including destinations, occupations, years of service in the colony, etc. Has index of places where the servants were bound. More than 3,000 names transcribed from microfilms of the original records at the Guildhall, London. Additions to this list are given in no. 2324, Galenson.

*   *   *

3700

KAMINOW, MARION, and **JACK KAMINKOW,** editors. *Original Lists of Emigrants in Bondage from London to the American Colonies, 1719-1744.* Baltimore: Magna Carta Book Co., 1967, 211p. (Available from Tuttle, Rutland, Vt.)

From British Treasury Money Books in the Public Record Office (T53/27-42). About 6,300 names, keyed to place of origin, destination in America, date received on board, with Public Record Office reference. Mostly convicts guilty of misdemeanors rather than serious crimes. Many aliases. Most from southern England.

*   *   *

3705

KANELY, EDNA A., compiler. "Passengers on Ship *Goethe* Arriving in Baltimore, Maryland, April 22, 1854." In *Maryland Genealogical Society Bulletin,* vol.

21:2 (Spring 1980), pp. 98-101.

From a list in the Baltimore City Legislative Reference Archives, document no. 1581. Identifies 192 passengers from Bremen, Germany. Name, age, place of birth, occupation. Note that the *Bulletin* lacks page numbers, erroneously omitted, but the index indicates that the list is on pp. 98-101.

*   *   *

3710

KASPER, JOHANN. "Eifeler Auswanderer in Amerika und ihre Schicksale." In *Jahrbuch des Kreises Ahrweiler,* vol. 8 (1940), pp. 139-143; vol. 9 (1941), pp. 154-157.

Emigrants from the Eifel to America and their fate. The Eifel region lies between the Mosel and Ahr rivers, now in the West German state of North Rhine-Westphalia. Involves about 30 persons: heads of families and some of the family members. A few ages, birthdates, places of origin are given. migration occurred in the period 1840-1845 and settlement was in Michigan, Illinois, Minnesota, and Wisconsin, One group founded "Johnsburg," near McHenry County, Illinois. Data from letters of emigrants collected in 1930 and 1931 by the Institute for History of the Rhine Province (Institut fuer geschichtliche Landeskunde der Rheinprovinz) at the University of Bonn, West Germany, and copies of letters in the state archives at Koblenz.

*   *   *

3720

KAESSBACHER, M. "Vom Dilsberg." In *Der Familienforscher.*   Jahrgang 3:2 (Feb. 1928), pp. 76-80; Jahrgang 3:7 (July 1928), pp. 286-289.

Information from church registers of Dilsberg, Germany, on emigration to America, 1852-1858. Names, birthdates, marriage dates, maiden names of wives, places of origin if other than Dilsberg, dates of emigration.

*   *   *

3730

KAUFHOLZ, C. FREDERICK. "Emigrants from Duderstadt, Germany, to America, 1822-1865." In *The American Genealogist,* vol. 48:4 (Oct. 1972), pp. 203-207.

Taken from archives of the city of Duderstadt, and from the author's own collections.

*   *   *

3740

KAUFMANN, KARL LEOPOLD. "Auswanderung aus dem Kreise Malmedy." In *Rheinische Heimatpflege,* Jahrgang 12:3 (1940), pp. 355-360.

Emigration from the district of Malmedy (southern Eifel region of Germany). Excerpted from applications for permission to emigrate, 1843-1919. Contains data on 452 emigrants from the Malmedy area to North America and Brazil, 1843-1919. Includes name of individual emigrant or head of emigrant family, age, place of origin, year of emigration, number of family members accompanying, and sometimes mention of occupation.

*   *   *

3750
KAYE, VLADIMIR J., editor and compiler. *Dictionary of Ukrainian Canadian Biography: Pioneer Settlers of Manitoba 1891-1900.* Toronto: Ukrainian Canadian Research Foundation, 1975. 249p.

> Each entry has copious notes outlining the settler's family composition, so much so that it could have been entitled, "Genealogical Biographies of Ukrainian Canadian People." Includes ages, families, and, often, date and place of landing. Some naturalization details.

*   *   *

3760
KEEN, G.B. "The Eighth Swedish Expedition to New Sweden." In *The Pennsylvania Magazine of History and Biography,* vol. 8:1 (1884), pp. 107-108.

> Original in the Royal Archives in Stockholm; this taken from a copy in the Historical Society of Pennsylvania. Tells of passengers who accompanied Hans Amundson to New Sweden in 1649. Also in no. 9120, Tepper, *Emigrants to Pennsylvania, 1649-1819,* pp. 4-5. (Lancour 194)

*   *   *

3766
KEEN, G.B. "The Third Swedish Expedition to New Sweden." In *The Pennsylvania Magazine of History and Biography,* vol. 3:4 (1879), pp. 462-464.

> Original record in the Royal Archives in Stockholm; this taken from a copy in the Historical Society of Pennsylvania. Emigrants on the *Kalmar Nyckel* and the *Charitas* for New Sweden in 1641. Intended to accompany an article by Odhner, no. 6351. Also in no. 9120, Tepper, *Emigrants to Pennsylvania,* pp. 1-3; and no. 8002, Scharf. (Lancour 193)

*   *   *

3776
KELKER, LUTHER R. "Lists of Foreigners Who Arrived at Philadelphia, 1791-1792." In *The Pennsylvania Magazine of History and Biography,* vol. 24:2 (1900), pp. 187-194; vol. 24:3 (1900), pp. 334-342.

> Supplementary to no. 1804, Egle, included in part in nos. 9041 and 9042, Strassburger. Also in no. 9120, Tepper, *Emigrants to Pennsylvania,* pp. 240-256. (Lancour 189)

*   *   *

3786
KELL, J.H., and **A. JAKOB.** "Die Auswanderungen aus den Buergermeistereien Haustadt und Hilbringen im 19. Jahrhundert." In *Saarpfaelzische Abhandlungen zur Landes- und Volksforschung,* vol. 2, Lieferung (fascicle) 3 (1938), pp. 432-456.

> Emigration from the mayoral jurisdictions of Haustadt and Hilbringen. From files stored in each place. Concerns about 300 emigrants from the vicinity of Merzig in the Saar to America, 1816-1908. Names, ages or birthdates, villages of origin, year of emigration, some family data, occupations. This article is an amplification of no. 3788 by Kell and Werner.

*   *   *

3788
KELL, J.H., and **JOS. WERNER.** "Die Auswanderungen aus dem Kreise Merzig im 19. Jahrhundert." In *Verein fuer Heimatkunde im Kreise Merzig, 3.* Jahrbuch, [193-], pp. 9-54.

> Emigration from the district of Merzig, 1817-1874. The section includes a list of names and planned destinations. For amplification of this see no. 3786, Kell and Jacob. Text not seen by editor.

*   *   *

3796
KELLOGG, LUCY MARY. "Ship List of the *Orient,* 19 May 1842." In *The Detroit Society for Genealogical Research Magazine,* vol. 26:2 (Winter 1962), pp. 63-64.

> From Port of New York records in the National Archives, Washington, D.C. Lists 188 passengers from Falmouth, England, 1842, to New York. Name, age, occupation given. Also in no. 9144, Tepper, *New World Immigrants,* vol. 2, pp. 443-447. (Lancour 257)

*   *   *

3801
KENYON, HUGH. *Kirdford: Some Parish History.* [Kirdford, Sussex: St. John the Baptist Church] 1971, pp. 24-25.

> Names of a few emigrants who left Kirdford in West Sussex, England. They settled in the extreme south of Ontario, Canada, 1832. See also no. 8775, Sockett.

*   *   *

3816
KING, FANNIE BAYLY (Mrs. W.W.), "Augusta County Early Settlers, Importations, 1739-1740." In *National Genealogical Society Quarterly,* vol. 25:2 (June 1937), pp. 46-50.

> Legal proceedings before Orange County Court, Virginia, where settlers proved their entitlement to enter public lands. Also in no. 5831, Morton; no. 2302, Fry; in no. 0720, Boyer, *Ship Passenger Lists, the South,* pp. 91-95; and in no. 9144, Tepper, *New World Immigrants,* vol. 2, pp. 133-135. (Lancour 228)

*   *   *

3830
KIRK, CLAIRE. *Ellis County, Texas, Naturalization Records.* Waxahachie, Texas: Ellis County Genealogical Society, 1980. 72p.

> Gives dates of arrivals in U.S. and declarations of intent to acquire citizenship, 1858-1929, when naturalization proceedings were transferred from Galveston to Dallas. Of 457 persons listed, 80 percent were from Austria or Czechoslovakia. List partially published in vol. 1:4 (Fall 1977) of *Searchers and Researchers,* pp. 24-32.

*   *   *

3848

KLINGELHOEFFER, HANS. "Auswanderungen aus der Standesherrschaft Stolberg-Gedern im 18. Jahrhundert." In *Mitteilungen der Hessischen Familiengeschichtlichen Vereinigung,* vol. 1:4 (Jan. 1927), pp. 122-123.

Emigrations from the noble estate of Stolberg-Gedern in the 18th century. Found in a payment book containing entries for the fees paid by the subjects of the noble land owner in order that they might emigrate. The book is stored in the Revenue Office in Gedern among the archives of the Princes of Stolberg-Wernigerode. Most of the emigrants went to Hungary or Pomerania; however, six are listed departing for Pennsylvania in 1748-1749. Names, places of origin, some occupations and family relationships given.

*　　*　　*

3872

KLUEBER, KARL WERNER. "Aus Hamburger Schiffslisten II: Russlanddeutsche Auswanderer nach Nordamerika im Jahre 1874." In *Genealogie,* vol. 7:12 (Dec. 1965), pp. 816-819.

Russian-German emigrants to North America in the year 1874. From the ships' passenger lists of Hamburg, stored in the Hamburg State Archives. Klueber fixed upon 1874 as the peak year of emigration for German Mennonites from Russia, since in that year, on Jan. 13, the Russian government enacted a mandatory military service act. He found that 27 ships containing Russian-Germans left Hamburg bound for New York. Ship names, departure dates, number of Russian-Germans and Mennonites on board. The work closes with a list of the surnames and Russian places of origin found in these passenger lists.

*　　*　　*

3879

KLUEBER, KARL WERNER. "Auswanderer-Angaben in Staatsanzeigern u. Schiffslisten. Ein Vergleich." In *Genealogie,* vol. 11:1 (Jan. 1972), pp. 20-27.

Covers emigration in the period 1849-1855, from two regions, Oberfranken and Oberfalz. Ports of destination most frequently indicated were New York and Quebec. Texas and Chile were also reported. Compares material from the Hamburg lists with information published in Bavarian newspapers.

*　　*　　*

3886

KLUEBER, KARL WERNER. "Auswanderer aus Anhalt und den preussischen Regierungsbezirken Magdeburg und Merseburg 1850-1852." In *Mitteldeutsche Familienkunde,* vol. 3:3 (July-Sept. 1972), pp. 337-344.

Emigrants from Anhalt and from the Prussian administrative districts of Magdeburg and Merseburg. From the Hamburg ships passenger lists stored in state archives in Hamburg, Germany. Involves 200 emigrants, chosen on the basis of place of origin as given in the Hamburg ships lists, moving to the Americas or Australia. Some research on the ancestry of the Ahlfeld family from the Anhalt area to America, latter half of the 19th century. Much family information.

*　　*　　*

3893

KLUEBER, KARL WERNER. "Auswanderer eines suedwestdeutschen Dorfes (Wangen) nach Ungarn und Amerika." In *Archiv fuer Sippenforschung und alle Verwandten Gebiete,* Jahrgang 16:5 (May 1939), pp. 141-146.

Emigrants from a southwest German village (Wangen) to Hungary and America. From records in Wangen. Twenty emigrants, 1834-1880, with names, some ages, some family data, and exact year of emigration.

*　　*　　*

3914

KLUEBER, KARL WERNER. "Dresdener Auswanderer nach Uebersee 1850-1903." In *Mitteldeutsche Familienkunde,* vol. 3:3 (July-Sept. 1971), pp. 193-198.

Emigration from Dresden [Germany] overseas, 1850-1903. From Hamburg ships' passenger lists and elsewhere. Names 180 emigrants to New York, San Francisco, Quebec, South America, and Australia. Includes some ages, family data, names of ships, and dates of departure.

*　　*　　*

3921

KLUEBER, KARL WERNER. "Der erste deutsche Ozeandampfer machte nur drei Ueberfahrten." In *Genealogie,* vol. 8:3 (Mar. 1967), pp. 656-664.

The first German steam-powered ocean liner made only three Atlantic crossings. From Hamburg emigration records for 1850 and articles in the newspaper, *Allgemeine Auswanderungs-Zeitung,* 1850. This article lists the passengers on board that vessel, the *Helena Sloman,* which made three voyages, Hamburg to New York, before sinking off Newfoundland. Names, ages, occupations, and places of origin.

*　　*　　*

3928

KLUEBER, KARL WERNER. "Die ersten deutschen Mormonen wanderten 1853 nach Amerika aus. Mit Ahnen und Verwandtschaftslisten des Bischofs Daniel Friedrich Lau." In *Genealogie,* vol. 9:7 (July 1969), pp. 625-638.

The first German Mormons emigrated to America in 1853: the forebears and lists of relatives of Bishop Daniel Friedrich Lau. Ship's passenger list for 1853, Liverpool to New Orleans, arriving October 28, 1853. Names 17 German Mormons, with ages, destinations, and extended family history of Bishop Lau.

*　　*　　*

3935

KLUEBER, KARL WERNER. "Die Hamburger Auswandererlisten (Schiffslisten)." In *Mitteilungen der Westdeutschen Gesellschaft fuer Familienkunde,* vol. 23:5 (Mar. 1968), cols. 277-282.

Ships passenger lists for the port of Hamburg, stored in the Hamburg, Germany, State Archives. Discusses the genealogical and demographic value of the Hamburg passenger lists and describes the state of the indexing project up to 1968. Names 35 passengers whose origins were in the Rhineland, traveling via Hamburg for destinations in North and South America, 1850-1851. Nineteen came to North America. Names, occupations, dates of departure, ships names, and ports or countries of destination.

*   *   *

3941
KLUEBER, KARL WERNER. "Die Hamburger Schiffslisten: eine wertvolle Quelle fuer die Uebersee-Auswandererforschung auch fuer Bayern." In *Zeitschrift fuer bayerische Landesgeschichte,* vol. 30:1 (1967), pp. 412-417.

The Hamburg [Germany] ships' lists: a valuable source for research on overseas emigration even from Bavaria. Lists for the years 1850 and 1851. Supplements no. 0598, Blendinger, and includes names not in Blendinger. Name of head of emigrant group, some ages, place of origin (or last place of residence), date of embarkation, destination of ship, and number emigrating in a given family.

*   *   *

3948
KLUEBER, KARL WERNER. "Die Hamburger Schiffslisten: Eine wertvolle Quelle zur mitteldeutschen Uebersee-Auswanderung im 19. und 20. Jahrhundert, mit einer Liste ausgewanderter Thueringer aus dem Jahre 1850." In *Mitteldeutsche Familienkunde,* vol. 1:4 (Oct.-Dec. 1965), pp. 289-294.

The Hamburg ships' lists: a valuable source for overseas emigration from central Germany in the 19th and 20th centuries. Includes a list of emigrants from Thuringia for 1850. From files on the port of Hamburg, stored in the Hamburg State Archives: 337 emigrants from Thuringia to the Americas. Ports include New York, San Francisco, Galveston, Quebec, and some South American cities. Names of individuals or heads of groups with occupation, place of origin, port of destination, ship, and date of departure for each.

*   *   *

3956
KLUEBER, KARL WERNER. "Aus Hamburger Schiffslisten, I: Indirekte Auswanderung: Deutsche wanderten ueber England nach New York aus." In *Genealogie,* vol. 7:11 (Nov. 1965), pp. 774-779.

From Hamburg ships' lists: I. Indirect route—Germans emigrating via England to New York. Lists 180 emigrants who traveled first to Hull, England, and subsequently shipped from Hull or Liverpool to New York. The records for the first quarter of 1860 are stored in the state archives at Hamburg. Names, places of origin, some occupations, most ages.

*   *   *

3960
KLUEBER, KARL WERNER. "Leipziger Auswanderer nach Uebersee 1850-1855." In *Mitteldeutsche Familienkunde,* vol. 2:1 (Jan.-Mar. 1969), pp. 273-281.

From ships' passenger lists for the port of Hamburg [Germany], 1850-1855, stored in the Hamburg State Archives. Names 363 emigrants from Leipzig, and the annexed suburbs of Reudnitz and Connewitz, destined for various North American (including Canadian) and South American ports.

Indicates heads of emigrant groups, some ages, dates of departure, ships names, ports of destination.

*   *   *

3967
KLUEBER, KARL WERNER. "Wiedergefundene Bremer und Hamburger Auswandererlisten." In *Genealogie,* vol. 8:8 (Aug. 1966), pp. 329-332.

Rediscovered emigration lists from Bremen and Hamburg, Germany. From two ships' lists published in the newspaper *Allgemeine Auswanderungs-Zeitung,* Jahrgang 1849, no. 94, p. 375; and for 1850, no. 137, p. 547. The ship *Itzstein and Welcker* departed from Bremen for New Orleans October 27, 1850, and the ship *Deutschland* departed from Hamburg for New York, Oct. 27, 1849. The first vessel listed 254 passengers and the second, 94 passengers. Gives names of individual emigrants, heads of emigrant groups, and places of origin.

*   *   *

3983
KNITTLE, WALTER ALLEN. "The Board of Trade List of the First Party of Palatines in London, May 3, 1709." In *Early Eighteenth Century Palatine Emigration.* Philadelphia, Pa.: Dorrance & Co., 1937, pp. 244-247. Reprinted by Genealogical Publishing Co., 1965.

Many of the Palatines came to America shortly after 1709. For the first of four lists of Palatines compiled up to June 11, 1709, by the Rev. John Tribbeko and the Rev. George A. Ruperti, see item no. 9214. A complete list of 12,000 names is in nos. 4772-4773 and 5013.   (Lancour 91A)

*   *   *

3990
KNITTLE, WALTER ALLEN. "The Embarkation Lists from Holland." In *Early Eighteenth Century Palatine Emigration.* Philadelphia: Dorrance & Co., 1937, pp. 248-274. Reprinted by Genealogical Publishing Co., Baltimore, 1965.

Lists five separate sailings for 11,000 persons from Holland to England, many of whom came to America shortly after. Supplementary to nos. 4772 and 4773, *List . . . ,* and no. 5013, MacWethy.   (Lancour 93)

*   *   *

3997
KNITTLE, WALTER ALLEN. "The Kocherthal Party — the 1708 Immigration to New York." In *Early Eighteenth Century Palatine Emigration,* Philadelphia: Dorrance & Co., 1937, pp. 243-244. Reprinted by Genealogical Publishing Co., Baltimore, 1965.

Names 53 Palatines who came to Newburgh, New York, under the leadership of the Reverend Kocherthal. For other references to Kocherthal, see index.   (Lancour 90)

*   *   *

4003
KNITTLE, WALTER ALLEN. "The New York Subsistence List." In *Early Eighteenth Century Palatine*

Emigration. Philadelphia: Dorrance & Co., 1937, pp. 282-291. Reprinted by Genealogical Publishing Co., Baltimore, 1965.

> Names 847 debtors to the British Government for subsistence given them in New York City or in Hudson River settlements after their arrival here between 1710 and September 1712. From a manuscript in the Public Record Office, London. Also printed in no. 1811, Ehle.   (Lancour 97)

*   *   *

4010
KNITTLE, WALTER ALLEN. "The Simmendinger Register." In *Early Eighteenth Century Palatine Emigration.* Philadelphia: Dorrance & Co., 1937, pp. 291-299. Reprinted by Genealogical Publishing Co., Baltimore, 1965.

> Appendix of Ulrich Simmendinger's pamphlet, *Warhoffte und glaubwuerdige Verzeichniss jeniger Personen...* Reutlingen, about 1717. Also printed in no. 8480, Simmendinger, where there is an explanation of the "Register."   (Lancour 94A)

*   *   *

4019
KNOLL, ANNA. *The Volga Germans in Ellis County, Kansas, 1876-1976.* Washington, D.C.: the author, 1975. 89p.

> Immigrants mentioned throughout the work. Page 5 has short list of those landing in Baltimore from the *Ohio,* November 23, 1875, arriving in Kansas the same month. Page 7 lists those arriving at the port of New York, July 29, 1876, reaching Victoria, Kansas, in August. Arrivals on page 7 are also listed in no. 4497, Laing.

*   *   *

4026
KNUDSON, KNUD S., and others. "The First Norwegian Settlers in Texas." In *Quarterly of the Central Texas Genealogical Society,* vol. 10:3 (July-Sept. 1967), pp. 9-14.

> Newspaper article submitted by Judge Derwood Johnson of Waco, in Norwegian language, 1900. Names many early Norwegian settlers of Bosque, Texas, and adjoining counties. 1840s and 1850s.

*   *   *

4033
KOCH, CONRAD. "Die 'Herbolzheimer Auswandererliste.'" In *Genealogie,* vol. 8:4 (Apr. 1966), pp. 167-170.

> List of emigrants from Herbolzheim. From unpublished documents in city and state archives in the state of Baden, Germany, letters from emigrants, and church registers of Herbolzheim and other localities. Published as a correction to Karl W. Klueber's, "Badische Auswanderer nach Venezuela," in the German periodical, *Genealogie,* vol. 7:5 (May 1965). Contains only a few names of the approximately 300 inhabitants of Baden who sailed to Venezuela in 1842 to establish the colony of Tovar.

*   *   *

4040
KOCH, HERBERT. "Achthundert Auswanderer aus Sachsen-Weimar (1854)." In *Archiv fuer Sippenforschung,* vol. 27:3 (Aug. 1961), pp. 131-136.

> "Eight hundred emigrants from Saxony-Weimar, 1854." Actually involves 1,047 emigrants to America, the names arranged alphabetically. For some adult emigrants, places of origin and occupations are given. See also no. 4046, Koch. For English translation, see no. 8590, Smith.

*   *   *

4046
KOCH, HERBERT. "Neunzig Auswanderer aus Sachsen-Weimar 1859." In *Praktische Forschungshilfe: Das Suchblatt fuer alle Fragen der Familienforscher,* n.s. vol. 2:2 (May 1969), p. 88-89.

> Ninety emigrants from Saxony-Weimar, 1859, from official police records of emigrants from the Grand Duchy of Saxony-Weimar-Eisenach. Mostly adults named, with places of origin and some occupations. All to America. This and no. 4040, Koch, were combined and translated by Smith in no. 8590.

*   *   *

4056
KOEHLER, ALBERT F. *The Huguenots or Early French in New Jersey.* Mimeographed. Bloomfield, N.J.: the author, 1955. 34p.

> History of the Huguenots who settled in New Jersey between 1677 and 1710. Pages 1-24 give names, birth dates, and birthplaces. Also in no. 0714, Boyer, *Ship Passenger Lists, New York and New Jersey,* pp. 222-237.   (Lancour 112)

*   *   *

4066
KOSS, DAVID H. "Advertisements for Missing Relatives in *Der Christliche Botschafter,* 1839-1865." In *National Genealogical Society Quarterly,* vol. 66:1 (Mar. 1978), pp. 33-41.

> Search notices for 110 missing Evangelicals, mostly Germans. The advertisements mention place of birth, place of residence in Germany, and often the approximate date of arrival in America.

*   *   *

4079
KRAUSE, NANCY, compiler. "The Nacogdoches Archives: 1835 Entrance Certificates and Citizen Applications." In *Stirpes,* vol. 15:2 (June 1975), pp. 43-50; vol. 15:3 (Sept. 1975), pp. 84-112; vol. 15:4 (Dec. 1975), pp. 152-157.

> Names, date of application, and names of witnesses, all 1835. Index compiled from the R.B. Blake transcripts of the Nacogdoches Archives, Texas. See also no. 1752, "Early East Texas Citizens."

*   *   *

4085
KREBS, FRIEDRICH. "American Emigration from

Baden-Durlach in the Years 1749-1751." Translated and edited by Don Yoder. In *Pennsylvania Folklife,* vol. 22:3 (Spring 1973), pp. 41-46.

> List of 63 families compiled from petitions to emigrate found in the records of the Court Council and Revenue Office of Baden-Durlach, Germany, in the Baden state archives. Baden-Durlach was a small duchy in the vicinity of Karlsruhe. Additions to this are in no. 9960, Yoder. See also the following items: no. 4089 for the year 1738; no. 4435 for the year 1751; nos. 4094 and 4417 for the year 1752; no. 4095 for the year 1753; and no. 4322 for the years 1749-1755.

*   *   *

4089

KREBS, FRIEDRICH. "Amerika-Auswanderer aus Baden-Durlach im Jahre 1738." In *Senftenegger Monatsblatt fuer Genealogie und Heraldik,* vol. 4:1 (Nov. 1956), cols. 17-18.

> Emigrants from Baden-Durlach in 1738. From a series of articles based on minutes of the Privy Councillor's office and treasury office records *(Hofrats- und Rentkammer-Protokolle)* in the *Generallandesarchiv* in Karlsruhe, Germany. Names individuals and heads of families applying for permission to emigrate; places of origin given but not ages. Krebs has attempted to link the names with entries in nos. 9041-9042, Strassburger. Also in no. 0702, Boyer, *Ship Passenger Lists, National and New England,* p. 53. For other years, see the following items: 4287 covering the year 1749; 4085, the years 1749-51; 4435 for the year 1751; 4094 and 4417, the year 1752; 4495 for the year 1753; and no. 4322 for the period 1749-55. (Lancour 17)

*   *   *

4094

KREBS, FRIEDRICH. "Amerika-Auswanderer aus Baden-Durlach im Jahre 1752." In *Senftenegger Monatsblatt fuer Genealogie und Heraldik,* vol. 3:9/10 (Mar.-Apr. 1956), cols. 289-292.

> Emigrants to America from Baden-Durlach in the year 1752. From minutes of the Privy Councillor's office and the treasury office (the *Hofrats- und Rentkammer)* of Baden-Durlach, preserved in the *Generallandesarchiv* of Baden in Karlsruhe, Germany. Names 50-60 emigrants, with places of origin, some family data, some intended destinations in America. Krebs has attempted to link the emigrants' names with entries in nos. 9041-9042, Strassburger. For English translation, see no. 4417, Krebs. For other years, see the following items: no. 4287 covers the year 1749; no. 4085, the years 1749-51; no. 4435 the year 1751; no. 4417, the year 1752, as docs the present entry by Krebs; no. 4095, the year 1753; and no. 4322 spans 1749-55. (Lancour 177A)

*   *   *

4095

KREBS, FRIEDRICH. "Amerika-Auswandcrer aus Baden-Durlach im Jahre 1753. In *Senftenegger Monatsblatt fuer Genealogie und Heraldik,* vol. 4:3 (Jan.-Feb. 1957), p. 204, cols. 79-80.

> Emigrants to America from Baden-Durlach, 1753. From minutes of the Privy Councillor's office and the treasury office records (the *Hofrats- und Rentkammer Protokolle)* of Baden-Durlach for 1753, stored in the *Generallandesarchiv* in Karlsruhe, West Germany. Names about 40 emigrants, indicating

heads of families and some family data, places of origin, some intended destinations. Krebs has attempted to link the names with entries in no. 9041-9042, Strassburger. Supplementary to nos. 4287, 4322, and 4417 (all Krebs). See also no. 0717, Boyer, p. 204; and nos. 4085, 4094, and 4435 for different years in that era. (Lancour 181)

*   *   *

4112

KREBS, FRIEDRICH. "Amerika-Auswanderer aus dem Oberamt Oppenheim 1742-1749." In *Hessische Familienkunde,* vol. 3:6 (June 1955), cols. 341-344.

> Emigrants to America from the jurisdiction of Oppenheim. From records of the former German Electoral Palatine jurisdiction of Oppenheim, stored in the Oppenheim city archives. About 50 emigrants to Pennsylvania, matched with entries in nos. 9041 and 9042, Strassburger. Supplies names, places of origin, and date of the certificate granting permission to emigrate. For English translation of this article, see no. 4397. (Lancour 163)

*   *   *

4119

KREBS, FRIEDRICH. "Amerika-Auswanderer aus den kurpfaelzischen Oberaemtern Heidelberg und Mosbach fuer die Jahre 1749/50." In *Badische Heimat,* vol. 33:1 (1953), pp. 76-77.

> Emigrants to America from the Electoral Palatine jurisdictions of Heidelberg and Mosbach for the years 1749-1750. Taken from minutes of the German Electoral Palatine jurisdictions stored in the *Generallandesarchiv* in Karlsruhe. Names 32 emigrants from Heidelberg, 1749-1750, and eight from Mosbach in 1749. Includes date of emigration and some names of accompanying family members. Matched with entries in nos. 9041-9042, Strassburger.

*   *   *

4121

KREBS, FRIEDRICH. "Amerikaauswanderer aus Odernheim am Glan." In *Nordpfaelzer Geschichtsverein,* Jahrgang 40, no. 1 (Mar. 1960), p. 407.

> Emigrants to America from Odernheim-on-the-Glan, Germany. From file "Zweibruecken III Nr. 1982" for May 2, 1748, in the state archives at Speyer, Germany. Concerns three male heads of families who emigrated to America in 1748. Krebs attempts to match their names against names of individuals appearing in nos. 9041-9042, Strassburger, who arrived in 1748 and 1749. See also no. 0780, Braun, for clarification and supplement to this article.

*   *   *

4122

KREBS, FRIEDRICH. "Amerikaauswanderer des 18. Jahrhunderts aus dem Akten des Staatsarchivs Speyer." In *Pfaelzische Familien- und Wappenkunde,* (Mitteilungen zur Wanderungsgeschichte der Pfaelzer, 4, 1964) vol. 5:4 (1964) p. 125-127.

> Some 18th century emigrants to America named in the files of the state archives in Speyer [Germany]. Covers emigration in the period 1727-1768. Indicates places of origin and some

family data. Krebs has attempted to link the names with entries in nos. 9041-9042, Strassburger.

*   *   *

4126

KREBS, FRIEDRICH. "Amerika-Auswanderer des 18. Jahrhunderts aus dem deutschen Suedwesten." In *Genealogie,* vol. 11:7, (July 1972), pp. 216-220.

Eighteenth-century emigrants to America from the southwestern part of Germany. From records deposited in the *Staatsarchiv* in Speyer and Ludwigsburg, and the *Generallandesarchiv* in Karlsruhe. Names and places of origin. Krebs has attempted to link these names with those in nos. 9041-9042, Strassburger. Period of emigration covered: 1739-1780.

*   *   *

4133

KREBS, FRIEDRICH. "Amerika-Auswanderer des 18. Jahrhunderts aus dem Gebiet der Pfaelz und dem ehemals pfaelzischen Unterelsass." In *Genealogie,* vol. 10:7 (July 1970), pp. 175-176.

Eighteenth-century emigrants to America from the Palatinate region and from the formerly Palatine Lower Alsace. From the Lutheran church register of Glanmuenchweiler and records in the state archives in Speyer concerning the area of Zweibruecken, specifically the former administrative units of Kleeburg and Katharinenburg. Concerns mostly emigrants who left without first obtaining permission to emigrate. Name, place of origin, and often age and family data.

*   *   *

4141

KREBS, FRIEDRICH. "Amerika-Auswanderer des 18. Jahrhunderts aus dem Gebiet des Herzogtums Zweibruecken." In *Pfaelzische Familien- und Wappenkunde* (Mitteilungen zur Wanderungsgeschichte der Pfalzer, 4, 1966), vol. 5:12 (1966), pp. 389-395.

Emigrants to America in the eighteenth century from the area of the Duchy of Zweibruecken. From records of the governments of Zweibruecken and Bergzabern, stored in the state archives at Speyer, Germany, and from the Reformed church register of Winden in Zweibruecken. Names 23 emigrants, 1709-1766, with some ages, family data, destinations in America, and dates of emigration. Krebs has attempted to link these names with those in entries numbered 9041-9042, Strassburger. Note that although this has the same title as no. 4145, the text is completely different.

*   *   *

4145

KREBS, FRIEDRICH. "Amerika-Auswanderer des 18. Jahrunderts aus dem Gebiet des Herzogtums Zweibruecken: aus den Akten des Staatsarchivs Speyer." In *Genealogie,* vol. 10:2 (Feb. 1970), pp. 50-53.

Emigrants to America in the 18th century from the area of the Duchy of Zweibruecken, according to records in the state archives at Speyer. Names 36 emigrants, 1728-1776, with places of origin, some ages, family data, destinations in America, and some dates of emigration. Krebs has attempted to link these names with those in entries nos. 9041-9042, Strassburger.

4147

KREBS, FRIEDRICH. "Amerikaauswanderer des 18. Jahrhunderts aus dem Gebiet des zweibrueckischen Amts Wegelnburg." In *Mitteilungen der Westdeutschen Gesellschaft fuer Familienkunde,* vol. 23:5 (March 1968), cols. 283-284.

Emigrants to America in the 18th century from the area of Wegelnburg in the jurisdiction of Zweibruecken. From receipts of the jurisdiction of Wegelnburg as well as file "Zweib. III Nr. 1838/II" in the state archives at Speyer, Germany. Names 30 emigrants, 1737-1765, and indicates some family relationships and places of origin. Krebs matched the data with entries in nos. 9041-9042, Strassburger.

*   *   *

4154

KREBS, FRIEDRICH. "Amerika-Auswanderer des 18. Jahrhunderts aus der heutigen Pfalz und der Nahe- und Hunsrueckgegend." In *Mitteilungen zur Wanderungsgeschichte der Pfaelzer* (Supplement to Pfaelzische Familien- und Wappenkunde), Folgen 11-12 (1954 –). pp. 62-66.

Emigrants to America in the 18th century from the present Palatinate and the Nahe and Hunsrueck regions [Germany]. Taken from various sources. Names 40 pre-Revolutionary War emigrants, mentioning places of origin, some ages, some destinations, some family data. See also no. 4203, Krebs. (Lancour 152)

*   *   *

4161

KREBS, FRIEDRICH. "Amerika-Auswanderer des 18. Jahrhunderts aus der Hunsrueck- und Nahegegend." In *Rheinische Vierteljahrsblaetter,* Jahrgang 19:1/2 (1954), pp. 240-241.

Emigrants to America in the 18th century from the Hunsrueck and Nahe regions. From records of Sponheim, Simmern, and Kreuznach preserved in the state archives of Koblenz and Lutheran church registers of Hueffelsheim, Germany. Names 52 emigrants, 1739-1768, with places of origin, some family data, and dates of emigration. Krebs has attempted to link the names with entries in nos. 9041-9042, Strassburger.

*   *   *

4168

KREBS, FRIEDRICH. "Amerika-Auswanderer des 18. Jahrhunderts aus der Nordpfalz (Ransweiler, Lettweiler, mit Auswanderer Briefen)." In *Nordpfaelzischer Geschichtsverein,* vol. 41 (1961), pp. 556-557.

Eighteenth-century [German] emigrants to America from the northern Palatinate (Ransweiler, Lettweiler), with letters from the emigrants. For English translation of this article, see no. 4343. Text not seen by editor.

*   *   *

4175

KREBS, FRIEDRICH. "Amerika-Auswanderer des 18. Jahrhunderts aus der Stadt Frankenthal." In *Mitteilungen der westdeutschen Gesellschaft fuer Familien-*

kunde, Jahrgang 47, vol. 19 (1959), pp. 577-580.

Eighteenth-century emigrants to America from the city of Frankenthal. Appears in a West German publication. See also 4147 and 4392, Krebs. Text not seen by editor.

* * *

4182
KREBS, FRIEDRICH. "Amerikaauswanderer des 18. Jahrhunderts aus pfaelzischen Gemeinden." In *Pfaelzische Familien- und Wappenkunde* (Mitteilungen zur Wanderungsgeschichte der Pfaelzer, 2, 1965), vol. 5:6 (1965), pp. 185-187.

Eighteenth-century emigrants to America from communities in the [German] Palatinate. From various Reformed Church registers and other sources. Emigrants for the period 1730-1764, with names, ages, places of origin, and family data. Krebs has attempted to link the names with entries in nos. 9041-9042, Strassburger. For English translation by A.A. Roth, see no. 4259, Krebs.

* * *

4189
KREBS, FRIEDRICH. "Amerikaauswanderer des 18. Jahrhunderts aus verschiedenen Kirchenbuechern und anderen Quellen." In *Pfaelzische Familien- und Wappenkunde* (Mitteilungen zur Wanderungsgeschichte der Pfaelzer, 1968), vol. 6:7 (1968) pp. 225-226.

Eighteenth-century emigrants to America noted in various church registers and other sources. Emigration period 1743-1784. Name, age, place of origin, and family data for the majority of the emigrants. Krebs has attempted to link the names with entries in nos. 9041-42, Strassburger.

* * *

4196
KREBS, FRIEDRICH. "Die Amerikaauswanderung aus dem kurpfaelzischen Oberamt Heidelberg in den Jahren 1737, 1738, 1751, 1753, und 1754." In *Badische Heimat,* Jahrgang 38:3/4 (Dec. 1958), pp. 303-304.

Emigration to America from the Electoral-Palatine division of Heidelberg, from records, the *Oberamtsprotokolle,* stored in the *Generallandesarchiv* in Karlsruhe, West Germany. Includes arrival information for emigrants whose names Krebs was able to locate in Strassburger's work, nos. 9041-42. Also printed in no. 4203, Krebs. Supplements nos. 4440 and 4450, Krebs. (Lancour 156)

* * *

4203
KREBS, FRIEDRICH. "Annotations to Strassburger and Hinke's *Pennsylvania German Pioneers.*" In *The Pennsylvania Genealogical Magazine,* vol. 21:3 (1960), pp. 235-248.

Emigrants from Heidelberg, Wuerttemberg, Oppenheim, from the present-day Rhineland Palatinate and the regions of Nahe and Hunsrueck, with name of ship and often the date of arrival. Many items contribute to the makeup of this work; see index for references to the places named above. Also in no. 9144, Tepper, *New World Immigrants,* vol. 2, pp. 17-30; and in

no. 0717, Boyer, *Ship Passenger Lists, Pennsylvania and Delaware,* pp. 100-113. (Lancour 141)

* * *

4210
KREBS, FRIEDRICH. "Ein Aufruf zur Auswanderung nach dem amerikanischen Staat Massachusetts aus dem Jahr 1751 (mit Auswandererliste aus dem Rhein-Maingebiet): Ein Beitrag zur Auswanderungsgeschichte des 18. Jahrh." In *Hessische Familienkunde,* vol. 5:8 (Oct. 1961), cols. 435-438.

An appeal for emigration to Massachusetts in the year 1751, (with a list of emigrants from the Rhine-Main region): a contribution to the history of emigration in the 18th century. From a printed notice dated December 17, 1751, filed in the state archives at Ludwigsburg, Germany. Covers 31 emigrants to Boston in 1751, with names of the adults and their places of origin. Most from central western Germany.

* * *

4214
KREBS, FRIEDRICH. "Auswanderer nach Amerika im 18. Jahrhundert aus dem ehemaligen Herzogtum Zweibruecken und dem kurpfaelzischen Oberamt Germersheim." In *Pfaelzische Familien- und Wappenkunde,* (Mitteilungen zur Wanderungsgeschichte der Pfaelzer, no. 3, 1967) vol. 6:3 (1967) p. 89-95.

Some 18th century emigrants to America from the former Duchy of Zweibruecken and the Electoral Palatine district of Germersheim [Germany]. From various church registers in the region of Landau and Zweibruecken, and other archives. Names 40 to 50 emigrants, 1738-1770, with places of origin, family data, and often ages. Some names correspond to entries in nos. 9041-9042, Strassburger. For English translation of this article, see no. 4266, Krebs.

* * *

4224
KREBS, FRIEDRICH. "Auswanderer nach den nordamerikanischen Kolonien im 18. Jahrhundert auf Grund der Eintraege im lutherischen Kirchenbuch von Freckenfeld." In *Blaetter fuer pfaelzische Kirchengeschichte und religioese Volkskunde,* vol. 19: 3/4 (1952), pp. 99-101.

Eighteenth-century emigrants to the North American colonies as reflected by the entries in the Lutheran Church registers at Freckenfeld [Germany]. About 40 emigrants, 1750-1753. Gives names, most ages, family data, year of emigration. Krebs has matched this information with entries in nos. 9041-9042, Strassburger, where names and years of emigration and arrival coincided. See also 4329, Krebs.

* * *

4231
KREBS, FRIEDRICH. "Auswanderer nach den nordamerikanischen Kolonien im lutherischen Kirchenbuch von Thaleischweiler." In *Mitteilungen zur Wanderungsgeschichte der Pfaelzer* (Supplement to) *Pfaelzische Familien- und Wappenkunde),* Folgen 3-4 (1952), pp. 21-24.

Emigrants to the North American colonies [who are named] in

the Lutheran church baptismal and marriage registers of Thaleischweiler [Germany]. About 50 emigrants to Pennsylvania during the 18th century before the Revolutionary War. Names, ages, family data. Matched with entries in nos. 9041-9042, Strassburger. Also in no. 0717, Boyer, *Ship Passenger Lists, Pennsylvania and Delaware*, pp. 176-181. See also no. 8470, Sigel.   (Lancour 159)

*   *   *

4245
KREBS, FRIEDRICH. "Beitraege zur Amerikaauswanderung des 18. Jahrhunderts aus Altwuerttemberg." In *Suedwestdeutsche Blaetter fuer Familien- und Wappenkunde,* vol.11:8 (Nov. 1961), pp. 186-189.

Materials concerning 18th-century emigration from Old Wuerttemberg. From records concerning the area around Freudenstadt preserved in the *Staatsfilialarchiv* of Ludwigsburg, Germany. About 100 emigrants, 1751-1752, with names, ages, family data, and places of origin. Many sailed on the *Duke of Wirtemberg.* Krebs has attempted to link these names with entries in nos. 9041-9042, Strassburger. Also in no. 0717, Boyer, *Ship Passenger Lists, Pennsylvania and Delaware,* pp. 196-199.   (Lancour 178)

*   *   *

4252
KREBS, FRIEDRICH. "18th Century Emigrants from Edenkoben in the Palatinate." Translated by Don Yoder. In *The Pennsylvania Dutchman,* vol. 4:9 (Jan. 1, 1953), p. 9.

Originally from the *Geschaefts Anzeiger* of August 2, 1952. Also in no. 9144, Tepper, *New World Immigrants,* vol. 2, pp. 174-75; and no. 0717, Boyer, *Ship Passenger Lists, Pennsylvania and Delaware,* pp. 187-89.   (Lancour 172)

*   *   *

4259
KREBS, FRIEDRICH. "Eighteenth Century Emigrants to America from Palatinate Parishes." Translated by Anthony A. Roth. In *Pennsylvania Genealogical Magazine,* vol. 26:1 (1969), pp. 33-36.

Mostly concerns Appenhofen. First published in German; no. 4182.

*   *   *

4266
KREBS, FRIEDRICH. "Eighteenth-Century Emigrants to America from the Duchy of Zweibruecken and the Germersheim District." In *Pennsylvania Folklife,* vol. 18:3 (Spring 1969), pp. 44-48.

Translated and edited by Don Yoder from original, no. 4214.

*   *   *

4273
KREBS, FRIEDRICH. "Einige Amerika-Auswanderer des 18. Jahrhunderts." In *Senftenegger Monatsblatt fuer Genealogie und Heraldik,* vol. 4:7 (Apr. 1958), cols. 195-198.

A few emigrants to America in the 18th century. From the

newspaper *Kayserliche Reichs-Oberpostamts-Zeitung* (Frankfurt am Main, Germany), supplemented by various church registers. Concerns about 20 emigrants, 1743-1764, with names, places of origin, some ages and family data. Krebs has tried to match this German data to the Strassburger ships' lists for Philadelphia. Also printed in no. 4203, Krebs; arrival dates supplied from nos. 9041-9042, Strassburger.   (Lancour 167)

*   *   *

4280
KREBS, FRIEDRICH. "Einige Amerika-Auswanderer des 18. Jahrhunderts." In *Senftenegger Monatsblatt fuer Genealogie und Heraldik,* vol. 5:2-3 (Oct.-Nov. 1960), cols. 79-82.

Some emigrants to America in the eighteenth century. From family records in the city archives of Wachenheim and elsewhere in Germany. Concerns 28 emigrants from the Palatinate to Pennsylvania and the Carolinas, 1732-1777. Names, places of origin, some family data, and a few ages. Krebs has tried to match this information to nos. 9041-42, the Strassburger ships' lists, for Philadelphia.   (Lancour 150)

*   *   *

4287
KREBS, FRIEDRICH. "Einige Amerika-Auswanderer des 18. Jahrhunderts." In *Senftenegger Monatsblatt fuer Genealogie und Heraldik,* vol. 5:4-5 (May-June 1961), cols. 123-126.

Some emigrants to America in the 18th century. From Privy Council and treasury office records (Hofrats- und Rentkammer-Protokolle) of Baden-Durlach, kept in the *Generallandesarchiv* in Karlsruhe, West Germany, and registers of the Reformed Church in Ottersheim in the Palatinate. Lists emigrants from Baden-Durlach to Pennsylvania in the year 1749. Also printed in no. 4203, Krebs.   (Lancour 168)

For emigration from Baden-Durlach in other years of that century, see items below:

Item No.	Year
4089	1738
4085	1749-1751
4435	1751
4094	1752
4417	1752
4095	1753
4322	1749-1755

*   *   *

4294
KREBS, FRIEDRICH. "Einige Amerika-Auswanderer des 18. Jahrhunderts." In *Senftenegger Monatsblatt fuer Genealogie und Heraldik,* vol. 6:1-2 (May-June 1966), cols. 60-64.

Some eighteenth-century emigrants to America. From files in the state archives at Speyer, Germany, and other sources. Concerns 39 emigrants from the Palatinate to America, 1727-1775, most with destination Philadelphia. Some ages, family data, occupations given. Place of origin indicated for all. Krebs has matched the German data with entries in nos. 9041-9042, Strassburger, wherever name and years of emigration and arrival coincide.

*   *   *

4301

KREBS, FRIEDRICH. "Einige Amerika-Auswanderer des 18. Jahrhunderts aus Otterberg." In *Nordpfaelzer Geschichtsverein*, Jahrgang 38, no. 2 (June 1958), p. 236.

Some eighteenth-century emigrants to America from Otterberg, Germany. From family files and old inventories in the Otterberg city archives. Mentions three emigrants with some family data, 1722 to late eighteenth century. Intended to serve as a supplement to entries in Fritz Braun's article, "Wege in die Welt," in *Otterberg und seine Buerger*. See no. 0891, Braun.

*   *   *

*4308

KREBS, FRIEDRICH. "Einige Amerika-Auswanderer des 18. Jahrhunderts aus Rheinhessen." In *Genealogie*, vol. 10:12 (Dec. 1970), pp. 337-338.

Some 18th century emigrants to America from Rhenish Hesse. From documentary records for the German towns of Alzey and Guntersblum. Concerns four emigrants who came to the colonies in the middle of the 18th century.

*   *   *

4315

KREBS, FRIEDRICH. "Einige Amerika-Auswanderer des 18. Jahrhunderts aus Wuerttemberg." In *Suedwestdeutsche Blaetter fuer Familien- und Wappenkunde*, Jahrgang 9:1 (Feb. 1957), pp. 442-443.

Some emigrants to America in the 18th century from Wuerttemberg. Found in minutes of the ruling council (Oberamt) of Wuerttemberg for 1749-1750, stored in the *Staatsfilialarchiv* in Ludwigsburg, Germany. Contains the names of ten adult male emigrants, places of origin, some family information, and date of emigration between the years 1749 and 1751. Krebs has tried to match this German data to nos. 9041 and 9042, the Strassburger lists of ships to Philadelphia. Also printed in no. 4203, Krebs.   (Lancour 170)

*   *   *

4322

KREBS, FRIEDRICH. "Emigrants from Baden-Durlach to Pennsylvania, 1749-1755." In *National Genealogical Society Quarterly*, vol. 45:1 (Mar. 1957), pp. 30-31.

From records of the court council and revenue office *(Hofrats und Rentkammer Protokolle)* of Baden-Durlach. List of 36 German emigrants to Pennsylvania in the years 1749-1755, mostly 1751. Ship name and arrival date frequently given. Personal names appear without umlauts, therefore care is needed to check more than one spelling. Also in no. 9144, Tepper, *New World Immigrants*, vol. 2, pp. 176-177; and no. 0717, Boyer, *Ship Passenger Lists, Pennsylvania and Delaware*, pp. 185-187.   (Lancour 171)

For other years in that era, consult the item numbers listed below:

Item No.	Year
4089	1738
4287	1749
4085	1749-51
4435	1751
4417	1752
4094	1752
4095	1753

4329

KREBS, FRIEDRICH. *Emigrants from the Palatinate to the American Colonies in the 18th Century*. Introduction by Milton Rubincam. (Pennsylvania German Society Special Study, 1) Norristown, [Pa.]: Pennsylvania German Society, 1953. 32p.

From church records of Frechenfeld, Billigheim, Thaleischweiler, Essenheim, Niederkirchen, Obermoschel, and Moersfeld in the Bavarian State Archives at Speyer, West Germany. Much information about emigrants and their families. For the German version, see no. 4364. See also no. 4224. (Lancour 132)

*   *   *

4343

KREBS, FRIEDRICH. "Emigrants of the 18th Century from the Northern Palatinate." Translated and edited by Don Yoder. In *Pennsylvania Folklife*, vol. 22:2 (Winter 1972-1973), pp. 46-48.

Originally published in no. 4168, Krebs. Many Mennonite families. Some ships named.

*   *   *

4350

KREBS, FRIEDRICH. "Emigrants to America from the Duchy of Zweibruecken: Excerpts from the Records of the Protestant Church of Zweibruecken." Translated by Ralph D. Owen. In *The Pennsylvania Genealogical Magazine*, vol. 23:4 (1964), pp. 255-256.
Covers period 1737-1750.

*   *   *

4357

KREBS, FRIEDRICH. "A List of German Immigrants to the American Colonies from Zweibruecken in the Palatinate, 1750-1771." Introduction by Don Yoder. In *The Pennsylvania German Folklore Society* [*Yearbook*], vol. 16 (1951), pp. 171-183.

From a manuscript in the *Kirchschaffenei Archiv* in Zweibruecken. Names 152 emigrants to Pennsylvania and Carolina, of whom 45 are identified in nos. 9041 and 9042, Strassburger. Also printed in no. 4364, Krebs. Additional material to that in no. 3193, Hinke and Stoudt. See also no. 9964, Yoder.   (Lancour 175, 175A)

*   *   *

4364

KREBS, FRIEDRICH. "Eine Liste deutscher Auswanderer nach den amerikanischen Kolonien aus Zweibruecken in der Pfalz 1750-1771." In *Familie und Volk*, Jahrgang 1:1 (Jan.-Feb. 1952), pp. 29-32.

A list of German emigrants from Zweibruecken in the Palatinate to the American colonies, 1750-1771. Names, family data, places of origin, and destinations: Pennsylvania and Carolina. No ages given. From a volume now deposited in the *Kirchschaffenei* archives of Zweibruecken for those years (i.e., archives of the church administrative offices). Adds to material in no. 3193, Hinke and Stoudt. The English version is no. 4357. Krebs has attempted to link these names with the entries in nos. 9041-9042, Strassburger.   (Lancour 175A)

4371

KREBS, FRIEDRICH. "More 18th-Century Emigrants from the Palatinate." In *The Pennsylvania Dutchman,* vol. 5:13 (Mar. 1, 1954), p. 12.

From records for the district of Neustadt. Ten emigrants granted permission to go to America, with ships' names and dates of departure supplied. Also in no. 9144, Tepper, *New World Immigrants,* vol. 2, page 180; and no. 0717, Boyer, *Ship Passenger Lists, Pennsylvania and Delaware,* page 205. (Lancour 182)

* * *

4378

KREBS, FRIEDRICH. "Notes on Eighteenth-Century Emigration to the British Colonies." Translated and edited by Don Yoder. In *Pennsylvania Folklife,* vol. 19:2 (Winter 1969-1970), p. 44.

Originally published in no. 4190, Krebs. Involves Palatines.

* * *

4385

KREBS, FRIEDRICH. "Palatine Emigrants from the District of Neustadt - 1750." In *The Pennsylvania Dutchman,* vol. 5:1 (May 1, 1953), p. 9.

Extracted from records of the district of Neustadt in the Palatine State Archives at Speyer. Names 13 persons applying for permission to emigrate, with ship and date supplied from nos. 9041 and 9042, Strassburger. Also in no. 9144, Tepper, *New World Immigrants,* vol. 2, pp. 172-173; and no. 0717, Boyer, *Ship Passenger Lists, Pennsylvania and Delaware,* pp. 191-192. (Lancour 174)

* * *

4392

KREBS, FRIEDRICH. "Palatine Emigrants of the 18th Century." Translated and edited by Don Yoder. In *Pennsylvania Folklife,* vol. 21:2 (Winter 1971-1972), pp. 41-43.

Compiled from community archives at Odernheim, city archives of Frankenthal, accounts of the Prefecture *(Vogtei)* at Wegelnburg, and the Palatine State Archives at Speyer. See also nos. 4147, 4175, Krebs.

* * *

4397

KREBS, FRIEDRICH. "Palatine Emigrants to America from the Oppenheim Area, 1742-1749." Translated and edited by Don Yoder. In *Pennsylvania Folklife,* vol. 22:1 (Autumn 1972), pp. 46-48.

English-language version of no. 4112, Krebs. The area is part of the present German state of Rhineland-Palatinate. Contained in records of the former Electoral Palatine district of Oppenheim. Some ships mentioned.

* * *

4404

KREBS, FRIEDRICH. "Palatine Emigration Materials

from the Neckar Valley, 1726-1766." Translated and edited by Don Yoder. In *Pennsylvania Folklife,* vol. 24:4 (Summer 1975), pp. 15-44.

Records housed in Baden State Archives at Karlsruhe, Germany. Names 141 persons, from various sources.

* * *

4409-4415

KREBS, FRIEDRICH. "Pennsylvania Dutch Pioneers." Translated by Don Yoder. In *The Pennsylvania Dutchman.*

4409

---Vol. 6:1 (June 1954), p. 40.

4410

---Vol. 6:2 (Sept. 1954), p. 37.

4411

---Vol. 6:3 (Winter 1954-1955), p. 39.

4412

---Vol. 6:4 (Spring 1955), pp. 37-38.

4413

---Vol. 7:3 (Winter 1956), pp. 38-39.

4414

---Vol. 7:4 (Spring 1956), pp. 38-39.

4415

---Vol. 8:1 (Summer 1956), pp. 57-59.

Gives names and genealogical data on several hundred emigrants from Germany to Pennsylvania in the years 1732 to 1785, with arrival dates and ship names from nos. 9041-9042, Strassburger. Translated from original in the state archives of Coblenz. Also in no. 9144, Tepper, *New World Immigrants,* vol. 2, pp. 34-60; and no. 0717, Boyer, *Ship Passenger Lists, Pennsylvania and Delaware,* pp. 143-166. (Lancour 151)

* * *

4417

KREBS, FRIEDRICH. "Pennsylvania Dutch Pioneers from Baden-Durlach: 1752. Translated by Don Yoder. In *The Pennsylvania Dutchman,* vol. 8:4 (Summer-Fall 1957), p. 48.

From records of the municipal council and revenue chamber *(Hofrats- und Rentkammer Protokolle)* of Baden-Durlach in the general state archives of Baden in Karlsruhe, Germany. Originally published in no. 4094, Krebs. Supplementary to nos. 4287, 4322, and 4095, Krebs. Also in no. 9144, Tepper, *New World Immigrants,* vol. 2, pp. 178-179; and no. 0717, Boyer, *Ship Passenger Lists, Pennsylvania and Delaware,* pp. 195-196. (Lancour 177)

For coverage of other years in that era, consult the item numbers listed below:

Item no.	Year
4089	1738
4287	1749
4085	1749-51
4435	1751
4094	1752
4095	1753

* * *

4422

KREBS, FRIEDRICH. "Pennsylvania Pioneers from the Neckar Valley, 1749-1750." In *The Pennsylvania Dutchman*, vol. 5:2 (June 1953), p. 13.

From records for the districts of Heidelberg and Mosbach, now part of the state of Wuerttemberg-Baden. Arranged chronologically by district, with name of ship and arrival date often supplied from Strassburger (nos. 9041-9042). First published in *Badische Heimat*, May 1953. Also in no. 9144, Tepper, *New World Immigrants*, vol. 2, pp. 169-171; and in no. 0717, Boyer, *Ship Passenger Lists, Pennsylvania and Delaware*, pp. 183-185.   (Lancour 169)

*   *   *

4428

KREBS, FRIEDRICH. "Pfaelzer Amerika-Auswanderer 18. Jahrhunderts." In *Familie und Volk*, (Jahrgang) vol. 5:2 (Mar.-Apr. 1956), pp. 60-62; vol. 5:4 (July-Aug. 1956), pp. 154-157; vol. 5:5 (Sept.-Oct. 1956), pp. 176-179.

Palatine emigrants to America in the 18th century. From files in the state archives at Speyer. Covers emigration between 1728 and 1792, with names, places of origin, approximate dates of departure, some family data. Gives ages in some instances, and links some of the names with entries in nos. 9041-9042, Strassburger.

*   *   *

4435

KREBS, FRIEDRICH. "Studien zur Amerikaauswanderung aus Baden-Durlach fuer das Jahr 1751." In *Badische Heimat*, vol. 36:2 (1956), pp. 155-156.

Studies concerning emigration to America from Baden-Durlach in the year 1751. From minutes of the municipal council and the treasury offices *(Hofrats- und Rentkammer)* of Baden-Durlach, stored in the *Generallandesarchiv* in Karlsruhe, Germany. Concerns 75 emigrants to America from communities then under the jurisdiction of Baden Durlach. Names individuals or heads of emigrant groups and places of origin. Sometimes gives the number of children accompanying parents. Krebs has matched the German data with entries in Strassburger, nos. 9041-9042, where name and years of emigration and arrival coincide. Other Baden-Durlach references: for the year 1738, no. 4089; for 1749, no. 4287; 1749-55, no. 4322; 1749-51, no. 4085; 1752, nos. 4417 and 4094; for 1753, no. 4095.

*   *   *

4440

KREBS, FRIEDRICH. "Zur Amerikaauswanderung aus dem kurpfaelzischen Oberamt Heidelberg 1741-1748." In *Zeitschrift fuer die Geschichte des Oberrheins*, vol. 106; n.s. Jahrgang 67:2 (1958), pp. 485-486.

Concerning emigration to America from the district of Heidelberg in the Electoral Palatinate for the years 1741-1748. Published in a journal on the history of the Upper Rhine from records of the Electoral Palatine district of Heidelberg, deposited in the *Generallandesarchiv* in Karlsruhe. Names heads of families and individuals applying for permission to emigrate, year of application, make-up of emigrating family, place of origin. Krebs has tried to match this German data with nos. 9041-9042, the Strassburger ships' lists for Philadelphia.

Also printed in no. 4203, Krebs. Supplementary to nos. 4450 and 4196, Krebs.   (Lancour 162)

*   *   *

4445

KREBS, FRIEDRICH. "Zur Amerika-Auswanderung des 18. Jahrhunderts aus Altwuerttemberg hauptsaechlich aus dem ehemaligen Oberamt Urach." In *Suedwestdeutsche Blaetter fuer Familien- und Wappenkunde*, vol. 9:2 (June 1957), pp. 464-465.

On emigration to America in the 18th century from within the earlier territorial limits of Wuerttemberg, mainly from the former jurisdiction of Urach. Found in minutes of the Upper Council of Wuerttemberg, stored in the *Staatsfilialarchiv* in Ludwigsburg, Germany. Concerns at least 56 emigrants to America in the years 1751-1754. Names, places of origin, some ages. Includes a list of emigrants from Dettingen, with ship names and arrival dates supplied from nos. 9041-9042, Strassburger. Krebs matched his data with entries in the Strassburger work, where ages and dates of emigration are given for colonists from this part of Germany. See also no. 2444, Gerber; and no. 0717, Boyer, *Ship Passenger Lists, Pennsylvania and Delaware*, pp. 192-194.   (Lancour 176)

*   *   *

4450

KREBS, FRIEDRICH. "Zur Fruehauswanderung aus dem kurpfaelzischen Oberamt Heidelberg nach Amerika (1726-1727). In *Suedwestdeutsche Blaetter fuer Familien- und Wappenkunde*, vol. 10:2 (June 1958), p. 512.

On early emigration to America from the Electoral Palatine district of Heidelberg, from records stored in the *Generallandesarchiv* in Karlsruhe. Concerns 16 emigrants to America in 1726 and 1727. Name, place of origin, date of emigration for each. Krebs has tried to match this German data to that in nos. 9041-9042, the Strassburger ships' lists for Philadelphia. Also printed in no. 4203, Krebs; and see nos. 4196 and 4440, Krebs. (Lancour 140)

*   *   *

4460

KRUEGER, GERHARD. *Auswanderer nach Uebersee aus dem Landkreis Cottbus im 19. Jahrhundert.* (Familienkundliche Heft fuer die Niederlausitz, 5.) Cottbus [Germany]: Verein fuer Heimatkunde, 1937. 20p.

Overseas emigration from the district of Cottbus in the 19th century, from a publication on Lower Lusatia. Contains data on 1,048 emigrants from the area around Cottbus, 1847-1886, to the Americas, Australia, the East Indies, and South Africa, about 350 of whom came to the Americas. Names of adults or heads of families are given, as well as year of emigration, place of origin, and continent or country of destination. The names are also given in the article cited in no. 4467, Krueger.

*   *   *

4467

KRUEGER, GERHARD. "Die Auswanderung aus dem Cottbuser Kreise um die Mitte des 19. Jahrhunderts." In Ekkehard: *Mitteilungsblatt deutscher genealogischer Abende*, Jahrgang 14:3 (June 15, 1938), pp. 284-285; 14:4

(Aug. 31, 1938), p. 301.

Emigration from the district of Cottbus around the middle of the 19th century. German source names 350 emigrants, 1847-1883, to Canada and elsewhere in North America and to several other locations. Indicates place of origin and date of emigration. See also no. 4460.

*   *   *

4477
KUHNS, MAUDE PINNEY. *The "Mary and John;" a Story of the Founding of Dorchester, Massachusetts, 1630.* Rutland, Vt.: Charles C. Tuttle Co., 1943. 254p. Reprinted 1971.

A reconstructed list of passengers who sailed from Plymouth, England, with genealogical accounts of them and their descendents. Pages 5 and 6 list 160 names. See also no. 0281, Banks; no. 3323, Hunt; and no. 6600, "Passengers on the *Mary & John.*" (Lancour 41)

*   *   *

4487
KUPILLAS, MRS. LAWRENCE O., contributor. "Passenger List, *Mercury,* Master: William Wilson. Emigrants from Parishes in Northern Switzerland, via The Netherlands, Qualified at Philadelphia, Pennsylvania, 29 May 1735." In *Districts I and II New York State Genealogical Records Commission. Downstate New York D.A.R. Cemetery, Church and Other Town Records,* 1976, vol. 458, pp. 78-90.

Typescript deposited in various libraries. Published by New York State Daughters of the American Revolution. Moritz Goetschy (Goetschius) and family came with 200 followers. See also no. 3000, Heidgerd; no. 7820, Rupp; nos. 1952 and 1960, Faust; and no. 9630, Weber.

*   *   *

4493
LAEUFER, H. "Auswanderer aus Dillgemeinden um 1700." In *Heimatkalender des Kreises Wetzlar,* 1958, pp. 59-62.

Emigrants from communities on the Dill River, ca. 1700. From minute books of the Dillheim *Landgericht* (district court). Concerns 17 adult males, Germany to America, 1670?-1719. Gives villages of origin, year of emigration.

*   *   *

4497
LAING, REV. FRANCIS B. "German-Russian Settlements in Ellis County, Kansas." In *Collections of the Kansas State Historical Society,* 1909-1910. Topeka, Kans.: 1910, vol. 11, pp. 489-528.

Lists of immigrants from places in Russia to America (Baltimore then to Kansas), 1875-1878, pp. 493-502. Reprinted as a separate pamphlet, 40p., 1910? The 1876 arrivals are also listed in no. 4019, Knoll. And see no. 1682, Freiling.

*   *   *

4502
LAMOND, ROBERT. *A Narrative of the Rise & Progress of Emigration, from the Counties of Lanark & Renfrew to the New Settlements in Upper Canada, on Government Grant . . . .* Glasgow: Chalmers & Collins, 1821. Facsimile ed. by Canadian Heritage Publications, Ottawa, 1978. 112p. Indexed.

Full details on the chartering of the ships *Earl of Buckinghamshire, George Canning, Commerce,* and *David,* all from Greenock, Scotland, to Quebec in 1821, with about 2,000 passengers on board. Contains various letters from emigrants and a partial port entry list.

*   *   *

4507-4511
"LAND NOTES, 1634-1655." In *Maryland Historical Magazine.*
4507
---Vol. 5:2 (June 1910), pp. 166-174; vol. 5:3 (Sept. 1910), pp. 261-271; vol. 5:4 (Dec. 1910), pp. 365-374.
4508
---Vol. 6:1 (Mar. 1911), pp. 60-70; vol. 6:2 (June 1911), pp. 195-203; vol. 6:3 (Sept. 1911), pp. 262-270; vol. 6:4 (Dec. 1911), pp. 365-373.
4509
---Vol. 7:2 (June 1912), pp. 183-196; vol. 7:3 (Sept. 1912), pp. 307-315; vol. 7:4 (Dec. 1912), pp. 385-394.
4510
---Vol. 8:1 (Mar. 1913), pp. 51-65; vol. 8:2 (June 1913), pp. 186-192; vol. 8:3 (Sept. 1913), pp. 257-270; vol. 8:4 (Dec. 1913), pp. 332-338.
4511
---Vol. 9:1 (Mar. 1914), pp. 38-46; vol. 9:2 (June 1914), pp. 170-182; vol. 9:3 (Sept. 1914), pp. 290-296.

Copied from Land Office records in Annapolis, Libers F, A, B. Much contained in no. 8510, Skordas. A few records beyond the year 1655.

*   *   *

4517
LANGGUTH, OTTO. "Auswanderer aus der Grafschaft Wertheim." In *Familiengeschichtliche Blaetter,* Jahrgang 30 (1932): part 3 (Mar.) cols. 53-60; part 4/5 (Apr./May) cols. 109-124; part 6 (June) cols. 155-164; parts 7/8 (July/Aug.) cols. 205-208; part 9 (Sept.) cols. 263-270; parts 10/11 (Oct./Nov.) cols. 299-304; part 12 (Dec.) cols. 343-352.

Emigrants from the county of Wertheim. Recorded in manuscript materials in the princely archive of Loewenstein-Wertheim-Rosenberg and Freudenberg, Germany. Period covered: 1750-1840, most dates being taken from the emigrants' applications for release from servitude to the rulers of Wertheim. Much information on the 272 emigrants, with ship identifications supplied from no. 9041-9042, Strassburger. Reprinted in the *Jahrbuch des historischen Vereins Alt-Wertheim,* 1935. English translation is no. 4525, Lohr. (Lancour 136A)

*   *   *

4525
LANGGUTH, OTTO. "Pennsylvania German Pioneers from the County of Wertheim." Translated and edited by Don Yoder. In *The Pennsylvania German Folklore Society* [*Yearbook*], vol. 12 (1947), pp. 147-289.

> Compiled from manuscripts in the princely archive of Lowenstein-Wertheim-Rosenberg. In the late 1740s, 272 immigrants from Wertheim in Franconia to Pennsylvania. Also printed as "Auswanderer aus der Grafschaft Wertheim." (no. 4517). Reprinted in *Jahrbuch des historischen Vereins Alt-Wertheim*, 1935. Also in no. 9964, Yoder. (Lancour 136).

*   *   *

4545
LEA, J. HENRY. "Genealogical Gleanings Among the English Archives: Bristol Apprentice Books." In *The New England Historical and Genealogical Register*, vol. 55:3 (July 1901), pp. 331-339.

> New England families in the *Bristol Apprentice Books, 1660-1684*. Also in no. 9151, Tepper, *Passengers to America*, pp. 158-166; and no. 0702, Boyer, *Ship Passenger Lists, National and New England*, pp. 170-173. (Lancour 56)

*   *   *

4555
LEDERLE, M. "Aus Lippstadt nach Amerika." In *Heimatblaetter*, vol. 44 (1963), p. 95.

> From Lippstadt to America. Text not seen by editor.

*   *   *

4565
LEE, MRS. CORINNE Mc N., and **MRS. LUCILLE S. MALLON,** copiers. "Petition & Record for Naturalization, U.S. District Court, Southern District of Alabama." In *Deep South Genealogical Quarterly,* vol. 1:3 (Feb. 1964), pp. 111-132; vol. 1:4 (May 1964), pp. 198-210; vol. 2:1 [published in error as vol. 1:5] (Aug. 1964), pp. 224-237; vol. 2:2 (Nov. 1964), pp. 278-290; vol. 2:3 (Feb. 1965), pp. 373-380; vol. 2:4 (May 1965), pp. 428-437; vol. 3:1 (Aug. 1965), pp. 470-478; vol. 3:2 (Nov. 1965), pp. 516-523.

> These naturalizations cover the years from the 1880s through 1930. Most entries give date and port of arrival in America. Much family information is included. Several nationalities. Copied from volumes 1-7 of the Naturalization Records at the U.S. District Court, Southern District of Alabama. Vols. 1 and 2 of the originals are in vol. 1:3 of the *Quarterly;* the remainder are in the *Quarterly*, vols. 1:4 through 3:2. Mrs. Lee and Mrs. Rochelle Farris copied only vol. 1:3, pp. 111-121; the remainder was copied by Mrs. Lee and Mrs. Mallon.

*   *   *

4575
LEESON, FRANCIS. "Records of Irish Emigrants to Canada, in Sussex Archives, 1839-1847." In *The Irish Ancestor,* vol. 6:1 (1974), pp. 31-42.

> Lists of heads of families and individuals, giving ages and dates of emigration. From the Petworth House Archives, set up by George Wyndham, Third Earl of Egremont. The archives contain details of the Petworth Emigration Committee's work.

*   *   *

4582
LEESON, FRANCIS. "West Sussex Emigration to Canada in the 1830s and 1840s." In *Sussex Family Historian,* vol. 1:2 (Sept. 1973), pp. 31-34.

> A study of the condition causing this emigration and the moving force behind it: the third Earl of Egremont. Index to emigrants to Upper Canada, 1832-1837, is on pp. 33 and 34 of the article.

*   *   *

4592
LE FEVRE, RALPH. *History of New Paltz, New York, and Its Old Families (from 1678 to 1820) Including the Huguenot Pioneers and Others Who Settled in New Paltz Previous to the Revolution . . . .* Albany, N.Y.: Fort Orange Press, 1903; Brandow Printing, 1909. 2nd ed., pp. 505-530. Reprinted by Genealogical Publishing Co., Baltimore, 1973.

> Also in no. 2924, Hasbrouck; and in no. 0714, Boyer, *Ship Passenger Lists, New York and New Jersey*, pp. 138-140. (Lancour 87A)

*   *   *

4596
LEISEN, GRETCHEN, contributor. "Emigrants to America, 1843-1877." In *Germanic Genealogist,* no. 15 (1978), pp. 357-371.

> Concerns the area called Imperial Circle of Vohenstrauss, the Bavarian part of the Austrian Empire. Gives names, year of emigration, and destination in America. Reprinted from Kurt Sander, *Ueber die Bewegung der Bevoelkerung des Kreises Vohenstrauss . . . ,* 1942, pp. 142-155.

*   *   *

4602-4604
LENT, ROBERTA LEE, abstractor. "Pioneers of Northern Minnesota." In *Genealogical Reference Builders Newsletter.*
4602
---Vol. 5:2 (May 1971), pp. 69-71; vol. 5:3 (Aug. 1971), pp. 149-151; vol. 5:4 (Nov. 1971), pp. 214-216.
4603
---Vol. 6:3 (Nov. 1972), pp. 220-223.
4604
---Vol. 7:1 (Feb. 1973), pp. 70-74.

> Abstracted from biographies in *History of Minnesota: Compendium of History and Biography of Northern Minnesota,* Chicago: Geo. A. Ogle & Co., 1902. Gives names and birth dates, origin, often date of emigration. Mostly Europeans, latter half of 19th century.

*   *   *

4612
"LIJST VAN EENIGE KOLONIERS DOOR KILI-

AEN VAN RENSSELAER IN DE JAREN 1636-1642 uit het Vaderland naar Zijne Kolonie Gezonden." In *Oud-Holland*, vol. 8 (1890), p. 296.

Has names of 29 colonists accompanying Kiliaen Van Rensselaer, 1636-1642, with their places of origin and occupations. Also in no. 0714, Boyer, *Ship Passenger Lists, New York and New Jersey*, pp. 92-93.   (Lancour 79)

*   *   *

4622

LILLY, MRS. GRANT E., contributor. "Passengers on the *Peter and Anthony*." In *The Huguenot*, no. 7 (1933-1935), pp. 153-155.

"List of All Ye Passingers from London to James River in Virginia, Being French Refugees Imbarqued in the Ship Ye *Peter and Anthony*, Galley of London, Daniel Perreau Commander." Passengers arrived September 1700. Also in no. 0953, Brock; and in no. 9143, Tepper, *New World Immigrants*, vol. 1, pp. 444-446. See other references in the index. (Lancour 223)

*   *   *

4627

LINDSAY, JOICEY H., contributor.   "Importation Oaths 1739-1741, Orange County [Virginia] In *Virginia Genealogical Society Quarterly*, vol. 17:2 (Apr. 1979), pp. 51-52; vol. 17:3 (July 1979), pp. 100-102; vol. 17:4 (Oct. 1979), pp. 121-123.

Includes facts about the person making the oath, the family accompanying him, and the date of the oath. Information found in Orange County Order Book, vol. 2 (1739-1741).

*   *   *

4632

"A LIST AND NUMBER OF PERSONS WHO HAVE ARRIVED IN NOVA SCOTIA FROM ENGLAND SINCE THE BEGINNING OF MAY 1774." In *Report, Board of Trustees, of the Public Archives of Nova Scotia*, 1935, Appendix C, pp. 34-39.

English settlers from Yorkshire arriving at Halifax. Gives personal and ships' names only. Note that pp. 26-66 of Appendix C give details of 900 ocean-going craft entering Halifax between July 4, 1778, and November 15, 1781.

*   *   *

4642

"LIST OF ARRIVALS PER *PENNSYLVANIA PACKET*, 1775." In *The Pennsylvania Magazine of History and Biography*, vol. 18:3 (1894), p. 379.

Copied from manuscripts in the Historical Society of Pennsylvania. List of British indentured servants bound for Philadelphia, March 15, 1775. Also in no. 9120, Tepper, *Emigrants to Pennsylvania*, p. 239.   (Lancour 187)

*   *   *

4652

"A LIST OF FOREIGN AND OTHER SETTLERS VICTUAL'D AT LUNENBERG IN THE PROVINCE OF NOVA SCOTIA Between the 24th Jany 1757 and the 15th May Following, Both Days Included (1313 Names in All)." In *Report, Board of Trustees of the Public Archives of Nova Scotia*, 1935, Appendix B, pp. 20-33.

Germans, Swiss, French Protestants, and others embarked at Halifax for Lunenberg (Canada.) Names only.

*   *   *

4662

"A LIST OF GERMAN EMIGRANTS, 1773." In *The Pennsylvania Magazine of History and Biography*, vol. 13:1 (1889), pp. 113-115.

A manuscript in the Historical Society of Pennsylvania tells of 53 German passengers who arrived on the *Britannia* on September 18, 1773. Incomplete lists are given in no. 7820, Rupp; no. 1804, Egle; no. 9041-9042, Strassburger; no. 1632, Diffenderfer. A complete list is in no. 9120, Tepper, *Emigrants to Pennsylvania*, pp. 236-238.   (Lancour 186)

*   *   *

4672

"LIST OF GERMAN PASSENGERS ARRIVED IN THE PORT PHILADELPHIA, IN THE SHIP *MARGARET*, FROM AMSTERDAM, C.E. Gardner, Master, September 19th, 1804. As Taken from the Original Immigrant List on File in the Division of Public Records, Harrisburg, Pa." In *The Journal of the Lycoming Historical Society*, vol. 1:3 (Mar. 1956), pp. 9-12.

Contains 91 names, with much information. Also printed in no. 1804, Egle; nos. 9041-9042, Strassburger; and in no. 9144, Tepper, *New World Immigrants*, vol. 2, pp. 325-328. (Lancour 191)

*   *   *

4682

"LIST OF LOYALISTS' FAMILIES Who Wish to Emigrate to the Island of Cape Breton this Fall [1784]." In Douglas Brymner, *Report on Canadian Archives*, 1891. Ottawa, Ont.: Printed by S. E. Dawson, 1892, p. 20.

Also in *Canadian Archives*, Series B., vol. 168, p. 43.

*   *   *

4692

"LIST OF PASSENGERS IN THE *MAYFLOWER*." In *IQH (Massachusetts Local History, New York Public Library)*, vol. 34, no. 14, 2p.

"Being the names of those who came over first in the year 1620...." Names preserved by Governor Bradford at the close of his *History* (no. 0756). Lists: p. 1, *Mayflower*, 1620; p. 2, *Fortune*, 1621; *Ann* and *Little James*, 1623. Other references to these ships are listed in the index.   (Lancour 34D)

*   *   *

4702-4703

"LIST OF PASSENGERS ARRIVING IN THE DISTRICT OF KEY WEST, FLA., 1837-1868." In *Deep South Genealogical Quarterly*.

4702
---Vol. 5:4 (May 1968), pp. 199-205.
4703
---Vol. 6:1 (Aug. 1968), pp. 35-42; vol. 6:2 (Nov. 1968), pp. 90-92; vol. 6:3 (Feb. 1969), pp. 152-156.

Abstract of passengers who arrived at the port of Key West between 1837 and 1848. Compiled by numerous persons, including Lois D. Mitchell.

*   *   *

4712
"LIST OF PASSENGERS, 1654-1664." In *Year Book of the Holland Society of New York,* (1902), pp. 5-37.

A better version than that given in no. 6291. From New York Colonial manuscripts, vol. 13, pp. 75, 88, 106; vol. 14, pp. 83-123. Additional information from James Riker's copy in the New York Public Library was published by Rosalie Fellows Bailey, no. 0220. Also in no. 0714, Boyer, *Ship Passenger Lists, New York and New Jersey,* pp. 117-134; and in no. 9143, Tepper, under the title, "Passengers to New Netherland," in *New World Immigrants,* vol. 1, pp. 166-193. See index for other references. (Lancour 83)

*   *   *

4722
"LIST OF PASSENGERS WHO CAME TO PLY-MOUTH IN THE *MAYFLOWER* on Her First Trip in 1620." In *Society of Mayflower Descendants, 1st Year Book,* New York, 1896, pp. 9-16.

Prepared by the historian of the Society. For references to numerous *Mayflower* lists, see index. (Lancour 33F)

*   *   *

4732
"LIST OF SERVANTS WHO SAILED FROM DUB-LIN FEBRUARY 25TH 1746/7 on the *Euryal,* and Arrived at Philadelphia April 11th." In *The Pennsylvania Magazine of History and Biography,* vol. 26:2 (1902), p. 287.

All women servants. Also in no. 9120, Tepper, *Emigrants to Pennsylvania,* p. 262. (Lancour 166)

*   *   *

4742
"A LIST OF SETTLERS VICTUALD AT THIS PLACE [HALIFAX] Between the Eighteenth of May & Fourth Day of June 1750, Both Days Included, with the Additions for June to Ye Last Day." In *Report, Board of Trustees of the Public Archives of Nova Scotia,* 1941. Halifax: 1942, Appendix B, pp. 21-45.

This contains the names of some New Englanders, though most were British English. It was taken from the Deschamps Manuscripts in the public archives of Nova Scotia in Halifax.

*   *   *

4752
"LIST OF THE PILGRIMS OF THE *WEL-*

COME." In *Memoirs of the Historical Society of Pennsylvania,* vol. 1 (1864), pp. 467-471.

Republished with notes and illustrations from no. 0132, Armstrong; no. 1342, Cowgill; no. 0242, Balderston; and no. 9143, Tepper, *New World Immigrants,* vol. 1, pp. 242-246. Names 99 of the estimated 100 passengers who accompanied William Penn in 1682. Original edition of this was published in 1826. For other references to the *Welcome,* see the index. (Lancour 119)

*   *   *

4762
"LISTE GENERALE D'ASSOCIES, DE COMMIS ET D'INTERPRETES qui passent l'hiver au service de la Compagnie du Nord-Ouest: dates et nature de leurs engagements respectifs, etc., etc." In *Report, Board of Trustees of the Public Archives of Nova Scotia,* 1935, pp. 53-56.

General list of partners, clerks and interpreters who spend the winter in the service of the Northwest Company, with the dates and nature of their respective contractual commitments. From the Archives du Canada, Canada Miscellaneous, Northwest Company Letter-Book, 1798. Name, occupation, place and date of contract, length of commitment beginning in 1797 and thereafter.

*   *   *

4772-4773
"LISTS OF GERMANS FROM THE PALATINATE Who Came to England in 1709." In *The New York Genealogical and Biographical Record.*
4772
---Vol. 40:1 (Jan. 1909), pp. 49-54; vol. 40:2 (Apr. 1909), pp. 93-100; vol. 40:3 (Oct. 1909), pp. 160-167; vol. 40:4 (Dec. 1909), pp. 241-248.
4773
---Vol. 41:1 (Jan. 1910), pp. 10-19.

Four Board of Trade lists of the first 6,520 Palatines to arrive in 1709, compiled in England by John Tribekko and George Ruperti, German clergymen (see no. 9214). Many came to America soon after arrival in London. There is much information on the immigrants. The first of these lists is printed in no. 3983, Knittle. Complete lists are in no. 9135, Tepper, *Immigrants to the Middle Colonies,* pp. 84-123. Abridged lists are in no. 5013, MacWethy. (Lancour 91)

*   *   *

4782
LOCKE, JOHN G. "Emigrants in Vessels 'Bound to Virginia.' " In *The New England Historical and Genealogical Register,* vol. 5:2 (Apr. 1851), pp. 248-249.

Shows that some of the passengers did not go to Virginia, but rather settled in Massachusetts, 1629-1635. Some Massachusetts names given. Also in no. 9151, Tepper, *Passengers to America,* pp. 108-110; and in no. 0702, Boyer, *Ship Passenger Lists, National and New England,* pp. 137-139. (Lancour 38)

*   *   *

4790
LOCKHART, AUDREY. *Some Aspects of Emigration*

from Ireland to the North American Colonies Between 1660 and 1775. New York: Arno Press, 1976, pp. 165-169, 170-174.

Names of indentured servants, 1749-1750, and felons 1735-1754; list compiled from Irish journals. Pages 175-193 give excellent tables of departures of emigrant ships from Irish ports, 1681-1775, excepting Ulster ports after 1717.

*   *   *

4803
LOEBER, N. "Die sogenannte Stephanische Auswanderung in den Jahren 1838 und 1839, unter besonderer Beruecksichtigung personeller, wirtschaftlicher und sozialer Folgen." In *Die Thueringer Sippe,* Jahrgang 5 (1939), pp. 120-126.

The so-called Stephan emigration in the years 1838 and 1839, with particular attention to personal, economic, and social consequences. Understood as a supplement to no. 4800, Loeber. Mentions several families who participated in the "Old Lutheran" emigration from Thuringia and the vicinity of Dresden, 1838-1839, to Missouri where they founded the villages of Altenburg, Wittenberg, Paitzdorf, Dresden, Frohna, and Seelitz. Names 42 persons.

*   *   *

4817
LOHR, OTTO. "Das aelteste deutsch-amerikanische Kirchenbuch." In *Jahrbuch fuer auslanddeutsche Sippenkunde,* Jahrgang 1 (1936), pp. 54-60.

The oldest German-American church register: Joshua Kocherthal's marriage register at West Camp, Province of New York. For the years 1708-1719, pp. 138-153, about 150 immigrants in 94 entries. For other mention of Kocherthal, see index. (Lancour 116, note)

*   *   *

4822
LOHR, OTTO. "Amerikadeutsche Familien des 17. Jahrhunderts." In *Jahrbuch fuer auslanddeutsche Sippenkunde,* Jahrgang 1 (1936), pp. 44-54.

German-American families of the 17th century. There is considerable misunderstanding concerning two items in Lancour: item 73: "Deutsche Einzeleinwanderer und Familien in Neu-Niederland," pp. 45-53; and item 116: "Einwanderer in Pennsylvania vor 1700," pp. 53-54. (Numbers 4830 and 4834 in the present work.) They appear to have been included in Lancour to prove Lohr's thesis, as iterated in the introductory section of his article cited above, that the German element in pre-1700 colonial America had been largely overlooked, that many Germans, because of intermarriage and assimilation by the Dutch of New Amsterdam and because of confusion regarding the terms "Dutch" (Netherlander) and "Deutsch" (German), had come to be regarded as immigrants from Holland. The first article, "German Immigrants..." is a list of arrivals before 1700, with place of origin, birth date or date of first appearance in American records, as well as some family information for most; some settled in New Jersey or Connecticut, the majority in New York. The second article, "Immigrants to Pennsylvania before 1700," includes, routinely, the date of immigration or date of first appearance in American records, and for many the place of origin. (Lancour 73 and 116)

*   *   *

4830
LOHR, OTTO. Deutsche Einzeleinwanderer und Familien in Neu-Niederland." In *Jahrbuch fuer Auslanddeutsche Sippenkunde,* Jahrgang 1 (1936), pp. 45-53.

German immigrants, both individuals and families, in New Amsterdam (or New Netherlands), 1610-1664. The majority were from coastal areas of present-day Germany. Most settled in New York, a few in New Jersey and Connecticut. See explanation in no. 4822, Lohr. Also in no. 0714, Boyer, *Ship Passenger Lists, New York and New Jersey,* pp. 14-25. (Lancour 73)

*   *   *

4834
LOHR, OTTO. "Einwanderer in Pennsylvanien vor 1700." In *Jahrbuch fuer Auslanddeutsche Sippenkunde,* Jahrgang 1, (1936), pp. 53-54.

Names of German families in Pennsylvania, with places of origin often indicated. See explanation in no. 4822, Lohr. Also in no. 0717, Boyer, *Ship Passenger Lists, Pennsylvania and Delaware,* pp. 7-9. (Lancour 116)

*   *   *

4846
LOMIER, DR. "Quelque Picards au Canada." (Les Provinces de France et la Nouvelle France.) In *Nova Francia,* vol. 1:2 (Oct. 1925), pp. 76-79; 1-3 (Dec. 1925), pp. 124-131; 1:5 (Apr. 1926), pp. 217-229; 1-6 (June 1926), pp. 273-278.

Some Canadian settlers from the ancient province of Picardy, France. A list of 17th and 18th century emigrants according to dioceses. Includes extensive descriptions of the Biencourt and Destroismaisons families. Name, alias, place of origin, names of spouse and parents, and date of arrival in Canada.

*   *   *

4860
LORD, MARY P. "Passenger List, Liverpool, England, 1830." In *The New England Historical and Genealogical Register,* vol. 93 (July 1939), pp. 298-300.

Names 109 passengers from Liverpool on the *Mexico.* Much information given. In 1963, the original list was in Mrs. Lord's possession. Also in no. 9151, Tepper, *Passengers to America,* pp. 459-461. (Lancour 246)

*   *   *

4870
LOUHI, EVERT ALEXANDER. *The Delaware Finns; or, The First Permanent Settlements in Pennsylvania, Delaware, West New Jersey and Eastern Part of Maryland.* New York: Humanity Press [1925], pp. 38-83.

Mention of new arrivals who went to Delaware and neighboring areas in the 1640s. Pages 82 and 83 have "The roll list of the colonists about to go to New Sweden, who have been examined and written down to the seventeenth of October 1655."

*   *   *

4880
LUCAS, HENRY STEPHEN. *Netherlanders in America: Dutch Immigration to the United States and Canada, 1789-1950.* (University of Michigan Publications, History and Political Science, 21.) Ann Arbor: University of Michigan Press, 1955, pp. 644-645.

> Table 3: Passengers. The list from the *Southerner*, Rotterdam to New York, Sept. 24-Nov. 17, 1846. Names 110 passengers and includes ages. Also in nos. 6875 and 6895, Prins.

*   *   *

4890
LUCAS, SILAS E., JR. *Index to the Headright and Bounty Grants of Georgia, 1756-1909.* Vidalia, Ga.: Georgia Genealogical Reprints, 1970. 741p.

> Names of 61,000 recipients of land grants, location of grant, number of acres, year of grant, and page reference in the grant book. In 1909 the Land Office Acts were repealed.

*   *   *

4894
LUECK, ALFRED. *Eisen, Erz und Abenteuer: Der Anteil einer kleinen Gruppe Siegerlaender Berg- und Huettenleute am industriellen und geistigen Aufstieg Amerikas.* Siegen, Germany: Huettenwerke Siegerland AG., [1956].

> Iron, ore and adventure: the contribution of a small group of Siegerland miners and smelters to the industrial ascent of America. Concerns twelve families (30 immigrants) who came in 1714 from the region around Siegen in Prussia to Virginia, where they founded the (now defunct) town of Germanna in what is presently Prince William County. Names all the adult immigrants and the places of their origin in the Siegerland (formerly part of the German principality of Nassau; now the southeast corner of the state of North-Rhine Westphalia in West Germany). Includes some ages, with much historical data surrounding this emigration and settlement.

*   *   *

*4898
LUEOEND, KARL. *Schweizer in Amerika: Karrieren und Misserfolge in der Neuen Welt.* [Olten?, Switzerland]: Walter Verlag A.G., 1979, pp. 292-315.

> Swiss in America: careers and failures in the New World; short biographies. About 100 persons named, with places of origin, birth and death years, places of settlement, and some family data. Covers the period from mid-sixteenth century to mid-twentieth century. Descendants of Swiss immigrants also treated.

*   *   *

4910
"A LYST OF THE PASINGERS ABORD THE SPEEDWELL OF LONDON, Robert Lock, Master, Bound for New England." In *The New England Historical and Genealogical Register,* vol. 1:2 (Apr. 1847), p. 132.

> Involves 41 persons to Boston, 1656. Also in nos. 1672 and 1674, Drake; no. 1352, Cox; no. 9151, Tepper, *Passengers to*

America, p. 462; and no. 0702, Boyer, *Ship Passenger Lists, National and New England,* p. 162.   (Lancour 54)

*   *   *

4916
MACCO, HERMANN FRIEDRICH, compiler. *Swiss Emigrants to the Palatinate and to America 1650-1800, and Huguenots in the Palatinate and Germany.* Arranged under the direction of Johannes F. Straumer; indexed by Helen J. Forrer. 6 vols. in typescript. Salt Lake City, Utah: The Genealogical Society of the Church of Jesus Christ of Latter-day Saints, 1954. 1,291p. and index of 160p.

> From parish records in Switzerland and the Palatinate and other records in official archives of the Swiss cantons of Basel, Bern, Aargau, and Zurich. This material is an alphabetical arrangement of the information contained in a manuscript (two loose-leaf binders), compiled by Macco during many years before 1945. The manuscript was purchased by the Genealogical Society from Macco's widow. Contains references to about 20,000 persons, with some family data on each. It supplements nos. 9041-9042, Strassburger and Hinke. May provide the exact information needed to continue research in Europe. Vol. 1, A-C; 2, D-G; 3, H-L; 4, M-R; 5, S-Z; 6, Index.

*   *   *

4918
McCOLL, HUGH. *Some Sketches of the Early Highland Pioneers of the County of Middlesex.* Strathroy [Ontario]: Gaelic Society of Toronto, 1904. Facsimile ed. by Canadian Heritage Publications, Ottawa, 1979. 55p., Appendex, xi; Index xvi.

> Names many early settlers, often with dates of arrival, mostly first half of 19th century. All from Scotland.

*   *   *

4920
McCONNEY, DR. E.J., compiler. "Prisoners of the '45 Rising." In *The Journal of the Barbados Museum and Historical Society,* vol. 31:2 (May 1963), pp. 73-90.

> Compiled from 18th century Treasury Money Books at the Public Record Office, London, and from Sir B.G. Seton and J.G. Arnot, *The Prisoners of the '45.* Concerns 269 prisoners sent to Barbados and Jamaica.

*   *   *

4930
McCORKLE, MRS. ELYZABETH S. "Canadian and Nova Scotia Refugees to New York." In *National Genealogical Society Quarterly,* vol. 53:2 (June 1965), pp. 116-118.

> These refugees arrived in 1775. "Canadian and Nova Scotia refugees entitled to lands in the State of New York, with the lots that were ballotted . . . ." Discussed in *Tree Talks,* vol. 4:2-3 (September and December 1964). Also in no. 6147, "New York State Ballotting Book."

*   *   *

4933
McCOWN, LEONARD J. "Index to Naturalization Records: Calhoun County, Texas." In *Stirpes*, vol. 19:2 (June 1979), pp. 88-101; 19:3 (Sept. 1979), pp. 177-188.

Taken from the District Clerk's Office, Port Lavaca, Texas. Much information in each entry, with court reference cited to facilitate further study. Covers latter half of 19th century; new citizens of European extraction.

*   *   *

4940
McCRACKEN, GEORGE E. "Passengers on the *Shield* 1684." In *The American Genealogist*, vol. 48:2 (Apr. 1972), p. 73.

Partial passenger list. From English certificates included in records of Falls monthly meeting. Found by Lewis D. Cook and published with comments by McCracken.

*   *   *

4950
McCRACKEN, GEORGE E. *The "Welcome" Claimants, Proved, Disproved and Doubtful, With an Account of Some of Their Descendants.* (Publications of the Welcome Society of Pennsylvania, 2) Baltimore: Genealogical Publishing Co., 1970. 660p.

Twenty-six English lists compared. Thousands of individuals in 2,000 families listed, 1852-1968. Exhaustive study.

*   *   *

4960-4963
McCRACKEN, GEORGE E. *"Welcome* Notes." In the *American Genealogist.*
4960
---Vol. 38:3 (July 1962), pp. 152-163.
4961
---Vol. 39:1 (Jan. 1963), pp. 4-15; vol. 39:3 (July 1963), pp. 164-169; vol. 39:4 (Oct. 1963), pp. 239-243.
4962
---Vol. 40:3 (July 1964), pp. 148-157.
4963
---Vol. 41:1 (Jan. 1965), pp. 38-40 (additions and corrections).

New information on some of the passengers on the *Welcome*. Compares several lists and finds no two the same. Also in no. 9143, Tepper, *New World Immigrants*, vol. 1, pp. 276-323. For other references to the *Welcome*, see the index. (Lancour 121)

*   *   *

4970
MacDONALD, A.D., compiler. *Mabou [Cape Breton Island, Nova Scotia] Pioneers: A Genealogical Tracing of Some Pioneer Families Who Settled in Mabou and District.* N.p.: the author, 195?, p. 639. Privately printed.

Contains a list from the ship *Catherine,* which sailed in 1843 from Tobermory, Scotland, to the Gut of Canso, Nova Scotia.

*   *   *

4980
MacDOUGALL, JOHN L. "List of Passengers Going in the Ship *Saint Lawrence* of Newcastile [probably Newcastle, England] . . . Bound for 'Ship Harbor, Cape Breton.'" In *History of Inverness County, Nova Scotia.* N.p. 1922, pp. 126-131.

List for a sailing in 1829 from the Scottish port of Leith to Ship Harbor, Port Hawkesbury, Nova Scotia. Scottish passengers: names, ages, former location (Island of Rum, Scotland), and port of landing (Gut of Canso).

*   *   *

4986
McGILL, JEAN S. *A Pioneer History of the County of Lanark.* Bewdley, Ont.: Clay Publishing Co., 1968. 4th pr., 1974, pp. 232-248.

Pages cited contain ship lists for the years 1815-1823, all to Canada, mostly from Scotland and Ireland. Many give township of settlement or former residence. Irish immigrants list ages.

*   *   *

4990
McHENRY, MRS. CHRIS, compiler. "Early Dearborn County [Indiana] Naturalizations." In *The Hoosier Genealogist,* vol. 19:1 (Mar. 1979), pp. 13-16.

Taken from the earliest extant Circuit Court Order Books nos. 1, 2, and 3. Early 1800s to 1830s. Various nationalities.

*   *   *

4998
MACHIR, VIOLETTE S. "They Came from Germany and Lived in Mason County, West Virginia, after 1880." In *The Genealogist's Post,* vol. 4:3 (Mar. 1967), pp. 5, 6, 8.

Excerpted from H.H. Hardesty, *Atlas,* 1883. Many arrived in and around the 1850s.

*   *   *

5000
McKAY, WILLIAM. [Passengers on the *Hector* on the voyage from Greenock, 1773, to Pictou, Nova Scotia.] In *The Nova Scotia Historical Quarterly,* vol. 3:2 (June 1973), pp. 126-129.

List attributed to Squire William McKay. See also no. 5007, G. MacLaren, *The Pictou Book.*

*   *   *

5002-5004
McKENZIE, DONALD A. "Upper Canada Naturalization Records (1828-1850). Nominal index to vols. 1 through 8." In *Families.*
5002
---Vol. 18:3 (1979), pp. 103-115, Part 1, to vols. 1-2 (1828-1830).

5003

---Vol. 19:1 (1980), pp. 36-56, Part 2, to vols. 3-4 (1831-1834); vol. 19:2 (1980), pp. 100-116, Part 3, to vols. 5-6 (1835-1841); vol. 19:3 (1980), pp. 131-149, Part 4, to vol. 7 (1842-1846).

5004

---Vol. 20:1 (1981), pp. 3-18, Part 5, to vol. 8 (1847-1850).

> Names of those naturalized, county or district, file year, and reference to entry number. Date of immigration is often given in the file.

*   *   *

5007

MacLAREN, GEORGE E. *The Pictou Book.* New Glasgow, N.S.: Hector Publishing Co., 1954. 267p.

> Names passenger ships from Scotland to Pictou, Nova Scotia, 1773 and 1801-1848. *Hector,* from Greenock, 1773, pp. 31-34; *Dove,* 1801 from Fort William, pp. 79-86; *Sarah* from Kilmorach and other ports, 1801, pp. 86-94. Lists emigrants from Scotland in 1815 who settled or resided in the area of Pictou in 1816, pp. 102-104. Other ships: *Lady Gray,* from Cromarty, 1841; some arrivals in Pictou and some in Quebec, pp. 104-105; *Ellen,* from Loch Laxford, Sutherland, 1848, pp. 108-110; *Hope,* from Glasgow, 1848, pp. 111-113; *London,* from Glasgow, 1848, pp. 113-114; *Lulan,* from Glasgow, 1848, pp. 114-118. The *Dove* was called the *Pigeon* in another work. A list of emigrant ships that arrived at Pictou, 1767-1849, pp. 118-124 of the MacLaren work. Some *Hector* passengers are listed in no. 5000, McKay.

*   *   *

5009

MacLEAN, J.P. *An Historical Account of the Settlements of Scotch Highlanders in America Prior to the Peace of 1783.* Cleveland [Ohio]: Helman-Taylor, 1900. Reprinted by Genealogical Publishing Co., Baltimore, 1968, pp. 110-11.

> A list of 28 persons from Argyleshire, probably from the Isle of Mull and the immediate vicinity of Oban, landing at Brunswick, N.C., Nov. 4, 1767. Includes names of the families to whom vacant lands were allotted in Cumberland or Mecklenburgh counties, North Carolina.

*   *   *

5011

McLEAN, MALCOLM D. "Migration Contracts." In *Stirpes,* vol. 16:1 (Mar. 1976), pp. 14-23.

> Excerpted from *Papers Concerning Robertson's Colony in Texas,* vol. 3 (Texas Christian University Press, Fort Worth, 1976). Early in 1830 Major Sterling C. Robertson had a contract form made for colonists who wished to sign up for migration to Texas. This list gives details of the date of signing, former address of colonist, amount of land given, and names of witnesses to the contract.

*   *   *

5013

MacWETHY, LOU D. "List of Palatines in 1709." In *The Book of Names.* St. Johnsville [N.Y.]: The Enterprise and News, 1933, pp. 75-111. Reprinted by Genea-

logical Publishing Co., Baltimore, 1969.

> Four London lists of Palatines from Germany, 1709, copied from a manuscript in the British Museum, London. See also nos. 4772-4773, "Lists of Germans . . . ;" no. 3990, Knittle; and no. 9214, Tribekko and Ruperti. (Lancour 92)

*   *   *

5015

MacWETHY, LOU D. "List of the Palatines Remaining at New York, 1710." In *The Book of Names.* St. Johnsville [N.Y.]: The Enterprise and News, 1933, pp. 120-123. Reprinted by Genealogical Publishing Co., Baltimore, 1969.

> Census of newly arrived immigrants who remained in New York. Also in nos. 6301, 6303, O'Callaghan; and no. 7820, Rupp.

*   *   *

5019

MacWETHY, LOU D., compiler. "Names of the Palatine Children Apprenticed by Gov. Hunter, 1710-1714." In *The Book of Names.* St. Johnsville, [N.Y.]: The Enterprise and News, 1933, p. 138. Reprinted by Genealogical Publishing Co., Baltimore, 1969.

> Gives name, age, parents' names, the name of the person to whom bound and that person's locality. Originally published in no. 6311, O'Callaghan, *The Documentary History of the State of New York.* The list also appears in no. 7820, Rupp. (Lancour 98)

*   *   *

5023

MacWETHY, LOU D. "West Camp; Statement of Heads of Palaten Famileys and Number of Persons in Both Towns of ye West Side Hudsons River. Winter, 1710." In *The Book of Names,* St. Johnsville, [N.Y.]: The Enterprise and News, 1933, pp. 123-124. Reprinted by Genealogical Publishing Co., Baltimore, 1969.

> A census of newly arrived Palatines living in the "west camp," 1710. Also in no. 6341, O'Callaghan. (Lancour 96A)

*   *   *

5028

MADUELL, CHARLES R., compiler. *Index of Spanish Citizens Entering New Orleans January 1820 Through December 1839.* New Orleans: the compiler, 1968. 50 copies, privately distributed. 88p.

> From microfilm in New Orleans Public Library. Mostly Spanish, including Spanish soldiers, and some French and Germans. For the years 1840-1865, see no. 5030.

*   *   *

5030

MADUELL, CHARLES R., compiler. *Index of Spanish Citizens Entering the Port of New Orleans Between January 1840 and December 1865.* New Orleans, the compiler, 1966. 50 copies, privately distributed. 75p.

Mostly from Havana, Cuba. Many lists missing. For the years 1820-1839, see no. 5028.

*   *   *

5040

MAHRENHOLTZ, HANS. "Auswanderer aus dem Lueneburgischen 1850." In *Norddeutsche Familienkunde,* Jahrgang 7:4 (Oct.-Dec. 1958), pp. 115-118.

Emigrants from the Lueneburg region, 1850. From files in the state archives at Hanover. About 150 emigrants from many communities, with places of origin, some ages, occupations, family data, and a few destinations. Similar information on other years in that era: no. 5109 covers 1849; no. 5111 covers 1851; and no. 5071 covers 1853.

*   *   *

5045

MAHRENHOLTZ, HANS. "Norddeutsche in aller Welt: Auswanderer aus dem Amte Diepholz 1823-1830 und 1831-1840." In *Norddeutsche Familienkunde,* Jahrgang 8:4 (Oct.-Dec. 1959), pp. 247-251.

North Germans the world over: emigrants from the jurisdiction of Diepholz, 1823-1830 and 1831-1840. About 50 departures, with places of origin, most ages, some family data, some places of destination, and names of a few relatives already in America. Information taken from files in the state archives at Hanover. For other information on German emigrants between the years 1825 and 1858, see item no. 5113 (which covers 1825-1840) no. 5051 (covering 1841-1849), and 5055 (covering 1841-1858).

*   *   *

5051

MAHRENHOLTZ, HANS. "Norddeutsche in aller Welt: Auswanderer aus den Amtern Diepholz 1841-1849 und Lauenstein 1841-1860." In *Norddeutsche Familienkunde,* Jahrgang 9:3 (July-Sept. 1960), pp. 82-84.

North Germans the world over: emigrants from the districts of Diepholz in the years 1841-1849 and Lauenstein, 1841-1860. Files of Diepholz containing applications for permission to emigrate; files of Lauenstein for the years 1841-1866, containing applications for release from obligation as subjects of the crown in order to emigrate. About 40 emigrants, with data on each. Items that cover similar time spans are no. 5045 for the years 1823-1840; no. 5113 for 1825-1840; and no. 5055 for 1841-1858.

*   *   *

5055

MAHRENHOLTZ, HANS. "Norddeutsche in aller Welt: Auswanderer aus dem Amte Diepholz (vorm. Amt Lemfoerde), 1841-1858." In *Norddeutsche Familienkunde,* Jahrgang 9:1 (Jan.-Mar. 1960), pp. 22-24.

North Germans the world over: emigrants from the domain of Diepholz (formerly Lemfoerde), 1841-1858. Names between 20 and 40 emigrants to America, with some other information. Taken from files concerning requests for permission to leave the former domain of Lemfoerde. For similar coverage, see

item no. 5045 on the years 1823-1840; no. 5113 on 1825-1840; and no. 5051 spanning 1841-1849.

*   *   *

5060

MAHRENHOLTZ, HANS. "Norddeutsche in aller Welt: Auswanderer aus dem Landdrosteibezirk Hildesheim." In *Norddeutsche Familienkunde,* Jahrgang 7:4 (Oct.-Dec. 1958), pp. 110-115; 8:2 (Apr -June 1959), pp. 185-188.

North Germans the world over: emigrants from the administrative district of Hildesheim. Names and places of origin of 150 emigrants. Has some ages, some occupations, and some destinations in America. From files in the state archives at Hanover.

*   *   *

5071

MAHRENHOLTZ, HANS. "Norddeutsche in aller Welt: Auswanderer aus dem Lueneburgischen 1853." In *Norddeutsche Familienkunde,* Jahrgang 8:1 (Jan.-Mar. 1959), pp. 154-155; 8:2 (Apr,-June 1959), pp. 186-188.

North Germans the world over: emigrants from the Lueneburg region, 1853. From files in the state archives at Hanover. Approximately 250 emigrants from several communities in the Lueneburg region. Some ages, occupations, family data, all with places of origin. Includes names of some family members. For similar information on other years in that era, see no. 5109 covering 1849; no. 5040 for 1850; and no. 5111 covering 1851.

*   *   *

5080

MAHRENHOLTZ, HANS. "Norddeutsche in aller Welt: Auswanderer nach Amerika, Polen, Venezuela, Neuseeland, 1753-1882." In *Norddeutsche Familienkunde,* vol. 7:3 (July-Sept. 1965), pp. 85-88.

North Germans the world over: emigrants to America, Poland, Venezuela, New Zealand, between 1753 and 1882. For the year 1845, there is a list of about 60 persons who emigrated, half of whom gave Texas as their destination. Some family information included. From records of the district of Calenberg.

*   *   *

5085

MAHRENHOLTZ, HANS. "Norddeutsche in aller Welt: Auswanderer nach Australien, Nord- und Suedamerika 1825-1846." In *Norddeutsche Familienkunde,* vol. 7:3 (July-Sept. 1966), pp. 215-221.

North Germans the world over: emigrants to Australia and to North and South America, 1825-1846. From files in the state archives of Lower Saxony, in Hanover, ref.: 84 I D No. 263. This article represents emigrants to America in the years 1845 and 1846 only. Mahrenholtz died in 1969, and a similar series was continued by Guenther Finke, no. 2053.

*   *   *

5093

MAHRENHOLTZ, HANS. "Norddeutsche in aller Welt: Auswanderer nach Neu-Schottland." In *Nord-*

deutsche Familienkunde, vol. 6:3 (July-Sept. 1962), pp. 80-82.

North Germans the world over: emigrants to Nova Scotia. Under the leadership of Thomas Christian Hammer, 65 emigrants originating partly in Hesse, partly in other parts of Germany, emigrated to Nova Scotia in 1753. Name, head of family, number in family group, and place of origin given. From files concerning the district of Stade in the kingdom of Hanover, kept in the state archives in Hanover.

*   *   *

5109

MAHRENHOLTZ, HANS. "Norddeutsche in aller Welt: Auswanderer aus dem Lueneburgischen 1849." In *Norddeutsche Familienkunde,* Jahrgang 7:3 (July-Sept. 1958), pp. 78-80.

North Germans the world over: emigrations from the Lueneburg region, 1849. From a file in the state archives at Hanover. About 150 emigrants from many communities in the vicinity of Lueneburg. Some ages, destinations, occupations, family data, with places of origin for all. For information on immediately succeeding years, see items nos. 5040, 5071, and 5111.

*   *   *

5111

MAHRENHOLTZ, HANS. "Norddeutsche in aller Welt: Auswanderungen aus dem Lueneburgischen 1851." In *Norddeutsche Familienkunde,* Jahrgang 7:1 (Jan.-Mar. 1958), pp. 23-25.

North Germans the world over: emigration from the Lueneburg region, 1851. Names about 200 emigrants from many communities in the area about Lueneburg. Some ages, destinations, occupations, and family data, with places of origin for all. From files in the state archives at Hanover. For items on adjacent years, see nos. 5109, 5040, and 5071 (for the years 1849, 1850, and 1853, respectively).

*   *   *

5113

MAHRENHOLTZ, HANS. "Norddeutsche in aller Welt: Auswanderungen aus dem Amt Lemfoerde 1825-1840 mit Auszug aus der Broschuere: 'Wohlgemeinter Rath der Deutschen Gesellschaft von Maryland an Deutsche . . . .' " In *Norddeutsche Familienkunde,* Jahrgang 9:4 (Oct.-Dec. 1960), pp. 118-124; 10:2 (Apr.-June 1961), pp. 173-178.

North Germans the world over: emigration from the jurisdiction of Lemfoerde, 1825-1840, with an excerpt from the pamphlet, "Well-intended Advice of the German Society of Maryland for Germans . . . ." Part 2 (Apr.-June 1961) has the subtitle, ". . . und Regierungsverordnungen und Massnahmen gegen die Auswanderung aus dem Bezirk Stade 1727-1761 (. . . governmental regulations and measures against emigration from the district of Stade, 1727-1761). Taken from files in the state archives at Hanover. Names 35 individual emigrants or heads of emigrant groups and gives places of origin, ages, occupations, some family data. Similar material in no. 5045 covering 1823-1840; no. 5051 for the years 1841-1849; and no. 5055 for the period 1841-1858.

*   *   *

5119

MAHRENHOLTZ, HANS. "Norddeutsche in aller Welt: Auswanderungen aus den Amtern Catlenburg-Lindau, Duderstadt und Gieboldehausen, 1831-1863 bzw. 1839-1866." In *Norddeutsche Familienkunde,* Jahrgang 10:4 (Oct.-Dec. 1961), pp. 245-249.

North Germans the world over: emigration from the jurisdictions of Catlenburg-Lindau, and Duderstadt and Gieboldehausen, 1831-1863 and 1839-1866, respectively. Files concerning emigrants and their release from the bonds of servitude, all in the state archives at Hanover. About 50 emigrants, places of origin, birthdates, family data, occupations, and some individual destinations beyond the general indication "America."

*   *   *

5125

MAHRENHOLTZ, HANS. "Norddeutsche in aller Welt: Auswanderungen 1860-1866 aus dem Amt Bruchhausen." In *Norddeutsche Familienkunde,* vol. 6:2 (Apr.-June 1963), pp. 181-184.

North Germans the world over: migration from the jurisdiction of Bruchhausen, 1860-1866. About 30 emigrants, with their birth dates, family data, occupations, and places of origin. Taken mostly from applications for permission to emigrate, which often mention relatives already residing in America. From a file in the state archives at Hanover.

*   *   *

5135

MAHRENHOLTZ, HANS. "Norddeutsche in aller Welt: Militaerpflichtige und arme Auswanderer, 1838-1858." In *Norddeutsche Familienkunde,* Jahrgang 6:4 (July-Aug. 1957), pp. 234-235.

North Germans the world over: emigrants obligated to military service and poor emigrants, 1838-1858. All from the Kingdom of Hanover in Germany to North and South America, with names, ages, and places of origin. From files concerning emigration between 1832 and 1868 in the state archives of Hanover.

*   *   *

5143

MAHRENHOLTZ, HANS. "Norddeutsche in aller Welt: Nachweise ueber 1830- bis 1848 nach Amerika auswandernde Niedersachsen." In *Norddeutsche Familienkunde,* Jahrgang 5:6 (Nov.-Dec. 1956), pp. 144-145.

North Germans the world over: documentation concerning citizens of Lower Saxony emigrating to America in the period 1830-1848. From files in the state archives at Hanover. Twelve emigrants from the jurisdiction of Harburg and from the prefecture of Caroxbostel, with names, some family data, occupations, exact years of emigration. This article inaugurated the series, "Norddeutsche in aller Welt."

*   *   *

5153

MAHRENHOLTZ, HANS. "Norddeutsche in aller Welt: Die Passagiere des an der britischen Kueste gestrandeten Auswandererschiffes *Burgundy.* " In *Nord-*

deutsche Familienkunde, Jahrgang 6:4 (July-Aug. 1957), pp. 233-234.

North Germans the world over: passengers on emigrant ship *Burgundy* stranded on the British coast. Two lists, prepared by British officials, of German emigrant passengers on board the American ship *Burgundy* from Bremen bound for New Orleans. The stranded passengers were harboured in Harwich and Ramsgate until they could be sent on to New Orleans. Names and places of origin given. From files concerning 1848 emigration in the state archives at Hanover.

*   *   *

5163
MAHRENHOLTZ, HANS. "Norddeutsche in aller Welt: Ueber Auswanderernachweise im Staatarchiv Hannover." In *Norddeutsche Familienkunde,* Jahrgang 6:2 (Mar.-Apr. 1957), pp. 183-186; 6:3 (May-June 1957), pp. 208-211.

North Germans the world over: items on emigration in the state archives in Hanover. Names, places of origin, and sometimes destinations. From files concerning emigrants to America between 1830 and 1837.

*   *   *

5183
MAK, MARTIN, transcriber. "S.S. *Patria* of Hamburg, Germany, to New York, 4 August 1899." In *The Pastfinder,* vol. 7:4 (Spring 1978), pp. 77-78.

A genuine ship passenger list, published as a sample to show readers what a passenger list includes. Gives name, age, sex, occupation, birth place, nationality, last residence, final destination, relatives in U.S., mother tongue, religion. This names 30 immigrants.

*   *   *

5193
MALLON, JOHN H., JR., contributor. "Naturalization Record I, 1856-1905: Application for Citizenship, State of Mississippi - Hancock County, Bay St. Louis, Miss., Court House. In *Deep South Genealogical Quarterly,* vol. 6:2 (Nov. 1968), pp. 96-98.

Name in full, country of origin, date of application.

*   *   *

5203-5204
MALLON, MRS. LUCILLE SIMMS, copier. "Early Ship Passenger Lists, 1820-1873." In *Deep South Genealogical Quarterly.*
5203
---Vol. 3:3 (Feb. 1966), pp. 569-573; vol. 3:4 (May 1966), pp. 652-656; 4:1 (Aug. 1966), pp. 721-729; vol. 4:2 (Nov. 1966), pp. 777-782; vol. 4:3 (Feb. 1967), pp. 834-838; vol. 4:4 (May 1967), pp. 895-897.
5204
---Vol. 5:1 (Aug. 1967), pp. 22-27.

Covers passengers arriving at the port of Mobile, 1832-1852, from many countries, but mainly Germany and Ireland. Cites full name, age, sex, occupation, country of origin, and often the destination. Many ships named. On p. 27 is a reference to

continuation of this material, but no further article on it appeared in the *Deep South Genealogical Quarterly.*

*   *   *

5213
MALLON, MRS. LUCILLE SIMMS, copier. English Inhabitants of the Tensas and Tombiggbee River Valley 1787." In *Deep South Genealogical Quarterly,* vol. 2:5 (i.e. 2:1) (Aug. 1964), pp. 265-266.

"Address to Commander in Chief of the Province of Louisianne . . . in the possible loss of Captain Favrot," January 15, 1787. Includes 60 names of English origin.

*   *   *

5218
MALLON, MRS. LUCILLE SIMMS, copier. "U.S. District Court, Selma, Alabama, Petition and Records for Naturalization, vols. 1 & 2." In *Deep South Genealogical Quarterly,* vol. 16:4 (Nov. 1979), pp. 205-207.

Full personal names, country of origin, and date of birth. Birth dates range from 1849 to 1904. No dates of naturalization given.

*   *   *

5223
MALLON, MRS. LUCILLE SIMMS, copier. "United States and Confederate Passport Records, 1855-1862. In *Deep South Genealogical Quarterly,* vol. 1:2 (Nov. 1963), pp. 58-62.

Provides full name, country of origin, some ages, filing date of record, and page reference. Originals are in U.S. District Court, Southern District of Alabama at Mobile - the only passports deposited there.

*   *   *

5243
MARSHALL, WILLIAM FORBES. "Names of Some Ministers, Licentiates, Students, or Emigrants Who Went from Ulster and Served in the Ministry of Presbyterian churches in North America During the Period 1680-1820, with the Presbytery of Oversight, or District of Origin Where These have been Ascertained, the Date or Approximate Date of Arrival, and the Provinces or States Where they Excercised Their Ministry." In *Ulster Sails West.* Belfast [Ireland]: The Quota Press [1943], pp. 61-68. Reprinted by Genealogical Publishing Co., Baltimore, 1977.

Also in no. 0702, Boyer, *Ship Passenger Lists, National and New England,* pp. 16-20. Boyer uses the unrevised Lancour work, where this is listed as no. 6   (Lancour 11-1)

*   *   *

5253
MARTELL, J.S. *Immigration to and Emigration from Nova Scotia 1815-1838.* Halifax, N.S.: Public Archives

of Nova Scotia, 1942, pp. 37-39.

> Archives Publication no. 6. Contains a list of Scottish emigrants from Great Britain in 1815 who settled in 1816 in the area of Pictou, Nova Scotia.

*   *   *

5263

MARTHALLER, AUBREY B, submitter. "Passenger Lists." In *Heritage Review,* no. 22 (Dec. 1978), pp. 46-47.

> Ships from Glasgow to New York, 1906; from Bremen to Baltimore, 1907. Lists passengers from Russia and Rumania.

*   *   *

5274

MARTIN, CHESTER BAILEY, selector. *Red River Settlement. Papers in the Canadian Archives Relating to the Pioneers.* Ottawa [Ontario]: Public Archives of Canada, 1910, pp. 10-13, 16-17, 24-27.

> Contains list of original Selkirk settlers in the years 1811-1814. From Miles Macdonnell Papers, Canadian Archives, M.155, pp. 145, 151, 165-168, and Selkirk Papers, vol. 2, M.734, Scotland, pp. 443-449, 558-562. Gives name, age, original location. Facsimile lists are contained in no. 3600, Jonasson. Other references to the Settlement in no. 0998, Bryce, and no. 6755, Phillips.

*   *   *

5284

MARWOOD, MRS. ALICE. "Passenger List-*Sierra Nevada."* In *The British Columbia Genealogist,* vol. 3:2 (Feb. 1974), p. 10.

> Information originally in *The Victoria Colonist,* Aug. 4, 1862. Passengers from San Francisco (and probably earlier from Britain) to Victoria, British Columbia.

*   *   *

5294

MARWOOD, MRS. ALICE. "Passengers on the steamer *Pacific* from San Francisco, Capt. Burns; from *The Victoria Colonist,* Aug. 15, 1862." In *The British Columbia Genealogist,* vol. 3:3 (May 1974), p. 3.

> Names only, and many of them without given names. Probably British, to British Columbia, Canada.

*   *   *

5304

MARWOOD, MRS. ALICE. "Ship's List - *Cyclone."* In *The British Columbia Genealogist,* vol. 3:1 (Nov. 1973), pp. 16-17.

> Passengers on the ship *Cyclone* from London, England, that arrived at Victoria, British Columbia, Canada, in 1862, as reported in *The Victoria Colonist.* Names, most of them only surnames and initials rather than full names.

*   *   *

5314

MARWOOD, MRS. ALICE. "Ship's List - *Mountain Wave."* In *The British Columbia Genealogist,* vol. 3:4 (Aug. 1974), p. 25.

> Passengers from the ship *Mountain Wave* that reached Victoria, B.C., September 1862, as recorded in The *Victoria Colonist* on September 23, 1862. British to Canada; listed mostly with surname and initials only.

*   *   *

5321

MARWOOD, MRS. ALICE. "Ship's List - *Tynemouth."* In *The British Columbia Genealogist,* vol. 3:3 (May 1974), pp. 11-12.

> The *Tynemouth* was also known as the *Brideship.* Its voyage was to San Francisco, leaving the latter port on September 12, 1862, and arriving at Esquimalt, British Columbia, Canada, September 17. Of 270 passengers from England, 34 left the ship at San Francisco. Information from *The Victoria Colonist.* Names only.

*   *   *

5328

MASSACHUSETTS. SUPERINTENDENT OF ALIEN PASSENGERS. *A List of Alien Passengers, Bonded from January 1, 1847, to January 1, 1851, for the Use of the Overseers of the Poor, in the Commonwealth.* Boston, Mass.: 1851. Reprinted by Genealogical Publishing Co., Baltimore, 1971. 99p.

> Often referred to as Munroe's *Alien Passengers,* because it was prepared under the direction of the Auditor of Accounts by J. B. Munroe, Superintendent of Alien Passengers for the Port of Boston.

*   *   *

5334

MASSEY, GEORGE VALENTINE, II. "Passengers on the Ketch *Endeavour."* In *Pennsylvania Folklife,* vol. 18:1 (Autumn 1968), pp. 36-39.

> From Liverpool to Pennsylvania, 1683; mouth of the Delaware River, September 1683. Refers to 23 Quaker families, totaling 87 passengers from Cheshire, England, including their servants.

*   *   *

5344-5346

MASSICOTTE, EDOUARD Z. "Les Colons de Montreal de 1642 a 1667."
5344
---In *Memoires de la Societe Royale du Canada,* 3rd ser., vol 7:1 (Section 1, 1913), pp. 3-65.
5345
---In *Le Bulletin des Recherches Historiques,* vol. 33:3 (Mar. 1927), pp. 170-192; vol. 33:4 (Apr. 1927), pp. 224-239; vol. 33:5 (May 1927), pp. 312-320; vol. 33:6 (June 1927), pp. 379-384; vol. 33:7 (July 1927), pp. 433-448; vol. 33:8 (Aug. 1927), pp. 467-482; vol. 33:9 (Sept. 1927), pp. 538-548; vol. 33:10 (Oct. 1927), pp. 613-625; vol. 33:11 (Nov. 1927), pp. 650-652.

5346

---Additions and corrections: vol. 37:12 (Dec. 1931), pp. 757-759.

> The colonists of Montreal from 1642 to 1667. A chronological list of the 1,500 persons who lived in Montreal from the foundation of the city until the second census. Name, household, place of origin. occupation, dates of birth, marriage, departure, death, and other biographical information. The title, "Les Colons de Montreal," changed with the ninth issue of the Bulletin (vol. 33:9) to "Les Premiers colons de Montreal" (The First Colonists of Montreal).

*   *   *

5354

MASSICOTTE, EDOUARD Z. "La Milice de 1663." In *Le Bulletin des Recherches Historiques,* vol. 32:7 (July 1926), pp. 405-418.

> A list of 139 volunteers for the 1663 militia in Montreal, Canada. Includes when available, rank, date of birth, date of arrival in Canada, occupation, and other biographical information.

*   *   *

5364

MASSICOTTE, EDOUARD Z. "Une recrue de colons pour Montreal en 1659: comment on immigrait autrefois." In *The Canadian Antiquarian and Numismatic Journal,* 4th ser., vol. 10 (Apr. 1913), pp. 63-96.

> A recruitment of colonists for Montreal in 1659: how immigration took place in former times. The article includes some names, with a few biographical notes, on pp. 79-90: "Estat des hom'es [sic], femmes et filles qui passerent a Montreal en 1659." (The condition of the men, women and girls who crossed to Montreal in 1659.) The discussion, but not the names, is also in *Le Bulletin des Recherches Historiques,* vol. 35:11 (Nov. 1929), pp. 671-678. See also no. 2662, Godbout.

*   *   *

5374

MASSICOTTE, EDOUARD Z. "La recrue de 1653: liste des colons qui partirent de France pour Montreal en l'annee 1653." In *Rapport de l'Archiviste de la Province de Quebec pour 1920-1921.* 1921, pp. 309-320.

> The recruitment of 1653: a list of French colonists who left for Montreal in 1653. The list includes mention of the wages paid to each volunteer, but limited biographical data is given. An introduction discusses the difficulties of recruitment and of the journey. The same list was published in 1913 in *The Canadian Antiquarian and Numismatic Journal,* 3rd series, vol. 10 (Oct. 1913), pp. 171-182. The subtitle differs - "La recrue de 1653: liste inedite des colons," but the texts appear to be identical. See also no. 5751, Mondoux; and no. 0172, Auger.

*   *   *

5388

MAYFLOWER DESCENDENTS AND THEIR MARRIAGES for Two Generations After the Landing, Including a Short History of the Church of the Pilgrim Founders of New England. Baltimore, Md.: Southern Book Co., 1956. Reprinted by The Bookmark, Knights-

town, Ind., 1977.

> Originally published in 1921 as *The Mayflower Passengers, Their Children and Grandchildren.* A second edition appeared in 1922 with the title, *Mayflower Descendents,* published by the District of Columbia's Bureau of Civil Achievement. The Bookmark reprint credits John T. Landis with the authorship.

*   *   *

5394

MERCER, GERALD A., copier. "Naturalization Records of Riverside County, California." In *Lifeliner,* vol. 11:1 (Sept. 1975), pp. 3-8; vol. 11:2 (Dec. 1975), pp. 39-44; vol. 11:3 (Mar. 1976), pp. 113-116; vol. 11:4 (June 1976), pp. 193-194.

> Naturalizations 1903-1911; resulting from immigration between the 1880s and the early 1900s. Origins: Canada, Great Britain, and elsewhere in Europe. Most entries include dates of arrival in the United States and witnesses' names.

*   *   *

5408

MERGEN, JOSEF. "Die Amerika-Auswanderung aus dem Amt Neumagen." In *Heimatkalender fuer den Kreis Bernkastel,* 1956, p. 56ff.

> Emigration to North America from the jurisdiction of Neumagen. In a publication of the Rhineland-Palatinate vicinity of Bernkastel, Germany. Text not seen by editor.

*   *   *

5422

MERGEN, JOSEF. "Die Amerika-Auswanderung aus dem Kreis Bitburg im 19. Jahrhundert." In *Eifel: Monatsschrift des Eifelvereins,* vol. 49 (1954), pp. 151-152.

> Nineteenth-century emigration to America from the Bitburg district. In a publication on the Eifel area of Germany west of the Rhine. Text not seen by editor.

*   *   *

5428

MERGEN, JOSEF. "Die Amerika-Auswanderung aus dem Kreis Pruem." In *Eifel: Monatsschrift des Eifelvereins,* vol. 48 (1953), pp. 99-101.

> Emigration to America from the district of Pruem. In a monthly journal on Eifel, a region west of the Rhine in Germany. Text not seen by editor.

*   *   *

5436

MERGEN, JOSEF. "Die Amerika-Auswanderung aus dem Regierungsbezirk Aachen." In *Heimatblaetter des Kreises Aachen,* Jahrgang 26:4 (1971).

> Emigration to America from the administrative district of Aachen [Germany]. Text not seen by editor.

*   *   *

5441-5445
MERGEN, JOSEF, compiler. *Amerika-Auswanderung aus dem Regierungsbezirk Trier im 19ten Jahrhundert.* 5 vols. Arranged and transcribed by Maria Cremer. Typescript. Salt Lake City, Utah: Genealogical Society, 1958. 700p.

> Emigration to America from the district of Trier [Germany] during the 19th century. Produced by the Genealogical Society from information given by Josef Mergen. Records name, age, place of origin, date of emigration, often the occupation and some family data for each of several thousand emigrants to North America in the 19th century.

*   *   *

5463
MERGEN, JOSEF. "Die Auswanderer von Kell nach Amerika." In *Trierischen Landeszeitung.* July 15, 1956.

> On emigrants from Kell to America. An article in the official gazette of Trier, called Treves in English, a city in the Rhineland Palatinate, Germany. Text not seen by editor.

*   *   *

5473
MERGEN, JOSEF. "Die Auswanderung aus Daleiden nach Nordamerika." In *Trierische Landeszeitung,* Sept. 28, 1954.

> Emigration from Daleiden to North America. Article published in the Trier (Treves) official gazette in the Rhineland Palatinate, Germany. Text not seen by editor.

*   *   *

5481
MERGEN, JOSEF. "Die Auswanderung aus dem Moselland nach Nordamerika im 19. Jahrhundert." In *Kurtrierisches Jahrbuch,* 4. Jahrgang (1964), pp. 70-84.

> Emigrants from the Moselle region to North America in the 19th century. Recorded in the state archives of Koblenz and elsewhere. Twenty-five emigrants, mostly well known inhabitants of the region.

*   *   *

5490
MERGEN, JOSEF. "Die Auswanderung aus Orenhofen nach Nord-Amerika." In *Trierische Landeszeitung,* Nov. 26, 1954.

> Emigration from Orenhofen to North America. Described in the offficial gazette of Trier (Treves), a city in the Rhineland, Germany. Text not seen by editor.

*   *   *

5540
MERGEN, JOSEF. "Trierer Amerika-Auswanderer 1855-1856." In *Porta: Heimatbeilage der Trierischen Landeszeitung,* Dec. 12, 1950.

> Emigrants to America from Trier (Treves), 1855-1856. Text not seen by editor.

*   *   *

5550
MERGEN, JOSEF. "Von der Eifel nach Nord-Amerika." In *Jahrbuch des Kreises Dueren,* 1973.

> From the Eifel region to North Ameria. Found in letters of emigrants and applications for permission to emigrate, 1845-1878. Names ten persons and indicates for each the place of origin, date of emigration, and some place of settlement in America. Published in an annual on the North-Rhine area about Dueren, Germany.

*   *   *

5583
MERIEUX, FRANCOIS. "L'Emigration Lyonnaise (1632-1760). In *Memoires de la Societe Genealogique Canadienne-Francaise,* vol. 9: 3-4 (July-Oct. 1958), pp. 205-208.

> A list of emigrants to Canada from the Province of Lyon during the French occupation (1632-1760) of "New France." Gives name, date of birth, facts of baptism or marriage, and limited biographical data (identification of some members of family and some occupations). Parish of origin given. No arrival dates, ships, or places of settlement mentioned.

*   *   *

5593
MERTZ, MARIAN SOWERS. "Juniata County, Pennsylvania, Naturalization Records." In *National Genealogical Society Quarterly,* vol. 55:1 (Mar. 1957), pp. 3-6.

> Lists naturalization applications of 65 persons, with declaration dates, 1789-1848. Extracted from two books in the Prothonotary's Office, Juniata County, Pennsylvania; petitions made before the Court of Common Pleas.

*   *   *

5603
METTLER, PETER, compiler. *Chronik des Deutschen Pionier-Vereins von Toledo, Ohio, sammt einer kurzen Geschichte der ersten deutschen Ansiedler in Toledo und Lucas County und der Nekrologie der verstorbenen Mitglieder des Vereins. Gegruendet am 10 Januar 1878.* Toledo [Ohio]: Gilsdorf Printing Co., 1898.

> A Chronicle of a German Pioneer Society of Toledo, Together with some Short Histories of the First German Immigrants in Toledo and Lucas County, and a List of Deceased Members of the Society, Founded January 10, 1878. Names, dates and places of birth in Germany, dates and ports of arrival (many in New York), covering 1770-1895.

*   *   *

5613
MEYER, MARY KEYSOR. "Passenger Arrivals at the Port of Baltimore." In *Maryland Genealogical Society Bulletin,* vol. 15:1 (Feb. 1974), pp. 38-43.

> List of 143 German immigrants on the *Neptune* who arrived in Baltimore, 1840. Original in Maryland Historical Society, Baltimore (MS. 1382). Gives origin, occupation, and intended place of settlement. Many to Ohio.

*   *   *

5623

MEYER, MARY KEYSOR, transcriber. "Passenger Arrivals in the Port of Baltimore. A List of Passengers on Board the Prussian Brig *Helena,* Capt. J.B. Sehlin from Havre, 19 August 1840." In *Maryland Magazine of Genealogy,* vol. 1:1 (Fall 1978), p. 12.

> From Maryland Historical Society, Baltimore (MS. 1382). Names 37 immigrants, with place of birth (Germany for most), destination, occupation, and age.

*   *   *

5635

MEYERS, CAROL M., compiler. *Early Immigrants to New Netherland: 1657-1664.* Gardena, Calif.: RAM Publishers, 1965. 26p.

> Taken from no. 6291, O'Callaghan.

*   *   *

5645

MIDDLEBROOK, LOUIS F. "The Ship *Mary* of Philadelphia. 1740." In *The Pennsylvania Magazine of History and Biography,* vol. 58:2 (Apr. 1934), pp. 127-151.

> Seven passengers who arrived in 1743 (three years after construction of the *Mary)* are named on pages 135 and 150. Also in no. 9120, Tepper, *Emigrants to Pennsylvania,* p. 262. (Lancour 160)

*   *   *

5655

MILLING, CHAPMAN J. *Exile Without End.* Columbia, S.C.: Bostick & Thornley, 1943, pp. 65-73.

> Appendix covers Acadians aboard the *Dolphin,* the *Cornwallis* and the *Endeavour;* Acadians incapable of labor, sick and infirm, the year 1756; Acadians sent to Prince Frederick's Parish, Winyaw; Acadian exiles and French prisoners arriving in South Carolina, years 1755-1756. Names as spelled in records and corrected from South Carolina *Council Journal,* for 1755-1756, and elsewhere. French spellings.

*   *   *

5665

MILLS, ELIZABETH SHOWN. "Certificates of Naturalization, Natchitoches Parish, Louisiana, 1820-1850." In *Louisiana Genealogical Register,* vol. 21:1 (Mar. 1974), pp. 85-93.

> Judicial copies of certificates of naturalization, now on file in the archives of Louisiana State University at Baton Rouge. Includes name, origin, and usually the date of declaration of intention. From box 5, folder 22, and box 6, folder 23.

*   *   *

5667

MILLS, ELIZABETH SHOWN. "Naturalization Applications and Certificates, Natchitoches Parish,

Louisiana, 1850-1877." In *Louisiana Genealogical Register,* vol. 22:3 (Sept. 1975), pp. 287-289.

> Selected items from the Natchitoches Parish naturalization files, Natchitoches Parish Records Collection, Department of Archives, Louisiana State University, Baton Rouge, Louisiana. From box 5, folder 6, and box 6, folder 23.

*   *   *

5675

MILNER, WILLIAM C. *Records of Chignecto.* (Collections of the Nova Scotia Historical Society, 15) Halifax [N.S.]: n.p., 1911. 86p.

> Yorkshire emigration from Hull, England, March 14, 1774, to Fort Cumberland, N.S., by ship *Albion,* pp. 40-43; also April 1775 on ship *Jenny* to Fort Cumberland, pp. 43-45; from the port of Newcastle on the *Providence* for Halifax, April 24, 1775; port of Poole to Halifax on the *Squirrel,* p. 45; and on the *Two Friends* from Hull to Halifax, March 1774, pp. 61-62. Names, ages, occupations, and reasons for immigration. See also no. 9975, "Yorkshire, England to Nova Scotia."

*   *   *

5685

MILZ, HEINRICH. "Mosellaendische Auswanderer." In *Mitteilungen der Westdeutschen Gesellschaft fuer Familienkunde,* vol. 10:2 (1938), columns 167-170.

> Emigrants from the Moselle region. Information gathered from church registers of the village of Foehren. Names 43 emigrants to America in 1764. Lists adults, including maiden names of wives, number of children or other family members in emigrant group, some other family data, and places of origin. An article by Heinrich Neu, in *Rheinische Vierteljahrsblaetter,* Jahrgang 6, p. 184, has these entries, but with some errors.

*   *   *

5695

"MINUTES OF THE COUNCIL AND GENERAL COURT, 1622-1624." In *The Virginia Magazine of History and Biography,* vol. 19:2 (Apr. 1911), pp. 113-148.

> From originals in the Library of Congress, Washington, D.C. Pages 131-134 list English emigrants who came to Virginia on the *Ann* and the *Bonny Bess* before February 1623. Also in no. 0720, Boyer, *Ship Passenger Lists, the South,* pp. 69-71; and in no. 9143, Tepper, *New World Immigrants,* vol. 1, pp. 17-20. (Lancour 215)

*   *   *

5705

MITCHELL, MRS. LOIS DUMAS, copier. "The Emigrants to Brazil: *Mobile Register and Advertiser,* March 25, 1866." In *Deep South Genealogical Quarterly,* vol. 3:2 (Nov. 1965), p. 536.

> Steamer *Margaret* of Mobile to the City of Para (or Belem), Brazil. A British complement of 34 passengers accompanying Major L.H. Hastings.

*   *   *

5715
MITCHELL, MRS. LOIS DUMAS, compiler. *Mobile Ship News.* Mobile, Ala., 1964. Vol. 1, 1821-1822. (No others published).

Lists of ships arriving, with crew and passengers and consignees. Approximately 550 passengers' names, pp. 4-106. Index to this volume appeared in *Deep South Genealogical Quarterly,* vol. 2:5 [i.e. 2:1] (Aug. 1964), pp. 238-242.

*   *   *

5719
MITGAU, HERMANN. "Amerikaauswanderer vor 100 Jahren. Aufzeichnungen aus Familienpapieren um 1849." In *Suedhannoverscher Heimatkalender,* (1964), pp. 112-113.

Emigrants to America 100 years ago; notes from family papers ca. 1849. Taken from letters in the possession of Hermann Mitgau. Concerns a family of four and one travel companion who emigrated from Holzminden, Germany, to Texas in 1849, arriving in New Orleans aboard the ship *Edmund,* May 10, 1849. Contains names and some family data.

*   *   *

5728
MOERSDORF, ROBERT. *Die Auswanderung aus dem Birkenfelder Land.* (Forschungen zur Rheinischen Auswanderung, Part 1) Bonn: Ludwig Roehrscheid Verlag, 1939, pp. 87-174.

Emigration from the Birkenfeld region, in a volume with eight tables and six maps in the text as well as three maps in the appendix. Pages 87-91 contain a list of emigrants from Germany's Birkenfeld region to America in the years 1697-1815 (Tabelle der Auswanderer des 17. und 18. Jahrhunderts . . .). Includes year of emigration, name of individual emigrant or head of emigrating group, village of origin, some wives' and children's names as well as a few maiden names, and the destinations. About 200 emigrants.
Pages 96-174 alphabetically list emigrants from the Birkenfeld region to America and to other parts of the world in the approximate period 1820-1899 (Tabelle der Auswanderer des 19. Jahrhunderts). Includes information similar to that for those who came in the earlier period. Involves about 3,000 individuals and families emigrating to the Americas. Pages 87-91 are also in no. 0702, Boyer, *Ship Passenger Lists, National and New England,* pp. 39-43. (Lancour 15 and 244)

*   *   *

5741
MOLERIO, DAGOBERTO. "A Passenger List for the Ship *William."* In *The New York Genealogical and Biographical Record,* vol. 101:3 (July 1970), pp. 142-144.

Tells of 41 passengers who sailed from the port of Greenock, Scotland in 1817. Found in files of the City Clerk in the Municipal Archives and Records Center of New York City. Also in no. 9135, Tepper, *Immigrants to the Middle Colonies,* pp. 152-154.

*   *   *

5751
MONDOUX, SOEUR. "Les 'Hommes' de Montreal." In *Revue d'Histoire de l'Amerique Francaise,* vol. 2:1

(June 1948), pp. 59-80.

Article about the 1653 recruitment and the crossing of the French to save Montreal. Sample contract included, and extracts from other contracts form the basis of the list. Gives names, places of origin, occupations, terms of contract, date, name of ship, and port of departure. No ages or biographical data given. Fuller lists in Massicotte, nos. 5344-46 and 5374. See also no. 0172, Auger.

*   *   *

5761
MONTAGNE, MME. PIERRE. *Tourouvre et les Juchereau.* Quebec: Societe Canadienne de Genealogie, 1965.

Tourouvre and the Juchereau Family. A history of 60 families from Tourouvre, in the Perche region of northwest France, who colonized Canada. Includes contracts signed by the recruits, legal documents pertaining to each recruit's family, and, when available, other biographical data on the colonists: e.g., dates of birth and death, year and age at departure, marital status, household, place of origin, port of arrival, etc. See also no. 2612, Godbout.

*   *   *

5771-5772
MONTGOMERY, MRS. L.E., copier. "Naturalization Records, McLennan County, Texas." In *The Family Tree* (Quarterly of the Central Texas Genealogical Society).
5771
---Vol. 12:2 (June 1969), pp. 5-10.
5772
---Vol. 12:3 (Sept. 1969), pp. 5-11.

Copied from an index of naturalization records in the Office of the District Clerk of McLennan County, Texas. Names only given. Period covered: 1850-1906.

*   *   *

5781
MOORE, CHARLES B. "Shipwrights, Fishermen, Passengers from England." In *The New York Genealogical and Biographical Record,* vol. 10 (Apr. 1879), pp. 66-76.

A study of the first settlers of New England, Virginia, and New York, containing names of immigrants to these and to American or West Indian islands, 1631-1635. Also in no. 9135, Tepper, *Immigrants to the Middle Colonies,* pp. 17-27; and in no. 0702, Boyer, *Ship Passenger Lists, National and New England,* pp. 21-27. Boyer omits many matters not related directly to immigration. (Lancour 7)

*   *   *

5791
MOORHOUSE, B-ANN. "Notices of Irish-Born Persons in New York City Newspapers." In *The Irish Ancestor,* vol. 5:1 (1973), pp. 24-27.

Names from newspapers, 1845-1907. The newspapers were often used to maintain Irish ties.

*   *   *

5801

MORALES, ADOLFO DE. "Catalogo de pasajeros al Reino del Peru desde 1560." In *Revista del Instituto Peruano de Lima: Investigaciones Genealogicas,* ano (vol.) 6:6 Apr. 1953), pp. 79-95; ano 7:7 (Nov. 1954), pp. 152-165; ano 8:8 (Dec. 1955), pp. 239-257.

> List of passengers to the Kingdom of Peru from 1560 on. Records from the archives of the [West] Indies (Archivo General de Indias) in Seville. Covers the period 1560-1594. Although it notes that the research will be continued, no further articles have appeared. This is a continuation of nos. 8870-8872, *Catalogo de Pasajeros* (Lancour 241), which covers the years 1509-1559. Names and places of origin (almost entirely from Spain). Most of the passengers were single.

*   *   *

5811

MORAS, C.B. "Angevins au Canada en Avril 1636." (Les Provinces de France et la Nouvelle France.) In *Nova Francia,* vol. 1:4 (Feb. 1926), p. 177, and a note by Chanoine F. Uzureau, vol. 2:1 (Oct. 1926), p. 39.

> Colonists from Anjou arriving in Canada, April 1636. Lists passengers from Anjou, France, aboard the ship *St. Jehan* destined for Canada. Gives name, household, occupation, and place of origin. The note by Canon Uzureau includes no names. See also nos. 2672 and 2682, Godbout.

*   *   *

5815

MORGAN, MARY M. "Pike County Ind. Naturalizations, Sept. 13, 1857-Nov. 5, 1906." In *The Hoosier Genealogist,* vol. 19:4 (Dec. 1979), pp. 90-93.

> From a Works Progress Administration worksheet giving name and date of naturalization or stating individual's intention to be naturalized. Provides name in full and specifies native country as well as date of acquisition of citizenship.

*   *   *

5821

MORRELL, JOHN D. "Passenger List." In *Wisconsin Helper,* vol. 2:3 (Feb. 1969), pp. 36-38.

> Passenger lists of vessels arriving at New York, 1847-1848. Only those whose destination was declared as Wisconsin are included. All are Germans who sailed from Bremen, Hamburg, or Rotterdam. Taken from microfilms in the National Archives, Washington, D.C. Names, ages, origin, and sometimes occupation.

*   *   *

5831

MORTON, OREN F. "Importations, 1739-1740." In *A History of Rockbridge County, Virginia.* Staunton, Va.: McClure Co., 1920, pp. 756-757.

> List of Augusta County settlers. Also in no. 3816, King; no. 2302, Fry; and no. 0720, Boyer, *Ship Passenger Lists, the South,* pp. 91-95. (Lancour 228A)

5841

MOYER, ROBERT V., abstractor. [Acts of the Legislature of New York State which Naturalized Citizens.] In *Tree Talks,* vol. 12:1 (Mar. 1972), p. 9. (Immigration and Naturalization, p. 39)

> Acts to naturalize persons in 1782 and 1785. British and German immigrants. For the years 1783 and 1784, see no. 1906, "Excerpts from the Laws of the State of New York."

*   *   *

5851

MUELLER, FRIEDRICH. "Auswanderungen aus Westfalen im 19. Jarhhundert." In *Auf roter Erde,* Jahrgang 18, n.s. no. 46 (Dec. 1962), p. 3.

> Emigration from Westphalia in the nineteenth century, seen in permits to emigrate from the district of Muenster in Westphalia. Concerns one family of five individuals who emigrated to America from Koeckelwick in the jurisdiction of Ahaus in the district of Muenster, 1846. Gives family names, maiden names, birthdates. Really a promotional article for Mueller's no. 5861, "Westfaelische Auswanderer." See no. 5861, Mueller.

*   *   *

5861

MUELLER, FRIEDRICH. "Westfaelische Auswanderer im 19. Jahrhundert — Auswanderung aus dem Regierungsbezirk Muenster, Part 1. 1803-1850." In *Beitraege zur westfaelischen Familienforschung,* vol. 22-24 (1964-1966), pp. 7-484.

> Westphalian emigrants in the 19th century - emigration from the governmental district of Muenster, part 1. From state archives in Muenster and in Detmold, West Germany. The lists cover pp. 57-389, with 6,453 numbered entries. Of 4,100 persons who emigrated officially, most went to America. Others left without permission, emigrating to different German principalities in Europe, possibly returning later to Westphalia. Part II, 1851-1900, is in typescript awaiting funds to publish.

*   *   *

5877

MUNDEL, HEDWIG. "A 1725 List of Wittgenstein Emigrants." Translated and edited by Don Yoder. In *The Pennsylvania Genealogical Magazine,* vol. 26:3 (1970), pp. 133-143.

> Names of 389 emigrants from Westphalia, approximately half of whom "secretly absconded to Pennsylvania."

*   *   *

5897

MURPHY, HON. HENRY C. [Extracts from the City Records at Leyden.] In Samuel G. Drake, *Result of Some Researches . . . Relative to the Founders of New England . . .* 1860, pp. 85-98.
> See nos. 1672 and 1674 for Drake's works.

*   *   *

5907

"MUSTER OF THE INHABITANTS IN VIRGINIA, TAKEN IN 1625. Total 1,095. The Muster of the

Inhabitants at Wariscoyack, Taken the 7th of February, 1625." In *William and Mary College Quarterly Historical Magazine*[1st series], vol. 7:4 (Apr. 1899), pp. 217-218.

Short lists of emigrants to Virginia, 1618-1623, with much information. From Isle of Wight County, Virginia, records of Wariscoyack and Basses Choyse. Also printed in no. 3520, Jester & Hiden; no. 0720, Boyer, *Ship Passenger Lists, the South,* pp. 67-68; and no. 9143, Tepper, *New World Immigrants,* vol. 1, pp. 1-2. (Lancour 212)

* * *

5917
MYERS, ALBERT COOK. "List of Certificates of Removal from Ireland Received at the Monthly Meetings of Friends in Pennsylvania, 1682-1750; with Genealogical Notes from Friends' Records of Ireland and Pennsylvania, Genealogies, County Histories, and Other Books and Manuscripts." In *Immigration of the Irish Quakers into Pennsylvania, 1682-1750, with Their Early History of Ireland.* Swarthmore, [Pa.]: the author, 1902, pp. 277-390. Reprinted by Genealogical Publishing Co., Baltimore, 1969.

(Lancour 126)

* * *

5924
MYERS, ALBERT COOK. *Quaker Arrivals at Philadelphia, 1682-1750; Being a List of Certificates of Removal Received at Philadelphia Monthly Meeting of Friends.* Philadelphia: Ferris & Leach, 1902. 131p. Reprint of 2nd ed. (1902) by Genealogical Publishing Co., Baltimore, 1957.

Certificates of removal from the different meetings of the congregations of Friends to which the immigrants had belonged in other countries. Supplemented by no. 3313, Hull. (Lancour 125)

* * *

5934
MYERS, MRS. LESTER F. "Abstracts from Aliens' Declarations of Intention to Become Citizens and Other Naturalization Proceedings. From Court of Common Pleas Records, Saratoga County [New York]." In *Tree Talks,* vol. 6:1 (Mar. 1966), pp. 9-10 (Immigration-Naturalization, pp. 7-8); vol. 6:2 (June 1966), pp. 61-62 (Immigration-Naturalization, pp. 9-10); vol. 6:4 (Dec. 1966), pp. 151-152 (Immigration-Naturalization, pp. 11-12).

British and Irish immigrants, early 1800s through 1830s. Although there is mention of continuations, none had appeared up to December 1979.

* * *

5942
MYERS, MRS. LESTER F. "Abstracts from the Minute Book of the Onondaga County Court of Common Pleas [New York], Recording Aliens' Declarations of Intentions to Become Citizens, and Other Naturalization Proceedings." In *Tree Talks,* vol. 11:1 (Mar. 1971), pp. 11-12 (Immigration and Naturalization, pp. 33-34); vol. 11:2 (June 1971), pp. 67-68 (Immigration and Naturalization, pp. 35-36); vol. 11:3 (Sept. 1971), pp. 133-134 (Immigration and Naturalization, pp. 37-38).

Mostly nationals of Great Britain; many Irish; a few French; 1830s.

* * *

5952
MYERS, ELEANOR (Mrs. Lester F.). "British Subjects Who Registered in Onondaga County 1812-1813." (Later entitled "Registration of British Subjects living in New York State in 1812-1813." In *Tree Talks,* vol. 15:2 (June 1975), pp. 96-109 (Society Page, 9-22); vol. 16:2 (June 1976), pp. 65-67 (Society Page, 7-9); vol. 17:2, (June 1977), pp. 71-72 (CNYGS, pp. 13-14); vol. 18:2 (June 1978), pp. 81-82 (CNYGS, pp. 15-16).

Gives full name, age, years in America, family residence, occupation. Registration was required because of the outbreak of the War of 1812. "Society Page" and CNYGS (for Central New York Genealogical Society) are references to subsections with separate pagination included in *Tree Talks.* Some of the work had the assistance of Mrs. Margaret Worden. Listings are "to be continued at a later date."

* * *

5962
MYERS, MRS. LESTER F. "Declarations of Intention and Naturalization Papers at the County Clerk's Office in Auburn, New York." In *Tree Talks,*

vol. 7:1 (Mar. 1967), pp. 14-15	(Imm./Nat. pp. 13-14);
vol. 7:2 (June 1967), pp. 69-70	(Imm./Nat. pp. 15-16);
vol. 8:1 (Mar. 1968), pp. 13-14	(Imm./Nat. pp. 17-18);
vol. 8:2 (June 1968), pp. 71-72	(Imm./Nat. pp. 19-20);
vol. 8:3 (Sept. 1968), pp. 128-129	(Imm./Nat. pp. 21-22);
vol. 8:4 (Dec. 1968), pp. 187-188	(Imm./Nat. pp. 23-24);
vol. 9:1 (Mar. 1969), pp. 14-15	(Imm./Nat. pp. 25-26);
vol. 9:2 (June 1969), pp. 78-79	(Imm./Nat. pp. 27-28);
vol. 9:3 (Sept. 1969), pp. 141-142	(Imm./Nat. pp. 29-30);

All Cayuga County immigrations, 1830s-1840s. Mostly British subjects. "Immigration and Naturalization" cited above is a subsection of *Tree Talks,* with its own pagination.

* * *

5972
MYERS, ELEANOR (Mrs. Lester F.). "Naturalization Records from Book of Common Pleas - on File in the Office of the County Clerk of Allegany County, New York, 1807-1828." In *Tree Talks,* vol. 12:3 (Sept. 1972), pp. 129-130 (Immigration and Naturalization, pp. 43-44). 1828-1841: vol. 13:4 (Dec. 1973), pp. 192-193 (Immigration and Naturalization, pp. 51-52). 1841-1850: vol. 14:1 (Mar. 1974), pp. 13-14 (Immigration and Naturalization, pp. 53-54).

Title varies. Mostly nationals of Great Britain and Ireland are recorded here. To be continued as more material becomes available.

5978

MYERS, ELEANOR (Mrs. Lester F.). "Naturaliza-
tion(s) Records from the Common Pleas Court Record
of Wayne County, N.Y." In *Tree Talks,* vol. 9:4 (Dec.
1969), pp. 201-202 (Immigration and Naturalization, pp.
31-32); vol. 18:3 (Sept. 1978), pp. 145-146 (Immigration
and Naturalization, pp. 59-60).

> Involves British and Irish and records mostly the 1830s. Refers
> to persons who came to America in the first quarter of the 19th
> century. Title varies.

*   *   *

5990

"NAMES AND OCCUPATIONS OF NEWBURGH
PALATINES." In *Olde Ulster; an Historical
and Genealogical Magazine,* vol. 9:4 (Apr. 1913),
pp. 102-103.

> All to New York in 1708 with Pastor Joshua Kocherthal,
> Newburgh, New York. Also in no. 9143, Tepper, *New World
> Immigrants,* vol. 1, pp. 447-448. For other references to
> Kocherthal, see index.   (Lancour 90B)

*   *   *

6003

NATURALIZATION APPLICATIONS FOR
MONTGOMERY COUNTY, INDIANA, 1850-1930.
Compiled and published by the "Who's Your Ancestor"
Genealogical and Historical Society, Crawfordsville,
Indiana, 1979. 67p.

> Gives full details on the persons acquiring citizenship, in-
> cluding date of immigration. Spans 1830s to 1920s.

*   *   *

6011

"NATURALIZATION OF MARYLAND SETTLERS
IN PENNSYLVANIA." In *Maryland Historical Magazine,* vol. 5:1 (Mar. 1910), p. 72.

> Names 23 Marylanders, who may have been Dunkers or
> Mennonites, who went to York, Pennsylvania, for naturali-
> zation, 1767-1772. Also in no. 0720, Boyer, *Ship Passenger
> Lists: the South,* pp. 19-20; and in no. 9144, Tepper, *New
> World Immigrants,* vol. 2, p. 533.   (Lancour 206)

*   *   *

6016-6019

"NATURALIZATIONS." In *The Colorado Genealogist.*
6016
---Vol. 37:2 (Summer 1976), pp. 54-57, 59.
6017
---Vol. 38:1 (Spring 1977), pp. 5-9; vol. 38:2 (Summer
1977), pp. 51-56; vol. 38:3 (Fall 1977), pp. 93-95.
6018
---Vol. 39:1 (1978), pp. 16-18; vol. 39:2 (1978), pp. 44-66;
vol. 39:3 (1978), pp. 97-101; vol. 39:4 (1978), pp. 125-126.

6019
---Vol. 40:1 (1979), pp. 19-22.

> Records copied from naturalization packets in the National
> Archives of the U.S. District Court, housed at the Federal
> Center in Denver, Colorado, location no. 468350. Gives packet
> designation, new citizen's name, origin or birthplace, county in
> which papers were filed, date papers were filed, list of
> documents contained in the packet. Various nationalities. Late
> 19th and early 20th centuries.

*   *   *

6021

"NATURALIZATIONS (from *The Publications of The
Huguenot Society of London,* vol. 24, 1921)." In *Virginia
Genealogical Society Quarterly,* vol. 11:3 (July 1973), pp.
75-76.

> Natives of Germany (with one exception); presumably Hu-
> guenots, 1743-1746.

*   *   *

6031

"NATURALIZATIONS, from U.S. Circuit Court Order
Book no. 9, 1811-1816." In *Virginia Genealogical
Society Quarterly,* vol. 7:3 (July 1969), p. 74; vol. 7:4
(Oct. 1969), pp. 97-98.

> Chiefly involves nationals of Great Britain, most of them late
> 18th-century immigrants.

*   *   *

6041

"NATURALIZATIONS, GERMANTOWN, PA.
3/7/1691/1692; Copia Naturalisationis of Francis
Daniel Pastorius and of 61 Persons More of German
Town from William Penn, Esq." In *National Genealogical Society Quarterly,* vol. 28:1 (Mar. 1940), pp. 7-8.

> A proclamation of William Penn declaring Francis Daniel
> Pastorius and 61 other foreigners freemen of the Province of
> Pennsylvania. From the Rolls Office, Philadelphia, now in the
> Juniata College Library, Huntington, Pennsylvania. Also in
> no. 9143, Tepper, *New World Immigrants,* vol. 1, pp. 434-435;
> and in no. 0717, Boyer, *Ship Passenger Lists, Pennsylvania
> and Delaware,* pp. 14-15.   (Lancour 129)

*   *   *

6047-6048

"NATURALIZED IN 1802." In *Laurel Messenger.*
6047
---Vol. 14:3 (Aug. 1974), p. 7.
6048
---Vol. 14:4 (Nov. 1974), p. 7. Title: "Naturalized Citizens." [1803-1827]

> Only names and countries of origin given. Many from
> Germany, Great Britain, and Ireland. Journal publishing this
> is focused on Somerset County, Pennsylvania.

*   *   *

6054-6056
NEIBLE, GEORGE W. "Servants and Apprentices Bound and Assigned Before James Hamilton, Mayor of Philadelphia, 1745." In *The Pennsylvania Magazine of History and Biography.*
6054
---Vol. 30:3 (July 1906), pp. 348-352; vol. 30:4 (Oct. 1906), pp. 427-436.
6055
---Vol. 31:1 (Jan. 1907), pp. 83-102; vol. 31:2 (Apr. 1907), pp. 195-206; vol. 31:3 (July 1907), pp. 351-367; vol. 31:4 (Oct. 1907), pp. 461-473.
6056
---Vol. 32:1 (Jan. 1908), pp. 88-103; vol. 32:2 (Apr. 1908), pp. 237-249; vol. 32:3 (July 1908), pp. 351-370.

> Chronological list of immigrant servants indentured in Philadelphia between October 2, 1745, and October 7, 1746. In volume 30 the material began with the title, "Servants and Apprentices . . .;" after the first instalment the title became "Account of Servants Bound and Assigned . . . ." Also in no. 9120, Tepper, *Emigrants to Pennsylvania*, pp. 54-179. See also nos. 8357 and 8358 "Servants and Apprentices . . . 1745." (Lancour 165)

*   *   *

6064
NEILL, EDWARD DUFFIELD. "Burgesses of the Assembly Convened at Jamestown, October 16, 1629." In *Virginia Carolorum: the Colony under the Rule of Charles the First and Second, A.D. 1625-A.D. 1685, Based Upon Manuscripts and Documents of the Period.* Albany, N.Y.: Joel Munsell's Sons, 1886, pp. 71-74.

> Covers 44 legislators of early Virginia, giving arrival dates in the Colony and other information. Also in no. 0720, Boyer, *Ship Passenger Lists, the South*, pp. 64-67. (Lancour 211)

*   *   *

6070
NEILL, EDWARD DUFFIELD. *The Founders of Maryland as Portrayed in Manuscripts, Provincial Records and Early Documents.* Albany, N.Y.: Joel Munsell, 1876, p. 64.

> Lists the passengers on the *Ark* and the *Dove*, St. Clement's Island, 1634. For full details of the *Ark* and the *Dove*, see no. 6157, Newman. For other references to the two ships, see the index. (Lancour 198C)

*   *   *

6077
NEILL, EDWARD DUFFIELD. "[Passengers on the *American Merchant*, 1714.]" In *Terra Mariae; or Threads of Maryland Colonial History.* Philadelphia, Pa.: J.B. Lippincott, 1867, p. 202.

> Names and occupations of seventeen men and boys who shipped on the *American Merchant*, 1714, to Maryland. Also in no. 0720, Boyer, *Ship Passenger Lists, the South*, pp. 11-12. (Lancour 201)

*   *   *

6087
NEISSER, GEORGE. "A List of the Bohemian and Moravian Emigrants to Saxony, Collected from Various Sources in Print and Manuscript, Begun and Completed at New York . . . June 2 -July 20, 1772." Translated and edited by Albert G. Rau. In *Transactions of the Moravian Historical Society* (Nazareth, Pa.) vol. 9 (1913), pp. 37-93.

> Original title: "Verzeichniss Emigrirter Boehmischer und Moehrischer Familien." Total of 648 persons, many found enumerated in Bishop Levering's *History of Bethlehem*. Most emigrated to America.

*   *   *

6097
NELSON, WILLIAM, editor. *Calendar of Records in the Office of the Secretary of State, 1664-1703.* Patterson, N.J.: The Printing Press and Publishing Co., 1899. 770p.

> First series, vol. 21 of the *Archives of the State of New Jersey;* vol. 21 of *Documents Relating to the Colonial History of the State of New Jersey.* Lists persons brought into the province, some of them imported indentured servants, with records of headlands for imported servants and others, as well as the passengers of the *Thomas and Benjamin* (1684) and the *Griffin* (1689). (Lancour 109)

*   *   *

6102
NESSLER, HANS. "Germanna und Germantown." In *Roland zu Dortmund: Zeitschrift der Genealogisch-Heraldischen Arbeitsgemeinschaft,* Jahrgang 6:8 (1972), pp. 143-145.

> Germanna and Germantown, Virginia. Names 30 of the emigrants who left the Duchy of Nassau-Siegen in 1713 and arrived in Virginia in 1714 to settle the colonies of Germanna and later Germantown.

*   *   *

6107-6108
"NEW CASTLE COUNTY, DELAWARE, NATURALIZATION RECORDS, 1826-1858." In *Maryland and Delaware Genealogist.*
6107
---Vol. 18:2 (Apr. 1977), pp. 38-39; vol. 18:3 (July 1977), pp. 62-63; vol. 18:4 (Oct. 1977), pp. 84-85.
6108
---Vol. 19:1 (Jan. 1978), p. 14.

> Name, date, and county of origin. Preserved in the collections of the Historical Society of Delaware.

*   *   *

6117
NEW JERSEY HISTORICAL RECORDS PROGRAM, Division of Community Service, Works Projects Administration. *Guide to Naturalization Records in New Jersey.* Newark, N.J.: The Historical Records

Program, 1941, pp. 32-38.

> Includes a chapter dealing with naturalization laws, colonial records, and the naturalizations in Samuel Allinson, *Acts of the General Assembly of the Province of New Jersey, 1702-1776*. Gives names, and dates of naturalization. The remainder of the 189 pages provides abstracts of the naturalization laws and studies of each county, indicating the location of particular records. Also in no. 9010, Stevenson.

*   *   *

6127

"NEW ORLEANS GERMAN SHIP REGISTER." In *Balkan and Eastern European American Genealogical and Historical Society Quarterly*, vol. 3:3 (June 1, 1966), pp. 3-25.

> Passengers from Bremen and Hamburg to New Orleans, 1845. Taken from original list. Name, age, occupation, destination, birthplace and name of ship. All family included.

*   *   *

6137

"NEW YORK GERMAN PROTESTANTS." In *Genealogical Reference Builders Newsletter*, vol. 1:2 (Feb. 1967), pp. 9-10.

> A petition to Mr. Secretary Boyle of the Board of Trade on behalf of Joshua de Kocherthal and fourteen other distressed Protestants lately arrived from the Palatinate and Holstein, asking that they and 41 Lutherans might remain in New York. Also published in *New York Colonial Documents*. Names, ages, trades or occupations.

*   *   *

6147

NEW YORK STATE. MILITARY BOUNTY LANDS. *The Balloting Book and Other Documents Relating to Military Bounty Lands in the State of New-York.* Albany [N.Y.]: Packard and van Benthuysen, 1825, pp. 185-188.

> "A list of the Canadian and Nova-Scotia refugees entitled to lands in the State of New York, with the lots that were balloted to them under the direction of the Commissioners of the Land-Office . . . ." See also no. 4930, McCorkle.

*   *   *

6157

NEWMAN, HARRY WRIGHT. "Documented List of the Adventurers on the *Ark* and the *Dove* and Those Who Were Early Identified with the Settlement." In *Flowering of the Maryland Palatinate.* Washington, D.C.: the author, 1961, pp. 339-341.

> Derived mostly from Patent Books in the Land Office, Annapolis, Maryland. For other references to the *Ark* and the *Dove*, see the index. (Lancour 198A)

*   *   *

6167

NEWSOME, A.R., editor. *Records of Emigrants from England and Scotland to North Carolina, 1774-1775.*

Raleigh [N.C.]: State Department of Archives and History, 1962. 30p. (Reprinted 1966)

> From transcripts in the North Carolina Historical Commission of original lists in the Public Record Office, London. Reprinted from *The North Carolina Historical Review* (no. 6169), where extra information is given. Also printed in part in no. 1088, Cameron. (Lancour 232)

*   *   *

6169

NEWSOME, A.R., editor. "Records of Emigrants from England and Scotland to North Carolina, 1774-1775." In *The North Carolina Historical Review*, vol. 11:1 (Jan. 1934), pp. 39-54; vol. 11:2 (Apr. 1934), pp. 129-143.

> From London and Newcastle to Carolina, 1774. Records of emigrants from Scotland, 1775, to North Carolina; Stranraer, Scotland, to New York, 1775; from Greenock, Scotland, to New York, 1774 and 1775. Several ships mentioned. Article made into a pamphlet: see no. 6167. Also in no. 0720, Boyer, *Ship Passenger Lists, the South*, pp. 130-155, and in no. 9144, Tepper, *New World Immigrants*, vol. 2, pp. 186-216. (Lancour 232A)

*   *   *

6179

NICHOLSON, CREGOE D.P. "Some Early Emigrants to America." In *Genealogists' Magazine* (London), vols. 12 and 13, 1955-1960. Reprinted by Genealogical Publishing Co., Baltimore, 1965, with the title: *Some Early Emigrants to America . . . .*

> Names about 1,000 persons who indentured themselves to serve in the plantations in 1683 and 1684, mainly in Maryland, Virginia, Barbados, and Jamaica, with a few for New York, New Jersey, Pennsylvania, and Carolina. Gives much information about the passengers. Also in no. 9143, Tepper, *New World Immigrants*, vol. 1, pp. 324-420. (Lancour 12)

*   *   *

6199

NIEPOTH, WILHELM. "Die Abstammung der 13 Auswanderer von Krefeld nach Pennsylvanien im Lichte niederrheinischer Quellen." In *Aus der Heimat*, vol. 24 (1953), pp. 2-9.

> The ancestry of 13 emigrants from Krefeld to Pennsylvania, in the light of Lower Rhenish source materials. Text not seen by editor.

*   *   *

6206

NORDDEUTSCHER LLOYD IN BREMEN. Passagier-Liste des Postdampfers "Salier," Captain C. Wiegand, von Bremen nach New York am 3. Mai 1882. Bremen [Germany]: Druck von Carl Schuenemann, 1882. [10p.]

> A complete list of 744 passengers on the steamer *Salier* in the spring of 1882, with names in full and places of origin. An incomplete list, of only 304 of those Bremen-to-New York passengers appears in no. 8130, Schultz.

*   *   *

6209
NORMAND, TED. "Naturalization Records: Avoyelles [Parish, Louisisana]." In *Lousiana Genealogical Register,* vol. 22:1 (Mar. 1975), pp. 12-14.

Partial list of persons who took the Oath of Allegiance. Indicates names, origin, date of birth, date and place of arrival. Involves immigrants from many countries; 19th century. Taken from records in the Avoyelles Parish Courthouse in Marksville, Louisiana.

*   *   *

6213
NOVA SCOTIA. PROVINCE. *House of Assembly: Journal and Proceedings, 1865.* Appendix 24, Immigration Agent's Report. Halifax, N.S.: Compton & Co., Printers to the Assembly, 1865.

Lists passengers on the following ships: *Euroclydon,* arriving in Halifax, April 1864, p. 5; *Kedar,* April 1864, p. 5; *Europa,* April 1864, p. 6; *Indian Queen,* June 1864, p. 6. All from Liverpool, England; English or Irish. Age, country of origin, and occupation given.

*   *   *

6219
NUGENT, NELL MARION, compiler. *Cavaliers and Pioneers: A Calendar of Virginia Land Grants, 1623-1800.* Vol.1:1-6. Richmond, [Va.]: Dietz Printing Co., [1929-1931].No others published.

Data on transactions of land grants in the years 1623 to the 1690s. The work was published finally in 1934, no. 6220, but the issue numbers there do not all agree with the numbers published here. No. 1, pp. 1-66; no. 2, pp. 67-105; no. 3, pp. 106-142; no. 4, pp. 143-179; no. 5, pp. 180-227; no. 6, pp.228-272.

*   *   *

6220
NUGENT,NELL MARION. *Cavaliers and Pioneers: Abstracts of Virginia Land Patents and Grants, 1623-1666.* Richmond [Va.]: Dietz Printing Co., 1934. Vol. 1, p. 767. Reprinted by Genealogical Publishing Co., Baltimore, 1963.

Record of 20,000 very early immigrants, with much relevant information. Taken from Patent Books 1 through 5. Title page states, "In 5 volumes," but to 1979 only three had appeared. See item nos. 6221 and 6223 for second and third volumes, published in 1977 and 1979. Issued originally by Nugent in parts between 1929 and 1931; the parts were then largely incorporated in this work, no. 6220. Stewart, item no. 9025, compiled the article, "Ancient Planters [1607]," pages xxviii-xxxiv.

*   *   *

6221
NUGENT, NELL MARION. *Cavaliers and Pioneers: Abstracts of Virginia Land Patents and Grants.* Indexed by Claudia S. Grundman, Vol. 2: 1666-1695. Richmond: Virginia State Library, 1977. 609p.

Abstracts from Patent Books 6 through 8. Chronicle of

immigrants, of freemen, slaves, and indentured servants to colonial Virginia. For other Nugent works, see nos. 6219, 6220 and 6223.

*   *   *

6223
NUGENT, NELL MARION, abstractor. *Cavaliers and Pioneers: Abstracts of Virginia Land Patents and Grants.* Vol. 3: 1695-1732. Richmond: Virginia State Library, 1979. 578p. Indexed.

Abstracts of Virginia Land Office patent books 9 through 14, covering the early decades of the eighteenth century. Includes numerous references to land patented by "French refugees," the Protestants (Huguenots) who fled France after Louis XIV revoked the Edict of Nantes in 1685. This completes the Nugent work: nos. 6219-6221 and 6223. The index is on pages 430-578.

*   *   *

6231-6232
OATES, ADDISON. "Naturalization Records . . . Texas." In *Copper State Bulletin.*
6231
---Vol. 10:3 (Fall 1975), pp. 69-74; vol. 10:4 (Winter 1975), pp. 107-112.
6232
---Vol. 11:1 (Spring 1976), pp. 17-22; vol.11:2-3 (Summer-Fall 1976), pp. 44-49.

Derived from records for the years 1846-1847 at Austin, Guadalupe, and Washington counties, Texas. Vol. 10, no. 3, contains records maintained at Belleville, Austin County; vol. 10, no. 4 contains records maintained at Austin, Guadalupe, and Washington counties. All supply names, origins, date of arrival in America, date of declaration, date of citizenship, name of county and date of arrival in county.

*   *   *

6238
OATES, ADDISON, copier. "Naturalizations Recorded in the Office of the District Clerk, Bastrop County, Texas." In *Copper State Bulletin,* vol. 11:2-3 (Summer-Fall 1976), pp. 50-51.

Name, date of arrival, age, origin, and date of declaration. Mostly involves immigrants from Europe, naturalized between 1851 and 1923.

*   *   *

6248
THE OATH OF ABJURATION, 1715-1716." In *The New-York Historical Society Quarterly Bulletin,* vol. 3:2 (July 1919), pp. 35-40.

From originals in The New York Historical Society. A chronological record kept by the Mayor's Court of the City of New York of the names of 125 foreigners who were naturalized under an act passed by the General Assembly in July 1715. Names only. Also in no. 0714, Boyer, *Ship Passenger Lists, New York and New Jersey,* pp. 162-166; and in no. 9143, Tepper, *New World Immigrants,* vol. 1, pp. 453-458. (Lancour 98/1)

6258

O'BRIEN, MICHAEL J., communicator. "Early Immigrants to Virginia (1623-1666), Collected by George Cabell Greer, Clerk, Virginia State Land Office, from the Records of the Land Office in Richmond." In *The Journal of the American Irish Historical Society,* vol. 13, (1914), pp. 209-213.

> Excerpts of the Irish names from no. 2772, Greer's *Early Virginia Immigrants.* Also published in nos. 6276 and 6280, O'Brien's *The Irish in America* (reprinted by Genealogical Publishing Co., Baltimore, 1965) pp. 43-47 and 158-162; and in no. 9143, Tepper, *New World Immigrants,* vol. 1, pp. 72-76. (Lancour 216A)

*   *   *

6264

O'BRIEN, MICHAEL J. "Grantees of Land in the Colony and State of Virginia, Copied from the County Records of Virginia." In *The Journal of the American Irish Historical Society,* vol. 13 (1913-1914), pp. 214-219.

> Names mostly of Irish origin, 1628-1878. Also in nos. 6276 and 6280, O'Brien, *The Irish in America,* pp. 48-53 and 163-168.

*   *   *

6267

O'BRIEN, MICHAEL J. "Irish Immigrants from English Ports in the Eighteenth Century." In *Irish Settlers in America,* Baltimore: Genealogical Publishing Co., 1979, vol. 1, pp. 525-532.

> Passengers of Irish origin, the names taken from no. 2151, Fothergill. Many settled in Maryland and Virginia. O'Brien's article was also published in *The Journal of the American Irish Historical Society,* vol. 18 (1919), pp. 208-215.

*   *   *

6270

O'BRIEN, MICHAEL J. "Irish Immigrants to New England - Extracts from the Minutes of the Selectmen of the Town of Boston, Mass." In *The Journal of the American Irish Historical Society,* vol. 13 (1914), pp. 177-187.

> Irish immigration between 1716 and 1769, most of it from 1762 through 1769. Also in nos. 6276 and 6280, O'Brien, *The Irish in America,* pp. 11-21 and 126-136, respectively; no. 0702, Boyer, *Ship Passenger Lists, National and New England,* pp. 187-193; and no. 9143, Tepper, *New World Immigrants,* vol. 1, pp. 461-471. (Lancour 66)

*   *   *

6276

O'BRIEN, MICHAEL J. *The Irish in America: Immigration, Land, Probate, Administrations, Birth, Marriage and Burial Records of the Irish in America in and About the Eighteenth Century.* Excerpted from *The Journal of the American Irish Historical Society,* vol. 13, 1914. Baltimore: Genealogical Publishing Co., 1965. 63p.

> Contains a number of articles by O'Brien, notably no. 6270, "Irish Immigrants to New England," pp. 177-187; "Some Interesting Shipping Statistics of the Eighteenth Century," pp.

25-35; no. 6258, "Early Immigrants to Virginia (1623-1666), Collected by George Greer," pp. 43-47; and no. 6264, "Grantees of Lands in the Colony and State of Virginia," pp. 48-53; as well as no. 6280, pp. 126-136, 140-149, 158-162, and 153-168. Throughout, the emphasis is on Irish immigrants in the period 1623-1878.

*   *   *

6280

O'BRIEN, MICHAEL J. *Irish Settlers in America: A Consolidation of Articles from The Journal of the American Irish Historical Society.* 2 vols. Baltimore: Genealogical Publishing Co., 1979, 644p; 638p.

> *The Journal of the American Irish Historical Society* was published from 1898 until 1941, when it was discontinued. Michael O'Brien was a prolific contributor to that *Journal,* and in all he wrote 132 articles, listing 25,000 Irish pioneers and settlers. Some contributions were in the form of passenger lists, five of which are included in this work: nos. 6258, 6264, 6267, 6270, and 6276. See also no. 3280, Hotten.

*   *   *

6286

O'CALLAGHAN, EDMUND BAILEY. "Early Highland Immigration to New York." In *The Historical Magazine and Notes and Queries Concerning the Antiquities, History and Biography of America,* ser. 1, vol. 5 (Oct. 1861), pp. 301-304.

> List of Scottish Highlanders led by Captain Lauchlin Campbell in 1736, and of later parties. Also printed in no. 6640, Patten; no. 0714, Boyer, *Ship Passenger Lists, New York and New Jersey,* pp. 167-173; and in no. 9144, Tepper, *New World Immigrants,* vol. 2, pp. 115-122. (Lancour 100)

*   *   *

6291

O'CALLAGHAN, EDMUND BAILEY. "Early Immigrants to New Netherland, 1657-1664." In *Documentary History of the State of New York.* Albany: Secretary of State, 1850, vol. 3, pp. 33-42; and Weed, Parsons and Co., 1850, vol. 3, pp. 52-63.

> Names of immigrants, with places of origin and ships taken. Also in no. 6520, "Passenger Lists, 1657-1664;" no. 5635, Meyers; and in O'Callaghan's *Lists of Inhabitants of Colonial New York* (Baltimore: Genealogical Publishing Co., 1979, pp. 163-174). See no. 6303. And see index for other references. (Lancour 86)

*   *   *

6296

O'CALLAGHAN, EDMUND BAILEY. "Emigrants to the Colonie on the Delaware River. List of the Colonists and Other Free People Who Have Entered to go to This City's Colonie in New Netherland." In *Documents Relative to the Colonial History of the State of New-York.* Albany [N.Y.]: Weed, Parsons & Co., 1858, vol. 2, p. 183.

> Thirty-eight persons named. Reference is to the year 1662. Also in 0717, Boyer, *Ship Passenger Lists, Pennsylvania and Delaware,* p. 219. (Lancour 197)

6301
O'CALLAGHAN, EDMUND BAILEY. "List of the Palatins Remaining at New York, 1710." In *Documentary History of the State of New-York.* Albany: Secretary of State, 1850, vol. 3, pp. 339-341; and Albany: Weed, Parsons & Co., 1850, vol. 3, pp. 562-565.

> Census of newly arrived immigrants who remained in New York. Much information given. Also in no. 5015, MacWethy; no. 7820, Rupp; and in no. 6303, O'Callaghan's own *Lists of Inhabitants of Colonial New York,* Baltimore, reprinted 1979, pp. 184-187.

*   *   *

6303
O'CALLAGHAN, EDMUND BAILEY. Lists of Inhabitants of Colonial New York, Excerpted from *The Documentary History of the State of New-York.* Indexed by Rosanne Conway. Baltimore: Genealogical Publishing Co., 1979. 351p.

> O'Callaghan's *The Documentary History of the State of New-York* contains a wealth of genealogical material, including lists which can be designated as passenger or related lists: no. 6291, pp. 163-174; no. 6301, pp. 184-187; no. 6311, pp. 188-190; no. 6321, pp. 193-194; no. 6326, pp. 37-39; no. 6341, pp. 191-192. *The Documentary History* was published in quarto and octavo editions, each with different pagination. Lists also in no. 5023, MacWethy.

*   *   *

6306
O'CALLAGHAN, EDMUND BAILEY. "Names of Settlers in Rensselaerswyck from 1630 to 1646; Compiled from the Books of Monthly Wages and Other Mss." In *History of New Netherland; or, New York under the Dutch.* New York: D. Appleton & Co., 1846, vol. 1, pp. 433-441.

> Also in no. 8360, "Settlers in Rensselaerswyck;" no. 0714, **Boyer**, *Ship Passenger Lists, New York and New Jersey,* pp. 38-45; and in no. 9143, Tepper, *New World Immigrants,* vol. 1, pp. 21-31. See index for other references. (Lancour 75)

*   *   *

6311
O'CALLAGHAN, EDMUND BAILEY. "Names of the Palatine Children Apprenticed by Gov. Hunter, 1710-1714." In *Documentary History of the State of New-York.* New York: Secretary of State, 1850, vol. 3, pp. 341-342; and Albany: Weed, Parsons & Co., 1850, vol. 3. pp. 566-567.

> Much information about orphaned and destitute Palatine children. Also in no. 5019, MacWethy; no. 7820, Rupp; and no. 6303, O'Callaghan, pp. 188-190. (Lancour 98)

*   *   *

6316
O'CALLAGHAN, EDMUND BAILEY. "The Names, Trades, &c., of the German Protestants to be Settled at New-York." In *Documents Relative to the Colonial History of New-York.* Albany: Weed, Parsons & Co.,

1855, vol. 5, pp. 52-53.

> Called "The Kocherthal Party." See also no. 5019, MacWethy; no. 7820, Rupp; no. 5990, "Names and Occupations . . . ;" and no. 9800, Williams. For other references to Kocherthal, see index. (Lancour 90C)

*   *   *

6321
O'CALLAGHAN, EDMUND BAILEY. "Palatine Volunteers for the Expedition Against Canada 1711." In *Documentary History of the State of New York,* vol. 3. [Albany, N.Y.]: Weed, Parsons and Co., 1850. (8vo ed., pp. 571-572; 4to ed., pp. 343-344.)
> Also in no. 6303, O'Callaghan, pp. 193-194.

*   *   *

6326
O'CALLAGHAN, EDMUND BAILEY. "The Roll Off Those Who Haue Taken the Oath Off Allegiance in the Kings County in the Province Off New Yorke the 26: 27: 28: 29: and 30th Day Off September in the Third Yeare of His Maytsh Raigne Annoque Domine 1687." In *The Documentary History of the State of New-York.* Albany: Secretary of State, 1850, vol. 1, pp. 429-432; Albany: Weed, Parsons & Co., 1849, vol. 1, pp. 659-661.

> From a manuscript in the Office of the Secretary of the State of New York. Also in no. 7680, *Holland Society Year Book,* 1896; no. 0714, Boyer, *Ship Passenger Lists, New York and New Jersey,* pp. 140-143; no. 9143, Tepper, *New World Immigrants,* vol. 1, pp. 426-433; and no. 6303, O'Callaghan, pp. 37-39. And see index. (Lancour 88)

*   *   *

6331
O'CALLAGHAN, EDMUND BAILEY. "Secretary Van Tienhoven's Answer to the Remonstrance from New Netherland." In *Documents Relative to the Colonial History of the State of New-York.* Albany: Weed, Parsons & Co., 1856, vol. 1, pp. 422-432.

> From a manuscript in the Royal Archives at the Hague, Netherlands. The defense by Cornelis van Tienhoven of the existing system of government in New Netherland, 1650. Has names of eleven colonists who signed the Remonstrance, with other relevent data. Also in no. 3490, Jameson; and in no. 9400, "Van Tienhoven's Answer . . . ." (Lancour 78)

*   *   *

6341
O'CALLAGHAN, EDMUND BAILEY. "Statement of Heads of Palaten Famileys and Number of Persons in Both Towns on ye West Side of Hudsons River. Winter, 1710." In *The Documentary History of the State of New-York.* Albany: Weed, Parsons & Co., 1850, vol. 3, p. 343; and in another ed., vol. 3, pp. 569-570.

> Census of newly arrived Palatines living in the "West Camp," 1710. Also in no. 5023, MacWethy; and in no. 6303, O'Callaghan, pp. 191-192. (Lancour 96)

*   *   *

6351
ODHNER, PROFESSOR C.T. "The Founding of New Sweden, 1637-1642." Translated by Professor G.B. Keen. In *The Pennsylvania Magazine of History and Biography*, vol. 3:3 (1879), pp. 269-284; 3:4 (1879), pp. 395-411.

Some passenger names in the text of the article; not really a passenger list. (No. 3766, Keen's "The Third Swedish Expedition . . ." accompanies Odhner's article.)   (cf. Lancour 193)

*   *   *

6381
OHLHAUSER, BETTY, collector. "Obituaries." In *Clues*, 1974 ed., pp. 35-43.

List of names from obituaries recorded in the denominational publication, *The Baptist Herald* (Forest Park, Illinois), pertaining to Germans from Russia. With the name of the deceased is given the dates of birth and death, date of departure from Russia, and name of spouse. Late 1800s to 1950s.

*   *   *

6401
OLD LAW NATURALIZATION RECORDS PROJECT. MISSISSIPPI. *Index to Naturalization Records, Mississippi Courts, 1798-1906, Prepared by Old Law Naturalization Records Project, Division of Community Service Programs, Works Progress Administration. Typescript.* Jackson, Miss.: Old Law Naturalization Records Project, 1942, 250p.
Reproduced from typewritten copy.

*   *   *

6406
OLIN, KARL. *Chisago Lake-Forsamlingen i Minnesota. Forteckning over de aldsta medlemmarna 1855-1867.* (Skriften Utgivna av Emigrantinstitutet, 2.) Lund, [Sweden]: Etnologiska Institutionen, 1973. 177p.

From the Chisago Lake meeting of the Congregational Church in Minnesota, a list of the oldest members, 1855-1867. Date of arrival in America, age, and family data given. From microfilms produced by the Emigration Institute with the Wallenberg Foundation. Names of members of the oldest Swedish congregation, Taylors Falls, with links to Linneryd, Aalmeboda, Ljunder, Algutsboda, and other places in Kronoberg County, Sweden.

*   *   *

6407
OLSON, VIRGINIA H. "Notes and Sources: Connecticut Loyalists Who went to Canada." In *Connecticut Ancestry*, vol. 17:1 (Sept. 1974), pp. 18-25; vol. 17:2 (Nov. 1974), pp. 51-59.

Most of the British Loyalists left Connecticut shortly after the Revolution. Information condensed from *The New York Genealogical and Biographical Record*, vols. 33-40; and Esther C. Wright, *The Loyalists of New Brunswick*, 1955, repr. 1972.

*   *   *

6411
OLSSON, NILS WILLIAM. *Swedish Passenger Arrivals in New York, 1820-1850.* Chicago: Swedish Pioneer Historical Society, 1967, 392p.

Also published as *Acta Bibliothecae Regiae Stockholmiensis*, 6. List of over 4,000 Swedes, the names derived from an examination of 33,000 ships' manifests documenting arrivals at the port of New York. Full genealogical details of arrivals, with list of place-names and an index of personal names.

*   *   *

6412
OLSSON, NILS WILLIAM. *Swedish Passenger Arrivals in U.S. Ports 1820-1850 (Except New York), with Additions and Corrections to Swedish Passenger Arrivals in New York 1820-1850.* Saint Paul, [Minn.]: North Central Publishing, 1979, 139p.

Complements no. 6411 by Olsson, where he deals only with New York arrivals. Contains additions and corrections to that work. Gives copious genealogical information about the arrivals.

*   *   *

6414
O'NEILL, DENIS P. *History of St. Raymond's Church, Westchester, N.Y.* Westchester, N.Y.: New York City Protectory Print, 1898. 23p.

Acadians from Canada in the 18th century. Page 13 has "the names of French neutrals sent by Gov. Lawrence from Nova Scotia to New York, with their location in the counties of Westchester, Richmond, Suffolk, Kings, and Queens. List of May 6, 1756." Pages 17 and 18 have "August 26, 1756, names of the heads of the French neutral families, the number of their children returned from Georgia and distributed through the counties of Westchester and Orange." They were not allowed to stay in Georgia because Georgia did not permit Catholics to live there. Many names were written phonetically and are therefore spelled incorrectly. Similar data appears in no. 3503, Jehn.

*   *   *

6417
O'RYAN, WILLIAM D. "A New Genealogical Source in the *Boston Pilot.*" In *The Irish Genealogist*, vol. 3:12 (Sept. 1967), pp. 520-524.

Notices in the *Boston Pilot*, placed in an effort to trace emigrant relatives and friends. Usually the notices indicate the date on which the person arrived in America; mostly 1830-1833. All Irish.

*   *   *

6421
OTTO, MRS. OLAF. *Naturalization Oaths of Allegiance Granted in Superior Court, Savannah, Georgia; 1790-1879, Inclusive.* n.p, n.d., 1-5p.

Original records located in the Georgia Historical Society. Only reference to this anywhere noted is in Neagles: *Locating Your Immigrant Ancestor: a Guide to Naturalization Records*

(2nd printing, Logan, Utah: 1975, p. 76.). Names, dates of naturalization, and reference citation to the court record.

*   *   *

6426
OVERTON, JULIA M. "Port of New York Immigrants with Ohio as Their Stated Destination, September 1-25, 1852." In *The Report* (Ohio Genealogical Society), vol. 19:3 (Fall 1979), pp. 105-112.

Lists taken from "Passenger Lists of Vessels Arriving in New York, September 1-25, 1852," National Archives Microfilm M-237, roll #119. Includes only passengers who specified their planned destination as either the state of Ohio, or a given place in Ohio. Name, age, sex, origin, occupation, etc.

*   *   *

6431
OYER, VERLE. "The Oyer Family Comes to America." In *Mennonite Heritage*, vol. 3:3 (Sept. 1976), pp. 25, 30-33, 35.

An article on the Oyer family, with passenger manifest of the ship *Superior*, December 4, 1830, Le Havre, France, to New Orleans, indicating members of the Swiss family, Oyer. Name, age, occupation, and country of origin given. Mostly Swiss Mennonites. Much genealogical background on the emigrants. Page 33 has three ship lists for crossings between 1831 and 1840, with possibly Mennonite or Amish passengers, chiefly from France and Germany.

*   *   *

6441
"PALATINES AND SERVANTS IMPORTED ON THE *KING OF PRUSSIA*." In *The Pennsylvania Genealogical Magazine*, vol. 27:1 (1971), pp. 54-61.

A business record of the firm of James and Drinker, merchants of Philadelphia, giving a list of 75 German and English immigrants (52 Palatines and 23 English servants) imported to Philadelphia in 1764.

*   *   *

6447
PARKIN, NONA. "This is the Story of a Plague Ship." In *The Genealogist's Post*, vol. 4:3 (Mar. 1967), pp. 2-3.

List of 75 persons who died of cholera while en route from Hamburg, Germany, to New York City on the S.S. *Lord Broughton* in 1867.

*   *   *

6450
PARKS, GARY W., transcriber. "The *Atlantic* Sailed the Atlantic in 1834." In *The New York Genealogical and Biographical Record*, vol. 111:2 (April 1980), pp. 93-94.

Taken from a file marked thus: Passenger Lists of Vessels Arriving in New York 1820-1897, microcopy no. M-237, roll #22, February 14-May 20, 1834. Lists 73 British passengers who landed in New York on May 19, 1834. Lancour no. 251 (our no. 8520) reprints a photostat of this manifest as published in *The Story of Sloane's* (New York: W. & J.

Sloane, 1950, p. 9). The *Atlantic* originated in Aberdeen, Scotland, and the founder of Sloane's was on board for this crossing.

*   *   *

6454
PARKS, GARY W. "Harford County, Maryland, Declarations of Oath and Naturalizations, 1830-1839 & 1857-1864." In *Maryland Magazine of Genealogy*, vol. 3:1 (Spring 1980), pp. 11-27.

From the Circuit Court Minutes in the Harford County Courthouse, Bel Air, Maryland. Lists 160 petitions of foreigners for either Declaration of Oath or Naturalization. Name, country of origin, age, date of pronunciation of the oath or naturalization, page reference in the court record. From Europe, with a preponderance from Ireland.

*   *   *

6460
"A PARTIAL LIST OF THE FAMILIES WHO ARRIVED AT PHILADELPHIA Between 1682 and 1687. With the Dates of Their Arrival." In *The Pennsylvania Magazine of History and Biography*, vol. 8:3 (July 1884), pp. 328-340.

From a manuscript in the Historical Society of Philadelphia. Also in no. 2313; Futhey & Cope; and in no. 9120, Tepper, *Emigrants to Pennsylvania*, pp. 6-18. (Lancour 124)

*   *   *

6463
"A PARTIAL LIST OF THE FAMILIES WHO RESIDED IN BUCKS COUNTY, Pennsylvania, Prior to 1687, with the Date of Their Arrival." In *The Pennsylvania Magazine of History and Biography*, vol. 9:3 (July 1885), pp. 223-233.

Compared, corrected, and retranscribed by Hannah Benner Roach, in no. 8370, Sheppard, *Passengers and Ships Prior to 1684*, pp. 159-175. Also in no. 9120, Tepper, *Emigrants to Pennsylvania*, pp. 19-29; and no. 0428, Battle. (Lancour 117A)

*   *   *

6468
"PASSENGER LIST . . . AMERICAN SHIP *MECHANIC* OF BALTIMORE . . . Sailed from Dublin, Ire., to Baltimore, Md., 28 May 1804." In *Genealogical Reference Builders Newsletter*, vol. 1:2 (Feb. 1967), p. 5.

Name, age, and origin of each passenger.

*   *   *

6478
"A PASSENGER LIST OF MENNONITE IMMIGRANTS from Russia in 1878." Edited by Harold S. Bender. In *The Mennonite Quarterly Review*, vol. 15:4 (Oct. 1941), pp. 263-276.

From a document in the Mennonite Historical Library at Goshen College, Indiana. Lists steerage passengers on the

North German Lloyd Steamer *Strassburg* from Bremen to New York, June 18, 1878. Gives place of origin and intended place of settlement, usually Kansas, Nebraska, Minnesota, or Dakota. Also in no. 9144, Tepper, *New World Immigrants*, vol. 2, pp. 514-527.   (Lancour 262)

* * *

6494

"PASSENGER LIST OF THE *ANN*." In *Georgia Pioneers Genealogical Magazine*, vol. 2:4 (Nov. 1965), pp. 15-16.

The *Ann* in 1733 brought the first settlers to the site which is now Savannah. Names of family head and members. See also nos. 1312, 1322, Coulter, and no. 3388. "Immigrants from Great Britain . . . ."

* * *

6500

"PASSENGER LIST OF THE SHIP *ELIZABETH*, Which Arrived at Philadelphia in 1819." In *The Pennsylvania Magazine of History and Biography*, vol. 25:2 (1901), pp. 255-258.

From the original in the Historical Society of Pennsylvania. Contains names of 83 emigrants from Amsterdam. Also in no. 9120, Tepper, *Emigrants to Pennsylvania*, pp. 257-260. (Lancour 192)

* * *

6510

"PASSENGER LISTS." In *Heritage Review*, no. 5/6 (June 1973), pp. 39-48.

Germans from Russia, to New York City, 1873. Name, age, sex, and occupation. Possibly researcher Gwen Pritzkau was the copyist.

* * *

6520

"PASSENGER LISTS 1657 TO 1664, from *Documentary History of New-York*, **vol. 3, pages 52-63."** In *Year Book of the Holland Society of New York*, 1896, pp. 141-158.

Also in no. 5635, Meyers; and no. 6291, O'Callaghan. (Lancour 86A)

* * *

6530

[PASSENGER MANIFEST OF THE SHIP *MAN-HATTAN*, 1820.] Manuscript. New York Public Library.

Documents the arrival in New York from Liverpool on August 18, 1820, of 18 passengers. Pages 38 and 39 of Lancour reproduce a photograph of this manifest and of a typed copy of the original. The data is in no. 0714, Boyer, *Ship Passenger Lists, New York and New Jersey*, 213 and 214. (Lancour 106)

* * *

6540

"THE PASSENGERS AND THE COMPACT." (The Mayflower Series of Papers, 2)   In *The Historical Bulletin*, Washington, DC., vol. 4:5 (May 1904), pp. 101-103.

Complete list of 102 persons, noting the 41 who signed the Compact and several not actually on the *Mayflower*. Also in no. 9143, Tepper, *New World Immigrants*, vol. 1, pp. 6-8. For numerous references to the *Mayflower*, see the index. (Lancour 33E)

* * *

6545

"PASSENGERS FOR NEW ENGLAND, March 20, 1635, Bound for New England from Waymouth." In *Genealogical Reference Builders Newsletter*, vol. 3:5 (Sept.-Oct. 1969), pp. 332-334.

Reprinted from no. 0124, Appleton. The Waymouth referred to is an older spelling and corresponds to Weymouth, England.

* * *

6550

"PASSENGERS FOR NEW ENGLAND." In *The New England Historical and Genealogical Register*, vol. 2:4 (Oct. 1848), p. 407.

Passengers on the *Arabella* bound for New England, May 27, 1671. Also in no. 9151, Tepper, *Passengers to America*, p. 463; and in no. 0702, Boyer, *Ship Passenger Lists, National and New England*, p. 183.   (Lancour 59)

* * *

6560

"PASSENGERS FOR NEW ENGLAND." In *The Essex Antiquarian*, vol. 4:9 (Sept. 1900), p. 137.

Passengers on the *Hannah and Elizabeth*, 1679, to Boston. Also in no. 9610, Waters; and in no. 9143, Tepper, *New World Immigrants*, vol. 1, p. 234.   (Lancour 60A)

* * *

6570

"PASSENGERS FOR NEW ENGLAND." In *The Essex Antiquarian*, vol. 11:2 (Apr. 1907), p. 65.

From Essex Registry of Deeds, four emigrants who left London in 1687. Also in no. 0702, Boyer, *Ship Passenger Lists, National and New England*, p. 187; and in no. 9144, Tepper, *New World Immigrants*, vol. 2, p. 531.   (Lancour 62)

* * *

6575

"PASSENGERS FROM IRELAND 1822." In *Irish-American Genealogist*, nos. 8-12 (Annual 1978), pp. 193-198.

Lists Irish arriving in the United States in the year 1822, abstracted from records in the National Archives, Washington, D.C. Name, sex, age, occupation. Continued from no. 6588, "Passengers: Irish . . . 1821."

* * *

6580

"PASSENGERS [FROM SCOTLAND, 1821-1822]."
In *Scottish Genealogical Helper,* no. 6 (Jan. 1976),
pp. 90-97.

Scottish passengers, with names and occupations listed, arriving at various ports. Extracted from shipping lists. Intended
to be continued.

*   *   *

6588

**"PASSENGERS: IRISH ARRIVING IN THE UNITED
STATES 1821 . . . ."** In *Irish Genealogical Helper,* no. 6
(Jan. 1976), pp. 81-83.

Abstracted from records in the National Archives, Washington, D.C. Name, age, sex, and sometimes occupation. The
following year's passengers (1822) are listed in no. 6575.

*   *   *

6600

"PASSENGERS OF THE *MARY AND JOHN,* 1634."
In *The New England Historical and Genealogical Register,* vol. 9:3 (July 1855), pp. 265-268.

In item no. 1672, Drake, pp. 68-71, it is mentioned that the
Hon George Lunt communicated this list. Article includes a
partial list of passengers on the *Hercules,* 1634. Also in no.
9151, Tepper, *Passengers to America,* pp. 73-76; no. 0702,
Boyer, *Ship Passenger Lists, National and New England,* pp.
142-145; no. 0281, Banks; no. 3323, Hunt; and no. 4477,
Kuhns.   (Lancour 45)

*   *   *

6606

"PASSENGERS ON THE SHIP *BEVIS* - 1638." In *The
Second Boat,* vol. 1:1 May 1980), p. 13.

The *Bevis* sailed from Southampton, England, in May 1638,
bound for New England.

*   *   *

6610

"PASSENGERS ON THE *WELCOME.*" In *The Pennsylvania Traveler,* vol. 3:1 (Nov. 1966), p. 4.

A note states "These are the passengers . . . accepted by the
Welcome Society of Philadelphia." For other references to the
Welcome, see index.

*   *   *

6620

**"PASSENGERS, *The ARK & The DOVE, John Curke-
of Crew on The Dove;* Nicholas Perrie-of The Crew on
Dove."** In *The Genealogist's Post,* vol. 3:2 (Feb. 1966),
p. 30.

Names only. For other references to the *Ark* and the *Dove,* see
index.

*   *   *

6630

**"PASSENGERS TO AMERICA: Various Communi-
cations and Sources."** In *The New England Historical
and Genealogical Register,* vol. 30:1 (Jan. 1876), pp.
39-43; vol. 30:4 (Oct. 1876), pp. 459-460; vol. 31:3 (July
1877), pp. 309-312; vol. 32:4 (Oct. 1878), pp. 407-411; vol.
33:3 (July 1879), pp. 307-310; vol. 37:3 (Apr. 1883),
pp. 162-163.

Miscellaneous ship and passenger data, mostly from manu-
scripts in the New England Historic Genealogical Society.
Contributors include Arthur M. Alger, Henry F. Waters, and
John S.H. Fogg. Title varies: "Passengers and Vessels that
(Have) Arrived in America," is in the later numbers. Also in
no. 9151, Tepper, *Passengers to America,* pp. 128-146; and in
no. 0702, Boyer, *Ship Passenger Lists, National and New
England,* pp. 174-182.   (Lancour 57)

*   *   *

6640

PATTEN, JENNIE M.   "The Argyle Patent and Ac-
companying Documents." In *History of the Somonauk
United Presbyterian Church Near Sandwich, De Kalb
County, Illinois, with Ancestral Lines of the Early
Members.*   Chicago: privately printed for James A.
Patten and Henry J. Patten, 1928, pp. 297-346.

Four lists of immigrants: "A List of ffamilies from the Island of
North Britane" who unsuccessfully petitioned for a grant of
land in Albany County in October 1738, pp. 298-299; "A List
of the Persons Brought from Scotland by Captain Lauchlin
Campbell to settle the Kings Lands at Wood Creek from 1738
to 1740," pp. 326-329; "List of Persons Brought From
Scotland by Capt. Lauchlin Campbell . . . 1738-1740," p.329-
355; and "A Further Account Delivered by Alexander
McNaught[on] and Duncan Reid of Persons Who Did Emigrate with Captain Campbell in 1738, 1739, and 1740 . . .," pp.
336-338. Also printed in part in O'Callaghan, no. 6286.
(Lancour 101)

*   *   *

6650

PATTERSON, REV. GEORGE.   *A History of the
County of Pictou, Nova Scotia.*   Montreal: Dawson
Brothers, 1877, p. 449-465. Reprinted, Pictou, [Nova
Scotia]: Pictou Advocate, 1916, pp. 281-293.

Material in Appendices A through I includes these: List of
grantees . . . 1783; List of . . . families in the district of Pictou;
List of passengers in ship *Hector,* compiled by William
McKenzie about 1837; Dumfries settlers, with places of
settlement; List of Highland emigrants, Halifax in 1784. The
Hector is also listed in no. 5007, McLaren.

*   *   *

6665-6666

**PENNSYLVANIA (COLONY). PROVINCIAL COUN-
CIL,** *Minutes of the Provincial Council of Pennsylvania,
from the Organization to the Termination of the Proprietary Government.* (Colonial Records of Pennsylvania,
vols. 3-4.) Harrisburg, Pa.: State of Pennsylvania, Theo
Fenn & Co.

6665

---Vol. 3, 1840, containing the Proceedings of the Council

from May 31, 1717, to January 23, 1735-1736. Pages 299-301, 303-305, 307, 346-348, 350-351, 390-392, 409-411, 414, 436-437, 440-442, 444, 457, 460-461, 483-490, 498-501, 554-559, 564, 614-616, 642-643, 647. Reprinted by Jo Severns & Co., Philadelphia, in 1852, with different pagination, starting on p. 283 and ending on p. 594.
6666
---Vol. 4, 1851, containing the Proceedings of the Council from February 7, 1735-1736, through October 15, 1745. Pages 58-60, 72-73, 99-100.

> Lists Palatines arriving in Pennsylvania between 1718 and 1742. Note that the first printing of vol. 3, 1840, has been used in no. 2048, Filby and Meyer. Also in no. 0717, Boyer, *Ship Passenger Lists, Pennsylvania and Delaware,* pp.48-86; and printed in part in no. 7820, Rupp.   (Lancour 138)

*   *   *

6680

PENNSYLVANIA (COLONY). SUPREME COURT. *Persons Naturalized in the Province of Pennsylvania [1740-1773].* In *Pennsylvania Archives,* ser. 2, vol. 2, 1876, pp. 345-486 (and in another ed., pp. 293-415). Excerpted and reprinted by Genealogical Publishing Co., Baltimore, 1967. 139p. Index pp. 125-139.

> Lists of foreign Protestants naturalized in Pennsylvania. About 3,000 persons, most of whom were Quakers, with place of residence and date of naturalization. More complete than no. 2564, Giuseppi.   (Lancour 161)

*   *   *

6695

PEREZ, L. "French Immigrants to Louisiana 1796-1800." In *Publications of the Southern History Association,* vol. 11:2 (Mar. 1907), pp. 106-112.

> Covers 99 immigrants to Louisiana from France in 1797. Settlements of Bastrop and Morehouse in the area of Ouachita, Louisiana. Also in no. 0720, Boyer, *Ship Passenger Lists, the South,* pp. 220-222; and in no. 9144, Tepper *New World Immigrants,* vol. 2, pp. 226-232.   (Lancour 242-1)

*   *   *

6710

PERRY, WILLIAM STEVENS, editor. "Liste generalle de tous les francois protestants refugies, etablys dan la paroisse du Roy Guillaume Comte d'Henrico en Virginia, y compris les femmes, enfans, veufes, et orphelins." In *Papers Relating to the History of the Church in Virginia, A.D. 1650-1776.* [Hartford, Conn.]: privately printed, 1870, pp. 193-195.

> A general list of all the French Protestant refugees established in the parish of King William village, Henrico County, Virginia, including women, children, widows, and orphans. These refugees arrived in Virginia about 1714. Also in no. 3640, Jones, and no. 0953, Brock.   (Lancour 226A)

*   *   *

6725

"A PETITION FOR THE RIGHTS OF A NATURAL BORN PERSON in the Province of Maryland . . . 1671

(and 1674)." In *The Genealogist's Post,* vol. 4:12 (Dec. 1967), pp. 17-21.

> Several petitions for naturalization by settlers from various countries, 17th century.

*   *   *

6740

PFALZ, TONI, compiler. "Liste der Apatiner in Amerika." In J. F. Senz, *Apatiner Heimatbuch . . .* (Donauschwaebische Beitraege no. 55), N.P.: Straubling, 1966, pp. 550-554.

> Home-book of the Apatin: rise, accomplishment and decline of the large community of Abthausen/Apatin, being Danube-Swabian, in the Batsch region of Hungary. These Hungarian-Germans, who trace their origins back to an emigration from Swabia in present-day Wuerttemberg to Hungary in the 18th century, emigrated from Hungary to America starting around 1900. The list is an address-list which Pfalz compiled from emigrants who were located in 1966, all with arrival dates between 1900 and the 1930s.

*   *   *

6765

PHILLIPS, JEAN BANNERMAN. "Sutherland Settlers at the Red River." In *Scottish Genealogical Helper,* no. 3, 1974, pp. 30-32.

> Concerns the Lord Selkirk settlers at Red River, Canada, many of whom were natives of Sutherland, Scotland, expelled for various reasons. Names passengers on board the *Prince of Wales,* from Orkney, arriving at Churchill Factory, Canada, late in 1813. Data includes ages and names of districts from which they came. Taken from nos. 0998 and 1000, Bryce. Also in no. 5274, Martin.

*   *   *

6785

"PIONEERS FROM BRAC." In *Balkan and Eastern European American Genealogical and Historical Society,* vol. 2:2 (June 1, 1965), pp. 57-58.

> Extract of persons from the Island of Brac, Dalmatia, known to have come to California before 1914. Name, year of arrival, location, 1891-1913.

*   *   *

6800

"POST-REVOLUTIONARY ARRIVALS at the Port of Philadelphia." In *The Pennsylvania Genealogical Magazine,* vol. 26:3 (1970), pp. 179-182; 26:4 (1970), pp. 263-266.

> Foreign arrivals at the port of Philadelphia, 1785-1788. Unofficial lists, usually thanking ship officers for the safe journey, published in various Pennsylvania newspapers, including the *Pennsylvania Packet and Daily Advertiser* and the *Pennsylvania Gazette.* The ships were from Irish ports, although the passengers were often classified as British.

*   *   *

6815
POTTER, ELISHA R. *Memoir Concerning the French Settlements and French Settlers in the Colony of Rhode Island.* (Rhode Island Historical Tracts, 5) Providence: Sidney S. Rider, 1879. 138p. Reprinted by Genealogical Publishing Co., Baltimore, 1968.

Genealogical notes on French immigrants who made an agreement in 1686 to settle on a plantation in Narragansett County. (Lancour 69)

*   *   *

6830
POULIN, JOSEPH-PHILIPPE. "Premiers colons du debut de la colonie jusqu'en 1700." In *Programme Souvenir, Sixieme Congres de la Societe Genealogique Canadienne Francaise,* October 8-10, 1960, Quebec, pp. 13-22.

First colonists from the beginning of the colony [New France] until 1700. Contains the names of first settlers who came to Quebec, "New France," between 1621 and 1700, the name of spouse and place of marriage, or the name of the parish, sometimes the year of baptism of the first-born child in each family. Page 22 lists land grants, 1650-1655; names of the first settlers at Trois-Rivieres; first colonists of Sorel, 1668-1681.

*   *   *

6860
PRINDLE, PAUL W. "Some Emigrants to America from the Ludwigsburg District, Wuerttemberg, Germany, 1738-1750." In the *New York Genealogical and Biographical Record,* vol. 93:2 (Apr. 1962), pp. 65-66.

Thirteen families who declared their intention to emigrate to Pennsylvania or New York, mentioned in archives of the city council of Poppenweiler, Ludwigsburg district. Also found in no. 9135, Tepper, *Immigrants to the Middle Colonies,* pp. 128-129; and in no. 0702, Boyer, *Ship Passenger Lists, National and New England,* pp. 54-55. (Lancour 17/1)

*   *   *

6875
PRINS, EDWARD. *Descendents of Albertus Christiaan van Raalte, Founder of Holland, Michigan, 1847-1972.* [Holland, Mich.] n.p., 1972.

Passenger list of the barque *Southerner* which carried the founder of Holland, Michigan, a Dutch community in the western part of that state, from Rotterdam to New York in 1846. Names, ages, occupations. Also in nos. 3880, Lucas, and 6895, Prins.

*   *   *

6890
PRINS, EDWARD. *Dutch and German Ships: Passenger Lists 1846-1856.* [Holland, Mich.]: the author, 1972. [250 p.]

Lists German and Dutch passengers, most arriving in New York. Many went to Holland, Michigan, to form part of the Dutch colony there. Names, ages, sometimes occupations, places of origin, and final destinations. Approximately 12,500 persons named.

6895
PRINS, EDWARD, compiler. "Rotterdam Passenger Lists." In *Family Trails,* vol. 3:1 (Spring-Summer 1970), pp. 20-25.

Passengers on the bark, *Southerner,* from Arnhem and Rotterdam in the Netherlands, to New York, Oct. 2 to Nov. 19, 1846. Also the *Antoinette Marie,* which first left Bentheim and then Rotterdam on April 4, 1847, and arrived in New York on May 23, 1847, its passengers finally settling in Graafschap, Michigan; and the *Vesta,* setting sail from Rotterdam on April 7, 1847, arriving at New York on May 27, 1847, its Frisian passengers settling in Vriesland, Michigan. Name, age, occupation, place or country of origin given. Also in no. 6875, Prins; and no. 4880, Lucas.

*   *   *

6904-6905
THE PRISONERS OF THE '45: Edited from the State Papers by Sir Bruce Gordon Seton, Bart. and Jean C. Arnot. (Publications of the Scottish History Society, 3rd. series, vols. 14-15.) Edinburgh: Scottish History Society, 1929, vols. 2-3.

Lists names, prison terms, ultimate disposal of each case, places of origin, ages, (sometimes), notes and authorities. Many are shown as having been transported to the American colonies or the West Indies, all in the late 1740s. Volume 1 discusses the trials of the prisoners, treatment, etc. The '45 was the Jacobite Rebellion, 1745-1746.

*   *   *

6920-6931
PRITZKAU, GWEN B. "Passenger Lists." In *American Historical Society of Germans from Russia, Work Papers.*
6920
---Work Paper, no. 9 (Oct. 1972), pp. 59-62. Hamburg to New York, 1873-1876.
6921
---Work Paper, no. 10 (Dec. 1972), pp. 51-54. Hamburg to New York, 1876; Hamburg to Rio de Janeiro and Paranagua, Brazil, 1878.
6922
---Work Paper, no. 11 (Apr. 1973), pp. 49-55. Hamburg to Paranagua, Brazil, 1878; Hamburg to New York, 1875-1878.
6923
---Work Paper, no. 12 (Aug. 1973), pp. 61-64. Hamburg to New York, 1874-1877.
6924
---Work Paper, no. 13 (Dec. 1973), pp. 50-53. Hamburg to New York, 1874-1875.
6925
---Work Paper, no. 14 (Apr. 1974), pp. 50-56. Hamburg to New York, Paraguay, and Brazil (La Plata), 1874-1877; Hamburg to Buenos Aires, Argentina, 1877.
6926
---Work Paper, no. 15 (Sept. 1974), pp. 49-53. Hamburg to New York, 1884-1898.
6927
---Work Paper, no. 17 (Apr. 1975), pp. 60-65. Hamburg to Baltimore, Boston, and New York, 1877, 1898-1899.

6928
---Work Paper, no. 20 (Spring 1976), pp. 77-80. Hamburg to America and Brazil, 1892, 1900-1901.
6929
---Work Paper, no. 22 (Winter 1976), pp. 44-49. Hamburg to New York, Halifax, South Africa (but many left the ships in London and took passage to America), 1877-1901.
6930
---Work Paper, no. 23 (Spring 1977), pp. 71-81. Hamburg to Paraguay, Rio de Janeiro, and North America, 1876-1880.
6931
---Work Paper, no. 24 (Fall 1977), pp. 78-82. Hamburg to New York and Rio de Janeiro, 1876-1886.

> Lists persons coming from the German colonies in Russia to America. Compiled from the microfilms of the Hamburg shipping lists in the Genealogical Society Library in Salt Lake City. Some originals are indistinct, so some of the names may have been transcribed incorrectly. For some names not transcribed in papers 9 through 14, which cover the years 1873 to 1877 or 1878, see no. 2960, Haynes.

*   *   *

6940-6943
PRITZKAU, GWEN B. "Passenger Lists." In *Heritage Review.*
6940
---No. 12 (Dec. 1975), pp. 41-44. Passengers from Russia, 1892, 1900.
6941
---Nos. 13-14 (Apr. 1976), pp. 55-58. Passengers from Russia to New York, 1900-1901.
6942
---No. 15 (Sept. 1976), pp. 15-18. Passengers from Russia to New York, 1849; from Hamburg to New York, 1872.
6943
---No. 17 (Apr. 1977), pp. 55-61. Passengers from Russia, 1884, 1889, 1901, from Hamburg to New York.

> All originally from Germany before move to Russia then to the United States.

*   *   *

6950-6951
PRITZKAU, GWEN B. "Passenger Lists." In *Heritage Review,* 1979.
6950
---No. 24 (Sept. 1979), pp. 37-41. Bremen to Baltimore, Germans from Russia, 1874-1876.
6951
---No. 25 (Dec. 1979), pp. 37-41. Crossings from Hamburg to New York, Halifax, and South America, 1902-1909. All Germans from Russia.

*   *   *

6954
PRITZKAU, GWEN B. "Passenger Lists." In *Heritage Review* (Germans from Russia Heritage Society), vol. 10:3 (Aug. 1980), pp. 43-46.

> Germans from Russia who came through Hamburg to Halifax, Nova Scotia, and New York, 1902-1903.

7035
PUNCH, TERRENCE M. "Irish Ancestors in the "Lost and Found" of the *Boston Pilot,* January - April 1846." In *The Irish Ancestor,* vol. 9:2 (1977), pp. 79-84.

> Culls 75 advertisements for missing relatives and often includes emigration data. Concerns U.S. immigrants of the 1830s and 1840s.

*   *   *

7050
PUNCH, TERRENCE M. "Irish Deserters at Halifax, Nova Scotia, During the Napoleonic Wars." In *The Irish Ancestor,* vol. 8:1 (1976), pp. 33-35.

> Military deserters, named in a list published April 1805 or 1806.

*   *   *

7058
PUNCH, TERRENCE M. "The Irish in Halifax, Nova Scotia, Before 1830." In *Canadian Genealogist,* vol. 1:3 (1979), pp. 173-180.

> Pages 174 and 175 list persons from Cornwallis's ships, 1749, and the early victualling list for Halifax, 1750. Derived from no. 0800, Akins. Names only.

*   *   *

7065
PUNCH, TERRENCE M. "Irish Repealers at Halifax, Nova Scotia, in 1843." In *The Irish Ancestor,* vol. 10:1 (1978), pp. 6-13.

> List of immigrants who signed for repeal of the Act of Union, 1801, which formed the United Kingdom of Great Britain and Ireland.

*   *   *

7072
PUNCH, TERRENCE M. "Loyalist Refugees, 1778." In *Genealogical Newsletter of the Nova Scotia Historical Society,* no. 23, vol. 2:2 (Spring 1978), p. 50.

> Found in the Public Archives, Nova Scotia, R. G. 1, vol. 369, pp. 416-421, with title, "A list of refugees for receiving rations of provisions, Halifax, 1778, Sept. 5th." Names 87 men, 154 women, and refers to 169 children. (Children's names not given) Total of 130 listed with names only.

*   *   *

7080
PUNCH, TERRENCE M. "The Passengers on the *Polly.*" In *The Irish Ancestor,* vol. 8:2 (1976), pp. 82-84.

> The brig *Polly* arrived in Halifax in the spring of 1799 from either Belfast, Ireland, or Greenock, Scotland.

*   *   *

7088
PUNCH, TERRENCE M. "A Scottish Passenger List,

1803." In *Genealogical Newsletter of the Nova Scotia Historical Society,* no. 23, vol. 2:2 (Spring 1978), p. 51.

Passengers from Perthshire who sailed from Port Glasgow in Scotland on the vessel *Commerce,* August 10, 1803, for Pictou, Nova Scotia. Taken from the Melville Papers: Scotland, 1784-1807, MS. 1053, ff. 104-109, in the National Library of Scotland. Name, age, occupation, with children listed. Includes 70 persons.

*   *   *

7095-7098
PUNCH, TERRENCE M. "Some Irish Immigrant Weddings in Nova Scotia." In *The Irish Ancestor.*
7095
---Vol. 6:2 (1974), pp. 101-112. Covers 1801-1817.
7096
---Vol. 7:1 (1975), pp. 39-54; vol. 7:2 (1975), pp. 104-120. Covers 1818-1830.
7097
---Vol. 8:1 (1976), pp. 53-69; vol. 8:2 (1976), pp. 124-139. Covers 1831-1840.
7098
---Vol. 9:2 (1977), pp. 133-146. Covers 1841-1845.

Extracts from the marriage records at St. Peter's Church in Halifax, Nova Scotia (now known as St. Mary's Basilica). Few precise dates of immigration but all were from Ireland at the end of the 18th century or early in the 19th century. Many settled on the Eastern seaboard, especially in Boston. No later instalments published up to January 1980.

*   *   *

7111
PUTNAM, EBEN. "Two Early Passenger Lists, 1635-1637." In *The New England Historical and Genealogical Register,* vol. 75:3 (July 1921), pp. 217-226.

Passengers on the *Hercules* of Sandwich. Additions and corrections to no. 0378, Bartlett. Also in no. 0702, Boyer, *Ship Passenger Lists, National and New England,* pp. 145-148; and in no. 9151, Tepper, *Passengers to America,* pp. 111-119. (Lancour 46)

*   *   *

7134
RAGSDALE, FLOYD. "Scotch Immigrants in Knox County, Illinois." In *Knox County Genealogical Society Quarterly,* vol. 2:1 (Jan. 1974), pp. 9-15.

Taken from Galesburg newspaper, *The Republican Register,* vol. 55, no. 232, September 30, 1925, "Scotch Came Here Early." Names, with dates of arrival and county of origin in Scotland. Dates covered: 1828-1909.

*   *   *

7141
RASKOB, JOHN JACOB. "The *Ark* and the *Dove.* A Description of the Settlement of the Colony of Maryland, as Found in the State House at Annapolis, Md." In *Raskob-Green Record Book,* Archmere, Claymont, Delaware: privately printed, 1921, pp. 95-97. Reprinted by Tradition Press, Hatboro, Pa., 1967.

Passengers with Governor Leonard Calvert, 1633, who arrived in 1634. For other references to these ships, see the index. (Lancour 198)

*   *   *

7156-7162
RASMUSSEN, LOUIS J. *San Francisco Ship Passenger Lists.* Colma, Calif.: the author.
7156
---Vol. 1. 1965. Reprinted by Genealogical Publishing Co., Baltimore, 1978. 273 p. Covers 1850-1864, but mostly the year 1850.
7158
---Vol. 2. 1966. 384p. 2nd printing, 1969. Covers April 6, 1850-November 4, 1851.
7160
---Vol. 3. 1967. 448p. Covers November 7, 1851 - June 17, 1852. Includes addenda to vol. 1, corrections to vols. 1 and 2.
7162
---Vol. 4. 1970. 471p. Covers June 17, 1852 -January 6, 1853. Includes addenda to vols. 1-3.

Names of passengers arriving through the port of San Francisco in mid-nineteenth century. San Francisco was the main port of entry in settlement of the West, and it is probable that many immigrants had already landed at New York and then taken ship to San Francisco, particularly in the Gold Rush days. Passengers came from all over the world, and vessels often called in other ports en route, embarking extra passengers. San Francisco ship passenger lists were formerly printed in the *San Francisco Genealogical Bulletin* (later *San Francisco Historic Record and Genealogy Bulletin),* 1963-1965. See nos. 7875-7891.

*   *   *

7171
RATH, GEORGE. *The Black Sea Germans in the Dakotas.* Freeman, S. Dak.: Pine Hill Press, 1977, 436p.

Lists passengers in several ships, mostly from Odessa, Russia, to Germany, embarking at Hamburg, with some transferring at Liverpool, England, for New York, arriving 1872 or 1873. All then proceeded to the Dakotas. Provides name, sex, age of each. There are also family histories, with dates of arrival and settlement. Lists are pp. 60-66, 82-84, 385-393, 403-425.

*   *   *

7177
RAVEN, JOHN J. "Families in Fressingfield, Eng., 1836, Wishing to Emigrate to America." In *The New England Historical and Genealogical Register,* vol. 49:3 (July 1895), pp. 337-338.

Fressingfield is in Suffolk, in the eastern part of England. There, 35 passengers were loaned money by the parish for the purpose of emigrating to America. Names and ages only. Also in no. 9151, Tepper, *Passengers to America,* pp. 478-479. (Lancour 253)

*   *   *

7192
RAVENEL, DANIEL, compiler. *"Liste des Francois et Suisses" from an Old Manuscript List of French and Swiss Protestants Settled in Charleston, on the Santee and at the Orange Quarter in Carolina Who Desired Naturalization.* Prepared probably about 1695 or 1696. New York: Knickerbocker Press, 1888. 77p. Reprinted by Genealogical Publishing Co., Baltimore, 1968.

Enumerates 154 French and Swiss refugees who declared themselves willing to be naturalized in anticipation of the Act of Naturalization of 1696. List, pp. 44-68. Originally published in the *Southern Intelligencer,* Charleston, S.C., June 1822. (Lancour 234)

*   *   *

7207
"RECORD OF INDENTURES OF INDIVIDUALS BOUND OUT as Apprentices, Servants, Etc. and of German and Other Redemptioners in the Office of the Mayor of the City of Philadelphia, October 3, 1771, to October 5, 1773." In *The Pennsylvania-German Society Proceedings and Addresses,* vol. 16 (1905), Lancaster, Pa.: 1907. 325p. Reprinted with added index by Genealogical Publishing Co., Baltimore, 1973. 364p.

Original volume, from which this was taken, is among the holdings of The American Philosophical Society in Philadelphia. Much information on persons indentured. Printed in part in nos. 7222-7223.   (Lancour 184)

*   *   *

7222-7223
"RECORD OF SERVANTS AND APPRENTICES BOUND and Assigned before Hon. John Gibson, Mayor of Philadelphia, December 5th, 1772-May 21, 1773." In *The Pennsylvania Magazine of History and Biography.*
7222
---Vol. 33:4 (1909),pp. 475-491.
7223
---Vol. 34:1 (1910), pp. 99-121; vol. 34:2 (1910), pp. 213-228.

Copied from Record Book in the Historical Society of Pennsylvania. Also in no. 7207, "Record of Indentures . . ." and no. 9120, Tepper, *Emigrants to Pennsylvania,* pp. 180-235. (Lancour 185)

*   *   *

7237
REDSTONE, VINCENT B. "American Traders, Planters and Settlers: Notes Drawn from Original Papers, 1628-1640." In *The Genealogical Magazine* (Boston), vol. 3 (1916), pp. 139-144.

Describes expeditions from England to the New World, 1628-1640. Includes three short lists. Also in no. 0702, Boyer, *Ship Passenger Lists, National and New England,* pp. 30-33, and in no. 9143, Tepper, *New World Immigrants,* vol. 1, pp. 77-82. (Lancour 9)

*   *   *

7252
REIMER, GEORG. "Schleswig-Holsteiner im Staate Iowa, USA." In *Mitteilungen der Gesellschaft fuer Schleswig-Holsteinische Familienforschung und Wappenkunde,* 1958, Heft 9 (Oct.) pp. 120-121.

People from Schleswig-Holstein in the state of Iowa, U.S.A. An alphabetical listing of 37 emigrants from Schleswig-Holstein, selected by Reimer from Joseph Eiboeck's *Die Deutschen von Iowa und deren Errungenschaften . . .,* Des Moines, Iowa, 1900. (Germans in Iowa and their achievements.) Most are listed with birthdate, place of origin, and place of settlement in Iowa. Some entries include additional biographical data.

*   *   *

7267
REINCKE, ABRAHAM. "A Register of Members of the Moravian Church . . . 1727-1754." Translated by W. C. Reichel. In *Transactions of the Moravian Historical Society,* vol. 1 (1876), pp. 283-426.

Members in the United States and abroad. Serves as a list of those who came to America and some who lived elsewhere.

*   *   *

7282
REINDERS, ALICE. "Delaware Settlers, 1693." In *National Genealogical Society Quarterly,* vol. 53:3 (Sept. 1965), pp. 205-206.

A list of Swedish families in Delaware or "New Sweden," in 1693, with the number of persons in each family. First published in no. 3263, Holm, and later in no. 1999, Ferris. See also nos. 0040-41, Acrelius.

*   *   *

7312
REMBE, HEINRICH. "Emigration Materials from Lambsheim in the Palatinate." Translated and edited by Don Yoder. In *Pennsylvania Folklife,* vol. 23:2 (Winter 1973-74), pp. 40-48.

Concerns the 18th and 19th centuries. Much is taken from Rembe's *Lambsheim: die Familien von 1547 bis 1800.* See no. 7314.

*   *   *

7314
REMBE, HEINRICH. *Lambsheim: Die Familien von 1547 bis 1800—fuer Maxdorf bis 1830—mit Angaben aus Weisenheim a.S., Eyersheim, und Ormsheim.* Kaiserslautern, Germany: Heimatstelle Pfalz, 1971. 297 p.

Lambsheim: families from 1547 to 1800; Maxdorf to 1830; and data on Weisenheim am Sand, Eyersheim, and Ormsheim. Pages 22-23 cover about 40 emigrants from Lambsheim to Pennsylvania in the years 1709 to 1764. Names of heads of emigrant groups or of individuals traveling alone; a few ages, occupations, dates of emigration, some ships' names.

*   *   *

7318

RENNER, EDNA, and **LAVINA WALTON.** *Naturalization and Citizenship: Partial List of Applications for Citizenship,* Schuyler County, Illinois. [Rushville, Ill.: Schuyler County Historical Musuem, ca. 1978-1979] 12p.

> Involves immigrants from Europe, including Great Britain. Covers the years 1828-1886. Prepared for the Schuyler-Brown Historical and Genealogical Society.

*   *   *

7328

"RETURN OF LOYALISTS AND DISCHARGED SOLDIERS Embarked on Board the Provincial Vessels for Chaleur Bay, Quebec, 9th June 1784." In *Report on Canadian Archives* by Douglas Brymner, Archivist, 1891. Ottawa: printed by S.E. Dawson, 1892, pp. 18-20.

> Loyalists were embarked aboard the brigs *St. Peter, Liberty,* and *Polly.* The data also appear in Canadian Archives, Series B, vol. 168, p. 30.

*   *   *

7343

REVILL, JANIE. *A Compilation of the Original Lists of Protestant Immigrants to South Carolina, 1763-1773.* Columbia [S.C.]: State Company, 1939. 163p. Reprinted by Genealogical Publishing Co., Baltimore, 1968.

> From the *Journals of the Council* of the Colony of South Carolina. Names and land allotments under the Bounty Act of 1761. (Lancour 238)

*   *   *

7355

REY, TIMOTHY. "Passenger List of *Catherine* (August 14 - September 19, 1850), Excerpted from 'Paulus den Bleyker: Type and Prototype." In *Michigan Heritage,* vol. 2:1 (Autumn 1960), pp. 15-16.

> Names 29 passengers from Amsterdam to New York, 1850, with much information. Ultimate destination, Kalamazoo, Michigan. Also in no. 9144, Tepper, *New World Immigrants,* vol. 2, pp. 512-513. (Lancour 259, under "Passenger List ...")

*   *   *

7365

RICE, BERNARDINE. "The Irish in Texas. In *Genealogical Reference Builders Newsletter,* vol. 1:1 (Jan. 1967), p. 3.

> Discusses Irish settlers who arrived in 1829 at the colony of San Patricio in Texas. See also Rountree, nos. 7740 and 7745.

*   *   *

7375

RICHARDSON, HESTER DORSEY. "An Inaccurate List of the Adventurers." In *Side-Lights on Maryland History* .... Baltimore: Williams and Wilkins, 1913, vol. 1, pp. 8-15, 411-418. Reprinted (2 vols. in 1) by Tidewater Publishers, Cambridge, Md., 1967, and by Genealogical

Publishing Co., Baltimore, 1967.

> Tells of the first Maryland adventurers who arrived in Maryland waters on the *Ark* and the *Dove,* March 25, 1633, landing on St. Clements Island, March 28, 1634. The names on pp. 411-418 are inaccurate. For other references to the *Ark* and the *Dove,* see the index. (Lancour 198D)

*   *   *

7385

RICHARDSON, HESTER DORSEY. [Names of Those Who Were Sent Over as King's Rebels in the Ship *Friendship* of Belfast, August 20, 1716, to Maryland.] In *Side-Lights on Maryland History* .... Baltimore: Williams & Wilkins, 1913, vol. 1, pp. 214-215. Reprinted (2 vols. in 1) by Tidewater Publishers, Cambridge, Md., 1967, and by Genealogical Publishing Co., Baltimore, 1967.

> Lists 80 prisoners, mostly Scottish. Also in no. 7983, Scharf. (Lancour 202A)

*   *   *

7395

RICHARDSON, HESTER DORSEY. "[Second Shipload of Scottish Rebels Sent to Maryland, October 18, 1716, on the *Good Speed.*]" In *Side-Lights on Maryland History* .... Baltimore: William & Wilkins, 1913, vol. 1, p. 215. Reprinted (2 vols. in 1) by Tidewater Publishers, Cambridge, Md., 1967; and by Genealogical Publishing Co., Baltimore, 1967.

> Fifty-five Scottish prisoners on the *Good Speed.* Also in no. 7990, Scharf. (Lancour 203A)

*   *   *

7405

RICHTER, HANS. "Texasauswanderung aus Rheinhessen." In *Volk und Scholle,* Jahrgang 7:11 (1929), pp. 346-349.

> Emigration to Texas from Rhenish Hesse. From the 1845 report of the Mayor of Buedesheim to the District Council in Bingen, stored in the Hessian State Archives [Germany]. Names about 15 emigrants of approximately 70 who came from Buedesheim to Texas in 1845. Voyage was from Antwerp to Galveston.

*   *   *

7415

RIDER, SIDNEY SMITH. *The History of Denization and Naturalization in the Colony of Rhode Island, 1636-1790.* n.p.: 1905? 14p.

> A general account of the Rhode Island law of naturalization before the adoption by Rhode Island of the Constitution of the United States in 1790. Indicates that about a dozen foreigners were naturalized between 1701 and 1766. Also in no. 0702, Boyer, *Ship Passenger Lists, National and New England,* pp. 197-200. (Lancour 70)

*   *   *

7422
RIEDEL, GERHARD. "Schlesische Auswanderer im 19. Jahrhundert." In *Schlesische Rundschau* [Wangen/ Allgaeu, Germany], Jahrgang 8:20 (July 15, 1956), p. 7.

Silesian emigrants in the 19th century. Data on three families, 20 emigrants, from villages in Silesia to America, 1839-1843. Names of parents, including mothers' maiden names, the number of children emigrating with each couple, villages of origin, year of emigration, some family data. Supposed to have been part of the "Old Luterhan" wave of emigration from Silesia.

*   *   *

7430
RIEDER, MILTON P., JR., and **NORMA GAUDET RIEDER,** compilers. *The Acadian Exiles in the American Colonies, 1755-1768.* Metairie [La.]: the compilers, 1977. 54p.

Acadians banished from their homes in the 18th century. Fourteen transports from Minas Basin, Nova Scotia, carried 1,600 Acadians from Grand Pre and 1,300 from Pisquid and Cobequid. Another 1,900 Acadians on two transports from Beau Bassin joined the fleet in Nova Scotia. Some landed in Boston, Connecticut, New York, Pennsylvania, Maryland, and Georgia; 1,000 in the Carolinas. Names, including names of wives and other family data, for most. See also no. 3500, Jehn.

*   *   *

7445
RIEDER, MILTON P., and **NORMA GAUDET RIEDER,** compilers and editors. *The Crew and Passenger Registration Lists of the Seven Acadian Expeditions of 1785; a Listing by Family Groups of the Refugee Acadians Who Migrated from France to Spanish Louisiana in 1785.* Metairie, La.: the compilers, 1965, 103 leaves.

Gives names, ages, occupations, indication of relationships. Covers about 1,000 passengers in seven ships arriving in New Orleans between July 29 and December 12, 1785.

*   *   *

7460-7461
RIEDER, MILTON P., JR., and **NORMA GAUDET RIEDER,** compilers. *New Orleans Ship Lists.*
7460
---Vol. 1: 1820-1821. Metairie, La.: the compilers, 1966, 93p.
7461
---Vol. 2: 1822-1823. Metairie, La.: the compilers, 1968, 105p.

Passengers on many ships, mostly from Europe. Includes many Americans from other American ports. Taken from copies in the U.S. National Archives, compared against abstracts maintained at New Orleans Public Library and customs lists in the Louisiana State Museum Library, New Orleans.

*   *   *

7495
RIMPAU, HANS HELMUTH. "The 'Brunswickers' in Nordamerika, 1776-1783." Translated by Claus and Ina Rimpau. In *Archiv fuer Sippenkunde,* no. 43 (Aug. 1971), pp. 204-219; no. 44 (Nov. 1971), pp. 293-308; no. 45 (Feb. 1972), pp. 346-355.

Introduction in English, French, and German. Material taken from original in state archives, Wolfenbuettel, Germany, 38B Alt. No. 260. Name; place of birth; age, time, and place of leaving; but data is not always accurate. Item no. 8560, Smith's *Brunswick Deserter Immigrants* is taken from Rimpau.

*   *   *

7507
RIMPAU, HANS HELMUTH. "Passagier-Listen von Einwanderer-Schiffen nach den USA." In *Genealogie,* vol. 7:5 (Sept.-Oct. 1964), pp. 280-284; 7:6 (Nov.-Dec. 1964), p. 354.

Passenger list of the bark *Friedrich Lucas* (registered in Germany as the *Friedrich Jacob),* departed Bremerhaven November 8, 1842, and arrived at New Orleans January 1, 1843. Original list stored in the U.S. National Archives, D.C. Names 185 passengers, most from northwest Germany, specifying age, place of origin, some occupations, and religion. Corrections are given in vol. 7:6, p. 354.

*   *   *

7524
RITTER, ERNST. "Auswanderungen aus dem Rheinland im 19. Jahrhundert." In *Pfaelzisch-Rheinische Familienkunde* (Mitteilungen zur Wanderungsgeschichte der Pfaelzer, no. 3, 1979), vol. 9:6 (1979), pp. 331-340.

Emigration from the Rhineland in the 19th century. Involves about 300 emigrants in the late 1700s and up to 1860. Gives names, places of origin, some family data, approximate year of emigration. Accompanying wives and children are seldom named. Taken from the official gazettes *(Amtsblaetter)* of Speyer, Germany, for 1818, and of Koblentz, Germany, for various years spanning 1824-1860.

*   *   *

7537
RITZ, ALBRECHT. "Auswanderung." In *Gestalten und Ereignisse aus Beihingen am Neckar.* Ludwigsburg [Germany]: Buchdruckerei Otto Eichhorn, 1939, pp. 238-258.

Names emigrants from Beihingen on the Neckar (River). Pages 238-246 list departures prior to about 1850; pages 247-258 cover later movement to about 1895. Information includes date of birth, port, and year of arrival. Also in no. 0702, Boyer, *Ship Passenger Lists, National and New England,* pp. 46-52. (Lancour 16-1)

*   *   *

7552
RITZ, ALBRECHT. "Von der Auswanderung aus dem Heidenheimer Gebiet." In *Nattheim und Oggenhausen im Kranz der Nachbargemeinden.* Heidenheim [Ger-

many]: Heidenheimer Verlagsanstalt, 1951, pp. 231-245.

> Record of emigrants from Nattheim, Oggenhausen, and **Fleinheim. Spans the years 1793 to the 1920s, but mostly 1850s to 1880s**. Emigrants prior to 1825 are also listed in no. 0702, Boyer, *Ship Passenger Lists, National and New England,* pp. 56-57. (Lancour 19-1)

*   *   *

7570
ROACH, HANNAH BENNER. "The First Purchasers of Pennsylvania." In Sheppard, Walter Lee, Jr., *Passengers and Ships Prior to 1684.* Baltimore: Genealogical Publishing Co., 1970, pp. 195-208.

> "An accompt of the Land in Pennsylvania granted by William Penn, Esqr., Sole Propietary Governour of that Province, to several purchasors within the Kingdom of England . . . ." Supplies the names of those who were granted land in Pennsylvania by Penn, 1681-1682. Also published in no. 2979, Hazard; and no. 0032, "An Account of the lands . . . ," from *Pennsylvania Archives.*

*   *   *

7585
ROACH, HANNAH BENNER. "The Philadelphia and Bucks County Registers of Arrivals, Compared, Corrected and Re-Transcribed." In Sheppard, Walter Lee, Jr., *Passengers and Ships Prior to 1684.* Baltimore: Genealogical Publishing Co., 1970, pp. 159-175.

> Retranscription of no. 2313, Futhey & Cope, *History of Chester County, Pennsylvania;* no. 0428, Battle, *History of Bucks County, Pennsylvania;* and no. 6463, "A Partial List of the Families Who Resided in Bucks County . . . ."

*   *   *

7600
ROACH, HANNAH BENNER. "Post-Revolutionary Arrivals in the Delaware River." In *The Pennsylvania Genealogical Magazine,* vol. 28:2 (1973), pp. 81-85.

> Irish immigrants to New Castle, Delaware, in 1789, who expressed their thanks for a safe voyage. Printed first in the *Pennsylvania Packet and Daily Advertiser.*

*   *   *

7610
ROBERTS, CHARLES R. "Germanic Immigrants Named in Early Pennsylvania Ship Lists." In *The Pennsylvania German Society Proceedings and Addresses,* vol. 39 (1928), 20p.

> A separate offprint in volume 39. Given as a speech in 1924 and containing excerpts of names from various lists preserved in the State Library (Department of Public Records) in Harrisburg. Also in no. 9144, Tepper, *New World Immigrants,* vol. 2, pp. 1-16; and in no. 0717, Boyer, *Ship Passenger Lists, Pennsylvania and Delaware,* pp. 116-124. (Lancour 143)

*   *   *

7620
ROBERTSON, LOIS, contributor. "Ship List, North German Bark *Goeshe,* 3 Jul 1868." In *Midwest Genea-*

logical Register, vol. 12:1 (June 1977), pp. 44-45.

> Lists 51 passengers from Bremen, Germany, to New York, with full data on each emigrant. Found in U.S. National Archives microfilm M-237, roll 297.

*   *   *

7630
ROBINSON, MRS. EUNICE. "List of Second Cabin Passengers per R.M.S. *Empress of Ireland* . . . from Liverpool to St. John, N.B., April 1907." In *The British Columbia Genealogist,* vol. 3:5 (Nov. 1974), pp. 5-8.

> Gives names only; all British passengers to Canada.

*   *   *

7650
ROEMER, HERMANN. *Die Auswanderung aus Markgroeningen, Kreis Ludwigsburg: im Zusammenhang der wuerttembergischen Auswanderung sippenkundlich dargestellt.* (Deutsches Auslandsinstitut, Forschungsstelle Schwaben im Ausland, vol. 1.) Ludwigsburg [Germany]: Eichhorn Verlag Lothar Kallenberg, 1941. 207p.

> Emigration from Markgroeningen, district of Ludwigsburg, presented from a genealogical viewpoint in the context of emigration from Wuerttemberg. Concerns 2,000 inhabitants of Markgroeningen from the 1770s into the 1920s with their announced destinations in many parts of America and elsewhere. Supplies names, most birthdates, places of origin, occupations, much family information on many of them, date of emigration, and city or country of destination. Arranged alphabetically by surname.

*   *   *

7660
ROGERS, ALBERT R. *The Historic Voyage of the Arbella 1630; Official Souvenir of the Arbella, on Exhibition, Charles River Basin, Boston, 1930, under the Auspices of the Massachusetts Bay Tercentenary, Inc.* Boston: Arbella Co., [1930]. 32p.

> "Believed passengers in the *Arbella,*" by C.J. Bolton, p. 15; "Conjectural passengers," p. 17. Also in no. 0702, Boyer, *Ship Passenger Lists, National and New England,* pp. 139-140. (Lancour 39 and 40)

*   *   *

7680
"THE ROLL OFF THOSE WHO HAVE TAKEN THE OATH OF ALLEGIANCE in the Kings County in the Province off New Yorke the 26: 27: 28: 29: and 30th Day off September in the Third Yeare off His Magtsh Raigne Annoque Domine 1687." In *Year Book of the Holland Society of New York,* 1896, pp. 159-166.

> Also in no. 6326, O'Callaghan. (Lancour 88A)

*   *   *

7690

"ROLLE DE HOMES ENVOIES A MONTREAL en l'annee 1653 et de ce qui a este acorde de gages a chacun d'eux." In *Rapport de l'Archiviste de la Province de Quebec,* 1920-1921, pp. 314-320. Quebec: Proulx, 1921. Also in *The Canadian Antiquarian and Numismatic Journal,* 3rd ser., vol. 10 (Oct. 1913), pp. 183-191.

A list of men sent to Montreal in 1653 and the wages accorded to each.

*   *   *

7700

ROSDAIL, JESSE H. "The Original Sloopers." In *Sloopers, Their Ancestry and Posterity, the Story of the People on the Norwegian Mayflower, the Sloop "Restoration," 1825, New York.* Broadview, [Ill.?]: Norwegian Slooper Society of America, 1961, pp. 605-606.

Official list has never been found. Research seems to confirm 50 names out of the traditional 53 compiled by Anderson, no. 0115. See also no. 0714, Boyer, p. 214; no. 0117, Anderson; no. 0588, Blegen.

*   *   *

7720

ROTH, MRS. BERTHA, contributor. "Immigrants from Kratzka, Russia, Who Settled in Russell County, Kansas." In *Clues,* 1977, pp. 49-51.

Taken from an article in the March 1, 1948, edition of *The Russell Record.* Lists 73 persons from Russia who arrived in Russell in October 1876. Wives and children listed. Maiden name of each wife is given.

*   *   *

7730

ROTH, ERNST. "Auswanderung aus dem Dillkreis." In *Volk und Scholle,* part 1 (Jan.-Mar. 1942), pp. 11-15.

Emigration from the Dill district of Germany, from a chronicle kept by the magistrate of the village of Sechshelden and other, unnamed sources, covering 200 departures in the years 1850-1885. Names individuals and heads of emigrant groups, indicating the number of persons in the group, some places of origin, and the dates of emigration.

*   *   *

7740

ROUNTREE, JOSEPH G., II. *History of Bee County, Texas.* Beeville, Tex.: the author, 1960, pp. 8-10.

Pages 8 and 9 carry a manifest naming a group of families who, in 1829, arrived at the port of Aranzazu, now known as Copano, Texas, aboard the brig *New Packet* from New York. They intended to become colonists on the Nueces River in Texas. Also in no. 7745, Rountree. Pages 9 and 10 mention passengers who arrived at the port of Matagorda, Texas, aboard the *Albion* from New York. They were Irish families, also intending to become colonists on the Nueces River, 1829. See also no. 7365, Rice.

*   *   *

7745

ROUNTREE, JOSEPH G., II. "Manifest of the Group of Families Who Have Presented Themselves at the Port of Aranzazu, Now Known as Copano, Aboard the Brig, *New Packet,* Arriving from New York in 1829." In *Our Heritage,* vol. 15:1 (Oct. 1973), p. 117.

Fourteen Irish colonists with children, settling in Texas. In Rountree, no. 7740, as well.

*   *   *

7790

RUBINCAM, MILTON. "Passenger List of the Steamer *Fah Kee.*" In *National Genealogical Society Quarterly,* vol. 51:1 (Mar. 1963), p.60.

From Santiago, Cuba, to New York on March 29, 1866. Contained in U.S. National Archives microfilm. Includes genealogical information on some of the 10 passengers listed.

*   *   *

7800-7801

RUBIO Y MORENO, LUIS. *Passajeros a Indias, Catalogo Metodologico de las Informaciones y licencias de los que Alli Pasaron, Existentes en el Archivo General de Indias -Siglo Primero de la Colonizacion de America, 1492-1592.* Madrid, Spain: Compania Ibero-Americana de Publicaciones.

7800

---Vol. 1, 447p. 1930? *Coleccion de Documentos Ineditos para la Historia de Hispano-America,* vol. 8 (i.e., 9). Passengers in the years 1534 to 1575, pp. 54-216.

7801

---Vol. 2, 431p. *Coleccion . . .,* vol. 13. Passengers in the years 1576 to 1588, pp. 7-252.

Information derived from Spanish archives, where what is actually the ninth volume of the documents is erroneously numbered vol. 8. Overall title in English would be: Passengers to the [West] Indies: A Systematic Cataloging of Information on and Permits for Those Who Went There, Taken from the General Archives of the Indies in the First Century of the Colonization of America, 1492-1592."

*   *   *

7810

RULAND, FRITZ, editor. "Die Auswanderung im 19. Jahrhundert." In *Unser Leintal: Ein Heimatbuch aus dem Wuerttemberger Unterland.* Heilbronn am Neckar [Germany]: Gauss, 1951, pp. 173-189.

Emigration in the nineteenth century. From church registers of several communities in the Lein Valley (Leintal) west of Heilbronn (Germany); and from the newspaper *Koeniglich Wuerttembergische Staats- und Regierungsblatt,* 1807. About 400 emigrants from the Lein Valley, 1750-1883, but really 1807-1883 (only one in 1750). Villages of origin indicated.

*   * -   *

7820

RUPP, ISRAEL DANIEL. *A Collection of Upwards of Thirty Thousand Names of German, Swiss, Dutch,*

French and Other Immigrants in Pennsylvania from 1727 to 1776, with a Statement of the Names of Ships, Whence They Sailed, and the Date of Their Arrival at Philadelphia, Chronologically Arranged, Together with the Necessary Historical and Other Notes, Also, an Appendix Containing Lists of More Than One Thousand German and French Names in New York Prior to 1712. Leipzig, (Germany): Degener & Co., 1931. 478, 89p. Reprint of the 2nd revised and enlarged ed., 1876, with index from 3rd ed. by Ernst Wecken, 1931, and added index of ships. Reprinted by Genealogical Publishing Co., Baltimore, 1965. 583p.

An index by Marvin V. Koger, *Index to the Names of 30,000 Immigrants . . . supplementing the Rupp, Ship Load Volume,* 1935, 232p, is inferior to Wecken's index in the third edition (above). Page 449 contains "Names of the First Palatines in North Carolina, as Early as 1709 and 1710; and pages 449-451 contain "Names of Males, Salzburgers, Settled in Georgia, 1734-1741." Contrary to some opinions, this work by Rupp does not duplicate nos. 9041-9042 by Strassburger, although there are thousands of names which are duplicates. Strassburger's work, however, is more accurate and more reliable than Rupp's. See also no. 9330, Urlsperger. The Salzburgers mentioned above were immigrants from Salzburg, Austria. (Lancour 144)

*   *   *

7825

"RUSH COUNTY, INDIANA, NATURALIZATIONS, 1857-April 1868." In *The Hoosier Genealogist,* vol. 20:1 (Mar. 1980), pp. 15-18.

Abstracts of these entries are from the microfilmed Nook 1, Naturalization Records, Genealogy Division, Indiana State Library. Name, age, country of origin, and often date and port of arrival. Predominantly native Irish, 1838-1867.

*   *   *

7830

SACHSE, JULIUS FRIEDRICH. *The Wreck of the Ship "New Era" upon the New Jersey Coast, November 13, 1854. (A Narrative and Critical History,* Part 16.) Lancaster, Pa.: The Pennsylvania-German Society, 1907, pp. 36-47.

Names the passengers saved and indentifies some of the lost. Includes places of origin, almost all from Germany.

*   *   *

7850

SAINSBURY, W. NOEL, communicator. "Communication from Governor Francis Nicholson of Virginia to the British Lords of Trade Concerning the Huguenot Settlement with 'List of Ye Refugees, August 12th, 1700.'" In *Collections of the Virginia Historical Society,* new series, vol. 6, Richmond, 1887, pp. 61-67.

Mr. Sainsbury was with the Public Record Office, London. The list of refugees is on pp. 65-67 and is also contained in no. 0953, "Miscellaneous Papers, 1672-1865," edited by R.A. Brock. It includes some names not given in "Documents Relating to the Huguenot Emigration to Virginia," in *Collections of the Virginia Historical Society,* new series vol. 5. See other references in the index.

7860

SAMS, CONWAY WHITTLE. *The Conquest of Virginia: the Second Attempt: an Account, Based on Original Documents, of the Attempt . . . to Found Virginia at Jamestown, 1606-1610.* Vol. 2. Norfolk, Va.: Keyser-Doherty Printing, 1924. Reprinted 1929.

The first planters, 1606-1607, pp. 808-813; the "first supply," 1607-1608; pp. 815-819; the "second supply or third company," 1608, pp. 821-823; a partial list (supply) 1609-1610, pp. 825-826. Includes passenger lists. See also no. 9238, Tyler.

*   *   *

7875-7891

"[SAN FRANCISCO SHIP PASSENGER LISTS, 1849-1875]" In *San Francisco Genealogical Bulletin,* later *San Francisco Historic Record and Genealogy Bulletin.*

Item	Vol./ No.	Pub. Date	Pages	Year of Arrival
7875	1:1	(July 1963)	16-18	1855
7876	1:3	(Sept. 1963)	5-6	1855
7877	1:4	(Oct. 1963)	17-18	1860
7878	1:5	(Nov. 1963)	16-17	1855
7879	1:6	(Dec. 1963)	19-20	1855, 1860
7880	1:7	(Jan. 1964)	20-22	1855, 1860
7881	1:8	(Feb. 1964)	19-21	1850, 1860
7882	1:9	(Mar. 1964)	17-18	1850, 1860
7883	1:10	(Apr. 1964)	10-12	1849, 1855
7884	1:11	(May 1964)	11-13	1850, 1860
7885	1:12	(June 1964)	12-14	1850, 1856
7886	2:13	(July 1964)	21	1865
7887	2:14	(Oct. 1964)	9-11	1860
7888	2:15	(Jan. 1965)	14-15	1875
7889	2:16	(Apr. 1965)	25-26	1871
7890	3:17	(July 1965)	43-44	1849, 1872
7891	3:18	(Oct. 1965)	40-41	1872

No others published. L. J. Rasmussen, compiler of the Bulletin, then began publishing the *San Francisco Ship Passenger Lists* (items 7156-7162).

*   *   *

7906-7907

SAVAGE, JAMES. "Gleanings for New England History." In *Collections of the Massachusetts Historical Society.*
7906
---3rd ser., vol. 8 (1843), pp. 243-348.
7907
---3rd ser., vol. 10 (1849), pp. 127-146. "More Gleanings for New England History."

Many lists of early emigrants from Britain to New England, copied from original records in Rolls Court, London. Volume 10 has numerous corrections of volume 8. Also in no. 0263, Banks. Partly in no. 9143, Tepper, *New World Immigrants,* vol. 1, pp. 34-71. See also no. 8825, Somerby, for corrections of some data. (Lancour 46B and 47)

*   *   *

7921

SCHALL, NED, compiler. "Passenger List." In *Heritage Review,* no. 21 (Sept. 1978), pp. 42-43.

The S.S. *Herman* from Bremen, Germany, arrived at the port of Baltimore, Maryland, on May 9, 1889, with 111 immigrants listed as having come from Russia, many from the Liebenthal region of Poland. Destination given as Dakota, U.S.A.

*　　*　　*

7930

SCHALL, NED. "[Passenger Lists.]" In *Heritage Review,* no. 24 (Sept. 1979), p. 41.

Passenger list of the S.S. *Hohenzollern,* from Bremen to New York, April 20, 1895. These migrants moved from the Kutschurgan district of South Russia to North Dakota.

*　　*　　*

7931

SCHALL, NED, compiler. "Passenger Lists." In *Heritage Review,* no. 19 (Dec. 1977), pp. 45-46.

Germans from Russia to New York City, 1885, who founded the settlement known as "Elsaz" in the Dakota Territory, McIntosh and Emmons counties, North Dakota.

*　　*　　*

7934

SCHALL, NED, compiler. "Passenger Lists." In *Heritage Review,* no. 20 (Apr. 1978), pp. 43-45.

Passengers from Russia to New York, 1888. Most came from the Kutschurgan district, some from Strassburg and Selz. Many settled in McIntosh and Emmons counties, North Dakota.

*　　*　　*

7937

SCHALL, NED, compiler. "Passenger Lists." In *Heritage Review,* no. 22 (Jan. 1979), pp. 47-48.

Covers 166 emigrants who came from Russia by way of Bremen, Germany, to New York City on the S.S. *Lahn,* April 14, 1893.

*　　*　　*

7941

SCHALL, NED, compiler. "Passenger Lists." In *Heritage Review,* no. 23 (Apr. 1979), pp. 51-52.

"On April 11, 1893, the S.S. *Saale* arrived at the port of New York . . . ," with 101 emigrants from Russia by way of Bremen, Germany. Many eventually settled in the Dakotas, although other destinations, such as Galveston, Chicago, Pennsylvania, are also given.

*　　*　　*

7943

SCHALL, NED, contributor. [Passenger Lists.] In *Heritage Review* (Germans from Russia Heritage Soci-

ety), vol. 10:3 (Aug. 1980), pp. 47-48.

Passengers from Russia, via Hamburg, who settled in Dakota Territory, 1886 and 1900.

*　　*　　*

7967

SCHARDON, WILHELM. "Auswanderer aus Beindersheim nach Amerika." In *Pfaelzisch-Rheinische Familienkunde: Pfaelzische Familien- und Wappenkunde.* (Mitteilungen zur Wanderungsgeschichte der Pfaelzer, no. 2, 1977) vol. 8:11 (Aug. 1977), pp. 467-472.

Emigrants to America from Beindersheim, situated near Frankenthal, south of Worms in the Rhineland-Palatinate. Covers 100 departures during the 19th century, with considerable information on the families.

*　　*　　*

7976

SCHARF, J. THOMAS. "[List of "Gentlemen Adventurers and Their Servants," on *The Ark* and *The Dove.*]" In *History of Maryland from the Earliest Period to the Present Day.* Baltimore: John B. Piet, 1879, vol. 1., p. 66. Reprinted in 3 vols. with index, by Tradition Press, Hatboro, Pa., 1967. Available from Gale Research Co., Detroit, Mich.

Passengers to St. Clement's Island, Maryland, 1634. Also in no. 0720, Boyer, *Ship Passenger Lists, the South,* pp. 9-10. For other references to these two ships, see index. (Lancour 198E)

*　　*　　*

7983

SCHARF, J. THOMAS. "A List of Rebbells Transported in the Shipp *Friendship* of Belfast, Michael Mankin, Commander, the 20th of August, 1716." In *History of Maryland from the Earliest Period to the Present Day.* 3 vols. Baltimore: John B. Piet, 1879, vol. 1, pp. 386-387. Reprinted with new index by Tradition Press, Hatboro, Pa., 1967. Available from Gale Research Co., Detroit, Mich.

Names 80 political prisoners, mostly Scottish, deported after an uprising in 1715-1716. Taken from the Public Record Office, London. Also in no. 7385, Richardson; and in no. 0720, Boyer, *Ship Passenger Lists, the South,* pp. 12-14. (Lancour 202)

*　　*　　*

7990

SCHARF, J. THOMAS. "A List of Rebell Prisoners Transported into this Province in the Ship the *Good Speed,* on the 18th Day of October, Anno Domini 1716, with the Names of the Persons Who Purchased Them." In *History of Maryland from the Earliest Period to the Present Day.* 3 vols. Baltimore: John B. Piet, 1879, vol. 1, pp. 388-389. Reprinted with new index by Tradition Press, Hatboro, Pa., 1967. Available from Gale Research Co., Detroit, Mich.

The account involves 55 Scottish prisoners. Also in no. 7395, Richardson; and in no. 0720, Boyer, *Ship Passenger Lists, the South,* pp. 14-15. (Lancour 203)

7997

SCHARF, J. THOMAS. "[Names of Aliens Naturalized by Special Acts of the Provincial Legislature, 1666-1750.]" In *History of Maryland from the Earliest Period to the Present Day.* 3 vols. Baltimore: John B. Piet, 1879, vol. 2, p. 11. Reprinted with new index by Tradition Press, Hatboro, Pa., 1967. Available from Gale Research Co., Detroit, Mich.

> Concerns 175 foreigners naturalized in Maryland. Gives names only. Also in no. 0993, Brumbaugh; and in no. 0720, Boyer, *Ship Passenger Lists, the South,* pp. 10-11. (Lancour 200)

*   *   *

8000

SCHARF, J. THOMAS. [Passengers on the Fourth Swedish Expedition to Delaware 1643]. In *History of Delaware, 1609-1888,* Philadelphia: L.J. Richards, 1888, vol. 1, pp. 46-47.

> Nineteen passengers on the *Fama* and the *Svanen,* from Stockholm and Gottenberg (*sic*), 1642, arriving at Christina, Delaware, February 15, 1643, under the leadership of Lt. Colonel Johan Printz.

*   *   *

8002

SCHARF, J. THOMAS. [Passengers on the Third Swedish Expedition to Delaware 1641.]. In *History of Delaware, 1609-1888,* Philadelphia: L.J. Richards, 1888, vol. 1, pp. 44-45.

> Thirty-two passengers on the *Key of Kalmar* and the *Charitas,* from Stockholm to Delaware, 1641. Also in no. 3766, Keen.

*   *   *

8005

SCHARF, J. THOMAS. "[Scotch Prisoners Deported to Maryland on the Ship Johnson, 1747.]" In *History of Maryland from the Earliest Period to the Present Day.* 3 vols. Baltimore: John B. Piet, 1879, vol. 1, p. 435. Reprinted with new index by Tradition Press, Hatboro, Pa., 1967. Available from Gale Research Co., Detroit, Mich.

> Transported from Liverpool to Oxford, Maryland, 1747, were 96 Scottish prisoners taken at the battle of Culloden. *Johnson* passengers also in no. 1242, Coldham; and no. 0720, Boyer, *Ship Passenger Lists, the South,* pp. 18-19. (Lancour 205)

*   *   *

8017

SCHEBEN, JOSEPH. *Untersuchungen zur Methode und Technik der Deutschamerikanischen Wanderungsforschung an Hand eines Vergleichs der Volkszaehlungslisten der Township Westphalia, Clinton County, Michigan, vom Jahre 1860 mit Auswanderungsakten des Kreises Adenau (Rheinland); mit mehreren Tabellen, Diagrammen, Kartenskizzen und Kartogrammen, sowie einem Text- und Briefanhang.* (Research Series on Emigration from the Rhineland, Part 3). Bonn [Germany]: Ludwig Roehrscheid Verlag, 1939. 155p., with 4 tables.

> A study of emigration from Adenau [Germany] to America, through comparison of a census of Westphalia Township, Clinton County, Michigan, taken in 1860, with emigration records of Adenau from 1840 on. Gives name and national origin of every resident of the township in 1860 and name and place of birth of the emigrants from the Rhineland at Adenau. Pages 17-38 list the census, *die Volkszaehlungslisten von Westphalia,* of June 1, 1860. Tables 1-3 on Adenau. Table 4 is a map. (Lancour 256)

*   *   *

8030

SCHEIFFARTH, ENGELBERT. "Uebersee-Auswanderer aus Neiderheimbach, Kr. St. Goar." In *Genealogie,* vol. 9:7 (July 1969), pp. 644-645.

> Emigrants to overseas from Niederheimbach in the county of St. Goar. From church registers in the village of Niederheimbach, Germany. Covers emigration to Australia and North and South America in the years 1847-1900. Place of origin, age, family data, and, for most, the year of emigration.

*   *   *

8040

SCHELBERT, LEO. "Notes on Lists of Swiss Emigrants." In *National Genealogical Society Quarterly,* vol. 60:1 (Mar. 1972), pp. 36-46.

> An examination of *Lists of Swiss Emigrants in the Eighteenth Century to the American Colonies,* by Faust and Brumbaugh (item no. 1960), that uncovers many errors. Supplies corrections and additions to "Zurich Lists," additions to the "Bern Lists," and Gerber's corrections and additions to the "Basel Lists." These were incorporated in the Genealogical Publishing Company's 1976 reprint of item no. 1960.

*   *   *

8050

SCHELL, JACK S. "Emigrants from Bischweiler, Zweibruecken, 1760-1764." In *National Genealogical Society Quarterly,* vol. 59:1 (Mar. 1971), p. 38.

> List of 30 emigrants from Bischweiler, which was formerly part of the Duchy of Zweibruecken in Germany and is now Bischweiler in eastern France on the Moder River. For Zweibruecken emigrants in the years 1728-1771, see no. 3193, Hinke and Stoudt; and no. 4357, Krebs.

*   *   *

8054

SCHENK, PAUL. *The Colony Bernstadt in Laurel County, Kentucky, at the Beginning of Its Sixth Year.* Translated from the original, written in 1886, *Die Kolony Bernstadt in Laurel County, Kentucky,* by S.A. Mory, Sr., in 1939. London, Ky.: The Sentinel-Echo, 1940. 42p.

> The appendices contain a list of Swiss settlers, and tables I-VII reveal occupations of the immigrants. These Swiss began to arrive in the U.S. in 1881. Full name, sex, place of origin, year of arrival, and number of children are given.

8060
SCHERMERHORN, RICHARD, JR. "Representative Pioneer Settlers of New Netherland and Their Original Home Places." In *The New York Genealogical and Biographical Record,* vol. 65:1 (Jan. 1934), pp. 2-12.

New Netherland settlers, 1620-1664, with original places of residence in Holland, Belgium, and Germany. Also in no. 9135, *Immigrants to the Middle Colonies,* pp.6-16; and no. 0714, Boyer, *Ship Passenger List, New York and New Jersey,* pp. 26-37.   (Lancour 74)

*   *   *

8070
SCHERMERHORN, WILLIAM E. *The History of Burlington, New Jersey, from the Early European Arrivals in the Delaware to the Quarter Millenial Anniversary, in 1927, of the Settlement by English Quakers in 1677.* Burlington, N.J.: Enterprise Publishing Co., 1927. pp. 379-380 (appendix).

Names heads of families who came in the ship *Kent* to Wickaco and arrived and settled in the neighborhood of Burlington in October 1677, and in the *Martha,* November 1677. The *Shield* from Hull and other, unnamed ships from England in 1678 are also included. For corrections, see no. 3580, Johnson. Also in no. 8760, Smith.   (Lancour 111A)

*   *   *

8080
SCHEUERMAN, RICHARD D. "Immigration Lists from the Jagodnaja Poljana and Jeruslan River Viciniges, 1874-1916." In *Pilgrims on the Earth: a German-Russian Chronical.* Fairfield, Wash.: Ye Galleon Press, 1974, pp. 85-86 (Appendix C).

Partial compilation of the names of families who migrated to the Pacific Northwest, many through Kansas.

*   *   *

8090
SCHIEBLE, LEOPOLD. "Bevoelkerungsabgaenge in fuerstlich fuerstenbergischen und benachbarten Orten 1720-1806." In *Archiv fuer Sippenforschung und alle verwandten Gebiete,* Jahrgang 33, part 26 (May 1967), pp. 102-107; part 27 (Aug. 1967), pp. 221-223; Jahrgang 34, part 29 (Feb. 1968), pp. 365-372; part 30 (May 1968), pp. 456-460.

Losses in population in localities of the principality of Fuerstenberg and neighboring places, 1720-1806. From notices in the weekly newspaper *Donaueschinger Wochenblatt,* 1779-1806, preserved in the Fuerstenberg royal library in Donaueschingen. Reports on 769 individuals who left their native villages between 1720 and 1806 because of various crimes. Many may eventually have found their way to America, and a comparison with nos. 9041-9042, Strassburger, may prove rewarding. Five are noted as having come to America.

*   *   *

8094
SCHIERENBERG, E. "Die Deutschpennsylvanier. (Mit besonderer Beruecksichtigung der Auswanderung

aus Nassau.)" In *Nassovia: Zeitschrift fuer nassauische Geschichte und Heimatkunde.* Jahrgang 4:16 (Aug. 16, 1903), pp.. 194-196; 4:17 (Sept. 1, 1903), pp. 206-208; 4:18 (Sept. 16, 1903), pp. 218-220; 4:19 (Oct. 1, 1903), pp. 232-235.

The Pennsylvania Germans, with particular reference to emigration from [the former duchy of] Nassau [Germany]. Documents stored in the state archives at Wiesbaden. Concerns 67 emigrants, mostly to America in 1709. Names of individuals or heads of emigrant groups, some family members, and community of origin for most of the emigrants. Destinations given were Pennsylvania or Carolina.

*   *   *

8099
SCHLEGEL, RONALD M. *Passengers from Ireland: Lists of Passengers Arriving at American Ports Between 1811 and 1817.* Transcribed from *The Shamrock or Hibernian Chronicle.* Baltimore: Genealogical Publishing Co., 1980. 158p.

Lists 7,308 names. Supersedes no. 2859, Hackett, and no. 1742, Early, rectifying errors and omissions. Includes death notices and advertisements placed by persons seeking missing relatives in other parts of the country. The 1811 arrivals are also given in nos. 8795-8797.

*   *   *

8120
SCHOTT, PAUL. "Die Auswanderung in Schutterwald in den letzten 100 Jahren." In *Mein Heimatland* (Freiburg im Breisgau, Germany), Jahrgang 24:1 (1937), pp. 40-44.

Emigration from Schutterwald, in the province of Baden, Germany, in the past 100 years. Provides a list of the surnames of 81 emigrants who left Schutterwald between 1830 and 1935.

*   *   *

8130
SCHULTZ, ESTHER, contributor. "Passenger List of the Ship *Salier* from Germany to New York, 1882." In *The Topeka Genealogical Society Quarterly,* vol. 8:1 (Jan. 1978), pp. 3-5; vol. 8:2 (Apr. 1978), pp. 33-38.

Lists 300 passengers, names only. Not completed; for complete list, see no. 6206, *Norddeutscher Lloyd in Bremen.*

*   *   *

8134
SCHUMACHER, MURIAL. "Manufacturing and Industry in Renssalaerswyck [sic]." In *The Dutch Settlers Society of Albany,* vols. 38-39, 1962-1963, pp. 7-13.

Names workmen who arrived in Rensselaerswyck, New York, to engage in manufacturing, building, and trades, 1631-1655. Mostly Dutch and Scandinavian. Title page of the journal erroneously shows vol. 37, but 38-39 is correct.

*   *   *

8140
SCHWARZENBERG DE SCHMALZ, INGEBORG.
"Die deutsche Kolonie Huefel-Comuy in Chile." In
Genealogie, vol. 14:7 (July 1978), pp. 193-201; vol. 14:9
(Sept. 1978), pp. 282-293.

The German colony of Huefel-Comuy in Chile. Huefel-
Comuy is today called Faja Maisan and is located in the
province of Cautin in the ninth district. Settlers went there
between 1906 and 1912. Names, ages, family data, places of
origin, supplied from completed questionnaires sent to the
colonists by the German Foreign Institute around 1937. Before
the loss of the questionnaires during World War II, the author
extracted a great portion of data from them for her card file.

*   *   *

8150
SCHWEDLER, FERDINAND A. VON. "Deutsche
Einwanderer in Texas (USA) 1844." In *Genealogie,* vol.
9:5 (May 1968), pp. 154-158.

German immigrants in Texas in 1844. From lists prepared
by D.H. Klaener, agent in Texas in 1844 for the German
Society of Nobility (Deutsche Adelsvereinigung). Names persons who arrived on the first four ships organized by that
society for settlement of its holdings, which later became the
communities of New Braunfels in Comal County and Nassau-
Farm in Fayette County. Name, members of family and other
family data, and place (colony) of settlement. These are the
first four shiploads of colonists who arrived at the port then
known as Karlshafen, Texas, between July 8 and December 14,
1844.

*   *   *

8170
**"SCOTCH PRISONERS SENT TO MASSACHUSETTS
IN 1652, by Order of the English Government."** In *The
New England Historical and Genealogical Register,* vol.
1:4 (Oct. 1847), pp. 377-380.

List of passengers aboard the *John and Sarah* of London,
November 1651 - May 1652. Also in no. 0269, Banks; nos.
1672 and 1674, Drake; no. 8171, "Scotch Prisoners . . . ;" no.
9151, Tepper, *Passengers to America,* pp. 146-149; and in no.
0702, Boyer, *Ship Passenger Lists, National and New England,*
pp. 154-157. (Lancour 53)

*   *   *

8171
**"SCOTCH PRISONERS SENT TO MASSACHUSETTS
—1652."** In *The Genealogist's Post,* vol. 5:7 (July 1968),
pp. 9-12.

A list of the passengers aboard the *John and Sarah* of London,
John Greene, master, bound for New England. Names arranged alphabetically. Extracted from *The Massachusetts
Historical Society Magazine,* vol. 61, pp. 4-29. See also no.
8170.

*   *   *

SCOTT, MRS. GRACE R., contributor.
    See under
    CRIGLER, ARTHUR D., and **GRACE R.
SCOTT.**

8195
SCOTT, KENNETH, compiler. *British Aliens in the
United States During the War of 1812.* Baltimore,
Genealogical Publishing Co., 1979. 420p.

Listed by state; all have dates of arrival, or date can be
deduced from information given, so that in effect it is like
a passenger list. Indexed. Over 10,000 names.

*   *   *

8198
SCOTT, KENNETH. "Early New Yorkers and Their
Ages." In *National Genealogical Society Quarterly,* vol.
57:4 (Dec. 1969), pp. 274-297.

Concerns 700 early inhabitants of New Netherland and
New York. Based mostly upon Colonial Documents of
New York in the Manuscripts Division of the New York State
Library; manuscript collections of the New-York Historical
Society; and Historical Documents Collection, Queens Col-
lege. Considerable information on individual's place of origin,
trade or profession, and some data on 17th and early 18th
century migration.

*   *   *

8202
SCOTT, KENNETH. "Kennebec County, Maine, Naturalizations." In *National Genealogical Society Quarterly,* vol. 66:1 (Mar. 1978), pp. 29-32.

Covers 1780 to 1830, with list of 62 aliens who applied for
citizenship at the Court of Common Pleas of Kennebec
County. Includes much other information. Taken from U.S.
National Archives, Works Progress Administration Naturalization Papers.

*   *   *

8212
SCOTT, KENNETH. "Orphan Children Sent to New
Netherland." In *De Halve Maen,* vol. 49:3 (Oct. 1974),
pp. 5-6.

A list of 17 Dutch orphans sent to New Netherland in 1755, and
details of three marriages of Dutch immigrants.

*   *   *

8222
SCOTT, KENNETH. "Resident Aliens Enabled to Hold
Land in New York State, 1790-1825." In *National
Genealogical Society Quarterly,* vol. 67:1 (Mar. 1979),
pp. 42-57.

In colonial New York, aliens needed letters of denization from
the King of England or in New York from the Governor, or
had to be naturalized before they could hold or dispose of real
property. Then later, Acts of the Legislature between 1790 and
1825 named those enabled to hold and dispose of land. Names
given here in alphabetical order.

*   *   *

8232
SCOTT, KENNETH. "Rockingham County, N.H., Naturalizations." In *National Genealogical Society Quarterly,* vol. 66:2 (June 1978), pp. 112-116.

From documents in the Superior Court of Rockingham County, New Hampshire. Papers of 81 persons, most from the United Kingdom, between the years 1792 and 1849. Date of emigration often cited.

*   *   *

8242-8245
SCOTT, KENNETH. "Runaways, Excerpts from *The Pennsylvania Gazette, 1775-1783.*" In *National Genealogical Society Quarterly.*
8242
---Vol. 64:4 (Dec. 1976), pp. 243-260.
8243
---Vol. 65:1 (Mar. 1977), pp. 88-91; vol. 65:3 (Sept. 1977), pp. 211-217; vol. 65:4 (Dec. 1977), pp. 295-301.
8244
---Vol. 66:1 (Mar. 1978), pp. 57-60; vol. 66:2 (June 1978), pp. 127-129; vol. 66:3 (Sept. 1978), pp. 231-235.
8245
---Vol. 67:2 (June 1979), pp. 121-129.

Search notices in classified advertisements for runaways, deserters, missing indentured servants, slaves, and apprentices.

*   *   *

8258
SCOTT, KENNETH, and **ROSANNE CONWAY,** compilers. *New York Alien Residents, 1825-1848.* Baltimore: Genealogical Publishing Co., 1978. 122p.

In 1825, an Act of the New York Legislature enabled resident aliens to acquire, use, or hold real estate. Entries often give date of arrival in America.

*   *   *

8270
SCOTT, KENNETH, and **KENN STRYKER-RODDA.** *Denizations, Naturalizations, and Oaths of Allegiance in Colonial New York.* Baltimore: Genealogical Publishing Co., 1975. 120p.

Denizations and licenses of the 17th and 18th centuries, pp. 1-11; naturalizations, mostly 18th century, pp. 12-75; Oaths of allegiance, pp. 76-120.

*   *   *

8276-8277
SCOTT, MRS. MARY LOU. *Naturalizations from Circuit Court Proceedings, Washington County, Pa., 1795-1888.* [Roscoe, Pa.: Citizens Library,] 1974. 2 parts.
8276
---Part 1, 1795-1841. 101p.
8277
---Part 2, 1841-1888. 64p.

Correlated from three separate items of the Iams Manuscript Collection, Elisha B. Iams, archivist. The collection was given to the Citizens Library about 1973. List includes a pre-

ponderance of immigrants from the British Isles, primarily Irish. Name, sometimes names of family members, national origin, and file number.

*   *   *

8280
SEACORD, MORGAN HORTON. *Biographical Sketches and Index of the Huguenot Settlers of New Rochelle, 1687-1776.* New Rochelle, N.Y.: The Huguenot and Historical Association of New Rochelle, 1941. 54p.

Names emigrants who settled in New Rochelle prior to the American Revolution. Much information about settlers. Also in no. 0714, Boyer, *Ship Passenger Lists, New York and New Jersey,* pp. 144-159. (Boyer extracted material from pp. 9-54 of Seacord.)   (Lancour 89)

*   *   *

8290
SEEBERG-ELVERFELDT, ROLAND. "Auswanderer aus Thueringen und Sachsen nach Uebersee." In *Mitteldeutsche Familienkunde,* Jahrgang 12:3 (July-Sept. 1971), pp. 219-221.

Emigrants from Thuringia and Saxony overseas. From the author's family files and other sources. Information on 20 emigrants in the latter half of the 19th century to New York, Chicago, St. Louis, New Orleans, Texas, and South America. Names, family data, birth dates, places of origin.

*   *   *

8302
SEELE, HERMANN H., contributor. "German Immigration Ships of the Adelsverein in the Year of 1845." In *Our Heritage* (San Antonio), vol. 4:1 (Oct. 1964), pp. 13-17; vol. 4:3 (Apr. 1965), pp. 81-84; vol. 4:4 (July 1965), pp. 117-122.

Translated from the *German Year Book* (31st issue) and published by *New Braunfels Zeitung* for 1936 as a supplement to the regular issue of the *New Braunfels Zeitung,* July 9, 1936.

*   *   *

8317
SEELE, HERMANN H., contributor. "Ship Lists." In *Our Heritage* (San Antonio), vol. 7:4 (July 1966), pp. 117-119.

Lists arrivals and their places of origin, translated from German-language newspaper *Galveston-Zeitung,* 1851, which published them as an extra. Ships were the *Magnet* and the *Reform,* which sailed from Bremen to Galveston in 1851. Also listed in no. 2514, Geue.

*   *   *

8330
SEIWERT, JEAN M., abstractor. "Passenger List of the S.S. *Scythia.*" In *The Detroit Society for Genealogical Research Magazine,* vol. 41:4 (Summer 1978), pp. 169-172.

Names about 250 emigrants from Ireland, England, and

Germany, who crossed from Liverpool, England, to New York, arriving July 3, 1878.

*   *   *

8345

"SELKIRK SETTLERS LANDED TODAY IN 1803." In *The Guardian*, Charlottetown, Prince Edward Island, August 7, 1974.

List published on the 171st anniversary of the arrival of the *Polly* with Scottish settlers from Selkirk to Prince Edward Island. Also has data covering pioneering families up to 1890. For earlier crossings of the *Polly*, see nos. 7080 and 7328.

*   *   *

8350

SELLERS, JOHN. "Naturalization Record Book One, Cooke County, Texas." In *Stirpes*, vol. 18:2-3 (June Sept. 1978), pp. 46-51.

Gives names, with date of naturalization, and usually the age, date of arrival, and port. Covers mostly 1880s through 1905. Emigrants from Europe: many Germans, British, and Irish.

*   *   *

8354

SELLINGSLOH, DAISY P., compiler. "Applications for Citizenship, Chester Co., South Carolina." In *The Quarterly, Local History and Genealogical Society* (Dallas, Texas), vol. 13:2 (June 1967), p. 11.

All were immigrants from Ireland, 1807-1815. See also no. 0069, Ainsworth.

*   *   *

8357-8358

"SERVANTS & APPRENTICES BOUND AND AS-SIGNED, 1745." In *Your Family Tree*.
8357
---Vol. 6:5-6 (Nov. 1953-Feb. 1954), pp. 81-83.
8358
---Vol. 7 (Mar.-May 1954), pp. 12-13, 51-52, 75.

Records of indentured servants and apprentices bound by James Hamilton, Mayor of Philadelphia, in 1745. And see nos. 6054-6056, Neible.

*   *   *

8360

"SETTLERS IN RENSSELAERSWYCK from 1630 to 1646, Compiled from the Books of Monthly Wages and Other MSS." In *Year Book of The Holland Society of New York*, 1896, pp. 130-140.

Considerable information on settlers. Also in no. 6306, O'Callaghan, and no. 9365, Van Laer. (Lancour 75A)

*   *   *

8370

SHEPPARD, WALTER LEE, JR., compiler and editor.

Passengers and Ships Prior to 1684. (Publications of the Welcome Society of Pennsylvania, 1.) Baltimore: Genealogical Publishing Co., 1970. 245p.

This excellent work contains over 3,000 names and an index to vessels. Reprints the following articles with corrections, additions, and new materials: "The Real Welcome Passengers," by Marion Balderston (no. 0246) pp. 1-26; "Pennsylvania's 1683 Ships," (no. 0236), pp. 75-120; "William Penn's Twenty-Three Ships," (no. 0248) pp. 27-69; "Early Shipping to the Jersey Shore of the Delaware," by Sheppard and Balderston (no. 8390) pp. 135-138; "The Philadelphia and Bucks County Registers of Arrivals," compared, corrected, and re-transcribed by Roach (no. 7585) pp. 159-175, from Futhey and Cope, no. 2313, and Battle, no. 0418. Includes "The Names of the Early Settlers of Darby Township, Chester County, Pennsylvania," by Bunting (no. 1018) pp. 179-185; "The Sailing of the Ship Submission in the Year 1682," by Dickson (no. 1587); "The First Purchasers of Pennsylvania," by Roach (no. 7570) pp. 195-208. Also includes "Digest of Ship and Passenger Arrivals in the Delaware" by Sheppard, pp. 121-126.

*   *   *

8380

SHEPPARD, WALTER LEE, JR. "Some Early Immigrants from Ireland to New Jersey." In *The American Genealogist*, vol. 50:1 (Jan. 1874), pp. 153-155.

Covers period 1687-1741. Discoveries made concerning those who travelled with a Shepherd family (various spellings), who came in 1687, or who joined the colony of New Jersey later.

*   *   *

8390

SHEPPARD, WALTER LEE, JR., and **MARION R. BALDERSTON.** "Early Shipping to the Jersey Shore of the Delaware." In Sheppard, *Passengers and Ships Prior to 1684.* Baltimore, Md.: Genealogical Publishing Co., 1970, pp. 135-148.

Lists passengers on several ships arriving between 1676 and 1681. See no. 8370, Sheppard.

*   *   *

8400

SHERWOOD, GEORGE. *American Colonists in English Records: A Guide to Direct References in Authentic Records, Passenger Lists not in "Hotten," &c., &c., &c.* Series 1-2. London: G. Sherwood, 1932-1933. 2 vols. Reprinted, 2 vols. in 1, by Genealogical Publishing Co., Baltimore, 1961.

Collection of items from various English records. Series 1 contains pp. 1-100 and series 2, pp. 101-216. Additions made by Smith and Gardner: see no. 8715. Excerpts in no. 0225, Bair. (Lancour 4)

*   *   *

8410

SHIMMICK, LILLIAN, and **HARWOOD G. KOL-SKY.** *Big Timber 1873-1976, Altory Township, Decatur County, Kansas - Cesko Narodni Hrbitov - A History of Big Timber Cemetery (Czech National Cemetery), the*

Final Resting Place of Pioneer Settlers from Czecho-slovakia & Germany . . . . n.p. [1976], pp. 4-5, 9-12.

A local history that contains copies of records from the U.S. National Archives' microfilm holdings of ships' manifests and passenger lists for the years 1858 to 1901. Names Czech and German families and supplies facts on individual's birth date, place of origin, year of marriage, dates of arrival in the U.S. and in Kansas, and date of death.

*   *   *

8420-8422
"SHIP LISTS OF PASSENGERS LEAVING FRANCE for Louisiana, 1718-1724." Translated by Albert Laplace Dart. In *The Louisiana Historical Quarterly.*
8420
---Vol. 14:4 (Oct. 1931), pp. 516-520.
8421
---Vol. 15:1 (Jan. 1932), pp. 68-77; vol. 15:3 (July 1932), pp. 453-467.
8422
---Vol. 21:4 (Oct. 1938), pp. 965-978.

Transcription in the library of the Louisiana Historical Society in the Cabildo Museum, New Orleans, entitled, "Louisiane. Passagers, 1718-1724." Announced to cover to the year 1724, but the last issue brings the lists to 1720. No further lists were published in *LHQ*. In 1970, N. J. Toups published the whole list: no. 9190, and reported discrepancies in the *LHQ* version. Boyer, no. 0720, *Ship Passenger Lists, The South,* pp. 189-220, and Tepper, no. 9143, *New World Immigrants,* vol. 1, pp. 472-515, copied the *LHQ* articles.   (Lancour 242)

*   *   *

8425
"SHIP PASSENGER LISTS." In *The Family Tree,* vol. 2:1 (July-Aug. 1970), pp. 54-61.

Emigrants from Scotland to America, 1774-1775. Passengers on the *Commerce* and the *Friendship,* for New York and Philadelphia respectively. Name, place of origin, age, occupation. These lists also appear in no. 1088, Cameron.

*   *   *

8430
SHIVELY, LOUIS F. "Palatine, Illinois." In *The Palatine Immigrant,* vol. 4:2 (Fall 1978), pp. 53-59.

Lists persons who came to Palatine, Illinois (Cook County), from the 19th century onward. Many came from other states. Some dates of arrival in America are given.

*   *   *

8440
SHURTLEFF, NATHANIEL BRADSTREET. "The Passengers of the *May Flower* [*sic*] in 1620." In *The New England Historical and Genealogical Register,* vol. 1:1 (Jan. 1847), pp. 47-53.

Also in no. 9151, Tepper, *Passengers to America,* pp. 1-7. For the many references to the *Mayflower,* see index. (Lancour 33A)

*   *   *

8450
SICKLER, JOSEPH S. "[Passengers on the *Griffin,* 1675.]" In *The History of Salem County, New Jersey, Being the Story of John Fenwick's Colony, the Oldest English Speaking Settlement on the Delaware River.* Salem, N.J.: Sunbeam Publishing Co., 1937, p. 25.

Passenger list of the *Griffin* (or *Griffith*), which came to the Salem River on November 23, 1675, bringing Major John Fenwick and the first permanent English-speaking settlers in the Delaware Valley. A better list than that in no. 8760, Samuel Smith. Printed in part in no. 3580, Johnson; and no. 1292, Cook. Also in no. 0714, Boyer, *Ship Passenger Lists, New York and New Jersey,* pp. 215-216. For other references to the *Griffin,* see index.   (Lancour 110)

*   *   *

8470
SIGEL, WALTER. "Auswanderungen im 18. Jahrhundert aus dem Kirchspiel Thaleischweiler." In *Pfaelzische Heimatblaetter,* Jahrgang 8:7 (1960), p. 55.

Eighteenth-century emigration from the parish of Thalcisch-weiler [Germany]. See also no. 4231, Krebs. Text not seen by editor.

*   *   *

8480
SIMMENDINGER, ULRICH. *True and Authentic Register of Persons Still Living, by God's Grace, Who in the Year 1709, under the Wonderful Providences of the Lord Journeyed from Germany to America or New World and There Seek Their Piece of Bread at Various Places* . . . . St. Johnsville, N.Y.: The Enterprise and News, 1934. 20p. Reprinted by Genealogical Publishing Co., Baltimore, 1962.

Originally entitled, *Warhoffte und glaubwuerdige Verzeichniss jeniger Personen* . . . . Reutlingen, Germany: ca. 1717. Names and ages, pp. 11-19. Also printed in no. 4010, Knittle. (Lancour 94)

*   *   *

8490
"THE 1683 IMMIGRANTS." In *The Palatine Immigrant,* vol. 3:4 (Spring 1978), p. 16.

German immigrants to the port of Philadelphia in the *America,* arriving on August 20, 1683. Short list of Mennonites. Other Mennonites arrived in Philadelphia on October 6, 1683, in the *Concord.* Thirteen families consisting of 33 persons; some are listed.

*   *   *

8500-8503
SKINNER, MRS. JEAN C., contributor. "Excerpts from Ship Passenger Lists." In *Wisconsin State Genealogical Society Newsletter.*
8500
---Vol. 24:1 (June 1977), pp. 2-3; vol. 24:2 (Sept. 1977), pp. 59-60; vol. 24:4 (Apr. 1978), pp. 165-166.
8501
---Vol. 25:1 (June 1978), pp. 13-14; vol. 25:3 (Jan. 1979), pp. 123-124; vol. 25:4 (Apr. 1979), p. 173.

8502
---Vol. 26:1 (June 1979), pp. 9-10.
8503
---Vol. 27:1 (June 1980), pp. 11-12.

Several ships, all 1852, sailing usually from Bremen to New York. Contains much information on the immigrants, many destined for Wisconsin. This series continues.

*   *   *

8510
SKORDAS, GUST, editor. *The Early Settlers in Maryland: an Index to Names of Immigrants, Compiled from Records of Land Patents, 1633-1680, in the Hall of Records, Annapolis, Maryland.* Baltimore: Genealogical Publishing Co., 1968, 525p.

Index from manuscript by Arthur Trader, Chief Clerk in the Maryland Land Commission, 1917. And see nos. 4507-4511, *Land Notes.*

*   *   *

8520
SLOANE, W. & J., Firm. "List or Manifest of . . . Passengers Taken on Board the Brig *Atlantic* from Aberdeen, Scotland, to Port of New York, Arriving 19 May 1834."] In *The Story of Sloane's.* New York: W. & J. Sloane, 1950, p. 9.

Photostat of a segment of the custom record, copied from original in the U.S. National Archives. The page shown in the Sloane book gives 73 names and was chosen for publication because it includes the name of the founder of the Sloane firm. For the whole manifest, see Parks, no. 6450. (Lancour 251)

*   *   *

8530
SMITH, CLIFFORD NEAL. *British Deportees to America, Part 1: 1760-1763.* (British-American Genealogical Research Monograph, 1). DeKalb, Ill.: Westland Publications, 1974. 97p.

Criminals and convicts named in British Home Office Papers in the Public Record Office, London. Similar lists are in nos. 1222-1223, Coldham, taken from municipal records and transportation registers in the Public Record Office, London. In an article in *Genealogical Journal,* Salt Lake City, vol. 8:3 (Sept. 1979), pp. 125-134, "Unrecognized Refugees from Injustice," Smith compares the work of Coldham with his own (above), listing variant name spellings, showing that both sources must be researched. Coldham's works are more ambitious than Smith's. Coldham cases the years 1617-1775; Smith, 1760-1765. Other transcripts are found in nos. 8534 and 8541.

*   *   *

8534
SMITH, CLIFFORD NEAL. "British Deportees to America, 1760-1763." In *Illinois State Genealogical Society Quarterly,* vol. 6:3 (Fall 1974), pp. 133-136.

Many were recruits, mainly to the 49th Regiment of Foot in Jamaica, later sent to New York. Only names given. Fuller details may be found in no. 8530, Smith.

8541
SMITH, CLIFFORD NEAL. *British Deportees to America, Part 2: 1764-1765.* (British-American Genealogical Research Monograph, 2) McNeal, Ariz: Westland Publications, 1979. 81p.

For earlier years, and annotation, see item no. 8530.

*   *   *

8560
SMITH, CLIFFORD NEAL. *Brunswick Deserter-Immigrants of the American Revolution.* (German-American Genealogical Research Monograph, 1.) Thomson, Ill.: Heritage House, 1973, [54p].

From the *Staatsarchiv* at Wolfenbuettel, Germany, where file 38B Alt. Nr. 260 is a summary list of Brunswick mercenaries sent to America in British service during the American Revolution. The detachment served mainly in Canada and northern New York. Most of the soldiers were captured at Saratoga and spent the war years as prisoners of war in Pennsylvania and Virginia, where many subsequently settled. The records supply names of the German birthplaces, thereby documenting the link between Germany and America for these elusive settlers. Some 3,000 did not return to Germany. Taken from no. 7495, Rimpau.

*   *   *

8562
SMITH, CLIFFORD NEAL. "Brunswick Deserter-Immigrants of the American Revolution." In *Illinois State Genealogical Society Quarterly,* vol. 6:2 (Summer 1974), pp. 77-81.

Summarizes no. 8560, Smith. Includes the names but not the places of origin in the former German state of Brunswick.

*   *   *

8570
SMITH, CLIFFORD NEAL. "Deserters, Dischargees, and Prisoners of War from the Fourth Regiment of Foot (King's Own) During the American Revolution." In *National Genealogical Society Quarterly,* vol. 66:3 (Sept. 1978), pp. 183-187.

List of British soldiers who probably remained in America after 1783, abstracted from British muster rolls. Lists show that soldiers deserted, were discharged, or were made prisoner.

*   *   *

8580-8581
SMITH, CLIFFORD NEAL. "Early German Settlers in Iowa." In *Illinois State Genealogical Society Quarterly.*
8580
---Vol. 7:1 (Apr. 1975), pp. 33-35; vol. 7:3 (Sept. 1975), pp. 145-147; vol. 7:4 (Dec. 1975), pp. 200-202.
8581
---Vol. 8:1 (Mar. 1976), pp. 28-30; vol. 8:3 (Sept. 1976), pp. 141-145.

Abstracted from a series of articles by Wilhelm Hauth (no. 2946), entitled "Deutsche Pioniere im Staate Iowa der USA"

(German Pioneers in the State of Iowa, USA). Places of origin and of settlement in Iowa specified.

*   *   *

8590

SMITH, CLIFFORD NEAL. *Emigrants from Saxony (Grandduchy of Saxe-Weimar-Eisenach) to America, 1854, 1859.* (German-American Genealogical Research Monograph, 4). DeKalb, Ill.: Westland Publications, 1974. 32p. Rev. ed., McNeal, Ariz., Westland, 1980.

Nos. 4040 and 4046, Koch, were combined for the title above. Refers to 890 emigrants from Saxony-Weimar. Names only.

*   *   *

8592

SMITH, CLIFFORD NEAL. "Emigrants from Saxony (Grandduchy of Sachsen-Weimar-Eisenbach), to America, 1854, 1859." In *Illinois State Genealogical Society Quarterly,* vol. 8:4 (Winter 1976), pp. 201-204.

A list of emigrants who came in 1854 or 1859 or shortly thereafter. Names with dates of arrival only. Other information is to be found in no. 8590, Smith.

*   *   *

8600

SMITH, CLIFFORD NEAL. "Emigrants from the Principality of Hesse-Hanau, Germany, 1741-1767." In *Genealogical Journal* (Salt Lake City), vol. 6:1 (Mar. 1977), pp. 19-23.

Verbatim translation of relevant sections of a manuscript in the state archives at Marburg, Germany, a bound register of the *Geheimer Rat* of the former principality of Hesse-Hanau. Not all the 190 emigrants from Hesse-Hanau came to the American colonies. Comparison of surnames appearing in nos. 9041 and 9042, Strassburger, with those appearing in the Hanau list makes it possible to indentify a number of passengers, to correct the spelling of their surnames, and to establish their places of origin. This article is a summary of no. 8602, also by Smith.

*   *   *

8602

SMITH, CLIFFORD NEAL. *Emigrants from the Principality of Hessen-Hanau, Germany, 1741-1767* (German-American Genealogical Research Monograph 6). McNeal, Ariz.: Westland Publications, 1979. 22p.

Indentifies immigrants to Pennsylvania and Carolina in the middle of the 18th century, with indication of their birthplaces. Refers to migration in Central European countries, as well. Discerns and corrects some of the surnames misspelled in items 9041 and 9042, Strassburger. Provides verbatim translation of relevant sections of the manuscript register in the *Staatsarchiv* at Marburg, Germany, and of the *Geheimer Rat* (Privy Council) of the former principality of Hessen-Hanau.

*   *   *

8610

SMITH, CLIFFORD NEAL. "German Immigrants on the *Indostan,* May 1804." In *National Genealogical Society Quarterly,* vol. 63:4 (Dec. 1975), p. 263.

Identifies 11 Prussian subjects who emigrated to America. Extracts from photostats in the Manuscript Division of the Library of Congress. Original papers are in the Prussian State Archives, Rep. A8, Magdeburg, now in the German Democratic Republic. Incomplete list.

*   *   *

8620

SMITH, CLIFFORD NEAL. "German Mercenaries of the American Revolution." In *National Genealogical Society Quarterly,* vol. 65:1 (Mar. 1977), pp. 75-81.

Good background study. Cites a few names as examples of information given. Specifies sources for the names listed.

*   *   *

8630

SMITH, CLIFFORD NEAL. "Hessian Laborers at Lancaster, Pennsylvania, 1777. In *National Genealogical Society Quarterly,* vol. 59:3 (Sept. 1971), p. 188.

Payroll of about 30 mercenaries, probably prisoners of war. From a manuscript of the Chicago Historical Society.

*   *   *

8634

SMITH, CLIFFORD NEAL. translator. *Immigrants to America and Central Europe from Beihingen am Neckar, Baden-Wuerttemberg, Germany, 1727-1934.* (German-American Genealogical Research Monograph, 11) McNeal, Ariz.: Westland Publications, 1980. 49p.

Translation from German of a section of no. 7537, Ritz. A considerable amount of family information is given.

*   *   *

8640

SMITH, CLIFFORD NEAL. *Mercenaries from Ansbach and Bayreuth, Germany, Who Remained in America After the Revolution.* (German-American Genealogical Research Monograph, 2) Thomson, Ill.: Heritage House, 1974. Reprinted, McNeal, Ariz.: Westland Publications, 1979. 52p.

Taken from no. 8905, Staedtler. Troops from Ansbach-Bayreuth (now Bavaria) fought in the American Revolution. This names birthplaces of a few of these "unofficial" immigrants and places where others deserted and settled in Canada and the United States. The index in the 1974 edition was by soundex, in which variant spellings of a name are listed together if they sound alike, but a new printing provided access by ordinary index as well as soundex.

*   *   *

8643

SMITH, CLIFFORD NEAL. *Mercenaries from Hessen-Hanau Who Remained in Canada and the United States After the American Revolution.* (German-American Genealogical Research Monograph, 5) DeKalb, Ill.:

Westland Publications, 1976. 105p.

> Names, ages, birthplaces, dates and places of desertion in Canada and the United States, as shown in German muster rolls.

* * *

8650

SMITH, CLIFFORD NEAL. *Muster Rolls and Prisoner-of-War Lists in American Archival Collections Pertaining to the German Mercenary Troops Who Served with the British Forces During the American Revolution.* (German-American Genealogical Research Monograph, 3, in three parts) DeKalb, Ill.: Westland Publications, 1974-1976. 177p. (Pt. 1, pp. 1-64; pt. 2, pp. 65-119; pt. 3, pp. 120-177.)

> These muster rolls and prisoner-of-war lists supplement various other Smith works on German mercenaries. From the American sources it is often possible to determine where deserter-immigrants and prisoners were held during the Revolution and, thereby, to guess where they are likely to have settled after the end of hostilities.

* * *

8652

SMITH, CLIFFORD NEAL. *Nineteenth-Century Emigration from Kreis Simmern (Hunsrueck), Rheinland-Pfalz, Germany, to Brazil, England, Russian Poland, and the United States of America.* (German-American Genealogical Research Monograph, 8) McNeal, Ariz.: Westland Publications, 1980. 35p.

> Simmern is an area in the Rhineland-Palatinate, German Federal Republic. Most of the emigration records are in the state archives in Koblenz. Emigrants listed in this monograph would have declared themselves to be Prussian subjects, because the area fell to the Kingdom of Prussia in 1815. The list of emigrants has been adapted and translated from two articles published by Walter Diener in 1935 (no. 1612) and 1938 (no. 1616). All listed came to America.

* * *

8655

SMITH, CLIFFORD NEAL. *Nineteenth-Century Emigration of "Old Lutherans" from Eastern Germany (Mainly Pomerania and Lower Silesia) to Australia, Canada, and the United States.* (German-American Genealogical Research Monograph, 7) McNeal, Ariz.: Westland Publications, 1980. 93p.

> Contains names of over 5,000 emigrants from the Kingdom of Prussia, 1835-1854, who left their homeland rather than participate in the merger of the Lutheran and Reformed Churches in the formation of the Prussian State Church. In the United States and Canada, the congregations formed the Buffalo Synod (later called the Evangelical Lutheran Synodical Conference of America: see Smith's *Encyclopedia of German-American Genealogical Research,* p. 43). Settlements were in upper New York State, southeastern Michigan (Detroit area), southeastern Wisconsin (Milwaukee and Madison areas), and in Texas. Summarizes data in no. 3474, Iwan, *Die altlutherische Auswanderung um die Mitte des 19. Jahrhunderts,* 1943. Australian immigrants' names not copied.

* * *

8656

SMITH, CLIFFORD NEAL. *Reconstructed Passenger Lists for 1850: Hamburg to Australia, Brazil, Canada, Chile, and the United States. Part 1: Passenger Lists 1 through 25* (German and Central European Emigration Monograph no. 1, pt. 1). McNeal, Ariz.: Westland Publications, 1980. 79p.

> Abstracted from microfilm roll number 1, Library of Congress, Manuscript Div., shelf number 10,897. About 2,500 names, sometimes occupations and places of origin. Destinations of these 25 ships: Quebec, San Francisco, New York, Galveston, Adelaide, Sydney, and a few Brazilian ports, totaling 18 to U.S. and Canadian ports. Parts 2 and 3, expected in 1980, will complete this series.

* * *

8660

SMITH, CLIFFORD NEAL. "Revolutionary War Refugees from Canada and Nova Scotia." In *National Genealogical Society Quarterly,* vol. 59:4 (Dec. 1971), pp. 266-273.

> A source of information on refugees from the American Revolution. Canadians who fought against the Crown had property seized. By an order of May 20, 1785, three townships adjacent to Lake Erie were set aside for 229 refugees.

* * *

8665

SMITH, CLIFFORD NEAL. "Some British and German Deserters During the American Revolution." In *National Genealogical Society Quarterly,* vol. 60:4 (Dec. 1972), pp. 267-275.

> Extracted from The George Washington Papers, Library of Congress Presidential Paper Series, microfilm roll 117, vols. 7-8 (British and German deserters, 1782-1783). Names those who were interrogated by American officers as deserters who crossed over to the American forces surrounding New York, 1782-1783.

* * *

8670

SMITH, CLIFFORD NEAL. "Some German Prisoners of War in the American Revolution." In *National Genealogical Society Quarterly,* vol. 59:2 (June 1971), pp. 105-109.

> Identifies some Germans captured during the American Revolution who were servants of officers and who stayed or may have stayed in the United States. This American prisoner-of-war list is especially rare and valuable because names of orderlies and officers' servants are not usually given on German muster rolls. Concerns the Braunschweiger (Brunswick) contingent in America, which arrived June 1, 1776, sailing from Dover to Quebec. Original list is in the Gunther Collection, Chicago Historical Society.

* * *

8690

SMITH, CLIFFORD NEAL. "Transported Jacobite Rebels, 1716." In *National Genealogical Society Quar-*

terly, vol. 64:1 (Mar. 1976), pp. 27-34.

> List of about 300 Scottish rebels captured at the Battle of Preston, Lancashire, in 1716 and transported variously to South Carolina, Virginia, Maryland, Jamaica, Leeward Islands, St. Christopher and Barbados. Also in no. 2989, Headlam, and partially in nos. 7385, Richardson, and 7983, Scharf.

*   *   *

8700
SMITH, CLIFFORD NEAL, and **ANNA PISZCZAN-CZAJA SMITH.** "Some German-Speaking Immigrants in Ohio and Kentucky, 1869." In *National Genealogical Society Quarterly,* vol. 62:1 (Mar. 1974), pp. 17-32.

> Taken from *Der Deutsche Pionier,* Cincinnati, Ohio, 1869. Gives personal names and places of origin.

*   *   *

8715
SMITH, FRANK. *Immigrants to America Appearing in English Records.* Logan, Utah: Everton Publishers, 1976. 117p.

> Records of many persons, collected from many sources, and provided by many correspondents. Includes 948 references more than are available in no. 8400, Sherwood. Note: the title page names Smith only, but the cover has David W. Gardner as well as Smith as author.

*   *   *

8730
SMITH, HENRY A.M. "Purrysburgh." In *The South Carolina Historical and Genealogical Magazine,* vol. 10:4 (Oct. 1909), pp. 187-219.

> Pages 208-210 contain "A List of the Germains and Switz Protestants under the Command of Collo Perry qualified before his Excellency Robert Johnson Esquire Governour of this province on the 22 and 23 dayes of December 1732," being the names of 93 alien settlers naturalized on those days. Only names and ages supplied. Pages 211-219 list land grants accorded between 1735 and 1745. Also in no. 0720, Boyer, *Ship Passenger Lists, the South,* pp. 158-160, (excerpted from pp. 208-210 of Smith book); and no. 9144, Tepper, *New World Immigrants,* vol. 2, pp. 82-114.   (Lancour 236)

*   *   *

8745
SMITH, CAPTAIN JOHN, of Willoughby by Alford, Lincolnshire. *Works, 1608-1631* . . . . Edited by Edward Arber. (The English Scholar's Library, no. 16) Birmingham [England]: privately printed, 1884, pp. 93-94, 107-108, 217, 310-311, 389-390, 411-412, 445-446, 549-560, 662-664, 731-732.

> Names the first settlers of Jamestown, 1607-1608. First planters, 1607, and those in the "first and second supplies," 1608. This served as a census of the inhabitants. Some additions in no. 3283, Hotten. Also appears in no. 9238, Tyler. The lists are repeated here in Smith, included twice because of the different spellings of names.   (Lancour 209 note)

*   *   *

8753
SMITH, REV. MATTHEW. "Voyage of the *Valiant.*" In *Pioneers on the Island,* edited by Mary Brehaut, part 1, pp. 87-88.

> Details of an 1898 interview in which the Rev. Matthew Smith recorded events of the crossing of the *Valiant* from Hull, England, to Charlottetown, Prince Edward Island, Canada.

*   *   *

8760
SMITH, SAMUEL. *The History of the Colony of Nova-Caesaria, or New Jersey: Containing, An Account of Its First Settlement, Progressive Improvements, the Original and Present Constitution, and Other Events, to the Year 1721* . . . . Burlington, N.J.: James Parker, 1765. 574p.

> Chapters 5 and 6, pp. 77-111, contain names of passengers on the *Griffith, Kent, Willing Mind, Martha, Shield,* and other, unspecified, ships. A second edition, published by William S. Sharp, is identical with the 1765 edition. Corrections in no. 3580, Johnson. Also in no. 0714, Boyer, *Ship Passenger Lists, New York and New Jersey,* pp. 217-220. Printed in no. 8070, Schermerhorn, with omission of the *Griffith* lists.   (Lancour 111)

*   *   *

8770
SMITH, W. BROADUS. *Naturalization Record(s), 1857-1870, Washington County, Texas.* N.P., 1968. 23p.

> Refers to arrivals in Texas from 1849 through 1867, the acquisition of citizenship occuring somewhat later, as the title indicates. Mostly Germans, principally from Prussia. About 90 names listed.

*   *   *

8775
SOCKETT, THOMAS. *Emigration. Letters from Sussex Emigrants Who Sailed from Portsmouth, in April, 1832, on Board the Ships "Lord Melville" and "Eveline," for Upper Canada.* 2nd ed. Petworth, Sussex, [England]: John Phillips, 1833, 47p.

> Contains letters from 33 emigrants; full names given. See also nos. 2688, Godman; 3801, Kenyon; and 0079, Young.

*   *   *

8777-8778
"SOME CHARLESTON NATURALIZATION RECORDS." In *The Carolina Herald."*
8777
---Vol. 7:2 (Oct. 1979), pp. 5-8.
8778
---Vol. 8:1 (Mar. 1980), p. 9. (In progress.)

> About a quarter of the holdings of the Clerk of Court's Office at Charles County, S.C., covering the 1840s to 1903. Gives name, date of petition, date of arrival, age, often the occupation, sometimes the residence. Many countries of origin.

*   *   *

8780

"SOME EARLY SETTLERS AND DATE OF THEIR ARRIVAL." In *Missing Links,* no. 27 (Oct. 1964), pp. 531-532.

Name, ship, date, sometimes place. British settlers, mostly to New England, 1630-1637.

*   *   *

8790

"SOME IMMIGRANTS TO AMERICA." In *English Genealogist,* no. 13, (1980), pp. 324-325.

Refers to emigrants from Londonderry, Ireland, and others from England, with dates and places of arrival often given. Covers the years 1620-1822. Taken from a number of sources, all of which have been included in this work.

*   *   *

8795-8797

"[SOME IRISH ARRIVALS IN NEW YORK and Other Ports in 1811 and 1812.]" In *The Recorder: Bulletin of the American Irish Historical Society.*
8795
---Vol. 3:5 (June 1926), pp. 2-19.
    Some Irish arrivals in New York in 1811, published in *The Shamrock,* a New York weekly, March 30 to August of that year.
8796
---Vol. 3:6 (Sept. 1926), pp. 17-21.
    Some Irish arrivals in New York, Philadelphia, and Baltimore in 1811. Passenger lists published in *The Shamrock; or Hibernian Chronicle,* July 18, 1811-August 17, 1811.
8797
---Vol. 3:7 (Dec. 1926), pp. 23-32.
    Some Irish arrivals in New York and other ports in 1811 and 1812. Includes passenger lists and other interesting items published in *The Shamrock; or Hibernian Chronicle,* September 14-December 21, 1811. In Lancour, as item 27A. See also no. 2859, Hackett; no. 8099, Schlegel; and no. 1742, Early, Charles M. In vol. 3:1 of *The Recorder* (Mar. 1925), on pp. 1 and 2, there is a list of ship arrivals from Ireland in 1811.

*   *   *

8810

"SOME OF THE PALATINES WHO CAME to Pennsylvania about 1727." In *Missing Links,* no. 37 (Aug. 1965), pp. 731-732.
    Names only.

*   *   *

8825

SOMERBY, HORATIO G., communicator. "Corrections of Names, Places, &c., Relating to New England Emigrants Wrongly Given in the Mass(achusetts) Hist(orical) Coll(ections) and in The N(ew) E(ngland) H(istorical) and G(enealogical) Reg(ister)." In *The New England Historical and Genealogical Register,* vol. 5 (Oct. 1851), p. 440.

Corrects data in *The Massachusetts Historical Collections,* 3rd ser., vol. 8 (1843), p. 319; and vol. 10 (1849), pp. 136-138, (our nos. 7906-7907, Savage); and in *The New England Historical*

and Genealogical Register, vol. 2 (1848), pp. 108-110 (our no. 8995, Stevens). No. 9151, Tepper, *Passengers to America,* p. 127, gives corrections to no. 8995, Stevens.

*   *   *

8835

SOMERBY, HORATIO G. "Emigrants for St. Christophers [and Barbados, etc.] 1634-1635." In *The New England Historical and Genealogical Register,* vol. 14:4 (Oct. 1860), pp. 347-359.

Also printed in nos. 1672 and 1674, Drake, pp. 99-114.

*   *   *

8845

SOMERBY, HORATIO G. "Items (1635)." In *The New England Historical and Genealogical Register,* vol. 2:4 (Oct. 1848), pp. 374-375.

Passengers for Virginia, 1635. Also in no. 1672, Drake, *Result of Some Researches . . . ,* 1860, pp. 71-72.

*   *   *

8855

SOMERBY, HORATIO G. "More Passengers to New England." In *The New England Historical and Genealogical Register,* vol. 25:1 (Jan. 1871), pp. 13-15.

See no. 0124, Appleton. Also in no. 9151, Tepper, *Passengers to America,* pp. 77-79, and no. 0702, Boyer, *Ship Passenger Lists, National and New England,* pp. 149-151. (Lancour 48)

*   *   *

8862

SOMERBY, HORATIO G. "Passengers for Virginia, 1635." In *The New England Historical and Genealogical Register,* vol. 2:1 (Jan. 1848), pp. 111-113; vol. 2:2 (Apr. 1848), pp. 211-212; vol. 2:3 (July 1848), p. 268; vol. 2:4 (Oct. 1848), pp. 374-375; vol. 3:2 (Apr. 1849), p. 184; vol. 3:3 (July 1849), p. 388-390; vol. 4:1 (Jan. 1850), p. 61; vol. 4:2 (Apr. 1850), pp. 189-191; vol. 4:3 (July 1850), pp. 261-264; vol. 5:1 (Jan. 1851), pp. 61-62; vol. 5:3 (July 1851), pp. 343-344; vol. 15:2 (Apr. 1861), pp. 142-146.

From originals of the Master of Rolls, London. Articles in various numbers of the register. The late appearance of the final list was because it had been lost. Also in no. 9151, Tepper, *Passengers to America,* pp. 80-127. (Lancour 217)

*   *   *

8870-8872

SPAIN, ARCHIVO GENERAL DE INDIAS, SEVILLE. *Catalogo de Pasajeros a Indias durante los Siglos XVI, XVII y XVIII.* Edited by the docents of the General Indian Archives under the Director of the Archives, Don Cristobal Bermudez Plata. Seville [Spain]: Imprenta Editorial de la Gavidia. 3 vols.
8870
---Vol. 1, 1509-1534. 1940. 515p.
8871
---Vol. 2, 1535-1538. 1942. 507p.

8872
---Vol. 3, 1539-1559. 1946. 529p.

Chronological list of passengers to Spanish America (including Florida and Louisiana, 1538-1559). From documents in the "Indian Archives" in Seville, 1509-1790. Provides name of emigrant, place of origin, place of departure, and destination. Vol. l supersedes an edition covering the years 1509-1533 (Madrid: Imprenta Espasa-Calpe, 1930). For continuation, 1560-1594, see no. 5801, Morales. No. 0720, Boyer, *Ship Passenger Lists, the South*, pp. 165-189, reconstructs pp. 233-285 of vol. 2 and reads: "Lancour suggests that the three-volume work contains lists [of sailings] from 1538 to 1559 to Florida and Louisiana, although in fact 'Louisiana' is a place name used in a later period, and all the names given for Florida are from the year 1538." (Lancour 241)

*   *   *

8880
SPENCER, WILBUR D. *Pioneers on Maine Rivers with Lists to 1651.* Portland, Maine: Lakeside Printing Co., 1930. 414p. Reprinted by Genealogical Publishing Co., Baltimore, 1973.

Pages 13-23 contain "Maine Visiting Lists before 1630," a list of pioneers, often with the names of ships in which they arrived. Mostly British settlers. Other settlements mentioned. (Lancour 30)

*   *   *

8890
SPENGEMANN, FRIEDRICH. *Die Reisen der Segelfregatten "Isabella," "Pauline," "Meta," und "Uhland" nach Nordamerika. nach Kaepitan Juergen Meyers Bordbuch.* Bremen, Germany: Buchdruckerei Vahland, 1937. 136p.

Lists of passengers on the *Isabella*, 1832-1839; the *Pauline*, 1839-1842; the *Meta*, 1842; and the *Uhland*, 1849, from Bremen to New York and Bremen to New Orleans. Names, ages, and places of origin. (Lancour 248)

*   *   *

8905
STAEDTLER, ERHARD. *Die Ansbach-Bayreuther Truppen im Amerikanischen Unabhaengigkeitskrieg 1777-1783: Forschungen zur Kulturgeschichte und Familienkunde.* (Freie Schriftenfolge der Gesellschaft fuer Familienforschung in Franken, vol. 8.) Nuernberg [Germany]: 1956, pp. 151-172.

The troops of Ansbach-Bayreuth in the American War of Independence, 1777-1783: researches in cultural history and genealogy. First issued as a doctoral thesis in Erlangen, Germany, 1955. The appendix, pp. 151-172, entitled, "Deserteure, Ueberlaeufer und Neusiedler in Amerika" (deserters, turncoats and settlers in America) has names alphabetically arranged. Name, military unit, date of desertion, etc. Concerns about 400 (Bavarian) soldiers. For English version, see no. 8640, Smith.

*   *   *

8925
STANARD, WILLIAM GLOVER. *Some Emigrants to Virginia: Memoranda in Regard to Several Hundred Emigrants to Virginia During the Colonial Period Whose Parentage is Shown or Former Residence Indicated by Authentic Records.* Richmond [Va.]: Bell Book and Stationery Co., 1911. 2nd ed., enl., 1915. Reprinted by Genealogical Publishing Co., Baltimore, 1965.

Alphabetical list of immigrants to Virginia, 1635-1800, from a variety of sources. (Lancour 218)

*   *   *

8935
STAPLETON, AMMON. "General List of Huguenot Immigrants to Pennsylvania." In *Memorials of the Huguenots in America, with Special Reference to Their Emigration to Pennsylvania.* Carlisle, Pa.: Huguenot Publishing, 1901, pp. 147-157. Reprinted by Genealogical Publishing Co., Baltimore, 1969.

Alphabetical list of immigrants to Pennsylvania during its provincial period, who are believed to have been of Huguenot origin. Extracts from no. 7820, Rupp, and no. 1804, Egle. Mostly French, some German. (Lancour 128)

*   *   *

8945
STEINEMANN, ERNST, editor. "A List of Eighteenth-Century Emigrants from the Canton of Schaffhausen to the American Colonies, 1734-1752." Introduction by Dr. Don Yoder. In *The Pennsylvania German Folklore Society* [*Yearbook*], vol. 16 (1951), pp. 185-196.

Alphabetical listing of 122 Swiss, individuals and heads of families, destined for Pennsylvania, Nova Scotia (Halifax), and Carolina. Appears as well in no. 8955, Steinemann. Also in no. 9964, Yoder. (Lancour 154)

*   *   *

8955
STEINEMANN, ERNST. "Zur schaffhauserischen Auswanderung." In *Beitraege zur Vaterlaendischen Geschichte.* [Switzerland]: Historisch-antiquarischen Verein des Kantons Schaffhausen, (1936), part 13, pp. 86-99.

Regarding emigration from Schaffhausen, from various sources. About 150 emigrants from the Canton of Schaffhausen, Switzerland, 1734-1752, are named, with places of origin, some occupations, year of emigration. Destinations were Pennsylvania, Nova Scotia (Halifax), and Carolina. This is a supplement to Steinemann's article "Die schaffhauserische Auswanderung und ihre Ursachen" (Emigration from Schaffhausen and its causes.) See also no. 8945, Steinemann. (Lancour 154A)

*   *   *

8965
STEPHENSON, JEAN. "Naturalization Register, United States District Court, Charleston, South Carolina, 1792-1800." In *National Genealogical Society*

Quarterly, vol. 30:4 (Dec. 1942), pp. 125-127.

> Record given to the Library of the Daughters of the American Revolution, Washington, D.C., compiled by Mrs. R.W. Hutson. See also no. 3020, Hemperley.

*   *   *

8980
STEPHENSON, JEAN. *Scotch-Irish Emigration to South Carolina, 1772. (Rev. William Martin and His Five Shiploads of Settlers.)* Washington, D.C.: the author, 1971. (Available from Mrs. Donna Hotaling, Washington, D.C.) 137p.

> Pages 30-31, 35, 42-101 name satisfied passengers listed in the *Belfast News Letter,* December 22, 1772, concerning the arrival of the *Mary and James* at "Charles-Town," S.C., October 18, 1772; and those of the ship *Lord Dunluce,* which arrived December 20, 1772, according to the *Belfast News Letter* of June 4-8, 1773. Full family information on persons from the *Lord Dunluce,* January 6, 1773. Varies from data found in the records. Warrants of survey: pp. 42-101.

*   *   *

8995
STEVENS, HENRY. "Passengers for New England, 1638." In *The New England Historical and Genealogical Register,* vol. 2:1 (Jan. 1848), pp. 108-110.

> Lists 110 passengers on the *Confidence* from London, April 11, 1638. Corrections to this in no. 8825, Somerby; also printed in corrected form in no. 0263, Banks; nos. 1672 and 1674, Drake; and in no. 9151, Tepper, *Passengers to America,* pp. 125-127. (Lancour 52)

*   *   *

9010
STEVENSON, JOHN R. "Persons Naturalized in New Jersey Between 1702 and 1776." In *The New York Genealogical and Biographical Record,* vol. 28:2 (Apr. 1897), pp. 86-89.

> Collected from Allinson's *Acts of the General Assembly of the Province of New Jersey . . . 1702 . . . to 1776.* Lists aliens naturalized by the Assembly of New Jersey between the dates of the union of the provinces of East and West Jersey in 1702 and commencement of the Revolutionary War. Contains names and dates, only occasionally the country of origin. Also in no. 9135, Tepper, *Immigrants to the Middle Colonies,* pp. 124-127. See also no. 6117, *Guide to Naturalization Records in New Jersey.* (Lancour 115)

*   *   *

9025
STEWART, ROBERT ARMISTEAD. "Ancient Planters [1607]." In Nell Marion Nugent, *Cavaliers and Pioneers: Abstracts of Virginia Land Patents and Grants, 1623-1666.* Richmond, Va.: Dietz Printing Co., 1934, vol. 1. p. xxvi-xxxiv (Introduction). Reprinted by Genealogical Publishing Co., Baltimore, 1963.

> List of persons known to have come to Virginia before the

close of 1616, with date of arrival and name of ship supplied when known. Information came from Patent Books 1 through 5. (Lancour 208)

*   *   *

9029
STIENS, ROBERT E., contributor. "Passenger List of the Steamship *Devonia,* Glasgow to New York 1893." In *Scottish-American Genealogist,* nos. 17-20. (1980 annual) pp. 72-74.

> Name, age, sex, native country, and last place of residence. Lists 112 passengers.

*   *   *

9031
STIENS, ROBERT E., contributor. "Passenger List of the Steamship *Trave,* 1893." In *Germanic Genealogist,* no. 19 (1979), pp. 84-91.

> The *Trave* crossed from Bremen and Southampton to New York, 1893. Article includes lists for the steamship *Steinhoft,* from Cuxhaven and Le Havre to New York, 1893, and the steamship *Stuttgart,* Bremen to New York, 1893. Names, ages, country of origin (most from Germany).

*   *   *

9034
STIENS, ROBERT E., contributor. "Three Passenger Lists 1893." In *Eastern & Central European Genealogist,* no. 3 (1979), pp. 120-154.

> Names individuals who arrived at New York or Baltimore in January 1893. The ships: the *Amalfi,* New York, January 5, 1893; the *Italia,* New York, January 3, 1893; and the *Weimar,* which arrived at New York, January 5, 1893, leaving about one-third of its passengers and proceeding to Baltimore. From U.S. National Archives microfilm, M 237 roll 602. Over 1,700 individuals from Eastern and Central European places. Name, age, sex, place of origin, ship.

*   *   *

9041-9042
STRASSBURGER, RALPH BEAVER. *Pennsylvania German Pioneers: a Publication of the Original Lists of Arrivals in the Port of Philadelphia from 1727 to 1808.* Edited by William John Hinke. Norristown [Pa.]: Pennsylvania German Society, 1934. Vols. 1 and 3 reprinted by Genealogical Publishing Co., Baltimore, 1964.
9041
---Vol. 1. 1727-1775. 776p.
9042
---Vol. 3. 1785-1808. 709p.

> Contains 29,800 names, with annotations written by Krebs (see no. 4203). Various references to the names in Strassburger will be found in other listings, mostly where authors have attempted to line up their information with that in Strassburger. This work (often referred to as Strassburger and Hinke) is much superior to no. 7820, Rupp, and no. 1804, Egle. It forms a revision with additions to Rupp and Egle, and was prepared and edited with great accuracy. Vol. 1 contains captains' lists, 1727-1775; vol. 2 has facsimiles of all signatures of signers of

oaths of allegiance and oaths of abjuration, and was not included in the G.P.C. reprint; vol. 3 has captains' lists from 1785-1808, and indexes to captains, ships, ports of departure, and surnames in all volumes. The set was originally vols. 42-44 of the *Pennsylvania German Society Proceedings*. (Lancour 146)

* * *

9055
STROBEL, PHILIP A. "Principal Residents at Ebenezer in 1741." In *The Salzburgers and Their Descendants: Being the History of a Colony of German (Lutheran) Protestants, who Emigrated to Georgia in 1734, and Settled at Ebenezer, Twenty-Five Miles Above the City of Savannah.* Baltimore: T. Newton Kurtz, 1855. Reprinted by the The University of Georgia Press, Athens, 1953. 318p.

References to immigrants and early settlers and, on p. 112, the names of 53 persons who no doubt were immigrants originally. To be found in a history of some former inhabitants of Salzburg, Austria. See also no. 9330, Urlsperger.

* * *

9061
STRUCK, WOLF-HEINO. *Die Auswanderung aus dem Herzogtum Nassau (1806-1866): Ein Kapitel der modernen politischen und sozialen Entwicklung.* (Geschichtliche Landeskunde, Veroeffentlichungen des Instituts fuer Geschichtliche Landeskunde an der Universitaet Mainz, vol. 4.) Wiesbaden [Germany]: Franz Steiner Verlag, 1966. 203p.

Emigration from the Duchy of Nassau (1806-1866): a chapter in modern political and social development. From notices of emigration published in the *Nassauisches Intelligenzblatt* for the years 1849 to 1868. Pages 134-203, an appendix, contain the names of about 4,000 emigrants from that region of Germany which was the Duchy of Nassau. Destinations include North and South America (Brazil, Venezuela, and Texas being indicated specifically). Names individuals or heads of emigrant groups. The fact that a wife, family, or children accompanied the head is stated, as well as the place of origin.

* * *

9070
STUCKY, HARLEY J. *The Swiss (Volhynian) Mennonite Ship List 1874 of the Immigrants Who Came from Russia.* North Newton, KS.: Mennonite Press, Faith & Life Bookstore, 1974. 37p.

The Swiss (Volhynian) Mennonites came to the United States from the Volga area of Russia in four groups on the ships *City of Richmond* and *City of Chester* to the port of New York. Most settled in South Dakota, a few in Kansas.

* * *

9085
SWIFT, R.G. "German Families." In *The Pennsylvania Magazine of History and Biography,* vol. 33:4 (1909), pp. 501-502.

List of German families arriving at Philadelphia from Hol-

land. Names and origins only. From an advertisement in Henry Miller's *Staats Bote* of February 9, 1758. Also in no. 9120, Tepper, *Emigrants to Pennsylvania,* p. 261. (Lancour 183, listed under R.G. Smith)

* * *

9100
TADICH, JOHN V. "The Jugoslav Colony of San Francisco on My Arrival in 1871." In *Balkan and Eastern European American Genealogical and Historical Quarterly,* vol. 4:2 (June 1967), pp. 81-95.

This study, written in 1932, discusses Yugoslavs in San Francisco between 1870 and 1875.

* * *

9110
TAYLOR, GEORGE. "Roger Williams." In *The Genealogist's Post,* vol. 1:5 (May 1964), pp. 3-9.

Lists some passengers on the *Lyon* from Bristol to Boston, 1631. Throughout the article there are references to other immigrants, with their dates of arrival, some having a connection with Rhode Island.

* * *

9115-9116
TENBARGE, ELEANOR. "Naturalization Records - Vanderburgh County, Indiana." In *The Tri-State Packet.*
9115
---Vol. 3:2 (Dec. 1979), pp. 28-38.
9116
---Vol. 3:4 (June 1980), pp. 5, 18.

Found in Court Order Book H, Circuit Court, 9-24-1850 to 8-11-1854. Date of declaration of intention, date of citizenship, oath, country of origin. This is a continuing series.

* * *

9120
TEPPER, MICHAEL, editor. *Emigrants to Pennsylvania, 1641-1819: A Consolidation of Ship Passenger Lists from The Pennsylvania Magazine of History and Biography.* Baltimore: Genealogical Publishing Co., 1975. 292p.

Fourteen articles on immigration, excerpted from *The Pennsylvania Magazine of History and Biography,* 1877-1934. Names 6,000 persons. Listed similarly in Boyer, nos. 0702, 0714, 0717, and 0720.

* * *

9135
TEPPER, MICHAEL, editor. *Immigrants to the Middle Colonies: A Consolidation of Ship Passenger Lists and Associated Data from The New York Genealogical and Biographical Record.* Baltimore: Genealogical Publishing Co., 1978. 178p.

Contains 15 articles taken from *The New York Genealogical and Biographical Record,* 1879-1970. About 5,500 names. Similar lists in Boyer, nos. 0702, 0714, 0717, and 0720.

9143-9144
TEPPER, MICHAEL, editor. *New World Immigrants: A Consolidation of Ship Passenger Lists and Associated Data from Periodical Literature.* 2 vols. Baltimore: Genealogical Publishing Co., 1979, 568p. and 602p.

Covers 27,500 immigrants from the years 1618-1878, with excellent index. All items were taken from Lancour's *Bibliography of Ship Passenger Lists . . . ,* 1963. Similar lists are in Boyer, nos. 0702, 0714, 0717, and 0720.

*   *   *

9151
TEPPER, MICHAEL, editor. *Passengers to America: A Consolidation of Ship Passenger Lists from The New England Historical and Genealogical Register.* Baltimore: Genealogical Publishing Co., 1977. 554p. Reprinted with new introduction and indexes, 1978.

Contains 35 articles excerpted from *The New England Historical and Genealogical Register,* 1847-1961. About 17,000 names. Similar lists in Boyer, nos. 0702, 0714, 0717, 0720.

*   *   *

9158
"THIRTY POUNDS REWARD." In *The Pennsylvania Genealogical Magazine,* vol. 25:1 (1967), p. 17.

Runaways from the ship *Amelia,* of Belfast, anchored in the Delaware River. Lists ten missing redemptioners and servants advertised for in the *Pennsylvania Journal and the Weekly Advertiser,* August 9, 1783.

*   *   *

9163
THWING, ANNIE HAVEN. "The Following Persons Embarked for New England in the *Susan and Ellen,* April 1635 . . . ." In *The New England Historical and Genealogical Register,* vol. 55 (July 1901), p. 345.

Names and ages of 24 passengers on the *Susan and Ellen,* 1635. Also in no. 9151, Tepper, *Passengers to America,* p. 462; and in no. 0702, Boyer, *Ship Passenger Lists, National and New England,* p. 153. (Lancour 50)

*   *   *

9170
"TIME OF THE ARRIVAL IN NEW ENGLAND of the Following Ministers." In *The New England Historical and Genealogical Register,* vol. 1:3 (July 1847), p. 289.

Names of 65 settlers listed under the year of arrival, 1630-1641. Also in no. 9151, Tepper, *Passengers to America,* p. 467; and in no. 0702, Boyer, *Ship Passenger Lists, National and New England,* p. 141. (Lancour 42)

*   *   *

9190
TOUPS, NEIL J., compiler and editor. *Mississippi Valley Pioneers.* Lafayette, La.: Neilson Publishing Co. [1970]. 135p.

Ships list of passengers who left France for Louisiana between

1718 and 1721. Names, with places of origin of persons immigrating under the auspices of The Western Company and The Company of the Indies. There were 37 vessels involved. Passengers are listed on pp. 23-127. Data from the Paris Archives, Ser. G 1, 464, and Ser. F 5b, 37, in the Archives of the Colonies. Transcriptions are in the Library of Congress; the University of Southwestern Louisiana (Dupre Library), Lafayette; and the Louisiana State Museum Library, New Orleans. Partly published in nos. 8420-8422, where there are discrepancies.

*   *   *

9198
TRAINOR, BRIAN. "Sources for the Identification of Emigrants from Ireland to North America in the 19th Century." In *Ulster Genealogical & Historical Guild Newsletter,* vol. 1:1 (1978), pp. 7-18; vol. 1:2 (1979), pp. 35-51.

Discusses passenger lists from Ireland and gives several, with much supporting data concerning passengers sailing from the port of Newry and elsewhere to the United States of America, 1803-1831. See also no. 1762, "Early Irish Emigrants . . . ." and no. 2151, Fothergill.

*   *   *

9200
TRAINOR, BRIAN, and **PATRICK McCORKELL.** "Sources for the Identification of Emigrants from Ireland to North America in the 19th Century." In *Ulster Genealogical & Historical Guild Newsletter,* vol. 1:3 (1979), pp. 76-90.

A study of the firm of William McCorkell & Co., specialists in the passenger trade. Lists crew members of the *Stadacona* who deserted at Philadelphia, May 2, 1864, and of the *Mohongo,* at Philadelphia, May-June 1864. Extracts from an order book of William McCorkell & Co., grain merchants & shippers, Londonderry, for passages to America paid to Robert Taylor & Co., Philadelphia, between 1864 and 1871, on *Minnehaha, Stadacona, Lady Emily Peel, Mohongo* and *Village Belle,* all crossings 1864. Name, address, age, and occupation of each passenger, the ship, date of sailing, and fare paid.

*   *   *

9214
TRIBEKKO, JOHN, and **GEORGE RUPERTI.** *Lists of Germans from the Palatinate Who Came to England in 1709.* Baltimore: Genealogical Publishing Co., 1965. 44p.

Lists about 6,500 emigrants, many of whom came to America. Names, ages, and family accompanying. Copied from original documents in the British Museum Library, London. First published in nos. 4772-4773, *The New York Genealogical and Biographical Record,* vols. 40 and 41, 1909-1910. Also in no. 9135, Tepper, *Immigrants to the Middle Colonies,* pp. 84-123.

*   *   *

9222
TRUDEL, MARCEL. *La Population du Canada en 1663.* Montreal: Fides, Collection Fleur du Lys, 1973. 368p.

Systematic analysis of the Canadian population in 1663.

Includes a list with the following information for each entry: name, sex, places of origin and settlement, marital status, household, occupation, property, literacy, and whether or not the individual was under contract. See pp. 163-320. No ships mentioned.

*   *   *

9224
TRUSDLE, MRS. MARGARET L., contributor. "Naturalization Intention Papers, Richland County, Ohio, 1875-1896." In *The Report: Ohio Genealogical Society,* vol. 11:3 (Fall 1971), pp. 122-128.

Gives individual's country of origin, date of arrival, name of witness. Some arrived in the 1840s and 1850s. Most from Germany.

*   *   *

9227
TUCKER, TERRY. *Bermuda - Unintended Destination, 1609-1610.* Bermuda: Island Press Ltd., 1978. 92p.

Pages 15-21 deal with the persons aboard the *Sea Venture,* which left Britain in 1609 for Jamestown but was wrecked off Bermuda. The names are given on pages 16 and 17. Genealogies of some of the passengers are on succeeding pages. "The names of the Originall Aduenturers for the plantacon of the Somers Islands . . . 1615" are on pages 83-85. Most were adventurers in The Virginia Company.

*   *   *

9230
TURNER, WALTER LeSUEUR, contributor. "Communication from Governor Francis Nicholson of Virginia Regarding Huguenot Refugees on Board Ship *Mary and Ann.*" In *The Huguenot,* vol. 6 (1933), pp. 82-86.

Lists refugees from London who arrived at the James River on July 23, 1700. Also in no. 0720, Boyer, *Ship Passenger Lists, the South,* pp. 86-89; and in no. 9143, Tepper, *New World Immigrants,* vol. 1, pp. 439-443. See other references in the index. (Lancour 222, under title of article)

*   *   *

9238
TYLER, LYON GARDINER. "Census of Inhabitants: Names of the First Settlers at Jamestown, 1607; Names of Those Who Came in the First Supply; Names of Those Who Came in the Second Supply; Names of Inhabitants of Jamestown in 1624." In *The Cradle of the Republic: Jamestown and James River.* Richmond [Va.]: The Hermitage Press, 1906. pp. 100-104.

Taken from no. 8745, John Smith. Also in no. 0720, Boyer, *Ship Passenger Lists, the South,* pp. 40-43. And see no. 7860, Sams. (Lancour 209)

*   *   *

9248
ULBRICH, HARALD. "Auswanderer aus Sachsen nach USA." In *Archiv fuer Sippenforschung und alle*

verwandten Gebiete, vol. 28:7 (Aug. 1962), pp. 394-395.

Emigrants from Saxony to America. From Saxon chronicles, articles on local history, etc. Represents between 200 and 300 emigrants who left the former Prussian province of Saxony for America, 1838-1900. Name, date of emigration, place of origin and, for most, the intended destination.

*   *   *

9258
UNITED STATES. DEPARTMENT OF STATE. *Letter from the Secretary of State, with a Transcript of the List of Passengers Who Arrived in the United States from the 1st October, 1819, to the 30th September, 1820.* Washington: Gales & Seaton, 1821. 288p. Reprinted with added index under the title, *Passenger Arrivals 1819-1820 . . .,* by Genealogical Publishing, Baltimore, 1967, pp. 289-342.

Record of 16th Congress, 2d session, Senate Document 118, Serial Number 45. Contains 10,247 names from Customs lists. Ships to American ports in various regions. Much information about the immigrants. This is the first official list of immigrants published by the U.S. Government. (Lancour 29)

*   *   *

9268
UNITED STATES. DEPARTMENT OF STATE. *Passengers Who Arrived in the United States, September 1821 - December 1823.* Indexed. Baltimore: Magna Carta Book Co., 1969. (Available from Tuttle, Rutland, VT.)

Derived from transcripts made by the State Department from National Archives records. Includes immigrants of many origins. Few names from the end of 1821 through 1823 (documents lost). Pages 1-357 list names; pages 359-427 provide an index of vessels and persons.

*   *   *

9280
UNITED STATES, WORKS PROJECTS ADMINISTRATION. *Index to Naturalization Records in Arkansas, 1809-1906.* (Immigration and Naturalization Records Indexing Project Service Division). Little Rock, Ark.: U.S.W.P.A., 1942. 6. 111p.
Limited to 75 copies.

*   *   *

9290-9314
UNITED STATES, WORKS PROJECTS ADMINISTRATION. *Index to Records of Aliens' Declarations of Intention and/or Oaths of Allegiance, 1789-1880, in United States Circuit Court, United States District Court, Supreme Court of Pennsylvania, Quarter Sessions Court, Court of Common Pleas, Philadelphia.* Compiled by W.P.A., Project No. 20837. [Harrisburg]: Pennsylvania Historical Commission, [1940?] 25 vols. in 11.

9290 v. 1, Letter A, 79p.	9293 v. 3, Letter D, 248p.
9291 v. 1, Letter B, 345p.	9294 v. 3, Letter E, 75p.
9292 v. 2, Letter C, 297p.	9295 v. 4, Letter F, 173p.

9296 v. 4, Letter G, 224p.
9297 v. 5, Letter H, 318p.
9298 v. 5, Letter I, 11p.
9299 v. 5, Letter J, 53p.
9300 v. 6, Letter K, 235p.
9301 v. 6, Letter L, 185p.
9302 v. 7, Ltr. M, p. 1-350
     v. 8, Ltr. M, p. 351-674
9303 v. 8, Letter N, 58 p.
9304 v. 9, Letter O, 88 p.
9305 v. 9, Letter P, 100p.

9306 v. 9, Letter Q, 18p.
9307 v. 9, Letter R, 191p.
9308 v. 10, Letter S, 370p.
9309 v. 11, Letter T, 98p.
9310 v. 11, Letter U, 8p.
9311 v. 11, Letter V, 24p.
9312 v. 11, Letter W, 218p.
9313 v. 11, Letter Y, 14p.
9314 v. 11, Letter Z, 18p.

Called Section II, *Alphabetical Index of Naturalization Records, 1794-1880, Maritime Records, Port of Philadelphia.* Entries include name of applicant, country of former allegiance, court of record, and declaration date. Reproduced from typewritten material. Only a few copies exist. (Lancour 188)

*   *   *

9330

URLSPERGER, SAMUEL, editor. *Ausfuehrliche Nachricht von den Salzburgischen Emigranten Die sich in America niedergelassen haben.* Halle, Germany: Waysenhaus, 1735. *Vierte Continuation . . .,* Halle: Waysenhaus, 1740, pp. 2307-2312.

Detailed account of early Salzburg emigrants who settled in America . . . fourth part. From reports of pastors overseeing the community in New Ebenezer, Georgia, to the Lutheran Church fathers in Augsburg and Halle, Germany. Provides the names and ages of about 230 settlers at New Ebenezer, Georgia, in 1739, including 65 who died between 1734 and 1739. Almost all these settlers were Protestant refugees from Salzburg, Austria, where they had been the object of persecution by the ruling Archbishop (in an otherwise totally Roman Catholic area). They fled first to northeastern provinces of Germany before then proceeding to the colony of Georgia in America, arriving in 1734. The book contains descriptions of the voyages to America, travel diaries of the two pastors in charge of the refugees, an historical account of conditions leading up to the emigration, and a contemporary description of Georgia. The Salzburgers in Georgia are also mentioned in no. 1134, Casteleiro; no. 7820, Rupp; and no. 9055, Strobel.

*   *   *

9350

VAILLANCOURT, EMILE. *La conquete du Canada par les Normands.* Montreal: G. Ducharme, 1933. 2nd ed. 252p., plus a table of place names in Normandy.

The Norman "conquest" of Canada. An alphabetical list of Norman French who emigrated to Canada in the sixteenth and seventeenth centuries. Gives fairly complete biographical information when available: names, aliases, occupations, places and dates of birth and death, names of parents, size of households, and dates and places of arrival and of marriage. The first edition, 1930 (250p.), has no table.

*   *   *

9365

VAN LAER, ARNOLD JOHAN FERDINAND, editor. "Settlers of Rensselaerswyck, 1630-1658." In *Van Rensselaer Bowier Manuscripts, Being the Letters of*

Kiliaen Van Rensselaer, 1630-1643, [*1657*], *and Other Documents Relating to the Colony of Rensselaerswyck.* Albany: University of the State of New York, 1908, pp. 805-846. Reprinted with 8-page index to Biographical Notices, by Genealogical Publishing Co., Baltimore, 1965. 54p.

Originally New York State Library Bulletin, History, 7. A record of the arrival of settlers in the colony from the date of its founding to the end of the administration of Jan Baptist Van Rensselaer. Much better and more comprehensive than no. 6306, O'Callaghan, and no. 8360, "Settlers . . . ." Also in no. 0714, Boyer, *Ship Passenger Lists, New York and New Jersey,* pp.45-81. (Lancour 76)

*   *   *

9370

VAN LAER, ARNOLD JOHAN FERDINAND. "Settlers of the Colony of Rensselaerswyck, 1637." In *The New York Genealogical and Biographical Record,* vol. 49:4 (Oct. 1918), pp. 365-367.

List immigrants indebted to the owners of the ship *Rensselaerswyck* for board from October 1, 1636, to their landing in New Netherland in 1637. Names 33 persons, with date of leaving the ship. From a manuscript in the New York State Library, Albany. Also in no. 9365, Van Laer; and in no. 9135, Tepper, *Immigrants to the Middle Colonies,* pp. 28-30. (Lancour 80)

*   *   *

9385-9387

VAN STIGT, K. *Geschiedenis van Pella, Iowa, en Omgeving,* 3 vols. [Pella, Iowa]: Weekblad Drukkerij, 1897.

9385

---Vol. 1, pp. 75, 76, 89-114.
     Names passengers who sailed from Rotterdam to Baltimore, Maryland, in 1847.

9386

---Vol. 2. pp. 42-44, 58-65.
     Emigrants from the Netherlands, 1848 and 1849.

9387

---Vol. 3. pp. 15-29, 79-93.
     Lists Dutch persons living in Pella or arriving from Rotterdam and elsewhere between 1849 and 1860.
     Translation of title: History of Pella, Iowa, and its Surroundings. Similar information in no. 0675, Booster Press.

*   *   *

9400

VAN TIENHOVEN, CORNELIS. "Van Tienhoven's Answer to the Vertoogh . . . [1650.]." In *Collections of the New-York Historical Society,* 2nd ser., vol. 2 (1849), pp. 329-338.

The defense by Cornelis (or Cornelius) Van Tienhoven of the existing system of government in New Netherland, 1650. Contains the names of eleven colonists, signatories to the Remonstrance. Also in no. 3490, Jameson; and in no. 6331, O'Callaghan. (Lancour 78A)

*   *   *

9412

"VARIOUS SAILINGS FROM SCOTLAND to Boston Between 1716 and 1766." In *The Scottish Genealogist,* vol. 7:4 (Oct. 1960), pp. 14-15.

Taken from "The Commissioners' Reports, Boston Records, vol. 29, Doc. 100, in the Massachusetts Historical Association, Boston, Mass., U.S.A." Contains short lists from eight voyages. Page 15 records some names of passengers, 1770-1774, to Island of St. John (later Prince Edward Island). Extracts from no. 9750, Whitmore. Also in no. 9143, Tepper, *New World Immigrants,* vol. 1, pp. 459-460.　(Lancour 65)

*　　*　　*

9424

VIDRINE, MRS. JACQUELINE OLIVIER. "Attakapas Area Families (Non-Acadians)." In *Louisiana Genealogical Register,* vol. 21:1 (Mar. 1974), pp.57-63.

Gathered from one volume of the church registers in St. Martinville, Louisiana, prepared by Father Michel Bernard Barriere while serving in the Attakapas Region, 1795-1823. Names, with places of origin.

*　　*　　*

9436

VILLERE, SIDNEY LOUIS, compiler. *The Canary Islands Migration to Louisiana, 1778-1783.* New Orleans, La.: Genealogical Research Society of New Orleans, 1971. 94p. Reprinted by Genealogical Publishing Co., Baltimore, 1972.

The history and passenger lists of the islander volunteer recruits and others, including family groups. Passenger lists of eight vessels, cataloging 2,000 immigrants, mentioning families, ages, and date of arrival.

*　　*　　*

9448

VIRKUS, FREDERICK A., editor. *Immigrant Ancestors. A List of 2,500 Immigrants to America Before 1750.* Baltimore, Genealogical Publishing Co., 1964. 75p.

In the years from 1925 to 1942, Frederick A. Virkus edited seven volumes with the title, *The Abridged Compendium of American Genealogy,* published in Chicago by The Institute of American Genealogy. Each volume has a section in the main body of the work, complete in itself, entitled "Immigrant Ancestors," containing much genealogical information: vol. 1, pp. 965-997; vol. 2, pp. 387-421; vol. 3, pp. 645-692; vol. 4, pp. 727-777; vol. 5, pp. 741-793; vol. 6, pp. 749-819; vol. 7, pp. 825-895. The section in vol. 7 appears to be the most complete and it has been reprinted. Thus that 1964 reprint list is the only one appearing in no. 2048, Filby, *Passenger and Immigration Lists Index.* The Virkus work supplies facts on birth, ancestry, time and place of arrival on this continent, marriage, and death of each immigrant that it includes. A more complete list of immigrants to America before 1750 whose surnames begin with the letter A or the letter B through "Battles" is contained in the material listed in item no. 9450.　(Lancour 3)

*　　*　　*

9450

VIRKUS, FREDERICK A., editor. *Immigrants to America Before 1750. An Alphabetical List of Immigrants to the Colonies, Before 1750, Compiled from Official and Other Records.* Surnames 'A through BAT.' Baltimore: Genealogical Publishing Co., 1965. 220p.

Published extracts from *The Magazine of American Genealogy,* section 4, nos. 1-27 (1929 - [1932]). Good compilation but incomplete, since publication of the magazine was suspended; it contains names from beginning of alphabet through 'Battles' only. Sources include manuscript and printed works and public and private records in great variety.　(Lancour 2)

*　　*　　*

9460-9461

VOELKER, FRIEDRICH. "Die amerikanische Nachkommenschaft der Familie Gutmann-Klungler." In *Genealogie.*
9460
---Vol. 9:7 (July 1969), pp. 646-649.
9461
---Vol. 11:2 (Feb. 1972), p. 47.

American descendants of the families of Gutmann and Klungler. Drawn from information from branches of the Gutmann (Goodman) and Klungler families on both sides of the Atlantic. Places of origin, even of many German-American individuals who married into these two families, with ages, places of settlement, and in many cases date of emigration. No. 9461 contains corrections to no. 9460.

*　　*　　*

9480

VOIGT, GILBERT P. *The German and German-Swiss Element in South Carolina, 1732-1752.* In *Bulletin of the University of South Carolina,* no. 113 (Sept. 1922), pp. 56-57, 59-60.

On pages 56 and 57 is a partial list of Saxe-Gothan settlers (German and Swiss settlers at Saxe-Gotha or Congaree, S.C.). Some have origin or settlement grant dates, 1742-1749. Pages 59 and 60 list Palatines, 136 German or German-Swiss settlers at Saxe-Gotha or Congaree: German-Swiss (Reformed) and the German (Lutheran). Also in no. 0720, Boyer, *Ship Passenger Lists, the South,* pp. 160-163; and in no. 9144, Tepper, *New World Immigrants,* vol. 2, pp. 164-168. (Lancour 237)

*　　*　　*

9510

VOTH, STANLEY E., editor. "Immigration Lists [1874-1879]." In *Henderson Mennonites from Holland to Henderson.* Henderson, Neb.: Henderson Centennial Committee, 1975, pp. 237-255.

Immigration lists for the years 1874-1879, and a few later. Family names and family members, age, village in Russia, place settled, and descendants. All Germans from Russia.

*　　*　　*

9520
VUJNOVICH, MILOS M. "South Slav Immigrants who Arrived at New Orleans on Regular Passenger Vessels from 1821 to 1870." In *Yugoslavs in Louisiana.* Gretna, La.: Pelican Publishing Co., 1974; San Francisco: R. & E., 1974, pp. 29-30.

From passenger lists of ships entering the port of New Orleans between 1813 and 1870.

*   *   *

9540
WALKER, ALEXANDER M. "Lists of Passengers from Gravesend Destined Principally to the New World, 1677." In *National Genealogical Society Quarterly,* vol. 53:4 (Dec. 1965), pp. 299-303.

From material designated as Public Record Office, Class E. 157/31; also identified by reference to the P.R.O. list, "Exchequer, King's Remembrancer Class list of records, 2, p. 153. Passengers destined for Barbados, Virginia, and Maryland, Also in no. 1252, Coldham.

*   *   *

9550
WALKER, ALEXANDER M. "Some Pioneers of North Carolina, 1674-1701." In *National Genealogical Society Quarterly,* vol. 53:3 (Sept. 1965), pp. 195-198.
Covers tithables 1674; quit rents 1675-1678; headrights.

*   *   *

9560
WALTERSCHEID, J. *Auswanderer aus dem Siegkreis.* (Forschungen zur Rheinischen Auswanderung, part 2) Bonn [Germany]: Ludwig Roehrscheid Verlag, 1939. 104p.

Emigrants from the Sieg district. Applications for permission to emigrate, filed in the state archives at Duesseldorf, Germany, under the heading "Regierung Koeln Ie 41 Band 1-11 (11 vols.)." Contains data on 1,673 emigrants in the years 1857-1889, from various jurisdictions in the North Rhine-Westphalian vicinity of Siegburg. In all, 1,500 emigrated to the Americas. Much information on each person. (Lancour 261)

*   *   *

9570
WALTON, F.S., (Mrs. John M., Sr.). "Manifest of All the Passengers Taken on Board the *Pyramid.*" In *New Orleans Genesis,* vol. 2:8 (Sept. 1963), pp. 379-383.

Copied from the U.S. National Archives, Record Group No. 36, Pub no.M-259, roll no. 32. Passengers mostly from France and Germany. Full name, occupation, age, sex, country of origin. Arrived at New Orleans, June 14, 1850, intending to become inhabitants of New Orleans (or of Louisiana).

*   *   *

9580
WAREING, JOHN. "The Emigration of Indentured Servants from London, 1683-86." In *Genealogists'*

Magazine (London), vol. 19:6 (June 1978), pp. 199-202.

Gives details on 1,701 servants known to have come to America, 1683-1686, and lists fourteen abstracts of agreements. Map shows destinations of 1,701 indentured servants "emigrating to His Majesty's Plantations in America, 1683-1686." See also no. 6179, Nicholson.

*   *   *

9590
WAREING, JOHN. "Some Early Emigrants to America, 1683-4. A Supplementary List." In *Genealogists' Magazine* (London), vol. 18:5 (Mar. 1976), pp. 239-246.

Records of indentured servants preserved in Middlesex Quarter Sessions files. Part of this series has appeared in no. 6179, Nicholson.

*   *   *

9596
WARREN, DOROTHY, compiler. "Plymouth County, Iowa, Naturalization Records, Second Papers, vol. 1, 1872-1886." In *Hawkeye Heritage,* vol. 11:2 (Apr. 1976), pp. 66-74.

Granting of citizenship to persons who had filed first papers (the declaration of intent) at least two years prior and who had lived in the United States continuously for five years and in the state of Iowa for one year. Name, place of birth, place where first papers where filed, date of citizenship.

*   *   *

9598
WARREN, MARY BONDURANT. *Citizens and Immigrants - South Carolina, 1768. Abstracted from Contemporary Records.* Danielsville, Ga.: Heritage Papers, 1980. 463p.

Details of immigration, ship lists, marine information - ship movements - taken from Governor's and Council Journals, Memorials and quit rents, Memorials Books of the Auditor General, and *The South-Carolina Gazette,* published in "Charles-Town." Primarily concerned with the year 1768. Since bounty money was paid to immigrants, many of the payment records serve as passenger information.

*   *   *

9600
WARREN, MRS. RUTH, contributor. "List of Inhabitants of Mobile." In *Deep South Genealogical Quarterly,* vol. 3:4 (May 1966), pp. 629-630.

Names the French who took the Oath of Allegiance and inhabitants of Mobile in what was then West Florida who took the Oaths of Allegiance and Fidelity, October 2, 1764. Official list on file in the British Public Record Office in London.

*   *   *

9610
WATERS, HENRY F. "More Passengers to New-

England, 1679." In *The New England Historical and Genealogical Register,* vol. 28:4 (Oct. 1874), pp. 375-378.

Names passengers of the *Hannah and Elizabeth* and the *Nathaniel* of Dartmouth. Extracted from Essex County Court papers and a book of notarial records in the Clerk's Office, County of Essex, Massachusetts. Also in no. 9151, Tepper, *Passengers to America,* pp. 167-170; and in no. 0702, Boyer, *Ship Passenger Lists, National and New England,* pp. 184-186. The list of the *Hannah and Elizabeth* appears also in no. 6560. (Lancour 60)

*   *   *

9620

WATERS, HENRY F. "Passengers to New England in 1670." In *The New England Historical and Genealogical Register,* vol. 28:4 (Oct. 1874), p. 447.

Receipt for the passage of a few persons on the *Happy Return* from Plymouth, England, to Boston in the year 1670. From court files of Essex County, Massachusetts. Also in no. 9151, Tepper, *Passengers to America,* p. 463, and in no. 0702, Boyer, *Ship Passenger Lists, National and New England,* p. 183. (Lancour 58)

*   *   *

9623

WATSON, JOHN F. *Annals of Philadelphia and Pennsylvania . . . and of the Earliest Settlements of the Inland Part of Pennsylvania . . . .* Vol. 2. [Philadelphia]: the author, 1854, pp. 230-232.

A list of 130 heads of families, with the number of persons each brought in at time of immigration. The list was made in 1693. See also nos. 0040, 0041, 1999, 3263, 7282.

*   *   *

9625

"WAYNE COUNTY, IND., Naturalization Intentions, August 1833-March 1840." In *The Hoosier Genealogist,* vol. 19:2 (June 1979), pp. 33-35.

Wayne County, Indiana, was formed during territorial days from Clark and Dearborn Counties. Immigrants in the period under review were mostly from England or Germany. Records were from Indiana's Wayne County Circuit Court Order Book E at Richmond.

*   *   *

9630

WEBER, LUDWIG. *Der Hinkinde Bott von Carolina* (The *Limping Messenger* from Carolina, or the Description of a Journey from Zurich to Rotterdam). Zurich [Switzerland]: n.p., 1735.

Original source for the article, no. 3161, Hinke. See also nos. 3000, Heidgerd; 4487, Kupillas; 7820, Rupp. (Lancour 153, note)

*   *   *

9640

WEHNER, GUSTAV. "Das Schicksal der Bremer Auswanderer-Listen." In *Norddeutsche Familienkunde,*

Jahrgang 1:3 (May-June 1952), pp. 74-78; Jahrgang 1:4 (July-Aug. 1952), pp. 96-98; Jahrgang 1:5 (Sept.-Oct. 1952), pp. 113-118.

The fate of the emigration lists of Bremen [lost]. Contains a name-index to no. 8890, Spengemann, which lists 2,645 passengers who were transported to America via Bremen between 1832 and 1849 by Captain Juergen Meyer of Bremen. This article contains only the names, but the original book, based on the logbook of Captain Meyer, indicates for the most part the place or land of origin for each passenger. The introduction provides details concerning the loss of the emigration lists maintained in Bremen beginning in 1832. Contains also a list of 52 names for the year 1834, which are likewise in no. 3080, Heyne.

*   *   *

9660

WEISER, FREDERICK S. "Johann Conrad Weiser und Birkenfelder Familien unter den Einwanderern in Nordamerika von 1709/10." In *Pfaelzische Familien- und Wappenkunde,* vol. 5:10 (1966), pp. 324-328; vol. 5:11 (1966), pp. 363-364.

Johann Conrad Weiser and some families from Birkenfeld among the Palatine immigrants to North America in 1709-1710. Includes information on Weiser, Feg, and Risch families and relatives, most of whom arrived in New York in 1709 or 1710. Gives place of origin for a few families, ages of members and family data for most.

*   *   *

9664

WEITZ, WILHELM. "Beitraege aur Auswanderung aus Ostfriesland im 19. Jahrhundert." In *Friesisches Jahrbuch. Jahrbuch des Nordfriesischen Vereins fuer Heimatkunde und Heimatliebe* (Aurich, Germany), vol. 32 (1958), pp. 110-135.

Data on emigration from East Frisia in the 19th century. Includes three ships' lists, *Ant je Brons,* Emden, Germany, to New York, 1855 and 1857; *Johannes,* Emden to Charleston, 1857. Contains 203 names with ages and places of origin.

*   *   *

9670

WELLS, FREDERIC PALMER. *History of Barnet, Vermont, from the Outbreak of the French and Indian War to Present Time . . . .* Burlington [Vt.]: Free Press Printing Co., 1923, p. 23.

Names of the seamen and a company of farmers who accompanied Colonel Alexander Harvey on a journey from Scotland to New York on the *Matty* in 1774. Also in no. 3670, "*Journal . . .*" and in no. 0714, Boyer, *Ship Passenger Lists, New York and New Jersey,* p. 174. (Lancour 102, 1A)

*   *   *

9680

WESTCOTT, THOMPSON. *Names of Persons Who Took the Oath of Allegiance to the State of Pennsylvania, Between the Years 1777-1789 . . . .* Philadelphia: Campbell, 1865, 145p. Reprinted by Genealogical Publishing Co., Baltimore, 1965.

> Contains details of many immigrations. Index is provided on pp. 119-145.

*   *   *

9689
WESTER, JUNE HART, abstractor. "Naturalizations from the Irwin County, Georgia, Superior Court Minutes, 1827-1847." In *The Georgia Genealogical Society Quarterly,* vol. 15:3 (Fall 1979), pp. 117-122.

> Mostly declarations of intent to acquire citizenship. Irish names, with date and place of arrival in America, 1828-1841. Ages given.

*   *   *

9695-9699
WESTERN PENNSYLVANIA GENEALOGICAL SOCIETY, Pittsburgh, compilers. *A List of Immigrants Who Applied for Naturalization Papers in the District Courts of Allegheny County, Pennsylvania.* Pittsburgh: the society, 1978, 1980.
9695
---Vol. 1, 1798-1840. 109 p. 4,500 names.
9696
---Vol. 2, 1841-1855. 139p. 6,000 names.
9697
---Vol. 3, 1856-1869. 112p. 4,800 names.
9698
---Vol. 4, section 1, 1870-1875. 1980. 78pp.
9699
---Vol. 4, section 2, 1876-1879. 1980. 107pp.

> Volume four (both sections), has about 8,600 names.

*   *   *

9725
WHITE, FRANK F., JR. "A List of Convicts Transported to Maryland." In *Maryland Historical Magazine,* vol. 43:1 (Mar. 1948), pp. 55-60.

> From a manuscript in the Maryland Historical Society. Pages 57-59 contain "A list of one hundred and fifteen felons & convicts shipped [in the year 1740] from Newgate by Andrew Reid Esq. on board the *York,* Capt Anthony Bacon Commander, bound for Maryland." Names only. Also in no. 0720, Boyer, *Ship Passenger Lists, the South,* pp. 15-18; and in no. 9144, Tepper, *New World Immigrants,* vol. 2, pp. 136-141. (Lancour 204)

*   *   *

9738
WHITEHEAD, WILLIAM A. "Names of Those Who Sailed on the *Henry and Francis,* 1685 from Leith, Scotland, to Perth Amboy, New Jersey, 5th September 1685." In *Contributions to the Early History of Perth Amboy and Adjoining Country.* New York: D. Appleton & Co., 1856, pp. 28-29.

> See also no. 2026, Fields; nos. 2590 and 2596, Glasgow; and no. 0973, Brown & Lindsay. For other references to the *Henry and Francis,* see index. (Lancour 113C)

9750
WHITMORE, WILLIAM H., compiler. *Port Arrivals and Immigrants to the City of Boston, 1715-1716 and 1762-1769.* Baltimore: Genealogical Publishing Co., 1973. 111p.

> Excerpted from *A Volume of Records Relating to the Early History of Boston Containing Miscellaneous Papers,* Registry Department of the City of Boston, 29th in the series formerly called *Record Commissioners' Reports,* Document Number 100, published 1900. This excerpt is taken from pp. 229-317 and has a reconstructed index. Irish names excerpted are in no. 1642, Donovan. (Lancour 64)

*   *   *

9760
WHYTE, DONALD. *A Dictionary of Scottish Emigrants to the USA.* Baltimore: Magna Carta Book Co., 1972. 504p.

> Covers era prior to 1855. Compiled from correspondence and monument inscriptions, 17th and, mainly, 18th century. Prepared for the Scottish Genealogical Society.

*   *   *

9770
WHYTE, DONALD. "Passenger List of the Schooner *Lady Mary.*" In *The Scottish Genealogist,* vol. 11:4 (Nov. 1964), pp. 21-24.

> The *Britannia,* crossing from Liverpool to New York in June 1842, sank near Newfoundland. More than 74 of its passengers ultimately reached New York on the *Lady Mary,* arriving August 24, 1842. The passenger lists are preserved in the National Archives, Washington, D.C.

*   *   *

9775
WHYTE, DONALD. "Scottish Emigrants to New York and Pictou, N.S., 1803: Two Unpublished Lists." In *Family History,* vol. 9:49-51 (Apr. 1975), pp. 15-21.

> From the papers of Henry Dundas, Viscount Melville, in the National Library of Scotland. Emigrants of Perthshire, sailing from Greenock to New York and from port of Glasgow to Pictou, Nova Scotia.

*   *   *

9780
WIESENTHAL, GEORG. "Darmstaedter Auswanderer aus dem Jahre 1847." In *Der Odenwald,* Jahrgang 4:3 (1957), pp. 81-83.

> Emigrants from Darmstadt in 1847. Lists 33 men who emigrated from the city of Darmstadt in Germany to found the colonies "Darmstaedter Farm" and "Bettina" near New Braunfels, Texas. Lists only the names and occupations of the emigrants.

*   *   *

9790
WILLIAMS, MILDRED C. "Bucks County, Penn-

sylvania, and Some Early Settlers." In *The Genealogist's Post*, vol. 1:2 (Feb. 1964), pp. 3-7.

Late 17th and early 18th centuries. Mostly English and Germans; some genealogical information.

*   *   *

9800
WILLIAMS, PASCOE. "London Documents: the Names, Trades, etc., of the German Protestants to be Settled in New York." In MacWethy, *The Book of Names*, pp. 51-52. Reprinted by Genealogical Publishing Co., Baltimore, 1969.

Additional names to the Kocherthal Records. Obtained in the State Library at Albany. List is dated June 28, 1708. For other references to Kocherthal, see index. See also no. 6316, O'Callaghan. (Lancour 90A)

*   *   *

9810
WILLISON, GEORGE F. *Saints and Strangers, Being the Lives of the Pilgrim Fathers and Their Families* . . . . New York: Reynal & Hitchcock, 1945. 513p. Reprinted by New Englandia, North Adams, Mass., 1973.

Pages 437-453 entitled, "The Pilgrim Company," have passenger lists from the *Mayflower*, 1620 and 1629; *Fortune*, 1621; *Shallop*, 1622, and other vessels. Names of immigrants are scattered throughout the book. For references to the *Mayflower*, see the index.

*   *   *

9820
WILSON, ISAIAH W. *A Geography and History of the County of Digby, Nova Scotia.* Halifax, [N.S.]: Holloway Brothers, 1900, p. 300. Reprinted (Canadian Reprint Series, 39) by Mika Studio, Belleville, Ont., 1972.

Contains a list from the schooner *Charming Molly*, May 5, 1760, of New England emigrants to be conveyed to the valley of Annapolis River. The vessel sailed from Boston and anchored in Annapolis, Nova Scotia, June 25, 1760. It made a second journey in July. See also no. 1072, Calnek.

*   *   *

9830
WINGO, BRUCE, contributor. "Naturalizations, Norfolk County [Virginia]." In *Virginia Genealogical Society Quarterly*, vol. 10:2 (Apr. 1972), pp. 56-57.
Ireland and other countries of origin, 1828-1854.

*   *   *

9840
WODROW, ROBERT. "[Lists of Scotch Prisoners Deported to New Jersey, 1685.]" In *The History of the Sufferings of the Church of Scotland, from the Restauration to the Revolution* . . . . Edinburgh [Scotland]: James Watson, 1722, vol. 2, pp. 481-487.

Names of Scottish prisoners ordered deported to plantations in East New Jersey. The list appears as well in vol. 4, pp.

216-223, of the 1830 edition (Glasgow: Blackie, Fullarton & Co.). Also in no. 0714, Boyer, *Ship Passenger Lists, New York and New Jersey*, pp. 239-248, from the 1830 edition. Other references to Scottish prisoners in the index. (Lancour 114)

*   *   *

9860
WOLFE, RICHARD J. "The Colonial Naturalization Act of 1740; With a List of Persons Naturalized in New York Colony, 1740-1769." In *The New York Genealogical and Biographical Record*, vol. 94:3 (July 1963), pp. 132-147.

From a manuscript in The New York Public Library. Names approximately 300 persons who were naturalized in the 18th century. More comprehensive than no. 2564, Giuseppi. Also in no. 9135, Tepper, *Immigrants to the Middle Colonies*, pp. 130-145. And see Hollander, no. 3253. The Jews in this list are named in no. 3303, Huehner. (Lancour 102)

*   *   *

9870
WOLFE, RICHARD J. "Early New York Naturalization Records in the Emmet Collection; with a List of Aliens Naturalized in New York, 1802-1814." In *Bulletin of the New York Public Library*, vol. 67:4 (Apr. 1963), pp. 211-217.

Roster of 115 aliens, most of them Irish, naturalized in New York, with much information on each. Also in no. 0714, Boyer, *Ship Passenger Lists, New York and New Jersey*, pp. 209-213; and in no. 9144, Tepper, *New World Immigrants*, vol. 2, pp. 242-248. (Lancour 105)

*   *   *

9880
WOOD, GREGORY A. *The French Presence in Maryland, 1524-1800.* Baltimore: Gateway Press, 1978. 234p.

Appendix 7 (pp. 186-201) lists 800 persons of French descent in the 1763 census of Acadians in Maryland, taken from "Au Duc de Nivernois, July 7, 1763, Affaires Etrangeres, Correspondance Politique Angleterre," vol. 450, pp. 438-446. To be found in a copy at the Hall of Records, Annapolis, Maryland, and in St. Martin Parish Library, St. Martinville, Louisiana. Appendix 8 lists some Acadians who took the Oath of Fidelity during American Revolution, 1778.

*   *   *

9890
WOOD, VIRGINIA STEELE. "Ship Passenger Lists, Savannah, Georgia, 1820-1868." In *National Genealogical Society Quarterly*, vol. 54:2 (June 1966), pp. 83-97.

Many ships from Liverpool, with British passengers mostly.

*   *   *

9900
WUST, KLAUS G. "[A List of Redemptioners Who Fled from the Ship *Capellen tot den Pol*, 1784. Notes and Documents: Maryland German Items in 18th Century

Newspapers.]" In *The Report, a Journal of German-American History*, vol. 33, 1968, p. 60.

> The 31 passengers of the *Capellen tot den Pol* in 1784 are listed in item no. 9902, Wust. The list of redemptioners is taken from *Philadelphische Correspondenz*, March 8, 1785.

* * *

9902
WUST, KLAUS G., editor. "[List of 31 Passengers Who Arrived in Baltimore in Fall, 1784. Notes and Documents: Items on Maryland in Early Pennsylvania-German Newspapers.]" In *Society for the History of the Germans in Maryland, 32nd Report, or The Report, A Journal of German-American History*, vol. 32, 1966, pp. 59-60.

> Originally in the *Philadelphische Correspondenz*, January 31, 1786, this concerns the vessels *Capellen tot den Pol* and *North America*, both from Holland. An article of praise from passengers for a safe voyage. Includes details of other *Philadelphische Correspondenz* notices, as well. Eighteenth century dates. See also Wust, 9900.

* * *

9916
WYAND, JEFFREY A., and **FLORENCE LEONE WYAND.** *Colonial Maryland Naturalizations.* Baltimore: Genealogical Publishing Co., 1975. 104p.

> Denizations, pp. 1-3 (1660-1771); naturalizations, pp. 5-71 (1666-1775). The compilation covers about 1,600 new citizens. Appendix: place names, clergymen and parishes.

* * *

9931-9932
YODER, DON, editor. "Lehigh County Naturalization Records." In *The Pennsylvania Dutchman.*
9931
---Vol. 1:6 (May 5, 1949), p. 6.
9932
---Vol. 2:22 (Jan. 1950), p. 6.

> List of German and Swiss immigrants who petitioned for naturalization before the Court of Common Pleas of Lehigh County, Pennsylvania, in accordance with a federal law of 1798. Copied from original papers in the Prothonotary's Office of the Lehigh County Courthouse in Allentown. Entries include name, place of origin, and date of arrival. Also in no. 9144, Tepper, *New World Immigrants*, vol. 2, pp. 233-239; and in no. 0717, Boyer, *Ship Passenger Lists, Pennsylvania and Delaware*, pp. 207-212. (Lancour 190)

* * *

9945
YODER, DON, editor. "A New Emigrant List." In *The Pennsylvania Dutchman*, vol. 1:3 (May 19, 1949), p. 6.

> Appeared originally in German as an advertisement for missing heirs in the early Allentown weekly *Der Friedens-Bothe* for June 17, 1825. Names 32 emigrants who arrived in

America during and after the Revolution. Also in no. 0702, Boyer, *Ship Passenger Lists, National and New England*, pp. 58-59; and in no. 9144, Tepper, *New World Immigrants*, vol. 2, pp. 224-225. (Lancour 22)

* * *

9960
YODER, DON, editor. "Pennsylvania Emigrants from Friedrichstal." In *Pennsylvania Folklife*, vol. 22:3 (Spring 1973), inside back cover [p. 49].

> Addendum to no. 4085, Friedrich Krebs. Period 1723-1739, from Germany.

* * *

9964
YODER, DON, editor. *Pennsylvania German Immigrants, 1709-1786: Lists Consolidated from Yearbooks of The Pennsylvania German Folklore Society.* Baltimore: Genealogical Publishing Co., 1980. 394p.

> Five lists originally published between the years 1936 and 1951. See no. 2444, Gerber; no. 4525, Langguth; no. 3193, Hinke; no. 4357, Krebs; and no. 8945, Steinemann. The lists cover emigrants from Wuerttemberg, Wertheim, Zweibruecken, and Schaffhausen. Indexed.

* * *

9975
"YORKSHIRE, ENGLAND, TO NOVA SCOTIA, 1774." In *Genealogical Reference Builders Newsletter*, vol. 1:9 (Oct.-Nov. 1967), pp. 4-5.

> A sailing from the port of Scarborough, Yorkshire, to Nova Scotia, 1774. No ship named. Passengers' names, ages, occupations. Includes (on p. 5) passengers from the port of Hull, Yorkshire, who sailed in the ship *Two Friends*, February 28 to March 7, 1774. See also Milner, 5675.

* * *

9979
YOUNG, GERARD. "Off to the New World with a Razor and a Bible." In *Bognor Regis Post*, October 12, 1968.

> An account of emigration from Sussex, England, to Canada during the 1830s and 1840s, made possible by the Petworth Emigration Committee. One sheet from a newspaper. See also no. 8775, Sockett; and no. 2688, Godman.

* * *

9985
ZUBER, RUDOLF. "Die Auswanderung aus dem Freiwaldauer Bezirk um die Mitte des 19. Jahrhunderts." In *Schlesien: Eine Vierteljahresschrift fuer Kunst Wissenschaft und Volkstum*, Jahrgang 19 (i.e. 14), Heft 2, pp. 100-106.

> Emigration from the district of Freiwaldau in Silesia around the middle of the nineteenth century. Presidential records of

the captaincy of Freiwaldau, beginning in 1850, stored in the Jauernig branch of the Freiwaldau district archives. Represents about 30 emigrants to America, 1850-1853. Names, dates of emigration, places of origin, and some destinations.

*   *   *

9995
ZUILL, WILLIAM E.S. "Emigrants to Bermuda, 1850." In *The Bermuda Historical Quarterly,* vol. 25:3 (Autumn 1968), pp. 77-85.

Discusses and lists a group of workhouse children from St. Pancras Parish, London, who were sent off to Bermuda on the Brig *James* to be apprenticed to Bermudian families.

*   *   *

Index

An Explanation of the Index

Reference is to the entry number of the individual item, not to a page.

The alphabetical arrangement used is known as the word-by-word system (e.g., New Jersey and New York come before Newcastle). In foreign words, the diacritical marks have been omitted: thus, in German, an umlauted vowel appears without the umlaut, but with an e after the vowel, and the word is alphabetized accordingly.

Generally, this index includes place-names, nationalities, ships' names, naturalizations, occupations, religious groups, military units, and categories of arrivals entered as prisoners or indentured servants. Some surnames are to be found in the bibliography, but relatively few.

Entries that could be identified by date have an indication of that before the reference number.

Ships' names are given in italics throughout the book: *Virginia,* therefore, is a reference to a ship; Virginia to the place; *Oxford,* to a ship; Oxford to the place.

The following abbreviations were used in the index:

c. = century	n.d. = no date
ca. = *circa*	N.S. = Nova Scotia

States have generally been indicated by the traditional standard abbreviations.

Perhaps it is worth pointing out that an expression like "Scottish departures" is a reference to Scots leaving their homeland for North America, not to the departure of Scots from this continent.

How to Use the Index for Rapid Reference

It is advisable to look first under the most specific place-names (of departure, arrival, or settlement) or the name of the people (the national name: French, Germans, etc.) from the country of emigration or the port of departure. Only if a nationality was not known from the material at hand was a given emigration assimilated to the nationality of the port of departure. Note that Silesia was divided between Poland and Czechoslovakia, but today some of it is in East Germany, and the source of the information and the port of departure may both be German. Whenever possible, therefore, multiple ways of access are provided in the index. The term *English* is used where the material refers explicitly to English places or people. If there is an indication that Scots, Welsh, or Irish were probably included aboard a sailing from an English port, the reference to that material may be found either under those groups, if they are identified, or under the more encompassing term *British.*

Use of the national names avoids excessive references to such terms as passengers, emigrants, immigrants, aliens, settlers, colonists, pioneers, pilgrims, etc., all of which were considered too general to be helpful as keywords in an index on this subject. It is recognized that national states were not formed until after the dates of many of the migration movements mentioned, but use of the national names does apply to the language groups, does spotlight the conscious national heritage of many families, and is convenient for present-day researchers who may more readily be able to identify given place-names within current frontiers. Mixed lists of people from various countries are indexed merely as arrivals or departures under the place-names involved, instead of by nationality.

A reader in search of an author name or (possibly) a book or article title should look in the alphabetical sequence of the main part of the bibliography. Authors and titles are not duplicated in the index.

Passenger and Immigration Lists Bibliography
Index

A

D

G

I

N

Q

R